Appeals Mechanism in International Investment Disputes

Appeals Mechanism in International Investment Disputes

Edited by

Karl P. Sauvant

Columbia Program on International Investment
Columbia Law School, The Earth Institute
Columbia University

with

Michael Chiswick-Patterson

OXFORD
UNIVERSITY PRESS

OXFORD
UNIVERSITY PRESS

Oxford University Press, Inc., publishes works that further Oxford University's objective of excellence in research, scholarship, and education.

Published by Oxford University Press, Inc.
198 Madison Avenue, New York, New York 10016

Library of Congress Cataloging-in-Publication Data

Appeals mechanism in international investment disputes / edited by Karl P. Sauvant.
p. cm.
Includes bibliographical references and index.
ISBN: 978-0-19-534156-0 (alk. paper) 1. Investments, Foreign (International law) 2. Dispute resolution (Law) 3. Arbitration and award, International. I. Sauvant, Karl P.
K3830.A64 2008
346.07--dc22

2007050084

Note to Readers:

This publication is designed to provide accurate and authoritative information in regard to the subject matter covered. It is based upon sources believed to be accurate and reliable and is intended to be current as of the time it was written. It is sold with the understanding that the publisher is not engaged in rendering legal, accounting, or other professional services. If legal advice or other expert assistance is required, the services of a competent professional person should be sought. Also, to confirm that the information has not been affected or changed by recent developments, traditional legal research techniques should be used, including checking primary sources where appropriate.

(Based on the Declaration of Principles jointly adopted by a Committee of the American Bar Association and a Committee of Publishers and Associations.)

Contents

Acknowledgments ix
Contributors xi
Participating Institutions xix
Foreword: Jeffrey D. Sachs xxi
Preface: David M. Schizer xxiii

PART I: INTRODUCTION

1 The Rise of International Investment, Investment Agreements and Investment Disputes 3
Karl P. Sauvant

2 The Multifaceted Nature of International Investment Law 17
Rainer Geiger

3 Implications for the Future of International Investment Law 29
José E. Alvarez

PART II: RECENT TRENDS IN INTERNATIONAL INVESTMENT LAW DISPUTES

4 A Coming Crisis: Expansionary Trends in Investment Treaty Arbitration 39
M. Sornarajah

5 Variation in the Substantive Provisions and Interpretation of International Investment Agreements 81
Patrick Juillard

6 Explanations for the Increased Recourse to Treaty-Based Investment Dispute Settlement: Resolving the Struggle of Life Against Form? 105
Jeswald W. Salacuse

Commentary:

7 The Proliferation of BITs: Conflicts of Treaties, Proceedings and Awards 127
Giorgio Sacerdoti

8 The Growing Diversity and Inconsistency in the IIA System 137
Anna Joubin-Bret

PART III: Promoting Consistency and Coherence

9 Challenges Facing Investment Disputes: Reconsidering Dispute Resolution in International Investment Agreements 143
Susan D. Franck

10 Transparency in International Dispute Settlement Proceedings on Trade and Investment 193
Hugo Perezcano Díaz

11 Provisions in the New Generation of U.S. Investment Agreements to Achieve Transparency and Coherence in Investor-State Dispute Settlement 201
Michael K. Tracton

12 Preliminary Rulings in Investment Arbitration 207
Christoph Schreuer

Commentary:

13 Transparency and Consistency in International Investment Law: Can the Problems Be Fixed by Tinkering? 213
Howard Mann

14 Improving the System of Investor-State Dispute Settlement: The OECD Governments' Perspective 223
Katia Yannaca-Small

PART IV: Critical Views on an Appellate Mechanism in Investment Disputes

15 Options to Establish an Appellate Mechanism for Investment Disputes 231
Barton Legum

16 Avoiding Unintended Consequences 241
Jan Paulsson

17 Implications of an Appellate Body for Investment Disputes from a Developing Country Point of View........ 267
Asif H. Qureshi & Shandana Gulzar Khan

PART V: Report to the Symposium

18 Examining the Institutional Design of International Investment Law........ 281
Christopher Brummer

Selected Bibliography 289
Brian J. Rapier

Appendix

1 Selection of BITs and FTAs with Provisions Relating to an Appellate Review Mechanism 301

2 ICSID Convention, Excerpts 319

3 ICSID, "Possible Improvements of the Framework for ICSID Arbitration"........ 321

4 ICSID, "Suggested Changes to the ICSID Rules and Regulations" 339

5 International Institute for Sustainable Development, "Comments on ICSID Discussion Paper, 'Possible Improvements of the Framework for ICSID Arbitration'" 353

6 UNCTAD, "Latest Developments in Investor-State Dispute Settlement, 2005" 377

7 UNCTAD, "Latest Developments in Investor-State Dispute Settlement, 2006" 391

8 OECD, "Novel Features in OECD Countries' Recent Investment Agreements: An Overview" 411

Index 431

Acknowledgments

The Columbia Program on International Investment held its first Symposium entitled "Transparency and Consistency in International Investment Law: Is There a Need for a Review Mechanism?" on April 4, 2006, at Columbia University. We would like to acknowledge the sponsors of that event, Mark and Gail Appel, without whom the Symposium would not have happened.

The co-organizers of the event were the Columbia Program on International Investment (a joint program of the Columbia Law School and The Earth Institute at Columbia University); the Center on Global Legal Problems, Columbia Law School; and the University of Paris I (Panthéon-Sorbonne), *Centre d'Études et de Recherches de Droit International.*

The core of this publication consists of original contributions prepared and presented at the Symposium. Special recognition is due to the distinguished authors of this volume and the rapporteur of the Symposium, for their contribution to the international debate on the issues of coherence and consistency in international investment law. They benefited from the feedback they received from the Symposium's participants and the active discussions chaired by José Alvarez and Rainer Geiger. Further, two presenters at the Symposium—Emmanuel Gaillard and George Bermann—helped this volume through their participation in the event and interaction with the authors. A special feature of this volume is that, after the Symposium was held, a number of eminent experts who could not attend the event itself provided their views on the question of an appellate mechanism for investment disputes; these are added to those of Barton Legum in Part IV of this volume. Further, Antonio Parra provided useful guidance on a number of issues related to this volume.

We recognize the assistance of Matthew J. Quint, the Program Coordinator at the Columbia Program on International Investment, in the preparation of both the Symposium and this book. Finally, thank you also to Vincent DeLuca for his role in organizing the Symposium, and Ipsita Aggarwal and

Ricardo Postigo for their assistance in this respect. Christopher F. Bush and Carmen Martínez López served ably and helpfully as note-takers at the event.

To all of them: thank you very much!

Karl P. Sauvant
Executive Director
Columbia Program on International Investment

Michael Chiswick-Patterson
Columbia Law School

Contributors

José E. Alvarez is the Hamilton Fish Professor of International Law and Diplomacy at the Columbia University School of Law. He is a graduate from Magdalen College, Oxford University and Harvard Law School. He was law clerk to Judge Thomas Gibbs Gee, U.S. Court of Appeals for the Fifth Circuit, and was in private practice at Shea & Gardner. Formerly attorney-adviser at the U.S. Department of State, Office of the Legal Adviser, he has also held appointments at Georgetown University Law Center, George Washington University Law School and the University of Michigan Law School.

Mr. Alvarez has been an International Affairs Fellow at the Council on Foreign Relations, where he is a member, and served on the Board of Editors of the *American Journal of International Law* and the *Journal of International Criminal Justice*. He has been a member of the Department of State Advisory Committee on International Law. His principal areas of publishing and teaching are international law, especially international organizations; international tribunals; war crimes; international legal theory; and foreign investment.

Christopher Brummer is an Assistant Professor of Law at Vanderbilt University School of Law. Prior to joining the academy, he practiced corporate law in London and New York for the firm of Cravath, Swaine & Moore.

Mr. Brummer earned a Ph.D. in Germanic studies from the University of Chicago, and his J.D. at Columbia Law School, where he was senior editor of the law review. Mr. Brummer's research focuses on trade and investment, the regulation of international securities, and globalization and the law. He is fluent in French and German.

Michael Chiswick-Patterson received his J.D. from Columbia Law School in 2007. He is now employed at Latham & Watkins LLP. His interests include international investment and business, trade law, and the role of those topics in U.S. foreign policy. He received his A.B. from Princeton University.

Susan D. Franck is an Assistant Professor at the University of Nebraska Law College. She has previously taught at the University of Minnesota Law School. She received her B.A. in Psychology and Political Science from Macalester

College in 1993 and her J.D. from the University of Minnesota in 1998. Ms. Franck practiced in the area of international dispute resolution as an associate in Wilmer, Cutler & Pickering's International Group in Washington, D.C., and in the International Arbitration Group at Allen & Overy LLP in London.

Ms. Franck's scholarship relates to the resolution of international disputes, including issues related to alternative dispute resolution and claims made under investment treaties. Ms. Franck teaches International Litigation and Arbitration, Investment Treaty Arbitration, Conflicts of Law, Mediation and Alternative Dispute Resolution.

Rainer Geiger is the Deputy Director for Financial and Enterprise Affairs and Head of the Middle East and North Africa Programme at the Organisation for Economic Co-operation and Development (OECD) in Paris. He is a graduate of the University of Heidelberg in Germany and Columbia Law School in New York, with a Ph.D. and an advanced law degree. He has been a Counselor in the Ministries of Economics and Economic Cooperation in Germany and Secretary of the Finance Commission of the Conference on International Economic Co-operation in Paris.

Mr. Geiger is Co-Chair of the Investment Compact Stability Pact for South East Europe. He is an Associate Professor of International Economic Law at the University of Paris I (Panthéon-Sorbonne), where he has published numerous articles on international economic law issues. He is a member of the German American Lawyers Association and the French Society of International Law.

Shandana Gulzar Khan is the Legal Affairs Officer at the Permanent Mission of Pakistan to the WTO in Geneva, responsible for negotiations on the Dispute Settlement Understanding, TRIPS and Rules. She is also an honorary member of the Asian Institute of Trade and Development based in Islamabad where she first started working as an international trade lawyer. She has also worked with the UNDP, the International Human Rights Law Group and in the Lower and High Court in Pakistan while teaching Law at various colleges in Islamabad and Peshawar. Ms. Khan has also published various articles on WTO matters.

Anna Joubin-Bret is Senior Legal Adviser with the Division on Investment, Technology and Enterprise Development of the UN Conference on Trade and Development (UNCTAD), based in Geneva. She is the technical assistance and training coordinator of the work program on international investment agreements. She oversees research for the program, including the publication of the UNCTAD series *Issues in International Investment Agreements*.

Ms. Joubin-Bret has been Legal Counsel in the legal department of the Schneider Group, General Counsel of the KIS Group and Director-Export of Pomagalski S.A. She has been appointed judge at the Commercial Court in Grenoble (France). She holds a post-graduate degree in Private International Law from the University of Paris I (Panthéon-Sorbonne), after having graduated in International Economic Law from that institution. Further, she holds a degree in Political Science from the *Institut d'Études Politiques.*

Patrick Juillard has been a Professor of International Law at the University of Paris I (Panthéon-Sorbonne) since 1983. He holds a Master of Comparative Law from Columbia Law School and a Doctorate of Law from the University of Paris.

Mr. Juillard has published extensively on international law, international economic law, international investment law, and foreign direct investment. He has taught at the University of Paris V (René Descartes), University of Paris (Nanterre) and the University of Michigan School of Law.

Barton Legum is Counsel in the Paris office of Debevoise & Plimpton LLP, focusing his practice on international arbitration and litigation. He previously served as Chief of the NAFTA Arbitration Division in the Office of the Legal Adviser, United States Department of State. In that capacity, he acted as lead counsel for the United States in defending over $2 billion (U.S.) in claims submitted to arbitration under the investment chapter of NAFTA. The United States won every case decided under his tenure. He is Programs Officer and a member of the Administration Committee and Council of the ABA Section of International Law. Mr. Legum received a D.E.A. from the University of Paris.

Howard Mann is a practicing international lawyer from Ottawa, Canada. He is also the Senior International Law Advisor to the International Institute for Sustainable Development (IISD). Mr. Mann represented IISD in the *Methanex v. United States* investor-State arbitration.

Mr. Mann has taught international sustainable development law at the Faculty of Law, University of Ottawa, and has published widely in the field. Prior to joining the private sector, he practiced international law for the Canadian Government, where he participated in the negotiation of several international environmental agreements. He holds a law degree from McGill University in Montreal, and his LL.M. and Ph.D. from the London School of Economics.

Jan Paulsson is head of the public international law and international arbitration groups at Freshfields Bruckhaus Deringer. He regularly advises governments and corporations around the world with respect to issues of international law. He has been counsel in hundreds of international arbitrations and sat as arbitrator in some 120 cases. Mr. Paulsson holds the Ibrahim Shihata Chair as Professor of International Investment Law at the University of Dundee, is a Yorke Distinguished Visiting Fellow at the University of Cambridge, and is a Visiting Professor at the University of Miami. He also teaches a course at the *Institut d'Études Politiques* in Paris. He is the author of several textbooks and numerous articles on the subject of international arbitration.

Hugo Perezcano Díaz is General Counsel for Trade Negotiations at Mexico's Secretariat of the Economy (formerly the Secretariat of Trade and Industrial Development). He is also lead counsel for Mexico in State-State dispute settlement proceedings initiated under the WTO and NAFTA, as well as in disputes brought by investors under NAFTA and bilateral investment agreements. Prior to being appointed General Counsel for Trade Negotiations, Mr. Perezcano was part of the Secretariat's legal team during the NAFTA and Uruguay Round Negotiations and was designated lead counsel for Mexico in trade negotiations with several Latin American countries.

Asif H. Qureshi is Professor of International Economic Law at the Law School, University of Manchester, Manchester, UK; and barrister attached to Quadrant Chambers in London, UK. He is also Editor-in-Chief of the *Manchester Journal of International Economic Law*; and a member of the International Law Association Committees on International Trade and International Law on Foreign Investment, respectively. He has published widely in International Economic Law; has held various visiting professorships; and acted as advisor to various governments and international organizations.

Brian J. Rapier is a member of the Class of 2008 at the University of Nebraska College of Law. He received a B.S. degree with majors in History and Political Science from the University of Nebraska at Omaha in 2005. He is interested in international law generally, international investment law and space law.

Giorgio Sacerdoti is Professor of International Law and European Law at Bocconi University in Milan, and has been a member of the Appellate Body of the WTO since 2001. Mr. Sacerdoti has held various posts in the public sector, including Vice-Chairperson of the Anti-Bribery Committee of the OECD. He has acted as consultant to the Council of Europe, UNCTAD and the World Bank. He is a member of the Committee on International Trade Law of the International Law Association.

Mr. Sacerdoti is also Counsel to Piergrossi Bianchini Eversheds, specializing in international litigation, arbitration, contracts, investments and transport law. He has often served as an arbitrator in international commercial disputes and at the International Centre for Settlement of Investment Disputes (ICSID).

Jeffrey D. Sachs is the Director of The Earth Institute, Quetelet Professor of Sustainable Development, and Professor of Health Policy and Management at Columbia University. He is also Special Advisor to United Nations Secretary-General Ban Ki-moon. From 2002 to 2006, he was Director of the UN Millennium Project and Special Advisor to United Nations Secretary-General Kofi Annan on the Millennium Development Goals, the internationally agreed goals to reduce extreme poverty, disease, and hunger by the year 2015. Sachs is also President and Co-Founder of Millennium Promise Alliance, a non-profit organization aimed at ending extreme global poverty. He is widely considered to be the leading international economic advisor of his generation. He is author of hundreds of scholarly articles and many books, including New York Times bestseller *The End of Poverty* (Penguin: 2005). He has won many awards and received many honorary degrees around the world. A native of Detroit, Michigan, Sachs received his B.A., M.A., and Ph.D. degrees at Harvard University.

Jeswald W. Salacuse is Henry J. Braker Professor of Law at the Fletcher School of Law and Diplomacy, Tufts University. Mr. Salacuse served as Dean of the Fletcher School and Dean of the School of Law of Southern Methodist University. He specializes in international negotiation, international business transactions and law and development.

Mr. Salacuse holds a J.D. from Harvard Law School, an A.B. from Hamilton College, and a diploma from the University of Paris. He has been a lecturer in law at Ahmadu Bello University in Nigeria, in private practice with a Wall Street firm, a professor of law and director of research at the National School of Administration in the Congo, the Ford Foundation's Middle East advisor on law and development, and later the Foundation's representative in the Sudan. He is currently president of an ICSID tribunal.

Karl P. Sauvant is the Executive Director of the Columbia Program on International Investment, Lecturer in Law at Columbia Law School and Co-Director of the Millennium Cities Initiative. He is also Guest Professor at Nankai University, China.

Until July 2005, he was Director of UNCTAD's Investment Division, where he created (in 1991) the prestigious annual United Nations publication *World Investment Report,* of which he was the lead author until 2004, and (in 1992) the journal *Transnational Corporations,* serving as its editor until 2005. He provided intellectual leadership and guidance to a series of 25 monographs on key issues related to international investment agreements (which were published in 2004/2005 in three volumes), and he edited (together with John Dunning) a 20-volume *Library on Transnational Corporations* (published by Routledge). Mr. Sauvant received his Ph.D. from the University of Pennsylvania.

David M. Schizer is Dean of Columbia Law School and the Lucy G. Moses Professor of Law. A graduate of Yale where he earned his B.A., M.A. and J.D., Dean Schizer clerked for U.S. Appeals Court Judge Alex Kozinski and Supreme Court Justice Ruth Bader Ginsburg. One of the nation's leading experts in tax law, Schizer worked at Davis Polk & Wardwell prior to joining the Columbia Law faculty in 1998. He was elected Dean of the faculty in 2004.

Dean Schizer continues to teach a colloquium on tax, and a course on professional responsibility. Before becoming Dean, he started a highly popular Deals course, bringing students academics and practitioners together to examine the art of the deal in the realworld.

Christoph Schreuer is Professor of Law at the University of Vienna. He has previously been the Edward B. Burling Professor of International Law and Organization at the Johns Hopkins University, and Professor at the University of Salzburg (Austria). Mr. Schreuer is currently a Member of the ICSID Panel of Conciliators and Arbitrators, with a term from 2002 until 2008. He is also the Chairman of the ILA Committee on the Law of Foreign Investment.

Mr. Schreuer holds a J.S.D. from Yale Law School, an LL.M. and a Diploma in International Law from Cambridge, and his initial law degree from the University of Vienna. He also received a *Universitätsdozent (venia legendi)* from the University of Salzburg.

M. Sornarajah is CJ Koh Professor of Law at the National University of Singapore. He was previously the Head of the Law School of the University of Tasmania. He is a Fellow of the Australian Centre for International Commercial Arbitration and is on the Regional Panel of the Singapore International Arbitration Centre. Mr. Sornarajah has been a Sterling Fellow at the Yale Law School; an International Law Fellow and Visiting Professor at American University in Washington, DC; a Professorial Fellow at the Centre for Petroleum and Natural Resources Law at the University of Dundee, Scotland; and a Research Fellow at the Max Planck *Institut fur Offentliches Auslandisches Recht* in Heidelburg, Germany.

Mr. Sornarajah has been arbitrator or counsel in several leading arbitrations and has published extensively in the area of international commercial arbitration and international investment law.

Michael K. Tracton is an investment negotiator with the Investment Office of the U.S. Department of State. He served on the team that developed the U.S. model bilateral investment treaty and has participated in several negotiations of U.S. investment treaties and investment chapters of free trade agreements. He has presented on international investment issues in the context of Asia-Pacific Economic Cooperation (APEC) and other fora. Mr. Tracton received his J.D. from the University of Maryland School of Law.

Katia Yannaca-Small is Legal Advisor to the Investment Division, Directorate for Financial and Enterprise Affairs, at the OECD. She is responsible for analytical work on all legal issues related to international investment agreements and in particular developments in investor-State dispute settlement. She manages the related activities of the OECD Investment Committee and proposes issues for discussion and possible policy development in this field. Previously, she was responsible for the analytical and organizational support of OECD anti-corruption efforts during the period leading to the OECD Anti-Bribery Convention; worked on foreign direct investment reviews of Central and Eastern European countries, in particular on the examination of the legal framework for and policies toward foreign investment; and addressed issues of corporate responsibility related to the OECD Guidelines for Multinational Enterprises.

Ms. Yannaca-Small holds a J.D. from the Athens University Law School, Greece, two postgraduate degrees on Public International Law and International Economic Law from the University of Paris I (Panthéon-Sorbonne), and is a graduate of the *École Nationale d'Administration* (ENA), France.

Participating Institutions

Columbia University School of Law, founded in 1858, stands at the forefront of legal education and of the law in a global society. Columbia Law School graduates have provided leadership worldwide in a remarkably broad range of fields—government, diplomacy, the judiciary, business, nonprofit, advocacy, entertainment, academia, science, and the arts. Led by Dean David M. Schizer, Columbia Law School joins its traditional strengths in international and comparative law, constitutional law, administrative law and human rights law with pioneering work in intellectual property, digital technology, sexuality and gender, and criminal law. For further information, visit http://www.law.columbia.edu.

The Earth Institute at Columbia University is the world's leading academic center for the integrated study of Earth, its environment and society. Led by Professor Jeffrey D. Sachs, The Earth Institute builds upon excellence in the core disciplines—earth sciences, biological sciences, engineering sciences, social sciences and health sciences—and stresses cross-disciplinary approaches to complex problems. Through research, training and global partnerships, it mobilizes science and technology to advance sustainable development, while placing special emphasis on the needs of the world's poor. For more information, visit http://www.earth.columbia.edu.

The Columbia Program on International Investment (CPII), launched in January 2006, seeks to be a leader on issues related to foreign direct investment in the global economy. Led by Dr. Karl P. Sauvant, its objectives are to analyze important topical policy-oriented issues related to FDI, develop and disseminate practical approaches and solutions, and provide students with a challenging learning environment. CPII is a joint program of the Columbia Law School and The Earth Institute at Columbia University, and is supported in part through the generosity of Mark and Gail Appel. For more information, visit http://www.cpii.columbia.edu.

Foreword

International investment law is evolving rapidly. Some 20 years ago, as observed in this volume, there was little that amounted to a coherent and consistent system of international investment law. Today, a multitude of treaties define the principal tenets of international investment law. This law continues to evolve, and we face the challenge of ensuring coherence and consistency in a process of continuing and rapid change.

This situation of continuing change is also an opportunity to ensure that international investment law evolves to address the concerns of all those who are directly involved in the investment process—firms, workers, host countries, home countries—and, beyond those, of the international community as a whole. Among the broader objectives, pride of place belongs to the promotion of long-term sustainable development, meaning a rise of incomes compatible with the protection of the environment. Investment law, after all, is a powerful tool to encourage investment and to encourage that investment to make the greatest possible contribution to global sustainable development.

I am deeply appreciative that the Columbia Program on International Investment, a joint undertaking of Columbia Law School and The Earth Institute, has taken on the challenge of the international investment law system. The April 2006 Symposium, the chapters of which are contained in this volume, was meant to be a first step in a series of events which will examine the future of international investment law and the challenges and opportunities of foreign investment and foreign investment law in the era of globalization.

*Jeffrey D. Sachs**

---

* Director of The Earth Institute at Columbia University, Quetelet Professor of Sustainable Development, and Professor of Health Policy and Management at Columbia University. He is also Special Advisor to United Nations Secretary-General Ban Ki-Moon. Email: Director@ei.columbia.edu.

Preface

Columbia Law School has a distinguished tradition of leadership in international law. From Francis Lieber during the American Civil War, to the legendary era of Wolfgang Friedman, Lou Henkin and Oscar Schachter during the 1950s and onwards, and now with our current generation of leaders in the field, the Columbia faculty has always had a strong international orientation.

Over the past few decades, and at an accelerating rate, international investment has surged to central importance in international economic relations. Parallel to that, an international regulatory framework is emerging to shape and rationalize this vitally important sector of worldwide business and economics. There are over 2,500 bilateral investment treaties, for example, with a range of variations as regards important substantive provisions. The area poses fascinating challenges for lawyers and policymakers.

The April 2006 Symposium at Columbia Law School, and this memorial volume, seek to foster research and thinking on this vitally important area. By convening international investment lawyers from government, academia, the private sector and non-governmental organizations, the symposium was an important step in the process of improving our understanding of the international regulatory regime. We are very proud of Columbia's leadership role in the field, and of the intellectual energy that emanates from the Columbia Program on International Investment (CPII). The combination of Columbia Law School's noted international faculty, the University's Earth Institute and its expertise in sustainable development, and the leadership at CPII of Dr. Karl P. Sauvant, the long-time Director of the Investment Division of the UN Conference on Trade and Development (UNCTAD), promises that Columbia University will become a leader in the study of the emerging international regulatory framework for investment.

*David M. Schizer**

---

* Dean, Columbia University School of Law, and Lucy G. Moses Professor of Law. Email: dschiz@law.columbia.edu.

PART I

Introduction

CHAPTER 1

The Rise of International Investment, Investment Agreements and Investment Disputes

*Karl P. Sauvant**

To set the scene and provide the context for this volume, I would like to make three points: (1) foreign direct investment (FDI) has become the most important vehicle to bring goods and services to foreign markets and to integrate national production systems; (2) this process has been accompanied by the rapid rise of international investment agreements (IIAs); and (3), most recently, we can also observe a substantial rise of international investment disputes.

The Rise of Foreign Direct Investment

Over the past 20 years, FDI[1] flows have expanded substantially, from around US$50 billion during the early 1980s, to US$1.3 trillion by the end of 2006; they are expected to stay roughly at this level during the next few years (Figure 1.1).

---

* Executive Director, Columbia Program on International Investment, and Co-Director, Millennium Cities Initiative. Email: karl.sauvant@law.columbia.edu. I would like to acknowledge with gratitude comments by Kenneth Vandevelde, Peter Muchlinski, Federico Ortino, and Luke Peterson, and the assistance by Michael O'Sullivan, Ted Platt and Hamed El-Kady.

1 FDI is defined as "an investment involving a long-term relationship and reflecting a lasting interest and control by a resident entity in one economy (foreign direct investor or parent enterprise) in an enterprise resident in an economy other than that of the foreign direct investor (FDI enterprise or affiliate enterprise or foreign affiliate)"; *see* UNCTAD, *World Investment Report 2007: Transnational Corporations, Extractive Industries and Development* (United Nations Publication: 2007) [hereinafter UNCTAD 2007], p. 245. This general definition of FDI is based on OECD, *Detailed Benchmark Definition of Foreign Direct Investment*, 3rd Edition (OECD: 1996) and International Monetary Fund, *Balance of Payments Manual*, 5th Edition (IMF: 1993).

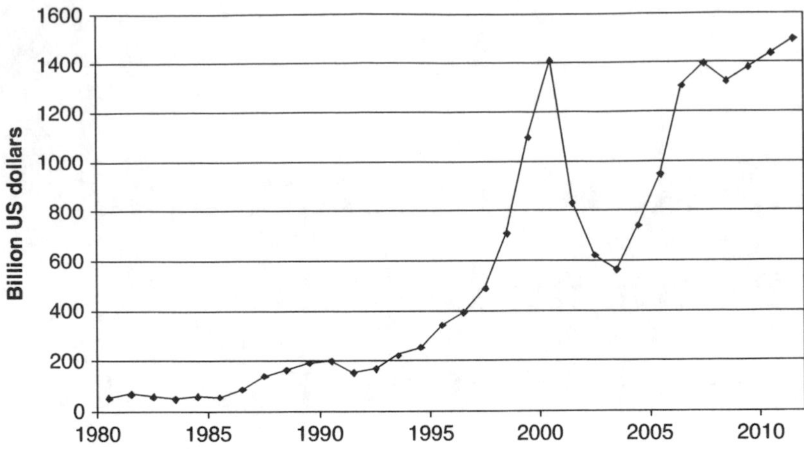

Figure 1.1 World inward FDI flows, 1980–2011 (Billion US dollars)
Source: UNCTAD (http://stats.unctad.org/fdi/) and Laza Kekic and Karl P. Sauvant, eds., *World Investment Prospects to 2011: Foreign Direct Investment and the Challenge of Political Risk* (The Economist Intelligence Unit Ltd.: 2007).

The lion's share goes to developed countries, although developing ones (and especially Asia) account for a substantial amount: approximately 30% in 2006 (Figure 1.2).[2]

Most of these flows are in the services sector (some three-quarters) and originate in developed countries, although a rising share comes from emerging markets—some US$210 billion in 2006.[3]

This investment is undertaken by more than 80,000 parent firms controlling over 800,000 foreign affiliates (many of them having entered corporate systems through acquisitions). Increasingly, firms from emerging markets[4] are also becoming multinational corporations (MNCs)—firms that control assets abroad—as they are subject to the same pressures as their counterparts from developed countries. These include: (1) the liberalization of FDI regulatory frameworks throughout the world—which increases the opportunities for firms to expand abroad; (2) progress in, especially, information and communication technologies—which creates the means to run global production networks;

---

2 UNCTAD 2007.

3 Laza Kekic and Karl P. Sauvant, eds., *World Investment Prospects to 2011: Foreign Direct Investment and the Challenge of Political Risk* (The Economist Intelligence Unit Ltd.: 2007).

4 Although emerging market MNCs, and some MNCs from economies in transition, have existed for some time, it is only recently that their activities have assumed important proportions. For a discussion of the issues to which this gives rise, *see* Karl P. Sauvant, with Kristin Mendoza and Irmak Ince, eds., *The Rise of Transnational Corporations from Emerging Markets: Threat or Opportunity?* (Edward Elgar: 2008).

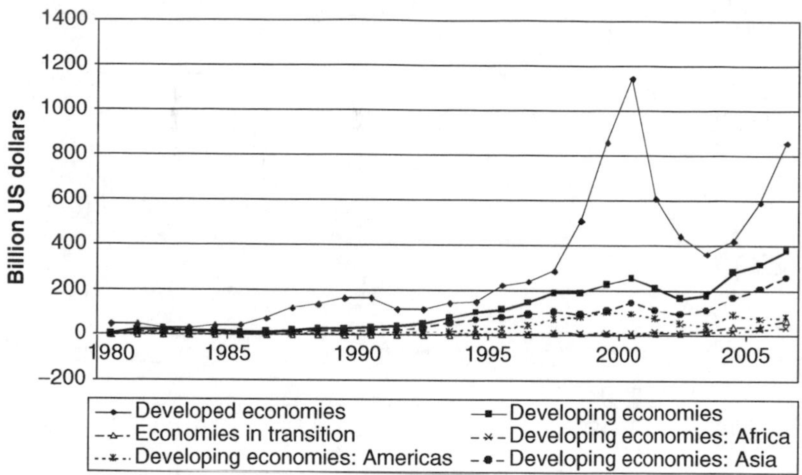

Figure 1.2 Inward FDI flows, by region, 1980–2006 (Billion US dollars)
Source: UNCTAD (http://stats.unctad.org/fdi/).

and (3) the pressures of competition—which lead firms to grasp these opportunities by undertaking outward FDI where the combination of ownership, locational and internalization advantages[5] makes this form of market entry superior to trade. Increasingly, indeed, any part of the production process can be located wherever it contributes most to a company's competitiveness, creating in this manner regional or global corporate production networks. In fact, foreign affiliates and such networks are more and more becoming a source of corporate competitiveness as they provide access not only to markets but also to various resources, ranging from natural resources and cheap labor to skills and technology. Hence the acquisition of a portfolio of locational assets becomes of key importance for firms, be they large or small, from developed countries or emerging markets.

The aggregation of these corporate networks is giving rise to an integrated international production system—the productive core of the globalizing world economy. Its importance can best be captured by looking at the accumulation of FDI flows, i.e., the stock of foreign direct investment. It stood at US$12 trillion in 2006 (Figure 1.3), roughly one-tenth of it accounted for by MNCs from emerging markets. (To this, one has to add various non-equity forms of control—such as management contracts and franchise agreements—through

---

[5] These are the main variables of the eclectic paradigm, the principal exploratory framework for FDI; *see* John H. Dunning, "The Eclectic Paradigm as an Envelope of Economic and Business Theories of MNE Activity," International Business Review, 9 (2000), pp. 163–192.

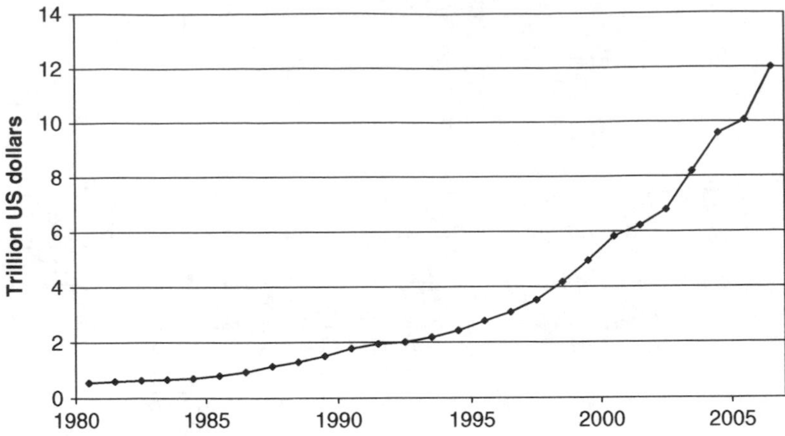

Figure 1.3 World inward FDI stock, 1980–2006 (Trillion US dollars)
Source: UNCTAD (http://stats.unctad.org/fdi/).

which additional economic activities are brought under the common governance of MNCs.) This FDI stock gave rise to an estimated US$25 trillion of sales by foreign affiliates (nearly twice the value of world exports in 2006), making FDI considerably more important than trade in terms of delivering goods and services to foreign markets, while, at the same time, integrating national production systems. In fact, roughly one-third of world trade takes place as intra-firm trade (i.e., trade among the various parts of the same corporate networks), and the bulk of technology is transferred within the framework of the integrated international production system. All of this means that FDI and the activities of MNCs have become central to the world economy, and to development.

The Rise of International Investment Agreements

No wonder, then, that all countries seek to attract FDI. For this purpose, the great majority of them have established investment promotion agencies (IPAs), in an increasing number of cases not only national ones but also sub-national ones. Their proliferation can best be seen from the growth of the World Association of Investment Promotion Agencies (WAIPA), which was established in 1995: by October 2007, it had 220 members (Figure 1.4).

Their role is to attract FDI, facilitate the establishment of foreign affiliates and provide after-investment services to those affiliates already established.

Perhaps even more impressively, all countries in the world have liberalized their FDI laws in an effort to attract more FDI, typically by opening more

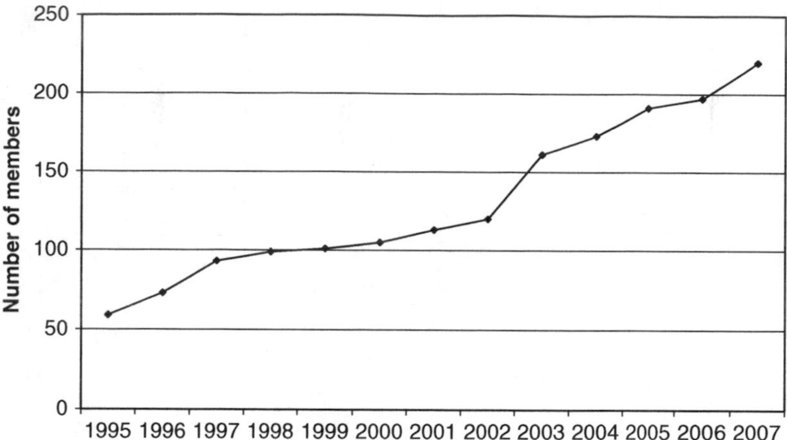

Figure 1.4 The growth of membership in WAIPA, cumulative, 1995–2007 (as of October 2007)
Source: WAIPA.

activities to foreign investors, reducing obstacles to the operation of foreign affiliates, providing a range of incentives, and offering various guarantees (for example, against nationalization) in their domestic laws, if not their constitutions. Of the 2,533 changes in FDI-related laws and regulations that took place between 1991 and 2006, some 90% were in the direction of making the investment climate more welcoming to FDI (Table 1.1). This is a pervasive trend, indeed.[6]

This trend is, furthermore, complemented by the rise of international investment law. Compared to the 1960s and 1970s, we have today a vastly different international investment law landscape. Back then, as Jeswald Salacuse writes in Chapter 6 of this volume, "foreign investors seeking the protection of international investment law found an ephemeral structure consisting largely of scattered treaty provisions, a few contested customs and some questionable general principles of law." Today, while no comprehensive multilateral investment treaty exists, international investment law is contained in a multifaceted, multilayered, increasingly complex network of international investment agreements (IIAs)—i.e., agreements that, in one way or another, address investment issues and involve virtually every country in the world.[7] Pride of place among these agreements belongs to bilateral investment treaties (BITs) for the promotion

---

6 There are however, signs of a backlash; *see* Karl P. Sauvant, "A Backlash Against Foreign Direct Investment?," *in* Laza Kekic and Karl P. Sauvant, eds., *World Investment Prospects to 2010: Boom or Backlash?* (The Economist Intelligence Unit Ltd.: 2006), pp. 71–77.

7 *See* UNCTAD, *International Investment Arrangements: Trends and Emerging Issues* (United Nations Publication: 2006), for a discussion.

Table 1.1 National regulatory changes, 1991–2006

Item	*1991*	*1992*	*1993*	*1994*	*1995*	*1996*	*1997*	*1998*	*1999*	*2000*	*2001*	*2002*	*2003*	*2004*	*2005*	*2006*
Number of countries that introduced regulatory changes in their investment regimes	35	43	57	49	64	65	76	60	63	69	71	70	82	102	93	93
Number of regulatory changes	82	77	100	110	112	114	150	145	139	150	207	246	242	270	205	184
More favorable to FDI[a/]	80	77	99	108	106	98	134	136	130	147	193	234	218	234	164	147
Less favorable to FDI[b/]	2	-	1	2	6	16	16	9	9	3	14	12	24	36	41	37

Source: UNCTAD, *World Investment Report 2005: Transnational Corporations and the Internationalization of R&D* (United Nations Publication: 2005, p. 26) and UNCTAD 2007, p. 14.

[a/] Includes further liberalization, or changes aimed at strengthening market functioning, as well as increased incentives.

[b/] Includes changes aimed at increasing control, as well as reducing incentives.

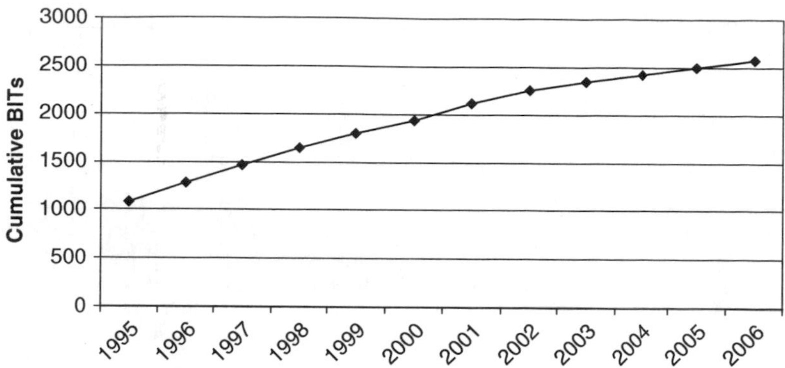

Figure 1.5 Number of BITs concluded, cumulative, 1995–2006
Source: UNCTAD (www.unctad.org/iia).

and protection of foreign investment. Their number had reached 2,573 at the end of 2006 (Figure 1.5), involving 179 countries. (*See* Appendices 6 and 7, *UNCTAD, IIA Monitors.*)

During 2006 alone, for example, 73 new BITs were concluded—more than one per week.[8] While early BITs were concluded primarily between developed and developing countries, their share of the stock of BITs had dropped to 40% by the end of 2006, while the share of BITs between developing countries had reached 27%.[9] Although the first BIT (between Germany and Pakistan) was concluded in 1959, BITs did not take off until the 1990s.[10] At that time, FDI flows became more important and countries, in their efforts to attract even more investment (and in the framework of overall more market-friendly policies), sought to signal the MNCs that they were prepared to guarantee an investment-friendly national regulatory framework through international agreements.

In addition to BITs, a number of other agreements also address investment matters, but as part of a range of other issues, most prominently among them

---

8 UNCTAD 2007. Unless otherwise indicated, the data used here come from this source. It should be noted that the number of BITs concluded per year has been decreasing since 2002, and a number of them are not (yet) in force (UNCTAD, "The Entry into Force of Bilateral Investment Treaties (BITs)," IIA Monitor, No. 3 (2006) (UNCTAD/WEB/ITE/IIA/2006/9)).

9 BITs between developed countries and countries of South-East Europe and the Commonwealth of Independent States accounted for 13%; between the latter group of countries and developing countries 10%; between developed countries 7%; and between countries of South-East Europe and the Commonwealth of Independent States 3%. *See* UNCTAD "Investment Instruments" on-line database (http://www.unctadxi.org/templates/Startpage____718.aspx).

10 There were fewer than 400 completed BITs in 1990.

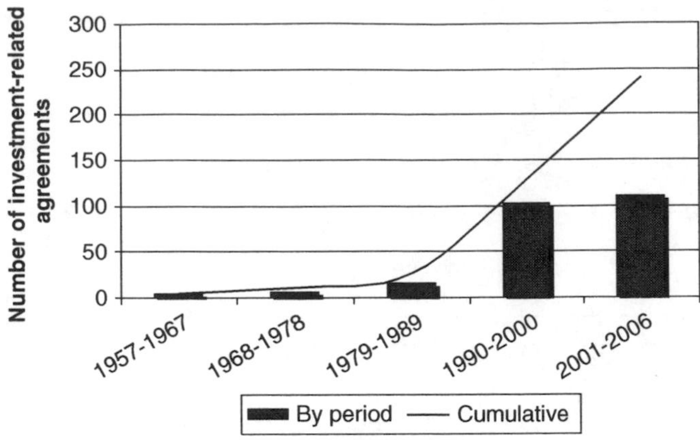

Figure 1.6 The growth of PTIAs, 1957–2006 (Number)
Source: UNCTAD 2007.

trade, but also *inter alia* intellectual property, competition and government procurement.[11] The number of such preferential trade and investment agreements (PTIAs) had reached 241 by the end of 2006, of which more than 90 involved developing countries only (Figure 1.6).

Developing countries participate in 79% of these PTIAs, compared to 54% for developed countries; as of end-2006, at least 72 additional agreements were under negotiation.[12]

These PTIAs represent an interesting development, in that they suggest a return to an earlier trend. Until the 1950s, investment matters were addressed (to the extent that they were covered at all) in comprehensive treaties akin to PTIAs; one example is the series of U.S. Friendship, Commerce and Navigation Treaties. Beginning in 1959, then, investment matters became the subject of separate treaties for the reasons mentioned earlier. BITs continue to be concluded, albeit at a decreasing rate, while investment matters are again being integrated into more comprehensive agreements, the PTIAs.[13] One of the

---

11 For a discussion of the rise of these agreements see OECD, "Novel Features in OECD Countries' Recent Investment Agreements: An Overview" (OECD: 2005), mimeo, reprinted in the annex of this volume. *See* also UNCTAD, *International Investment Arrangements: Trends and Emerging Issues* (United Nations Publication: 2006). Double taxation treaties (of which there were 2,651 by the end of 2006, *see* UNCTAD 2007, p. 16) are also important for MNCs; given their specialized nature, they are not discussed here.

12 UNCTAD 2007 and www.unctad.org/iia. For a full discussion of such agreements, *see* UNCTAD, *Investment Provisions in Economic Integration Agreements* (United Nations Publication: 2006).

13 This may also partly account for the decrease in the number of BITs concluded. However, the BITs in existence already cover most of the most important investment relationships, so it is only natural that the annual number of new treaties is declining. On the other hand, there are an increasing number of

reasons may well be that more comprehensive treaties allow more scope for trade-offs across issue areas.

Another reason may be that PTIAs typically are oriented more toward liberalization than BITs, i.e., they not only seek to protect investment that has already been made, but also tend to seek to reduce restrictions on investment. While it is true that some recent BITs also go beyond protection (e.g., those by the U.S., Canada and Japan that foresee national treatment at the entry stage), the overwhelming number remain focused on protection. In particular, they typically provide for national, most-favored-nation (MFN) and fair and equitable treatment; protection from expropriation (and rules for action if and when takings occur, including as regards compensation); and the transfer of funds. And, most importantly in the context of this volume, they typically contain provisions for investor-State dispute settlement.[14]

The Rise of International Investment Disputes

Foreign direct investment has not only become more important than trade, it is also more intrusive than (arm's length) trade, as it involves the entire range of issues related to the production process. This intrusiveness is accentuated by the fact that FDI not only has positive effects on host countries (e.g., it brings capital, technology, skills, access to markets), but can also have negative ones (e.g., it can lead to the crowding out of domestic firms or involve abusive transfer pricing, restrictive business practices or the control of sectors that, for one reason or another, are considered to be sensitive). Moreover, public policy and regulation concerning FDI take place in the context of several sets of tensions, both from the perspective of MNCs seeking a favorable investment climate and governments seeking to attract FDI and benefit from it as much as possible: the global corporate interests of MNCs vs. the national development interests of countries; foreign vs. domestic ownership; policies to attract FDI vs. policies to maximize its benefits; a country's interest as a host country vs. its interests as a home country; and the constraints imposed by the emerging integrated international production system, a globalizing world economy and international investment law vs. the need for policy space in the interest of national development. Combined with the rising number of IIAs containing

---

renegotiations of BITs; *see* UNCTAD, "International Investment Rule-Setting: Trends, Emerging Issues and Implications," TD/B/COM.2/73 (5 January 2007), mimeo.

14 For a full discussion of the contents of BITs, *see* UNCTAD, *Bilateral Investment Treaties 1995–2006: Trends in Investment Rulemaking* (United Nations Publication: 2007).

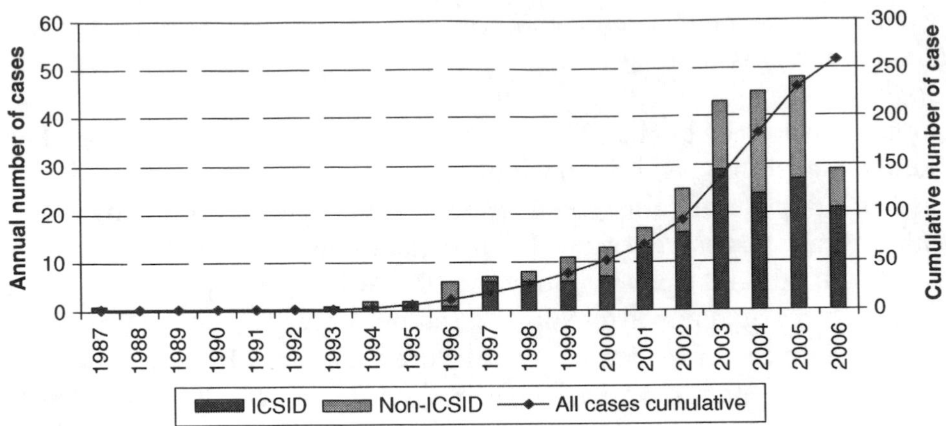

Figure 1.7 Known investment treaty arbitrations (cumulative and newly instituted cases, 1987–2006)
Source: UNCTAD 2007.

dispute settlement provisions and their growing complexity, all this makes it more likely that conflicts arise between foreign investors and host countries.

It is not known how many of such conflicts arise and are settled (amicably or otherwise) at the *national* level. What is a new and important development is that an increasing number of disputes are being brought to the *international* level, causing a veritable investment disputes explosion. (The reasons for this development are examined by Salacuse in Chapter 6.) More specifically, the number of known[15] treaty-based investor-State dispute settlement cases had reached 259 by the end of 2006 (Figure 1.7), virtually all of them initiated by investors.

The great majority of these cases (191 to be precise, or 74%) were filed since the beginning of 2002, with the currently highest number (50) filed in 2005.[16] For comparison: during the entire existence of GATT (1948–1994), a total of 101 disputes were brought, and another 369 disputes have been brought under the WTO from its inception through 25 September 2007.[17] It must be noted, however, that only States can use the WTO's dispute settlement machinery;

15 "Known" because the non-public nature of many disputes makes it likely that there are additional disputes not captured by the data reported here.

16 The data, here and below, are from UNCTAD, "Latest Developments in Investor-State Dispute Settlement," IIA Monitor, No. 4 (2006) (UNCTAD/WEB/ITE/IIA/2006/11) [hereinafter UNCTAD 2006], reprinted in the annex to this volume, and UNCTAD 2007. *See* UNCTAD 2006 for an instructive discussion of these disputes.

17 *See*: WTO "Chronological list of disputes cases." (http://www.wto.org/english/tratop_e/dispu_e/dispu_status_e.htm).

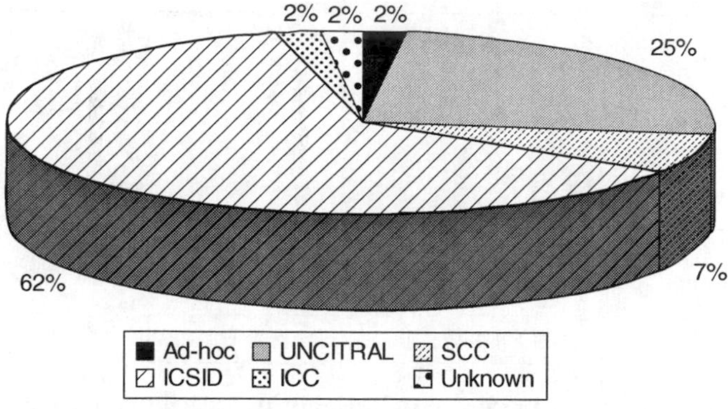

Figure 1.8 Disputes, by forum of arbitration, cumulative as of end-2006 (Percentage)
Source: UNCTAD 2007.
Note: SCC = Stockholm Chamber of Commerce; ICC = International Chamber of Commerce.

in the case of investment, on the other hand, and depending on the exact formulation of the applicable treaty, any of the 80,000-plus MNCs, 800,000-plus foreign affiliates and perhaps even their shareholders could potentially initiate a case.

Almost two-thirds of all known disputes have been brought before the International Centre for Settlement of Investment Disputes (ICSID) (or ICSID's Additional Facility), with the United Nations Commission on International Trade Law (UNCITRAL) providing the second most popular framework (Figure 1.8). The governments of 70 countries are involved, mostly of developing countries (44), but also of developed countries (14) and economies in transition (12) (Table 1.2). Argentina leads with 45 cases, all but three of them at least partly related to its recent financial crisis. Disputes have arisen

Table 1.2 Leading defendants in international investment disputes, as of end-2006

Defendant	*Number of claims*
Argentina	45
Mexico	18
Czech Republic	11
United States	11
India	9
Moldova, Republic of	9
Russia	9
Ecuador	8
Egypt	8
Canada	7
Poland	7
Romania	7

Source: UNCTAD (www.unctad.org/iia).

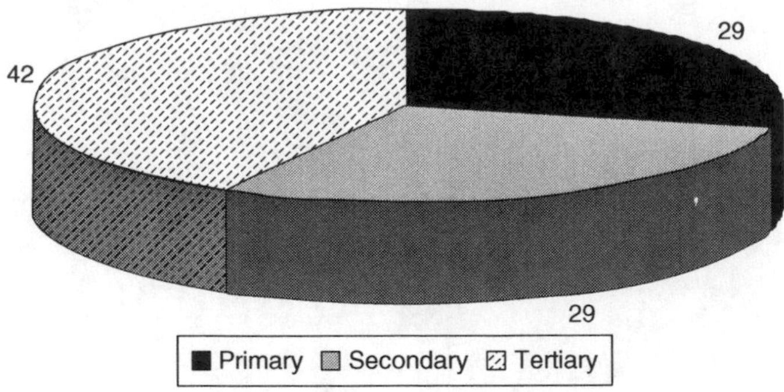

Figure 1.9 Sectors involved in known investment treaty arbitrations, as of end-2006 (Percentage)
Source: UNCTAD 2007.

roughly evenly in the services sector (including infrastructure), manufacturing and natural resources (Figure 1.9).

The issues that are or were involved in these disputes relate in particular to the interpretation of key elements of investment protection standards, especially as regards the principle of fair and equitable treatment, the international minimum standard of treatment, the scope of MFN treatment, and the meaning of "in like circumstances" as it relates to national treatment. Other issues include the question of regulatory takings, the scope of the umbrella clause, the notion of "effective control," and the definition of "investment," as well as, in relation to a number of cases involving Argentina, the question of whether a "state of necessity" existed, as a result of a national economic emergency, such as could excuse infringements of protection standards. As can be seen from this list, the subjects that are addressed in arbitration cases relate to key issues in international investment law.

There is little systematic information on the amount of damages awarded so far. Claims can be very high; in the case of three arbitrations brought by the majority shareholders in Yukos, they are reported to total US$33 billion.[18] But this does not mean that arbitrators will award high amounts, even if they find in favor of a claimant. For example, 21 disputes reached a conclusion during 2006; however, out of a total of US$1.63 billion in claimed damages, arbitrators awarded only US$241.2 million, or 15% of the claimed damages.[19]

---

18 UNCTAD, "Latest Developments in Investor-State Dispute Settlement," IIA Monitor, No. 4 (2005) (UNCTAD/WEB/ITE/IIT/2005/2), p. 6, reprinted in the annex to this volume.

19 UNCTAD 2006, p. 6.

But awards *can* be high: a tribunal awarded to CSOB under a contract case (on 29 December 2004) US$824 million (plus US$10 million as a partial contribution to the costs, expenses and counsel's fees) in its case against Slovakia; in the Lauder case, the claimant was awarded (3 December 2001) US$270 million (plus interest) against the Czech Republic; and CMS Gas Transmission Company was awarded (15 May 2005) US$133.2 million (plus interest) against Argentina.[20] In other words, awards can be substantial, without even counting the costs of litigation.[21]

This surge in investment disputes is not necessarily a problematic matter in and of itself, as disputes are normal in any rule-based system. In fact, it is surprising that the number of disputes had not started to rise much earlier and had not reached considerably higher magnitudes, considering the growth of the stock of foreign direct investment, the intrusiveness of FDI and the great number of IIAs with dispute settlement provisions. But things seem to be changing, judging from the developments during the past few years reported earlier. This raises questions related to the financial burden of awards and the costs of dispute settlement for the countries involved, the potential damage disputes can do to the relationship between investors and host countries, the capacity of countries to handle such disputes, and the effect the surge of disputes can have on the negotiation of IIAs. But it also raises the questions of whether the multitude of one-off tribunals established to deal with investment disputes can—and does—lead to inconsistencies in the interpretation of IIAs and how one can meet this challenge, including through the establishment of a review mechanism for arbitral decisions.

More specifically, against the background of the rise of FDI, IIAs and investment disputes, the contributions in this volume look, in its Part I, at the multifaceted nature of international investment law and the future of this law. Part II, then, deals with the evolving nature of international investment law, recent trends in international investment disputes and the reasons for the increase of such disputes. In Part III of this volume, a number of issues directly pertaining to investment disputes are addressed, before examining, in Part IV the question of an appellate mechanism in international investment disputes.

---

20 UNCTAD, *Investor-State Disputes Arising from Investment Treaties: A Review* (United Nations Publication: 2005), p. 9.

21 UNCTAD 2006, p. 6 observes: "a few recent decisions … seem to reinforce the recent trend that allocates (at least part of) the legal fees and arbitration costs to the losing party, whether the State or the investor." It continues to list a few cases, including the decision (2 October 2006) of the ADC tribunal to award the full costs of US$7.6 million (which included the investor's legal costs) to the defending country.

Most of these chapters were presented at the Columbia Program on International Investment Symposium on "Transparency and Consistency in International Investment Law: Is There a Need for a Review Mechanism?," 4 April 2006, held at Columbia University, in cooperation with the *Centre d'Études et de Recherches de Droit International* of Sorbonne University Panthéon-Sorbonne. A number of the commentaries made on that occasion are included as well, as is the summary by the rapporteur of the Symposium. Finally, the annex contains documents that bear directly on ICSID's proposal for the establishment of a review mechanism, as well as materials that provide context for this proposal and hence deal with the rise of international investment disputes and the proliferation of international investment agreements.

The international investment law system is in a phase of rapid change. Disputes, and reactions to them, contribute to that process. Making sure that the various components of this system are consistent and coherent, that its processes are transparent and that all participants feel that it serves their interest can only strengthen the rule of law governing this important economic activity, complementing—and reinforcing—the national regulatory investment frameworks of individual countries.

CHAPTER 2

The Multifaceted Nature of International Investment Law

*Rainer Geiger**

International investment has expanded exponentially over the past decades. While industrialized countries still account for the bulk of outward investment, emerging market economies are becoming major sources of investment as well. There is a growing consensus that investment is a driving force for economic development and that there is a common interest in providing favorable conditions for investment—which implies a transparent and equitable set of rules governing the relations between investors and governments. The importance of investment and private sector initiatives is recognized in the Monterrey Consensus and the United Nations' Millennium Development Goals.

Foreign direct investment (FDI) can bring significant benefits to host countries, but these benefits will only accrue if there is a coherent framework of rules ranging across a wide spectrum of policy areas that determine the scope for business activities.[1] These not only include the traditional areas of investment liberalization and investment protection, but also policies and rules relating to taxation, the environment, labor relations and the development of human resources, infrastructure development, efficient financial institutions, good governance in the public and corporate sectors and rules to ensure the

---

* Deputy Director, Financial and Enterprise Affairs, OECD; Associate Professor for International Law, University Paris I (Panthéon/Sorbonne). This chapter reflects introductory remarks and conclusions presented at the Symposium. It represents the personal views of the author. Email: Rainer.Geiger@oecd.org.

1 OECD, *Foreign Direct Investment for Development: Maximising Benefits-Minimising Costs* (2002).

competitive functioning of markets. If such a framework is in place, investment becomes an instrument for sustainable development. Responsible corporate conduct is another ingredient of a favorable investment environment; this means that corporations not only abide by the law, but also respect fundamental values of business behavior and take into account the interests of a wide range of stakeholders in the countries in which they operate.

The emerging consensus on the importance of investment and the need for policies conducive to investment has not yet translated into a consistent multilateral framework. Attempts to negotiate multilateral rules for investment have not been successful, as witnessed by the spectacular failure, within the Organisation for Economic Co-operation and Development (OECD), of a Multilateral Agreement on Investment (MAI) and the incapacity of the WTO to launch multilateral negotiations on investment. Today's international investment law is still characterized by a multifaceted system of rules, which is a source of complexity, imbalance and inconsistency. The challenges are to increase transparency, coherence and legal certainty. The focus is on dispute settlement under existing bilateral and regional investment treaties. Do present mechanisms of investor-State arbitration provide sufficient guarantees for procedural fairness and substantive justice? Can bilateral treaties provide a basis for developing a reliable and coherent set of interpretations? Would an appeals mechanism help? Is there scope for revival of more comprehensive multilateral approaches?

To set the scene for these discussions, this chapter provides a brief overview of the main features of the present system of international investment law.

The present landscape of international investment law is dominated by treaty provisions, contained in either bilateral, regional, plurilateral or multilateral instruments on various aspects of investment relations. Soft law approaches (i.e., non-binding standards) play an important role in the area of corporate responsibility and are increasingly used to define good practices for government policies in areas that did not yet lend themselves to multilateral rule setting (e.g., taxation, competition).

The Bilateral Treaty Network

There is a dense and still expanding network of bilateral investment treaties (BITs), most of which have been concluded between OECD countries and developing countries. European countries account for the largest number of these treaties. Non-European countries, in particular the U.S. and Mexico, have included investment provisions in trade agreements. With the growing volume of South-South investment, developing countries increasingly conclude BITs among themselves.

As demonstrated by a recent OECD study,[2] the treaty practice of most countries shows a certain degree of convergence in investment protection provisions. There is also an increasing emphasis on market access and right of establishment—not only in the BIT model pursued by the United States, but also in trade agreements with investment content. The aim is to ensure high standards of protection and to enhance liberalization of entry conditions for new investment. Most BITs contain dispute settlement clauses, both State-State and investor-State.

How can the proliferation of BITs be explained? Investment treaties are perceived as a tool to promote both outward and inward investment. They are designed to contribute to a rules-based system for international investment, with dispute settlement provisions that allow direct recourse by investors to arbitration. While no causal relationship between treaties and the attraction of investment can be clearly demonstrated, investment treaties provide a strong signal that investors can rely on the existence of international law obligations. Confidence and legal certainty are essential elements for mutually beneficial relations between investors and host countries.

By definition, each international treaty implies, for the contracting parties, a limitation to their sovereignty. This is accepted if the treaty pursues a common goal and is properly balanced in its definition of mutual rights and obligations. As compared to multilateral instruments, bilateral treaties reflect the bargaining power of the contracting parties. The interest of host countries is to promote investment, and often investment requires a degree of legal certainty that may not be seen to be available under the host country's own laws. On the other hand, even if an investment treaty contains reciprocal rights and duties, BITs concluded in the past referred to one-way situations where developing countries were always at the receiving end of the investment. As a consequence, they reflected the views of industrialized countries, which tended to impose on developing countries obligations they would not be ready to assume themselves. Sometimes, treaty provisions were adopted by host countries without serious negotiation, and key clauses were ambiguously drafted.

---

2 "Novel Features in OECD Countries' Recent Investment Agreements," Symposium organized by ICSID, OECD and UNCTAD, 2005. (This article is reproduced in Annex 8.)

Has the pendulum swung too far toward privileging FDI to the detriment of host countries' interests? Has sovereignty been for sale?

These concerns are amply demonstrated by the upsurge of litigation under investment agreements.[3] They are related to the mechanism of investor-State dispute settlement, where ad hoc arbitral tribunals may sit in judgment on regulatory acts of host countries touching areas of public interest like health, safety and the environment. But, even more importantly, these concerns are rooted in the way substantive provisions are drafted and interpreted. If a treaty lacks balance between the protection of investment and a government's right to regulate, signatories face the risk of large compensation awards in instances considered to be "measures tantamount to expropriation" or lack of "fair and equitable treatment".[4] The interpretation of the MFN clause found in most BITs has become a source of controversy as well: does it only cover substantive provisions of the treaty or does it also extend to the way dispute settlement mechanisms are defined?[5]

Today, the more diversified nature of investment relations—where industrialized countries themselves may become host to investment originating from developing countries—offers an opportunity to reconsider the balance of investment treaties. This may lead to a clarification of existing treaty provisions by the contracting parties. This happened, for instance, within NAFTA and the U.S. model BIT with respect to the issue of "regulatory takings" and the scope of the "fair and equitable" treatment standard. Consideration may also be given to insert into the text of future treaties language specifying the scope of public interest safeguards like national security, health and the environment.

Another avenue for evolving treaty practice would be to diversify dispute settlement mechanisms to avoid where possible the costly recourse to arbitration (for example small claims commissions, mediation and conciliation mechanisms). More explicit procedural safeguards like transparency of proceedings, consolidation of claims, systematic publication of awards and the possibility of third party intervention can also help provide balance between investor and

---

3 UNCTAD, *Investor-State Disputes Arising from Investment Treaties: A Review* (United Nations Publication: 2005).

4 Rainer Geiger, "Regulatory Expropriations in International Law," 11 N.Y.U. ENVTL. L. J. 1, 94–109 (2002).

5 Key legal concepts of investment agreements are discussed in: OECD, *International Investment Law: A Changing Landscape* (2005).

host country interests and increase procedural fairness. Views differ on the desirability and feasibility, under ICSID or similar mechanisms, of an appeals procedure. In the absence of a single multilateral text of reference, an appeals procedure that has to examine awards based on diverging treaty texts may not in itself be sufficient to increase coherence and to create the value of precedent.

Piecemeal Approaches at Plurilateral and Multilateral Levels

On a regional level, NAFTA, in its Chapter 11, sets out a high standard model for investment rules that applies to both the entry of investment and the treatment of established foreign-controlled enterprises. It also covers performance requirements as well as monopolies and State-owned enterprises to the extent that they affect investment. Investor-State dispute settlement is provided and has been relatively frequently used to challenge individual and regulatory measures of contracting parties.[6] The instances introduced, and the awards rendered, have generated controversy and abundant analysis of key investment protection issues of relevance for the interpretation of standard clauses of investment treaties, as mentioned above.

The NAFTA model is largely reflected in the Energy Charter Treaty (ECT), with the main difference that ECT negotiators did not succeed in extending the agreement to the entry of new investment. In its present form, ECT provides high standards for the treatment of existing investment and opens access to investor-State dispute settlement.[7] The treaty was designed to provide a framework for energy cooperation between Eastern European countries and Western partners, but its efficiency is greatly diminished by the fact that one of the key participants, Russia, has not ratified the agreement.

As a result of the Uruguay Round, WTO rules apply to specific aspects of investment relations: trade-related performance requirements (TRIMS), trade-related intellectual property rights (TRIPS) and services (GATS). After the failure of the 2003 Cancun Ministerial, attempts to launch WTO negotiations on a comprehensive set of multilateral investment rules have been abandoned.

---

6 *Cf.* "In the Cold Shadow of *Metalclad*: The Potential Change to NAFTA's Chapter 11," N.Y.U. ENVTL. L. J. Vol. 11, at 264 (2002).

7 *Cf.* C. Bamberger, "An Introduction to the Energy Charter Treaty," IEA/OECD 1995.

Within the OECD, binding and non-binding instruments apply to the liberalization and treatment of investment. The Code for Liberalisation of Capital Movements (1961, with subsequent amendments) provides, subject to specific exceptions, for the freedom of transfers and transactions related to direct investment as well as the right of establishment.[8] Its key principles are top-down (i.e., immediate application, except for measures protected by reservations), stand-still (i.e., prohibition of new restrictions), roll-back (i.e., progressive elimination of existing restrictions), and non-discrimination. This instrument, which is legally binding on OECD members, has no dispute settlement mechanism; implementation relies on peer pressure and periodic reviews of remaining restrictions. There is a general exception for measures motivated by national security and public order considerations.

The Declaration and Decisions on International Investment and Multinational Enterprises (adopted in 1976 and subsequently amended) extends national treatment to foreign controlled enterprises after establishment, again subject to exceptions formulated by members.[9] Due to the combined effect of both instruments, general controls on investment have virtually disappeared in OECD countries. However, investment in certain regulated areas is still subject to exceptions, and most recently trends have emerged to dissuade mergers and acquisitions by foreign enterprises, based on national security considerations and other reasons such as "economic patriotism."

The Draft Multilateral Agreement on Investment

In 1995, the OECD countries launched negotiations on a comprehensive set of investment rules. The new agreement was designed to consolidate all OECD investment instruments into a single text which would be open to signature by non-OECD countries.

The Multilateral Agreement on Investment was to be:

- State of the art: building on the highest standards of treatment contained in bilateral, regional and sector investment agreements;
- Comprehensive: covering all categories of investment (direct as well as portfolio), all sectors and activities of enterprises, all phases of the investment process (before and after establishment, privatization

8 *Cf.* "OECD Code of Liberalisation of Capital Movements," Annex E, 2006.

9 OECD, *National Treatment for Foreign Controlled Enterprises* (2005).

and de-monopolization) and applying at all levels of government (federal, state, provincial, regional, local);

- Evolutionary: setting a framework for progressive liberalization while respecting the regulatory authority of signatory countries and protecting important national interests;
- Balanced: recognizing societal interests such as labor and environment standards and highlighting the responsibilities of multinational corporations (MNCs) to behave as good corporate citizens in the countries in which they operate;
- Open: developing a free-standing treaty open to all countries willing and able to assume its obligations; and
- Enforceable: providing mechanisms for dispute settlement at State-to-State and investor-State levels.[10]

The above principles were reflected in key provisions of the draft agreement.[11] After initial momentum, the negotiations ran into political difficulties in 1997, were suspended for assessment in May 1998, and then were abandoned at the end of that year.

What lessons can be drawn from this failure of a promising exercise? What were the achievements and main difficulties?

On the positive side, the MAI produced a codification of high-quality rules on liberalization and investment protection, based on the NAFTA model. It also recognized explicitly the right of each contracting State to regulate, and attempted to strike a balance between investment rules and social and environmental considerations.

Negotiators were unable to cope with a number of fundamental difficulties that ultimately led to the breakdown of the negotiations:

- Lack of focus: there was no clear understanding of the coverage of the text—whether it should focus on direct investment or all types of investment-related transactions and assets;

---

10 Rainer Geiger, "Towards a Multilateral Agreement on Investment," 31 CORNELL INT'L L. J. 455 (1998).

11 The consolidated text of the draft MAI, the Chairman's proposals and other negotiating materials have been published on the OECD Website (http://www.oecd.org).

- Conceptual ambiguities: should the agreement be modelled as an investment agreement with top-down obligations, or follow a WTO approach of negotiated offers and commitments for market access and national treatment?
- Unresolved difficulties: lack of agreement between the U.S. and European member countries on issues ranging from cultural diversity and national security to the scope of dispute settlement.

Above all, the negotiating process suffered from poor management: developing countries for which the agreement was mainly designed were not invited to the negotiating table, the relations between the new approach and the WTO agreements remained unclear, the negotiations were expert-driven without strong backing through the political process, and until a late stage there was no information provided to the public, nor did meaningful stakeholder consultations take place. The emerging text received only lukewarm support from business and trade unions, and was vigorously opposed by the NGO community.

The Policy Framework for Investment

In May 2006, the OECD achieved a landmark result in adopting a tool for global and regional dialogue on investment, national policy assessment and peer review.[12]

The Policy Framework for Investment (PFI) is:

- Non-prescriptive: it does not stipulate rules; instead, it provides a checklist for national policies to improve the environment for both domestic and international investment;
- Comprehensive but non-exhaustive: it covers ten policy areas that are conducive to a favorable investment environment (investment policy, investment promotion and facilitation, trade, competition, tax, corporate governance, promoting responsible business conduct, human resource development, infrastructure, financial sector development, public governance). New chapters will be added as experience develops, and the whole text will be periodically reviewed;

---

12 OECD, *Policy Framework for Investment* (2006).

- Participatory: the PFI was developed by a Task Force composed of OECD and non-OECD countries, and benefited from active stakeholder participation (business, trade unions, NGOs).

The PFI is conceived as a contribution to development strategies based on the Millennium Development goals. National development agencies, represented in the Development Assistance Committee (DAC), will be asked to provide their support. The PFI is also expected to provide a strong basis for a continuing international investment dialog, in partnership between the OECD and key multilateral institutions such as the World Bank Group, UNCTAD and regional development banks.

In line with the fundamental objectives of international investment law, the PFI aims at promoting policy transparence, coherence of policy approaches and a rules-based system backed by public/private sector dialog and stakeholder participation. It will serve as a guidepost for regional cooperation through existing institutions like APEC, ECLAC, NEPAD and other arrangements like the MENA-OECD Investment Program and the Investment Compact for South East Europe.[13]

The Way Forward: How to Improve Transparency and Coherence?

Despite the confusing array and the fragmented nature of bilateral, regional and multilateral investment agreements, there is reason to hope that greater transparency, coherence and predictability can be achieved in the future development of international investment law. It is encouraging to note a growing international consensus that investment can serve as an important tool for sustainable development, that all countries, whether capital exporting or capital importing, share common interests in improving the investment environment and that global benchmarks like the PFI can successfully be translated into action through a global and regional investment dialog.

Major challenges remain for the immediate future. First, there is a need for clarifying the legal concepts underlying international investment agreements

---

13 On 17 February 2006, MENA countries (Middle East and North Africa) expressed support for a Ministerial Declaration setting forth principles and good practices for an improved investment environment; on 28 June 2006, Ministers from eight countries participating in the Investment Compact for South East Europe adopted a Regional Framework for Investment. Both texts are available on the OECD Website (http://www.oecd.org).

on the basis of the useful work already accomplished by the OECD and UNCTAD and through the NAFTA process of interpretation. The quality and consistency of BITs can be improved by providing developing countries with capacity-building support for negotiating and implementing these agreements. UNCTAD has taken a pioneering role in this respect, and regional cooperation programs organized by the OECD provide for the exchange of experience and the development of common approaches.

Second, there is a strong need to improve dispute settlement mechanisms, both in terms of procedural fairness and substantive justice. Existing arrangements could be diversified in order to avoid lengthy arbitration procedures, which can be extremely costly for the parties involved. For that purpose, consideration should be given to the promotion of mediation and conciliation facilities as well as the introduction of special procedures to process small claims. Procedural guidelines could be developed for investor-State arbitration on key aspects such as transparency of proceedings, third party intervention and consolidation of claims.

There is no consensus on the introduction of an appeals procedure for arbitral awards. It has been argued that such a procedure could help develop international case law to serve as a basis for more consistent interpretation of investment agreements. (See Annexes 3 and 4, *ICSID discussion and proposal papers*). But there are drawbacks related to the costs and delays created by an additional layer of dispute settlement. In addition, it is difficult to conceive how the coherence of awards would be increased by an ad hoc appeals procedure, in the absence of a permanent international tribunal that has no institutional basis in the current system.

Theoretically, a multilateral approach would be the best way to achieve coherence in international investment law. Yet all attempts, whether in the OECD or the WTO, to develop a comprehensive set of multilateral investment rules have run into the ground. Learning from the errors of the past and building on an emerging commonality of interests, is the time now ripe to consider a renewed approach to multilateral negotiations? Is there today a better chance to reach a result that would justify a new effort? Would a multilateral agreement add value to existing instruments or would it just reflect the least common denominator?

To be successful, a new multilateral effort would have to build on a strong international consensus on key elements. It would require the choice of a credible and effective negotiating forum, probably based on an ad hoc institutional arrangement. It would have to bring together all the key players in the investment process—both OECD and non-OECD. The process would have to be transparent from the beginning, backed by an effective information strategy, consultations of opinion leaders and stakeholder participation. Finally, consideration would have to be given to an acceptable international system of dispute settlement that could include a permanent claims tribunal serving as an instance of appeal.

To test the feasibility of such an effort, it would be advisable to create an international commission of experts tasked with developing a blueprint for a multilateral agreement. It would have to be composed of a limited number of independent persons with high standing in international investment law, supported by international organizations and entrusted to conduct a broad process of consultations with governments and non-governmental groups.

Even within the present system, additional institutional arrangements could be envisaged to provide research and capacity-building support to developing countries in the field of international investment law. The creation of an international institute that would function in close cooperation with existing organizations and regional initiatives could provide an efficient tool to improve the quality and coherence of investment agreements and to develop and support, at the national level, consistent mechanisms for implementation and enforcement.

CHAPTER 3

Implications for the Future of International Investment Law

*José E. Alvarez**

This volume, the product of a symposium on "Transparency and Consistency in International Law: Is There a Need for a Review Mechanism?" held at Columbia University on April 4, 2006, addresses a unique emerging regime that is neither the product of a single multilateral treaty nor the subject of an overreaching international institution. The international rules governing foreign direct investment (FDI) do not arise from anything resembling the enormous multi-year trade rounds that produced the World Trade Organization (WTO) and its impressive post-Uruguay Round dispute settlement system. Unlike the rules governing trade in goods, the world's FDI rules emerge instead from some 2,500 bilateral agreements as well as an increasing number of free trade agreements that contain investment guarantees, such as the North American Free Trade Agreement (NAFTA)'s Chapter 11. Even while WTO lawyers still debate the virtues of increased transparency—such as whether or when *amici* briefs from non-state entities ought to be considered by the WTO's dispute settlers or whether the emerging WTO case law has indeed generated harmonious interpretations over time—the WTO still inspires the envy of investment lawyers.

WTO lawyers, after all, have the luxury of a single set of "covered agreements" subject to a single and relatively binding mechanism for settling interpretative disputes (complete with elaborate and detailed time tables for attempts at non-judicial settlement in the shadow of establishing a formal panel). They enjoy the benefit of an appeals mechanism—a single Appellate Body that can correct

* President of the American Society for International Law, and Hamilton Fish Professor of International Law and Diplomacy at the Columbia University School of Law. Email: jalvar@law.columbia.edu.

panelists' errors of law (if not of fact) and that can direct remedial compliance once the Appellate Body has spoken on the merits. The Dispute Settlement Understanding (DSU) of the WTO acknowledges that the central role of trade dispute adjudicators is to provide "security" and "predictability" and urges them only to "clarify" the single set of obligations that all WTO members are subject to, but not to "add to or diminish the rights and obligations" provided in those agreements.[1] While the DSU suggests that the primary purpose of the system is to settle promptly disputes among members, it implicitly affirms that dispute settlers need to generate those consistent interpretations over time associated with the rule of law, since, after all, members would scarcely enjoy secure or predictable rights otherwise.

The contrast with the emerging FDI regime could not be starker. As the chapters of this volume suggest, despite repeated invocations of similar terminology among investment agreements—comparable invocations of national and most-favored-nation (MFN) treatment, similar admonitions to accord compensation upon expropriation, and injunctions to treat investors "fairly and equitably" consistent with international law—investment agreements differ in how these substantive guarantees are phrased. While these textual differences are often minute, and not always obvious to the non-lawyer, they are potentially of enormous significance, particularly with respect to the finely honed disputes that manage to evade peaceful settlement and require formal adjudication. The textual differences among investment agreements may be critically significant given the established rules for treaty interpretation used in this regime no less than for the WTO's—which, as all know, stress above all other interpretative factors the need to interpret a treaty in light of its "plain meaning."[2] Accordingly, it is important—and potentially devastating for hopes for harmonious global investment rules—that treaty clauses assuring national treatment sometimes extend to entry and post-entry treatment but may sometimes extend only to the latter; that MFN treatment sometimes applies to "all provisions" of an investment treaty (suggesting perhaps that it applies even with respect to procedural matters on dispute settlement) but sometimes only to the "treatment" of investors; or that investors are sometimes assured "fair" treatment only insofar as consistent with customary international law but sometimes this assurance is given *in addition* to such rights. (See Annex 8, *Novel Features in OECD Countries' Recent Investment Agreements.*)

---

1 Understanding on Rules and Procedures Governing the Settlement of Disputes, Uruguay Final Round, Article 3(2).

2 Vienna Convention on Treaties, Article 31(1).

Moreover, the ways investment disputes are settled potentially magnifies the textual differences among investment agreements and the ways these might be interpreted. While WTO claims are restricted to governments as litigants, investor-State dispute settlement relies on a private attorney general model of enforcement. Under the typical investment agreement, those eligible to bring claims—and to bring contentious or controversial interpretations forward for consideration—are not limited to the 150 or so States that are parties to the WTO. Tens of thousands of private investors throughout the world that invest in countries subject to an investment agreement can bring such claims—and thereby influence the direction of the emerging FDI case law. While it is true that private business interests remain in the background of WTO disputes and may exert great pressure on governments to pursue certain claims, the fact remains that WTO dispute settlement remains formally in the hands of governments—which ultimately can decide not to pursue certain controversial claims if this may delegate too much authority to the system's adjudicators. Whereas the creativity of WTO treaty interpretation is restricted to those that government lawyers are prone to advance (and are therefore hemmed in by governments' understandable fears that their creative views of the law may someday be reciprocally applied to them), such concerns play a much lesser role in investment disputes, where the creativity of a claimant's lawyers recognizes no such bounds.

The possibility of inconsistent results as between distinct ad hoc investment tribunals even when these are adjudicating identical treaty guarantees emerges from another difference between trade and investment arbitration. By contrast to the harmonious timetables and hierarchical appeals envisioned by the WTO's DSU, investment agreements rely on a motley collection of ad hoc arbitral systems and institutions, including the International Centre for Settlement of Investment Disputes (ICSID), its Additional Facility, and UNCITRAL. All of these are subject to distinct procedures and not entirely consistent ways of, for example, enforcing subsequent arbitral awards, admitting *amici*, applying rules on arbitrators' conflict of interest or permitting the discovery of documents or the testimony of experts. And, as every lawyer knows, the procedural niceties by which adjudication is conducted often have a significant outcome on the substance of the decisions reached.

Finally, in contrast to the WTO Appellate Body's established set of judges charged with overseeing the ad hoc panelists' views of WTO law, investment disputes have no institutionalized appeals process—unless you count the limited review authority some national courts have to set aside awards when asked to enforce them or ICSID's similarly limited annulment procedures. There is no single set of judges, or indeed any other single mechanism, available by which to harmonize even those arbitral decisions interpreting textually identical investment agreements that reach differing outcomes. Of course, international law itself—which does not even recognize a hierarchy among institutionalized dispute settlers and fails to make the judgments of the International Court of Justice binding on the rest—does not fill this gap.

Therefore, it comes as no surprise that the ad hoc nature of investor-State dispute settlement, including its lack of an appellate mechanism, should generate the types of concerns highlighted by the title of this symposium. As Thomas Franck, among others, has suggested, the legitimacy of international law is premised, among other things, on the coherency of its rules, that is, on observers' confidence that its primary rules consistently adhere to fundamental principles of first order importance.[3] The prospect that, over time, awards by different investor-State tribunals will expound different interpretations of comparable guarantees, albeit based on different treaties, sends chills up the spines of investment lawyers who fear that their emerging regime will self-destruct for failing the first test of any real "system" of rules. (See Annex 7, *UNCTAD, IIA Monitor, No. 4 (2006)*).

The chapters in this volume address this fear, as well as the underlying realities that prompt it. The contributors to this book accordingly address recent trends in foreign investment law. Some focus upon the rise in the number of investment agreements and in adjudicated investment disputes and attempt to explain both. Others tackle the question of whether investment agreements really do differ in significant respects among themselves. A number of the contributors consider possible remedies to promote greater transparency and/or consistency in the regime, whether through the changes that are being introduced into the latest wave of U.S. investment agreements or through a future appellate mechanism.

But some of the commentators—such as Barton Legum—warn us that some cures may be worse than the disease they purport to cure. The scholars and practitioners here are not uniform in advocating an investment appellate body, whether based in ICSID or regional arrangements. Perhaps they recognize that, notwithstanding the many touted merits of the WTO regime and its Appellate Body, that regime has its own legitimacy deficits. They warn that the WTO's reliance on a single body of powerful appellate judges is now seen by

---

3 *See, e.g.*, Thomas Franck, *The Power of Legitimacy Among Nations* (Oxford University Press: 1990).

some as part of the problem. Creating a super-tribunal of investment judges may be a solution in search of a problem—if the lack of consistent results proves not as serious in reality as in prediction, or if inconsistency will not be remedied by anything less than the negotiation of a single global multilateral investment treaty. It may also be a solution that inspires doubts about who the judges ought to be or whether they are sufficiently accountable, as does the WTO regime in some circles. Certainly not all nations, including especially the United States, are amenable to being second-guessed by a single, seemingly all-powerful supranational tribunal of judges selected by extra-constitutional means.

At the outset we also need to remember—as several of the contributors here remind us—that the emerging foreign investment regime (to the extent it can be described as a single "regime" and not merely a kaleidoscope of disparate treaties) faces broader challenges than even those of central focus here. Although lawyers understandably emphasize the fragmentation challenge inherent to this decentralized, under-institutionalized set of rules, the debate over transparency/consistency is nestled within a more general, and far more politically loaded, question: namely, are the emerging investment rules fair? Some of the commentators here cannot resist raising this more general challenge.

How do investment agreements relate to persistent doubts about whether the "golden straitjacket" that they impose on states, and especially on developing counties, is really more "golden" and less of a "straitjacket?"[4] Muthucumaraswamy Sornarajah's contribution contends that the emerging FDI regime is imbalanced, consisting entirely of rights for multinational corporations (MNCs) but imposing no duties upon them. As he and others here suggest, investment treaties are inherently suspect to many because they were initiated by rich nations who tended to present their model texts on a take-it-or-leave-it basis to developing countries who believed that they had little choice if they were to attract much needed capital from the companies based in the North. Although today's 2,500 bilateral investment agreements include a substantial number negotiated between developing countries and on the basis of model texts drafted by them, the ostensibly "colonialist" origins of the U.S. and European bilateral investment treaty programs still affect perceptions

[4] Compare Thomas Friedman, *The Lexus and the Olive Tree* (Anchor: 2000) (largely celebratory examination of the "golden straitjacket" imposed on developing countries by international institutions and other pre-conditions of "globalization").

and are difficult to overcome. The prospect that such an "imbalanced" set of norms will nonetheless benefit the poorest countries of the earth, that the regime's affirmation of the free market will produce a "win-win" situation that satisfies pent up demands for economic development and reduce global poverty, or the proposition that it will ameliorate persistent (if not growing) gaps between the global North and South (as well as rich and poor within both sets of nations)—all of these remain contested around the world, despite the ostensible popularity of investment agreements. At a time when a new wave of leaders, especially in Latin America, have been elected on the basis of populist ire directed at the symbols of globalization—including investment treaties—even a symposium directed at the lawyerly problems of transparency and consistency can scarcely ignore the prospect that the turn to investment agreements may prove short-lived either because these treaties fail to produce the economic results predicted or because they fail to recognize (or permit) governments to retain sufficient regulatory discretion to engage in experimental "pro-growth" policies.

For all these reasons, the chapters of this volume are more ambitious than the title of the symposium suggests. This scholarly collection is not just about whether or not an appellate mechanism is desirable or more *amicus* briefs ought to be permitted in investor-State dispute settlement. While those specific remedies are addressed, the broader questions posed are characteristic of those now being raised across a number of international regimes—from those of the UN system to international financial institutions and yes, including the WTO, the object of investment lawyers' envy.

The following chapters are part of a broader conversation about whether the Grotian premises that inspired both formal international organizations like the UN and the WTO, as well as more decentralized approaches—such as ICSID's ad hoc arbitral mechanism—remain valid. This conversation is therefore part of a broader (and still unresolved) debate about whether:

- international law-making needs to be pursued through top-down institutions or can be effectively undertaken in the decentralized, bottom-up fashion anticipated by investment agreements;
- regimes like those governing investment (or trade) are "self-contained" or relate to more general laws and principles;
- the leading superpower is as influential in this realm as it is in those regimes that rely on formal weighted voting (e.g., the UN Security Council or the IMF); and

- there is any such thing as an "international judiciary" governed by common notions of the judicial function even while operating in radically different adjudicative settings.

These far-reaching questions engage, and should interest, the entire "invisible college" of international lawyers—and not just a narrow cadre of investment experts.

PART II

Recent Trends in International Investment Law Disputes

CHAPTER 4

A Coming Crisis: Expansionary Trends in Investment Treaty Arbitration

*M. Sornarajah**

Investment treaties are entered into on the assumption that providing security for investment through the recognition of standards of treatment, compensation for expropriation and the repatriation of profits will result in larger flows of foreign investment (FDI) into developing countries. That assumption is now doubted in several studies by economists and others.[1] Moreover, since the award in *AAPL v. Sri Lanka*,[2] in which the tribunal found jurisdiction on the basis of the provisions of an investment treaty, the number of investment

---

* CJ Koh Professor of Law, Singapore Normal University, and Professorial Fellow, Centre for Petroleum and Natural Resources Law, University of Dundee, Scotland. Email: lawsorna@nus.edu.sg.

1 Eric Neumayer and Laura Spess, "Do Bilateral Investment Treaties Increase Foreign Direct Investment to Developing Countries," *at* (http://econwpa.wustl.edu:8089/eps/if/papers/0411/0411004.pdf); Elkins et al., "Competing for Capital: The Diffusion of Bilateral Investment Treaties, 1960–2000," *at* (http://papers.ssrn.com/sol3/papers.cfm?abstract_id=578961); Jennifer Tobin and Susan Rose-Ackerman, "Foreign Direct Investment and the Business Environment in Developing Countries: The Impact of Bilateral Investment Treaties," 2 May 2005, *at* (http://www.law.yale.edu/outside/html/faculty/sroseack/FDI_BITs_may02.pdf); Jeswald Salacuse and Nicholas Sullivan, "Do BITs Really Work: An Evaluation of Bilateral Investment Treaties and their Grand Bargain," 46 HARV. INT'L L. J. 67–130 (2005); Kevin P. Gallagher and Melissa Birch, "Do Investment Agreements Attract Investment? Evidence from Latin America," 2005, Forthcoming (Submitted to EURO. J. DEV. RESEARCH) (2006) 7 J. WORLD INV. & TRADE 6; J. P. Tumman and C. F. Emmert, "The Political Economy of U.S. Foreign Direct Investment in Latin America: A Reappraisal," LARR: 39(3), 9–29 (2004); Mary Hallward-Dreimeier, "Do Bilateral Investment Treaties Attract FDI? Only a bit…and it might bite," World Bank Policy Research Working Paper Series, Number 3121 (World Bank); UNCTAD, *Bilateral Investment Treaties in the Mid-1990s* (United Nations Publication: 1998).

2 30 ILM 577 (1991).

disputes subjected to arbitration on the basis of treaty provisions has reached explosive proportions. The question thus raised for developing countries, in light of those studies and a recent bevy of adverse awards against developing countries, is whether the advantages of entering into investment treaties outweigh their potential disadvantages.[3]

To a large extent, these doubts have come about due to the expansionary attitudes taken by arbitrators who have accepted the expansionary litigation theories of lawyers who are seemingly taking the law in investment treaties beyond what the parties had originally intended.

The gravity of this situation has been accentuated by the fact that for the first time, rich countries are at the receiving end of the law in such arbitrations, especially as a result of the investment chapter of the North American Free Trade Agreement (NAFTA). The United States and Canada have begun to see that devices of investment protection that they had created for their nationals investing abroad are now being used against them. They are feeling the discomfort that only developing countries felt in the past. The developed countries are the largest recipients of FDI, and thus now must face the restrictions on host country sovereignty that, in the past, applied primarily to the developing world.

The new model investment treaties produced by both the U.S. and Canada demonstrate backtracking from entrenched positions that had previously been taken on issues of investment protection by both countries; they have also acted to curtail the law that was contained in the provisions of the investment chapter in NAFTA. In particular, an interpretative statement of the NAFTA Commission defined the "fair and equitable" standard of treatment (hitherto regarded as a new standard of treatment desired by developed countries) as nothing more than what was already contained in customary international law.[4] The recent Comprehensive Economic Agreement between India and Singapore leaves out a reference to the "fair and equitable" standard of treatment altogether.[5] The tribunal in the award in *Methanex v. United States of America*[6] in 2005 restricted the scope of takings in investment treaties by effectively excluding regulatory takings from their scope. The regulatory exception in

---

3 The combined claims against Pakistan in the *SGS*, *Salineri* and *Hubco* arbitrations, for example, exceeded the national reserves of that state.

4 The text is in *UPS v. Canada*, Award on Jurisdiction, 22 November 2002, paras. 80–85.

5 For text, *see* U.S. Department of Commerce website (http://commerce.nic.in/ceca/toc.htm).

6 For final award and proceedings *see* U.S. Department of State website (http://www.state.gov/s/l/c5818.htm).

takings jurisprudence receives treatment in the new model treaties of the U.S. and Canada. The safeguard provisions in the Canadian model treaty are so extensive as to raise the issue as to whether they do not undermine the scope of the treaty. The investment chapter of the Australia–U.S. Free Trade Agreement leaves out provisions on investor-State dispute resolution altogether, leaving room for speculation as to the need for such a clause.[7] States that have been affected by recent peculiarities in the process have expressed dissatisfaction with treaty-based arbitration.[8] In sum, there is backtracking taking place in the practice of developed countries in the area of investment protection.

A Crisis of Legitimacy

A crisis of legitimacy is being created by the large number of arbitrations[9] that have been initiated (almost exclusively by investors), especially, also, because they may extend the law in a manner not contemplated by the original drafting of the parties. It is a recognized phenomenon that, when a court or a tribunal considers a statute or a treaty, it may give it meanings that may not have been intended by the drafters of the text. But, in these circumstances, there are control mechanisms that allow for a review of the decisions made. One problem with investment arbitration is that decisions usually are made by ad hoc tribunals established for the express purpose of the dispute at hand. No control mechanisms exist within that type of system. An annulment of the contemplated appellate procedures will lead to the same uncertainties as are involved in the making of the award itself. These procedures for challenging an award are not suitable for developing country respondents. They would add to the costs of developing countries in dealing with such arbitrations and therefore will prove unattractive to them.

---

7 One view is that Australia has not been comfortable with the idea of such arbitrations. It had had a dispute with the U.S. concerning a U.S. mining company. The facts are in the domestic litigation concerning the dispute (*Dillingham Moore v. Murphyores*, 136 CLR 1 (1979)). The matter is that there is no need for such provisions as the courts of the two States are trusted by the investors. If so, why have investment provisions in the treaty at all? Further, *see* William Dodge, "Investor-State Dispute Settlement Between Developed Countries: Reflections on the Australia–United States Free Trade Agreement," 39 Vand. J. Transnat'l L. 1 (2006) (suggesting that a likely reason was to avoid the experience of the U.S. and Canada under NAFTA).

8 The Czech Republic, a country that faced inconsistent decisions in the *Lauder* cases, and Argentina, which faces a multiplicity of arbitrations, are examples. The interest in investment treaties has cooled in Latin America and in the former socialist countries of Central and Eastern Europe.

9 Statistics as to the number of arbitrations up to 2005 are provided in "Latest Developments in Investor-State Dispute Settlement," UNCTAD IIA Monitor, No. 4, 2005 (http://www.unctad.org/en/docs//webiteiit20052_en.pdf) (Annex to this volume).

Further, the tribunals, unlike courts and other tribunals within constitutional systems, are constituted largely of persons having experience in commercial arbitration. Hence, they tend to lean toward commercial solutions based on commercial prudence and give little concern to the predicament of a State faced with fashioning policy in the context of circumstances that may have undergone changes. The pronouncements of commercial arbitrators on substantial issues of international law involved in treaty-based investment arbitration can be open to question. Tribunals can consist of judges or arbitrators inexpert in matters of international law or without a long period of experience in the field, which makes it difficult to speak authoritatively as representative tribunals of the international community.[10] The further charge, made by some, is that they may have an ideological predisposition toward solutions that favor international business.[11]

This issue of legitimacy has been accentuated in recent times by several incidents. The Czech Republic won and lost cases on the same facts before two different arbitral tribunals.[12] Argentina faces over 30 arbitrations resulting from measures taken during an economic crisis. The claims are based on measures alleged to be expropriations or as amounting to wrongful treatment under the treaties. There is little doubt that Argentina would use its domestic courts to question the validity of these awards.[13] In Asia, Pakistan and Indonesia faced a series of arbitrations resulting from regime changes.

Governments have, not surprisingly, reacted against this situation. The Pakistani government sought antisuit injunctions from its courts against the arbitrations. In Argentina, the constitutional validity of the investment treaties is being queried. In Indonesia, the spate of arbitrations that resulted from the overthrow of Suharto was subjected to antisuit injunctions by the Indonesian courts. In one of the arbitrations, *Karah Bodas v. Pertamina*,[14] the Indonesian

---

10 The tribunals are called upon to speak on issues of international law. Thus, the tribunal in *SD Myers v. Canada* had to decide on a conflict involving Canada's treaty obligations. Such issues are best decided by persons with a competence in international law rather than persons with a competence in commercial arbitration.

11 On this allegation, *see* M. Sornarajah, "Power and Justice in Foreign Investment Arbitration," 14(3) J. Int'l Arb. 103 (1997).

12 Conflicts in opinion between tribunals on issues of the law have occurred in the past—*see e.g.*, the Libyan Oil Nationalization cases, *Texaco*, *BP* and *Liamco*. These cases involved differing uses of the law to resolve disputes arising from the same nationalization decree. But the Czech cases involved contrary results on the basis of the same facts.

13 Carlos Alfaro and Pedro Lorenti, "The Growing Opposition of Argentina to ICSID Arbitration Tribunals," 3 Journ. World Invest. 22 (2005).

14 In the U.S., the Second Circuit Court of Appeals has decided a case on the enforcement of the award, *Karaha Bodas v. Perusahaan*, 190 F Supp. 2d 936 (S.D. Texas 2002). Litigation concerning the award is before courts in Canada, Hong Kong and Singapore.

state-related entity against which the award was made is strenuously resisting its enforcement.[15] This may well become a pattern for the future, and a situation of normlessness[16] may result. Difficulties associated with sovereign immunity and acts of state may make the resulting awards unenforceable, in the absence of cooperation by the respondent States.

In the related area of dispute settlement in international trade, despite the fact that such dispute settlement takes place in the context of constitutional documents to which States are parties and that the mechanism operates entirely between States, the problem of legitimacy has still been raised, due to the manner in which members of the panels have expanded the original intent of the parties.[17] If such criticism is made of the more institutionalized system of dispute settlement within the World Trade Organization, the criticism could be made with even greater vigor in the case of investment arbitration by ad hoc tribunals without any control mechanism.

It is evident that countries are beginning to think freshly about treaty-based investment arbitration. As indicated, the recently released Canadian and U.S. model investment treaties show considerable rethinking on the issue of commitments by introducing the possibility of defences to liability. More importantly, the investment chapter in the recently concluded free trade agreement between India and Singapore takes this rethinking further and gives insights as to how developing countries are going to approach this problem in the future. The investment chapter in this Agreement dispenses with references to treatment standards, which has been the focus of much of the new litigation in the field. It is necessary to take these developments into account in viewing the future of treaty-based investment arbitration.

---

15 Though it has lost in the U.S. courts and in the court of first instance in Hong Kong, the enforcement proceedings in Singapore are still pending. There is an appeal pending in Hong Kong.

16 The term "normlessness" is similar to the notion of *anomie*, which was used by the sociologist Robert Merton to indicate a clash of norms and a resulting situation in which norms become weak or not accepted by groups. Disequilibrium will come about if the supporters of the different set of norms have equal strength. The term was used to explain group or gang crimes of violence. Freda Adler, ed., *The Legacy of the Anomie Theory* (Transaction Publishers: 1995).

17 *See generally*, Richard Steinberg, "Judicial Lawmaking at the WTO: Discursive, Constitutional and Political Constraints," (2004) 98 Am. J. Int'l L. 247 ("Most of those characterizing WTO dispute settlement as activist do so pejoratively, and some have suggested that this activism might warrant an extreme policy response, such as threatening unilateral U.S. withdrawal from the WTO"). Bhupinder Chimni, "The World Trade Organization, Democracy and Development: A View from the South," 40 (1) Journal of World Trade 5 (2006).

These developments evidence the displeasure of countries with the trend that has been set in motion in investment arbitration. They will require that a rethinking be done on treaty-based investment arbitration. Contemplating merely to institute an appellate system is hardly sufficient: if the base is weak, as a problem cannot be dealt with by building another layer on top of weakness.[18] The strategy of addressing issues of substantive imperfection through procedural reform is hardly likely to produce the necessary reform. The system is in danger of crumbling altogether if the expansive nature of arbitrations is not curbed. The need for such arbitration exists, no doubt. But the system has been led astray by those who have set it on a track in which the balance between the interests of the State and the interests of the foreign investor has been upset. If this trend goes unchecked, the system itself may collapse.

While this trend is unfolding, its defenders are developing theories to support the system. Faced with the fact that efforts at creating a multilateral investment agreement have largely met with failure, it is argued that the mounting number of investment treaties constitute customary international law[19]—when, in fact, the internal balance in the different treaties varies considerably. It would appear that this attempt has now been given up as its lack of foundation has been sufficiently exposed.[20] A more recent attempt is to argue that the system of investment arbitration has resulted in the formation of a global administrative law in the field.[21] This is too hasty a conclusion. There are no institutional structures supporting investment arbitration agreed upon by the international community for such a claim to be made. It is an indication that theoretical grounds are suggested in order to occupy the ground that has been captured by expansionary trends; but the difficulty is that the trends themselves have been checked and may be in retreat.

---

18 The International Centre for Settlement of Investment Disputes (ICSID) has suggested the creation of an appellate system. That effort itself is an indication of the acceptance of the fact that there is much amiss with investment arbitration. The creation of an appellate system will not cure the issues of credibility that afflict the existing system. The strategy of addressing issues of substantive imperfection through procedural reform is hardly likely to produce the necessary results. The U.S. model treaty also requires the exploration by the parties of an appellate system.

19 For discussion, *see* M. Sornarajah, *International Law on Foreign Investment*, 2nd Edition (Cambridge University Press: 2004), pp. 205–206.

20 It would appear that of the 2,500 BITs, many are yet to be ratified. South Africa has not ratified treaties it signed after 2003. Brazil's treaties also await ratification. Many states, like the Philippines and the Czech Republic, are considering the issue of whether the obligations assumed under these treaties are counter-productive.

21 Gus Van Harten and Martin Loughlin, "Investment Treaty Arbitration as a Species of Global Administrative Law," EUROPEAN J. OF INT'L L.121 (2006).

This chapter attempts to identify possible ways of avoiding the undermining of the utility of investment arbitration by ensuring that the essential balance that should exist in such arbitration is restored. First, the problem is identified. Expansionary trends in treaty-based arbitration are examined in the subsequent section. In conclusion, possible pathways to restoring the lost balance are considered.

The Theoretical Basis of the Problem

Investment treaties of the modern variety began in 1959, the first being the treaty between Pakistan and Germany signed that year. Early treaties were designed to establish rules between the parties as to investment security, simply because the existing international law on foreign investment protection was unclear.[22] They focused on expropriation and required payment of compensation in the event of expropriation. Many treaties were concluded between 1959 and 1990. They contained a variety of standards of protection that depended on the negotiating balance between the parties. They were always made between a capital-exporting State and a capital-importing State, indicating the existence of an obvious asymmetry. Preambular statements in treaties that encouraged reciprocal flows of investment were an inexactitude, as in reality the treaties protected the one-way flow that took place between the exporters and the recipients. This asymmetry itself sets these treaties apart from other treaties. There was no consideration of these treaties contributing to customary international law at that stage, for it was evident that, though the outer shell of these treaties contained similarities, their contents varied significantly. The terminology used in the treaties was typically imprecise,[23] giving scope for arbitrators to give meanings to the law that extend beyond the intention of the parties.[24]

---

22 This lack of clarity existed throughout the history of international investment law. The U.S. claim to an international minimum standard of protection was resisted by the Latin American countries through the Calvo Doctrine, which articulated the supremacy of national law. After decolonization in the middle of the twentieth century, the Calvo Doctrine was espoused by the newly independent states of Africa and Asia, whereas the Europeans supported the international minimum standard. *See* M. Sornarajah, *International Law on Foreign Investment*, 2nd Edition (Cambridge University Press: 2005).

23 Indeed, lawyers long recognized that these treaties were crafted in vague, open-ended terms. In the words of one arbitration lawyer, they "are maddeningly imprecise as to the substantive legal standard to be applied by the tribunal". William D. Rogers, "Emergence of the International Centre for Settlement of Investment Disputes (ICSID) as the Most Significant Forum for Submission of Bilateral Investment Treaty Disputes," presentation to Inter-American Development Bank Conference, 26–27 October 2000.

24 The self-interest of arbitrators is analyzed by Yves Dezaley and Bryant G. Garth, *Dealing in Virtue: International Commercial Arbitration and the Construction of Transnational Legal Order* (University of Chicago Press: 1996).

In the early 1990s, the picture changed dramatically. A confluence of circumstances led to the triumph of market capitalism: the fall of the Soviet Union, the sudden crisis relating to sovereign lending, the drying up of foreign aid, and the success of the Asian Tigers. The view prevailed that, in the rapidly globalizing world economy, the liberalization of flows of foreign investment and capital would bring about development and prosperity. The "Washington Consensus" was formed. Conditions under which loans were given by the International Monetary Fund (IMF) and the World Bank required conformity to the prescribed model. Evidence of following the model was provided by entering into investment treaties, which, unlike those of the previous generation, were more uniform, with rights enforceable through secure processes of arbitration.[25] This approach accounted for the great boost in the number of investment treaties concluded in the final decade of the past century.[26]

The figures show that treaty activity peaked in the 1990s.[27] Three important areas of the world added significantly to the number of the treaties.

- The first group included the countries of Central and Eastern Europe, newly liberated from communism. Eager to underline their embrace of the free market, they were responsible for a large number of investment treaties in the belief that the signing of the treaties would show that they had turned a new page and that it would bring in much needed FDI. The competition that these new countries engaged in for such investment was another factor leading to the increase in treaties.
- A second large group comprised Latin American countries, also turning a new page and showing a new vigorous embrace of the free market philosophy. Deserting the Calvo Doctrine that shielded them from foreign litigation in this area, Latin American countries, including Argentina, the home of Carlos Calvo, signed large numbers of investment treaties. Both regions have now shown that they need to retreat from their original fervor for the treaties but are locked into a system that they had voluntarily entered.

---

25 Previous treaties had shown a diversity of patterns relating to arbitration. Some made arbitration optional. Others required further criteria to be satisfied before arbitration could be triggered. Some had compulsory arbitration. The treaties also were increasingly based on models prepared by the negotiating parties, especially developed countries.

26 Francis Fukuyama, *After the Neocons: America at the Crossroads* (Profile Books: 2006).

27 UNCTAD, *World Investment Report 2006: FDI from Developing and Transition Economies: Implications for Development* (United Nations Publication: 2006).

- Third, China entered into a large number of treaties. But the Chinese treaties are finely nuanced and the possibility of arbitration under them is rather remote.[28] The subjection of the definition of investment to the regulatory structure of the domestic legal system and the confining of dispute settlement to disputes arising from outright expropriation ensures that, despite being a heavy practitioner in the field of investment treaties, China will avoid significant disputes.[29] For China, the treaties were signalling devices that it had moved away from the old position of hostility to foreign investment. The protective content in the treaties is minimal. This has been so until now, despite the fact that China is among the largest recipients of investment.[30] It is noteworthy also that Southeast Asia has escaped much litigation; again, this is because its treaties typically have sufficient escape clauses that reduce the likelihood of litigation. They require that investments should receive prior approval if they are to be protected under the treaty.[31]

It is evident from this cursory description of the spurt of treaties that different aims and concerns underlie them. In that context, the claim that they give rise to customary international law is questionable. It is partly based on the treaties made with the liberalization of investment flows in mind, containing rights of entry and establishment and strict protection standards. However, treaties based on the philosophy of liberalization are largely concluded only by the U.S. and Canada and, more recently, Japan and the Republic of Korea. One cannot extrapolate for the world from the treaties of a few countries; even the practice of a few powerful States is not sufficient to generate customary international law. Besides, even if there are over 2,600 BITs, the fact is that nearly one-third remain unratified.[32] (See Annex 6, *UNCTAD, IIA Monitor, No.4 (2005).*) Is not the fact that States do not ratify these treaties (for whatever reason) also a matter of practice that may indicate that States are reluctant to take the final steps necessary to create obligations affecting their sovereignty?

---

28 But, *see* the 25 November 2005 treaty between China and Germany, which gives broader rights of arbitration to the foreign investor.

29 Chinese views are usefully stated in Chen Huiping, *OECD's Multilateral Agreement on Investment: A Chinese Perspective* (Kluwer: 2002). But newer Chinese treaties have stronger dispute resolution clauses that may presage change. *See* China-Germany Investment Treaty.

30 Shan Wenhua, *The Legal Framework of E.U.-China Investment Relations* (Hart Publishers: 2005), pp. 277–279.

31 *Grueslin v. Malaysia*, 5 ICSID Rpts 483 (2000) was an arbitration in which jurisdiction was refused because there was no prior approval of the investment. *See also Yaung Chi Ooo v. Myanmar*, 42 ILM 430 (2003).

32 *See* website of UNCTAD (http://www.unctad.org).

The effort to boost international investment law through the argument that BITs create customary international law appears to be a strategy of strengthening the global law of foreign investment protection at a time when efforts to create such a law through multilateral treaties have resulted in failure.[33]

The strategy of the multilateralization of investment protection also manifests itself in the claim that the treaties have created inherent rights for foreign investors. The comparison is made with human rights law. But that comparison itself is misplaced: human rights instruments are multilateral. Moreover, human rights are inherent to an individual. They are designed to protect the hapless citizen or the fleeing refugee from the awesome might of States. It would be belittling the human rights movement to compare the interests of large multinational corporations (MNCs) as being in need of protection through a law akin to human rights law. Further, the recognition that an MNC has inherent rights would also need to be seen in the context that the personality of these corporations for purposes of responsibilities remains a matter of controversy.[34] The efforts that are made in this area so as to create a new theory to secure the interests of MNCs are indeed surprising.

There are also other considerations to be taken into account. Human rights are secured for citizens of a State. Citizens are an ascertainable group owing allegiance to the State. The State owes a duty of protection to them. In the case of foreign investors, their existence is unknowable to a host country until entry is made. Even after entry, the vagaries of corporate nationality and shareholdings in companies are such that the class to whom protection is due cannot be ascertained with any certainty. There are conceptual difficulties that stand in the way of the argument that investment protection is an inherent right. Such a right, if recognizable, is a variant of a property right, which does not have universal recognition in the absolute manner asserted by the proponents of the theory that MNCs have an inherent right to the protection

---

33 *See* OECD's effort at a Multilateral Agreement on Investment (MAI) and the WTO's decision at the Cancun Ministerial not to pursue a multilateral investment agreement. *See* also M. Sornarajah, *The International Law on Foreign Investment* (Cambridge University Press: 2004).

34 For views that multinational corporations lack personality to be subjected to liability, *see* Wybo P. Heere, *From Government to Governance* (Cambridge University Press: 2003), pp. 175–212. It is interesting to note that some international lawyers still believe that MNCs lack personality to be subjected to liability but accept that they enjoy rights (Janet Dine, *Companies, International Trade and Human Rights* (Cambridge University Press: 2005)). As Dine points out, these corporations are given personality when it suits their interests and denied personality when not.

of assets.[35] Property rights are not protected in the absolute in many liberal states. The Canadian Bill of Rights has no reference to property rights.[36] The standards of property protection vary even in the constitutions of the nations of the British Commonwealth, which have common legal roots.[37]

The statements of property rights in most human rights instruments appear with heavy qualifications, subjecting them to public interests. In respect to land ownership, the U.S. view on the taking of property is quite at odds with the views taken in Europe, where the social function of property is stressed as more important than an individual's claim to property. The tension is equally present in U.S. law, though some judges would tend to recognize the market-oriented notion of an absolute property right[38] to the exclusion of historical notions as to the appropriate use of property.[39] The argument is that these qualifications are removed, and an absolute right to property is created in MNCs, through the network of investment treaties.[40] Such an absolute right is absent even in the most advanced of the developed countries.

But this seems to be the tenor of the arguments that have resulted from a number of treaty arbitrations.[41] It has been alleged that these arbitrations take the protection of property rights beyond even what is to be found in constitutional systems that tend toward an absolute right to property.[42] Assuming that

---

35 Many scholars have questioned whether investment treaties create rights greater than promised in constitutions which are considered as stating the right almost without qualification. The issue has been raised in the U.S., where constitutional protection of property is considered to be very strong. A constitutional challenge mounted on these grounds has been refused in Canada.

36 Neither does the European Convention on Human Rights, where it is stated in the First Protocol to the Convention. The original Convention did not contain a right to property, presumably because Europe had many socialist governments at the time of its drafting. The case law that has emerged under the European Convention accepts to a larger extent the public and social function of property and makes compensation for takings revolve around the extent to which there is a social justification for the interference with property rights of the individual.

37 Tom Allen, *The Right to Property in Commonwealth Constitutions* (Cambridge University Press: 2000); Laura Underkuffler, *The Idea of Property* (Oxford University Press: 2003).

38 Justice Scalia in *Lucas v. South Carolina Coastal Commission*, 505 U.S. 1003 (1992) provides an example.

39 For the view that the tension exists in U.S. law as well, *see* Gregory Alexander, *Commodity and Propriety: Competing Visions of Property in American Legal Thought* (University of Chicago Press: 1997).

40 *See also* M. Sornarajah, "The Clash of Globalizations and International Investment Law," the Simon Reisman Lecture, Ottawa (2004) (http://www.carleton.ca/ctpl/pdf/papers/sornarajah.pdf).

41 The writings referred to in the note below indicate that rights more extensive than the constitutional rights to property in many countries, including Canada and the U.S., are recognized in the modern arbitrations, particularly under NAFTA.

42 Vicki Bean, "Global Fifth Amendment? NAFTA's Investment Protection and the Misguided Quest for an International Regulatory Takings Doctrine," 78 N.Y.U. L. Rev. 30 (2003); David Schneiderman, "Investment Rules and New Constitutionalism," 25 Law and Social Inquiry 757 (2000).

there is a uniform right to property in the world, it has to be juxtaposed with other credible rights with which it may clash, for example the right to development, the right to an environment, the right to air quality and the right to water and other essentials such as electricity. Such clashes concern the international community as a whole and are incapable of balanced disposal by commercial arbitrators whose prime concern may be for contractual sanctity. They may pay less attention to competing notions of property, and the notion that contractual sanctity has been eroded in many systems by competing considerations such as unfair bargaining power, undue influence and economic duress or that the situation may be different in the case of State contracts.

Competing objectives may combine with competing international obligation, forcing decisions about which should have priority. In *SD Myers v. Canada*,[43] the conflict was between Canadian obligations under a multilateral treaty, the Basel Convention on the Transport of Hazardous Wastes, and the right of a U.S. investor under NAFTA. In *Santa Helena v. Costa Rica*,[44] the conflict was between the obligation to protect the habitat of the black puma and the right of the investor under the U.S.–Costa Rica investment treaty. In *SPP v. Egypt*,[45] the competing interests related to the protection of cultural artefacts covered by the World Heritage Convention and an investor's contractual right to continue building a tourist resort. In all such situations, arbitrators have held that contractual and treaty rights of the investor trump obligations that are owed to the international community as a whole. The instances could be multiplied.[46]

Thus, care has to be taken that a worthwhile system of balance and compromise is maintained in investment treaties as well as in international arbitration to ensure that States do not become wary of signing such treaties in the future because they fear facing large numbers of arbitration suits based on an expansive interpretation of international investment law and a lack of sufficient attention to competing objectives. In order to restore a balance and legitimacy to the system, the expansionary trends that have been set in motion must first be identified. Ways must then be found of curbing the excesses that have come about.

Not for once is it claimed that there should be no arbitration of investment disputes. No developing country takes such a position. States err. Hapless foreign

---

43 ILM 1408 (2001).

44 5 ICSID Rpts 153 (2002).

45 3 ICSID Rpts 189 (1992).

46 They are discussed in M. Sornarajah, *The Settlement of Foreign Investment Disputes* (Kluwer: 2001).

investors, once they have entered a country, are at the mercy of the sovereign power of the State. Commitments made prior to entry may be callously withdrawn. There must be protection for the foreign investor in such circumstances. Equally, there cannot be a system that is entirely protective of the rapacious foreign investor who harms the development goals of a host country through misconduct. Neither should there be protection when the State is compelled to intervene in a situation in which public interests require such an action. In the latter circumstances, prudent adjustments of rights of investors in the light of the circumstances may be necessary, and these functions are best performed by neutral tribunals sensitive to the balance that the competing interests require. There must be a balanced system that provides justice against errors and wanton acts of both parties. Investment arbitration is such a system and it must be preserved. What is claimed is that excesses have occurred in the present system, particularly as a result of trends initiated in the past few years. Such excesses, if left unchecked, could destroy a worthwhile system that could survive and provide remedies to foreign investors in appropriate situations. It is in this context that the expansionary trends that have been instituted must be analyzed in the hope that they can be corrected. No generic attack is made on arbitration. It is a system that is well accepted across the globe. It is so accepted only because the fairness inherent in the process has not been thwarted. So, too, a balanced system of investment arbitration will be acceptable to developing country international lawyers if the biases in the present system can be removed.

Expansionary Trends in Foreign Investment Arbitration

Treaties merely state propositions. As with legislation, life is blown into them by judges, arbitrators and other decision-makers who ascribe meanings to the propositions contained in them and determine their outer scope. Judges, however, can be corrected if they exceed the mandate of the constitution and misinterpret the law. Investment arbitrators cannot be so corrected as there is no mechanism for the making of such correction. Sometimes, arbitrators keep extending the outer scope of the principles in the treaties. What has happened in the past decade and a half is an increase in arbitration as a result of "arbitration without privity."

"Arbitration without Privity"

"Arbitration without privity" is an approach that sacrifices accuracy to flamboyance. That there can be no arbitration without privity would be clear even to a neophyte in the field. An agreement between the parties is central to any arbitration. *AAPL v. Sri Lanka* initiated a particular trend on the basis of investment treaties.[47] All that was done in that case was to take the provision on dispute settlement in the U.K.–Sri Lanka treaty that contained a unilateral offer and convert it into an agreement upon the investor indicating a willingness to initiate arbitration proceedings before ICSID. An agreement to arbitrate between the parties was constructed on this basis. That was not arbitration without privity, but a construction of an agreement between the parties based on the existence of earlier offers of arbitration and its subsequent acceptance. As an afterthought, justification was found in an ICSID memorandum which stated that the arbitration agreement need not be in the same document. A number of investment arbitrations that have taken place in recent times have been on the basis of treaty provisions containing unilateral promises of arbitration.

It is too late to contest the premises on which this technique of construction rests. It is striking that the U.K.–Sri Lanka treaty (as well as other treaties containing the same language) existed for many years previously and had been commented upon.[48] But, if so striking a change had been initiated by the State parties themselves, it would have been announced or made known to investors. Had it been so obvious, it would have been attempted before *AAPL v. Sri Lanka*. This raises the issue as to whether the states making these treaties intended the result that was accomplished in *AAPL*. Once the case was decided in 1990, this approach was emulated by others.

Though it is perhaps too late, it would be good to pause to consider whether the technique is reconcilable with the theory of international law on treaties. The making of a contract that contains clauses in favor of third parties had been problematic in most legal systems. English common law, until recently, had a difficulty with the concept due to the existence of the doctrine of consideration. Systems based on Roman law had difficulty in recognizing a *stipulatio alteri* but overcame the difficulty quicker than the common law system did. It is interesting to note that, what has been considered a primitive

47 *SPP v. Egypt*, 22 ILM 752 (1983) did the same as far as unilateral offers in State legislation on foreign investment was concerned. But, this has not been the most significant basis for claiming jurisdiction in later cases.

48 The description of British treaties by Eileen Denza and Shelagh Brooks, "Investment Protection Treaties: The British Experience," 36 ICLQ 1069 (1987), written three years before *AAPL v. Sri Lanka*, does not contain any reference to this possibility. Both writers were Foreign Office legal officers with experience in drafting British investment treaties. Mann, who commented on the U.K.–Philippines treaty, makes no reference to the possibility (FA Mann, "British Treaties for the Promotion and Protection of Investment," 52 BYIL 241 (1981)). The conclusion that the technique was an afterthought is not far-fetched.

legal system, had evolved a *stipulatio alteri* of an infinite variety in investment law, and that too in favor of entities which purportedly have no standing in international law.

In the international law of treaties, the idea that treaties could be made in favor of third parties was seldom contemplated, though slowly categories of rights conferred on third States through treaties did emerge.[49] In the context of this development, the idea that a treaty could grant rights to entities like MNCs, whose personality in terms of international law is doubted by some scholars,[50] would at least appear problematic, though it has never been raised in the context of the arbitrations that have resulted from investment treaties.[51] Not only is that a problem because rights are conferred on a large class of entities that have no personality, but also because rights are conferred on potentially unknown and unknowable persons.[52] As the issues that have arisen in connection with corporate nationality demonstrate, the right to arbitration can—through notions of corporate personality—be used by a limitless number of persons or foreign companies simply through the technique of incorporation, or through "migration" to states in which they can find protection.[53]

A case like *Fedax v. Venezuela*[54] illustrates that the mere transfer of documents held by nationals of a State to foreigners having treaty protection may engage the jurisdiction of tribunals to provide protection. The possibility that protection could be created through the transference of shares of a company to nationals of States with protection has been contemplated.[55] The issue of round-tripping—in which nationals of a State obtain protection

---

49 The parallel drawn with human rights treaties is not apposite. These treaties recognize inherent rights, not newly created rights of investment protection. Human rights treaties work on the theory of a pre-existence of rights that treaties simply declare and provide a mechanism to protect.

50 Malcolm Shaw, *International Law*, 5th Edition (Cambridge University Press: 2004), p. 224.

51 Mixed Claims Commissions were entirely different from the present systems, though there are superficial parallels.

52 For example, in *Fedax v. Venezuela*, 37 ILM 1378 (1998), jurisdiction was established by transferring bonds issued by Venezuela to its own citizens by transferring the bonds to foreigners with treaty protection. In *Aguas del Tunari v. Bolivia*, ICSID Case No. ARB/02/3/ (2006), jurisdiction was established on the theory that companies can migrate, the company in the case migrating to a State that had treaty protection.

53 This arises as a consequence of *Aguas del Tunari, supra, note 52.*

54 37 ILM 1378 (1998).

55 *Aguas del Tunari, supra*, note 52.

by incorporating a company in the other State party to the investment treaty—divided a tribunal rather acrimoniously.[56]

Do domestic legal systems admit the possibility of such wide notions of the *stipulation alteri*? Would countries have agreed to such a situation had they known that they were opening such a Pandora's box? Having opened it, many are now seeking to find a way out of this situation through the use of antisuit injunctions, constitutional challenges to investment treaties and threats of review of awards by domestic courts. The original flaw may have been in the theory underlying the technique, but it may be too late to challenge the basis of the technique of constructing consent on the basis of the arbitration provisions of investment treaties. But, States that seek to turn away from the situation may reopen the debate as to whether the intention behind the arbitration provision in investment treaties was indeed to hold out a unilateral offer of arbitration to an unlimited and unidentifiable class of investors.[57]

Why the intention should be so relevant is that, in arbitration of any type, success and eventual enforcement depends largely on the actual consent of the parties, not on consent that is artificially constructed. This is very much so in domestic arbitration where courts and arbitrators are careful in ensuring that they do not go beyond the bounds of the arbitration provisions. There does not seem to be similar caution displayed in investment arbitration. Yet, the need for such caution in situations in which sovereign countries are involved is greater simply because the existence of consent involves a surrender of sovereignty. The construction of such a surrender of sovereignty should not be lightly inferred. Constructing consent without caution could eventually undermine the very existence of treaty-based investment arbitration.

---

56 *Tokio-Tokeles v. Ukraine* dealt with the phenomenon of round-tripping, whereby citizens of a state go into another state which has an investment treaty with their state, incorporate a company there and receive protection from the treaty. The issue of round-tripping was also raised in *Yaung Chi Oo Ltd v. Myanmar*, 42 ILM 430 (2003).

57 Note Bolivia's argument in *Aguas del Tunari* that jurisdiction should be limited to circumstances that a State can reasonably contemplate, as consent is the cornerstone of arbitration (para. 194). Also, note the expert opinion of Dolzer in the case (para. 199) that the "circle of beneficiaries" was carefully limited by the treaties. In a separate opinion in *Aguas del Tunari*, arbitrator Alberro-Semerena accepted the Bolivian argument. The manner in which the tribunal interpreted control favors the MNCs, whose structures are in a multiplicity of countries. Again, by creating structures of control, MNCs could diversify the nature of the protection that they obtain beyond the limits intended by the States making relevant treaties.

The Expansion of Jurisdiction: Further Techniques

A diversity of techniques has been used to expand jurisdiction, as well as the substantive law on liability after jurisdiction is found. They are evident in the awards made in the past few years, during the growth in the number of arbitration cases after the notion of "arbitration without privity" took hold. They are usually based on interpretations that take the view that the securing of economic development is the objective behind the conclusion of investment treaties and that a purposeful interpretation securing these objectives should be sought.

a. Use of the Most-Favored-Nation Clause

The expansion of jurisdiction that is inherent in the notion of a constructed consent has been further enhanced through the application of the most-favored-nation (MFN) standard provision that appears in most investment treaties. The way in which this could be done was demonstrated in *Maffezini v. Spain*.[58] In this case, an Argentine investor in Spain, not finding a unilateral offer to arbitrate investment disputes in his State's investment treaty with Spain, used the MFN treatment clause in the Spain–Argentina treaty to support the argument that he should be able to use the better provisions contained in the treaty between Spain and Chile which involved a unilateral offer of arbitration. The argument succeeded. *Maffezini* therefore makes it possible for investors to expand the scope of a treaty's jurisdiction by scouring the treaty network of a State and picking a treaty that is most favorable to them to base jurisdiction, again a technique that was probably not contemplated by the countries upon the signing of the treaties. The technique that was used in *Maffezini* could be employed not only in connection with dispute settlement but also for other substantive and procedural rights in investment treaties. As a result, the content of the treaties could be subjected to expansion depending on the nature of the network of treaties that the MFN clause attracts.

Maffezini was followed in other awards.[59] The curtailment of this trend in some later disputes is to be welcomed.[60] If permitted, the *Maffezini* argument could

---

58 5 ICSID Rpts 396 (2000); further, *see* Dana Freyer and David Herlihy, "Most Favoured Nation Treatment and Dispute Settlement in Investment Arbitration," 58 ICSID Review—Foreign Investment Law Journal (2004).

59 *Siemens v. Argentina, Camuzzi v. Argentina* and *Gas Natural v. Argentina* (text for all cases: http://ita.law.uvic.ca).

60 *See Palma Consortium v. Bulgaria; see also Salini Construttori v. Jordan* (text for all cases: http://ita.law.uvic.ca).

have led to an indefinite expansion of the basis of jurisdiction beyond the actual or presumed consent of States.

Maffezini could be seen as reflecting another effort at bringing about a world system of investment protection. Had the technique suggested been given full scope, it would have been possible to arrive at a solution that isolates the treaties that give the best protection and ensure that the same protection is afforded through all treaties that contain widely drafted MFN clauses. This effort seems now to have been stifled.

b. Use of Corporate Nationality

Another avenue for expansion of jurisdiction is through corporate nationality. Since mere incorporation is sufficient under many treaties for the acquisition of corporate nationality, the simple technique of incorporation alone assures that nationals unrelated to the State that is a party to an investment treaty can acquire the protection of the treaty. *Lauder v. The Czech Republic* contained just such a situation: U.S. interests incorporated in the Netherlands before proceeding to invest through a company incorporated in the Czech Republic.[61] In fact, many states make treaties that facilitate this situation. They operate on the basis of a platform concept so that MNCs would locate within their territories and proceed out from there. As a result, they may reap some of the advantages, including repatriation of profits through their banks, in exchange for, among other things, the protection provided by the treaties. The Netherlands, Mauritius and some of the smaller countries of Southeast Asia adopt such policies. They again expand the scope for arbitration by companies using treaties of countries to which they are quite unrelated. No doubt, the purposes of the host country and the foreign investor are well served as a result of such treaties; but the host country does create problems for itself when it enters into that type of agreement.[62]

Round-tripping is another issue that has come into the fore as a result of *Tokio-Tokeles v. Ukraine*.[63] Nationals of Ukraine incorporated a company in a

---

61 The Netherlands was also featured in *Fedax v. Venezuela*, 37 ILM 1378 (1998). Nationals, not paid under bonds issued by their government, transferred the bonds to a Dutch Antilles company and the company successfully brought arbitration proceedings under the Dutch treaty.

62 The case filed by Enron against India was based on the treaty between Mauritius and India.

63 ICSID (2004). The issue of round-tripping was also raised in *Yaung Chi Oo Ltd v. Myanmar*, 42 ILM 430 (2003); *see also Champion Trading Company v. Egypt*, ICSID Case No. ARB/02/9 (2003), where a company formed and controlled in the U.S. by nationals holding dual nationality and hence not entitled to protection in their own rights, was held to be entitled to bring a claim under the U.S.–Egypt treaty.

country with which Ukraine had an investment treaty and directed their investment back into Ukraine through that company. The tribunal held that the company was entitled to treaty protection, despite the protest of the Chairperson of the Tribunal, who resigned after filing a strong dissent to the majority opinion. Corporate nationality can thus be seen as being manipulated so as to increase the scope for jurisdiction. It is a result quite unintended by the State parties to the treaties who had in the pre-existing law stressed the need for a link based on nationality before jurisdiction could be established.[64]

The assumed purpose of an investment treaty is to enable foreign investment flows through its protection. This objective is not furthered by giving protection to citizens who cycle their investments through the other State in the treaty. Increasingly, States now limit the notion of corporate nationality either by requiring that the corporation claiming jurisdiction under the treaty should have majority control located in the hands of nationals of the other country or by requiring that effective management of the company be located within the territory of the other State. Yet, the problem will remain an issue. Incorporation in tax havens like the Dutch Antilles and some protectorates[65] may secure not only tax advantages but also the protection of investment treaties.

In *Aguas del Trigas*,[66] the possibility is held out that companies could "migrate" by establishing themselves in countries that have treaty protection and thereby secure the protection of investment treaties, even though such "migration" did not have the consent of the host country. In this manner, a foreign investor has the opportunity to enhance protection at will, thereby altering the status that existed at the time of the conclusion of the foreign investment contract. The notion of corporate "migration" increases the potential for a company, which in the theory of law has personality only in the legal system that created it, to choose the nature of the protection subsequently simply by "migrating." This again is an expansive interpretation that increases the category of persons protected beyond what a host country could have anticipated at the time it signed a treaty. It, no doubt, benefits platform States as it attracts more established companies to "migrate" into their territories for the purposes of protection. But the traditional host countries of an investment, which made the investment treaties, have to shoulder the burden of protection of an investment not

---

64 *Nottebohm Case*, ICJ Rpts 4 (1955).

65 In *AAPL v. Sri Lanka*, the British treaty was extended to Hong Kong companies. But, the British Virgin Islands are excluded from the scope of protection of many British treaties.

66 ICSID Case No. ARB/02/3 (2006).

attracted into the state by the treaty but in respect of an already existing investment.[67] The tribunal in *Aguas del Tunari*[68] concerned itself only with the issue as to whether "migration" was possible under the domestic laws of the two countries involved in the migration, not its impact on the issue of whether the host country's obligation as to protection could be enlarged through such migration. The technique of "migration" will enable MNCs to shop for the nature of the protection they desire. They could, in anticipation of disputes, locate in the best haven, depending on the nature of the treaties that exist. A refugee law in reverse, a law for the protection of firms, could thus be created, tainting thereby the legitimacy of the international investment law system.

Waiver Clauses

There seems also to be a tendency to discard exclusive jurisdiction and waiver clauses in several arbitral awards. This is a carry-over from the days prior to investment treaties when the waiver of rights of recourse to diplomatic intervention was construed as having no effect, as the right that was being waived in the contract was the right of the home country of the foreign investor.[69] That reasoning was slightly spurious, because what was waived could be the personal right of investors to seek such protection by confining themselves to the remedies under local law, without recourse to which the issue of diplomatic protection could not arise. In any event, the local remedies law mandated that such remedies be sought. There must first be a wrong to the foreign investor before there could be a wrong that could be espoused by the home country. Similar ruses are used in overcoming waiver clauses in investment arbitration. The conventional view that has come about is that a contract is distinct from treaty rights, and that waiver and exclusive jurisdiction clauses in a contract are to be restricted to issues of breaches arising from the contract.[70] This seems

---

67 A "platform State" is usually a small entity, like Mauritius, Hong Kong or Singapore, which makes treaties in the hope of attracting companies to locate themselves within their territories and use them as gateways into larger economies like China or India. An investment treaty may have this specific objective.

68 Paras. 168–180; the tribunal did not address the issue raised (para. 183) by Bolivia that the claimant was a new company with enhanced rights under the protection of the Dutch BIT.

69 The *North American Dredging Co.* case, as discussed in Donald Shea, *The Calvo Clause* (University of Minnesota Press: 1955).

70 *Compania de Agual del Aconquija SA and Vivendi Universal v. Argentina*, 40 ILM 426 (2001); *Vivendi Annulment Award* (2002); *Azurix v. Argentina*, ICSID Case No. ARB/01/12 (2003); in *SGS v. Philippines*, ICSID Case No. ARB/02/06 (2003), the clause was interpreted as creating obligations, but it did not feature in creating liability.

logical as far as treatment standards are concerned, as these standards are extraneous to the contract.

However, expropriation usually involves a breach of contract and cannot logically be said to give rise to a claim outside the contract. Besides, for an expropriation claim to arise, there must be a denial of due process. There could not have been due process if the claimant had not attempted recourse to the local tribunals. A distinction must necessarily be draw in this regard between claims based on expropriation and claims based on treatment that can arise only from the treaties. The issue of whether claims based on expropriation could be covered by the waiver requires further thought. Such further thinking is unlikely to occur simply because of the fact that arbitrators seemed to have foreclosed such inquiry by taking an early stance on the issue.

Jurisdiction and the Umbrella Clause

The presence of "umbrella clauses" in investment treaties has caused problems and exposed schisms within investment treaty arbitration. It has been generally accepted that a mere violation of a foreign investment contract does not create international liability in the State and that disputes as to contract violation must be dealt with in municipal law through the methods prescribed in the contract.[71] Umbrella clauses are catch-all provisions, usually tucked away in the text. Their precise scope would have puzzled developing country negotiators had they noticed it or paid attention to it.

The concept of the umbrella clause remained uninterpreted as used in the two cases collectively known as *SGS*.[72] They arrived at opposite conclusions as to the use of such clauses. The effect of the umbrella clause in an investment treaty would be to enable the rights negotiated in the contract by the parties to be given protection by the States parties to the treaty. It would have meant that foreign investors could have indefinitely extended the extent of the treaty protection through provisions they secured through negotiation of the foreign investment contract. *SGS v. Pakistan* refused to give the clause protecting the contract such a wide definition. A contrary conclusion would have the effect of extending the scope of protection indefinitely, as the State would become

---

71 *Noble Ventures v. Romania*, ICSID Award (2005); *Azininian v. Mexico* 14 ICSID Rev. 563 (1999), para. 87 ("indeed, NAFTA cannot possibly be read to create such a regime, which would have elevated a multitude of ordinary transactions with public authorities into potential international disputes").

72 *SGS v. Pakistan*, ICSID Case No. ARB /02/06 (2003); *SGS v. Philippines*, ICSID Case No. ARB /02/6 (2004).

liable for any breach of the contract it occasions by its measures if it leads to an interference of negotiated contractual rights of the foreign investor. Such a treaty device would have been unique in that a third party to the treaty, even a foreign investor purportedly lacking status in international law, would have the power of extending the scope of the treaty.

The direct way of stating this in the treaty itself would have been to include contractual rights as assets in the definitional provision on investment in the text, or to indicate in the dispute settlement provision that disputes could arise from violation of contractual rights and could be subjected to arbitration. State sovereignty should not be toyed with by any tribunal, least of all by an ad hoc tribunal whose legitimacy to embark on such course would be suspect.[73] As the later award, *Joy Mining Machinery v. Egypt*,[74] put it, it would be difficult to accept that "an umbrella clause inserted in the treaty, and not very prominently, could have the effect of transforming all contract disputes into investment disputes under the treaty."

The problem with the umbrella clause is that it seeks to achieve indirectly purposes that are directly achieved in most treaties if parties think it necessary. For that reason, the umbrella clause and its interpretation have caused concern. Since the conflict depends on arbitrators taking sides on whether or not expansive interpretations should be made, this is an issue on which the scope for conflict could increase.

The contrary position is contained in *SGS v. Philippines*, which involved a U.K. investment treaty. In this case, the umbrella clause was quite similar to the U.K. treaty with Egypt dealt with in *Joy Mining*. The contrary position seeks to introduce the old view that a foreign investment contract is an internationalized contract through the back door—that is, the presence of an umbrella clause is made the occasion to internationalize the whole contract, ensuring that the violation of any contractual obligation receives treaty protection. If this aim is to be secured, the States that made the treaty would have made it abundantly clear and not stated in a clause usually tucked away in a treaty provision. Commentaries on investment treaties hardly gave space to the consideration of such a momentous clause having such consequences. It is as if the contract is incorporated in the treaty. Why have elaborate provisions in an investment treaty when all that is required is a provision to state that the

---

73 *Impreglio v. Pakistan*, ICSID Case No. ARB/03/03, Decision on Jurisdiction (2005).

74 *Joy Mining Machinery v. Egypt*, ICSID Case No. ARB/03/11 (2004), para. 81.

obligations negotiated by the parties are binding as if they were obligations under the treaty? The effort to confine the decision to situations in which the breach is made through the exercise of a governmental power is meaningless, because such an interference would amount to a taking.[75] Such an interpretation would make the taking clause in the treaty otiose. The broader interpretation that any breach would engage responsibility as a treaty violation adopts too wide an understanding. The wide interpretation in *SGS v. Philippines* is expansionary.

The efforts to confine it in subsequent awards indicate the embarrassment it has caused to the system of investment arbitration. The episode merely goes to illustrate that many States do not seem to understand the significance of clauses they accept in investment treaties—and how problematic an expansive interpretation of specific treaty clauses can be.

Courses of Action

Treatment Standards

Treatment standards were hardly the foundation of treaty-based arbitration in times when the focus of most arbitration was on expropriation of the assets of an investor; instead, emphasis shifted there only recently, during the period of liberalization.[76] Treatment standards rose to prominence because outright expropriation has become a rarity in modern times. Two outcomes have resulted. The first is that the focus has shifted to a violation of treatment standards. The second is that new theories of expropriation are being developed. The first trend of the emphasis on the violation of treatment standards has been accentuated particularly in the context of NAFTA arbitration between the two developed countries of Canada and the U.S. Expropriation is hardly likely in these States. Litigation between them, which is increasing, depends either on an expansionary view of expropriation or on the interpretation of treatment standards. The fear is that the legal strategies used in this context will permeate into general international law and affect investment arbitration against developing countries.[77]

---

[75] This narrower interpretation is suggested in dicta in *Impreglio* (para. 278), where it is suggested that the interference will not violate the umbrella clause unless the state had "exercised the specific functions of a sovereign authority." (See Annex 7, *UNCTAD, IIA Monitor, No. 4* (2006).)

[76] Joshua Robbins, "The Emergence of Positive Obligations in Bilateral Investment Treaties," 13 U. Miami Int'l & Comp. L. Rev. 403 (2006).

[77] The takings jurisprudence in U.S. constitutional law is complex and has given rise to much litigation over the whole period of that country's history. Litigation has moved through phases during which permissive

Treatment standards had hitherto hardly figured in investment arbitrations against developing countries but are now becoming regular features, as they have become an alternative standard on the basis of which awards are made; a claim of expropriation is now seldom made by itself but instead in association with a series of alleged violations of treatment standards. The situation that may come about is that, though a claim of expropriation fails, the claim based on treatment standards could succeed, as in *CMS v. Argentina*. In the process, the treatment standards in investment treaties come to be fleshed out by arbitrators, giving new meanings to the phrases that describe them, again, possibly well beyond the meanings that were originally contemplated by the parties.

a. Failure to Provide National Treatment

A main thrust of the recent investment treaties signed largely by Canada, the United States, Japan and the Republic of Korea has been to ensure the right of entry and establishment, thus ensuring that national treatment applies at the pre-entry stage as well. Most other treaties recognize only post-entry national treatment, in accordance with the idea that a State should have the right to decide whether or not to admit investment at the point of entry. Once admitted, foreign investment must be given national treatment. In deciding the scope of this treatment, ideas borrowed from international trade have seeped into the investment area so that the notion that non-discrimination should be between "like" investors in "like" circumstances has been advanced as a limiting factor in the application of the standard.

A number of cases have been instituted on the basis of an alleged violation of national treatment under NAFTA. These violations are usually coupled with violations of other treaty provisions.[78] *SD Myers v. Canada* was an award that highlighted issues relating to national treatment. It held that the standard was

---

approaches were taken to State takings, primarily in earlier times when the country in its developmental phase had to interfere with property rights to build necessary infrastructure; to a more strict view that takings must be compensated if there is permanent injury caused to the property interests of an owner. There are several texts that deal with the phases that U.S. law has gone through, *e.g.*, Gregory Alexander, *Commodity and Property: Competing Visions of Property in American Legal Thought* (University of Chicago Press: 1998). For the most recent case, discussing the earlier cases, *see Linda Lingle, Governor of Hawaii v. Chevron Inc.*, 544 U.S. 528 (2005). The suggestion that U.S. or European law on takings should be extrapolated into international law fails to take into account the fact that the law in these regions moved through different phases.

78 *SD Myers v. Canada*, 21 ILR 7 (2002); *UPS v. Canada Post* (pending 2007); *Marvin Feldman v. Mexico*, ICSID Case No. ARB (AF)/99/1 (2002); *ADF v. United States of America*, ICSID Case No. ARB(AF)/00/1 (2003).

violated on the facts of the case. The denial of the continued functioning of a toxic waste disposal facility provided by a U.S. firm in Ontario was held to be a violation of NAFTA provisions on national treatment. The waste was taken across the Canadian border into Ohio for treatment. This place was within a hundred miles of Ontario. The closest Canadian treatment facility was across Canada in Alberta, several hundred miles away. The Canadian minister's decision that the waste must be treated in Canada was held to be a violation of the national standard treatment. This was despite the fact that Canada may have had an obligation under the Basel Convention on the Transfer of Hazardous Wastes not to export toxic materials abroad. It was an instance of clashing treaty obligations. A controversy that the case gave rise to is whether in such instances an arbitration tribunal set up under an investment treaty should decide an issue involving a conflict of treaty obligations. The other treaty was a multilateral treaty creating obligations toward the entire international community. In these circumstances, the issue arises as to whether there is a doctrine of limiting the tribunal constituted under a BIT from considering an issue that implicates the interests of the whole international community.[79]

The pending NAFTA case, *UPS v. Canada*, also demonstrates how alleged violations of national treatment can be intrusive of domestic organization of sectors, like the delivery of postal services. Here, UPS alleges violation of national treatment, as the facility of collecting parcels from post offices is made available to a delivery service that operates as a commercial subsidiary of Canada Post, a national monopoly in postal services, but that facility is not made available to UPS, a foreign company. The fear that is raised is that such litigation may affect public sectors that are operated by State-owned companies with an obligation to provide services in all areas of the country. The internal organization of economic sectors, it is alleged, comes to be determined by external standards determined by external tribunals.[80]

b. International Minimum Standard of Treatment

The "international minimum standard" was a standard that was articulated in the context of the conflicts relating to state responsibility for physical

---

79 The classic U.S. analysis is contained in *Mitsubishi v. Soler Chrysler Ltd*, 473 U.S. 614 (1984), which takes a pro-arbitration stance. Similar stances are not taken in other jurisdictions.

80 On this basis, the constitutional validity of NAFTA was questioned by an intervenient in the arbitration, the Canadian Postal Workers Union, before the Ontario Courts. The primary courts have dismissed the challenge. An appeal is pending.

mistreatment of U.S. nationals in Latin America. The *Neer Claim* in 1926, which stated the rules of such responsibility, is still used as the best authority for that type of claim.[81] It was progressively extended to the protection of property in claims made by the U.S. There was ambivalence even among writers of that country to the making of this extension. Nevertheless, it has come to be accepted as international law in the majority of U.S. writings. Some arbitrators have regarded the international minimum standard as a part of the regional law confined to North America.[82] Its status as customary international law is by no means established.[83] However, to the extent that it is stated in investment treaties, it must be taken as constituting law as between the parties to the treaty.

Though repeated in investment treaties, the content of the international minimum standard cannot be ascertained outside the practice in the North American context. There seems to be authority for just two propositions: where there is a denial of justice by a local administration, usually the courts, State responsibility would be engaged; and full compensation must be paid for the expropriation of property.

The fact that there should be a denial of justice by the local courts in itself is an assertion of the initial competence over issues relating to aliens in the domestic tribunals. It is from the denial of justice that responsibility arises. It must not be an ordinary error of law, but rather one of manifest injustice that is readily and objectively recognizable as such. The inclusion of an international minimum standard in an investment treaty must, *prima facie*, be accepted as an assertion of the initial competence of local law and local tribunals. The inherent conflict this creates with the dispute resolution provision in a treaty has hardly been noticed in the discussion of issues relating to investment treaties.

---

81 *The Neer Claim* was decided by a Mexican Claims Commission, 4 UNRIAA 85 (1926). It held that responsibility for personal injury to an alien arose only if the treatment amounted to "outrage, to bad faith, to willful neglect of duty or to insufficiency of governmental action so far short of international standards that every reasonable and impartial man would readily recognize its insufficiency." The International Court of Justice approved the formulation in the case of *ELSI*, ICJ Rpts 1 (1989), which more directly involved foreign investment. In that context, the idea that *Neer Claim* is an old case reflecting positions in 1926 is not apposite. Its principle is still relevant.

82 The tribunals that so considered them had strong international lawyers.

83 Quite apart from the Calvo Doctrine, which was given up by the Latin American countries only in the 1990s (but may be revived in the context of events like the Argentinean economic crisis and the arbitrations precipitated by it), doctrines such as permanent sovereignty over natural resources have not yet been dismantled. It is unlikely that they would be. *See also* Mathew Porterfield, "An International Common Law of Investor Rights?," 27 U. PA. J. INT'L ECON. L. 79 (2006).

Case law generated on the international minimum standard does not provide any authority outside these two claims as regards the content of an international minimum standard. Expropriation is separately provided for in investment treaties.

So what is left is the rule relating to a denial of justice. What the content of this rule might be, outside the area of denial of justice, is still left an unfilled blank. Awards of tribunals have seldom sought to flesh out this blank. In most awards in which a violation of the standard was alleged, it was pleaded as an alternative ground for expropriation. Since expropriation was found, it was not necessary to make findings on the basis of violation of the minimum standard. The standard remains based on the notions of denial of justice, for which there is practice confined largely to the North American context. On the basis of denial of justice, it would be difficult to establish violation of minimum standards without prior recourse to the local courts of the host country, which is precisely what the dispute settlement procedures of investment treaties seek to avoid. To that extent, the international minimum standard would seem to be a surplusage in an investment treaty. But, it nevertheless remains. The inclusion of the standard may be in the hope that it could be given meaning by the arbitration tribunal in an appropriate context.

In *Mondev International v. U.S.*,[84] there is a suggestion made that, because the international minimum standard is repeated in several treaties, it has universal relevance. However, for it to have such relevance, its content must be identified with precision. A cipher, however many times it is multiplied, is still a cipher. The tribunal's view in *Mondev* that the international minimum standard as stated in *Neer*[85] is not a static concept is also questionable, because the content of this dynamic concept, if it is one, was not identified by the tribunal. A similar idea was repeated in *ADF Group v. U.S.*[86] This repetition merely accomplishes the task of conserving a concept in the hope that an opportune moment would arise for its use when more substance could be put into a presently vague concept.

84 42 ILM 85; 6 ICSID Rpts 192 (2003).

85 4 UNRIAA 85 (1926).

86 *ADF Group v. U.S.*, 6 ICSID Rpts 527 (2003), para 179: "Both customary international law and the minimum standard of treatment of aliens it incorporates are constantly in a process of development." If so, the trends in this development should be identified, instead of pronouncements that lay the basis for a future relaxing of the standards established in *Neer*. That case does not establish a substantive proposition but indicates that the breach of the treatment standard must be of a sufficient seriousness to merit State responsibility, the imposition of which should not be lightly made. The ICJ agreed with that proposition in *ELSI*. The only possible development that could be made is to relax the high threshold for the imposition of such responsibility."

Further, the fact that there must be a denial of justice for liability to arise takes wind out of the sails of dispute settlement under an investment treaty, because, in strict terms, denial of justice is seldom found by international tribunals, except in the most extreme circumstances.[87] Possibly, preparations are being made by debatable statements, such as those found in *Mondev* and *ADF*, to lower the threshold for the imposition of State responsibility on the basis of a violation of the international minimum standard of treatment.

The view that arbitrators are capable of filling in the content of standards through the exercise of a quasi-legislative power is debatable. Since they cannot make such law for their own countries, it is questionable to claim that they could or should make law for the whole of the international community. International rules must have some democratic legitimacy. The filling in of content through purported power that does not reside in them can hardly compel acceptance. The reasoning advanced on the basis of quasi-legislative power is spurious. This is so particularly because most of the tribunals are ad hoc tribunals consisting of persons whose competence in international law is not always clear. The analogy with law creation in a common law system is thus hardly apposite. There is a great difference between judges appointed to ongoing court systems in accordance with constitutional tenets and given a mandate to create law that can be set aside by a legislature if inappropriate, and ad hoc tribunals constituted by the parties to a specific dispute creating what they consider law applicable to the international community, lacking control or an oversight mechanism. It is strange that a system that insists on transparency in domestic law seeks to maintain a standard that lacks transparency and cannot be satisfied in advance by a State because it is too vague until its scope is identified. Such a situation is unsustainable and suspect.

c. Fair and Equitable Standard of Treatment

If the international minimum standard lacks content, the fair and equitable standard is even more lacking in substance. It too is being used in the hope that it can be fleshed out when necessary. According to an early commentator, this standard is higher than the international minimum standard.[88]

---

87 For an allegation of denial of justice, see *Loewen Group v. United States*, 7 ICSID Rpts 434 (2003). Despite the characterization of the trial as "a disgrace," the tribunal found no liability in the State, as all remedies up the appellate ladder had not been followed. Denial of justice seldom gives rise to State responsibility, except when there is an inordinate and extreme denial that shocks the conscience; *ELSI Case*, ICJ Rpts 15 (1989).

88 F.A. Mann, "British Treaties for the Promotion and Protection of Investments," 52 BYIL 241 (1981).

When the fair and equitable standard was made a basis of claims under NAFTA in *Pope and Talbot v. Canada*,[89] the NAFTA Commission, realizing that this concept could be fleshed out by arbitrators, released an interpretive statement[90] indicating that this standard had no meaning other than the international minimum standard of customary international law. Thus, at least among the NAFTA parties, this phrase is another surplusage without content. The Singapore–U.S. FTA, as well as the new model BIT of the U.S., adopts a similar position.[91]

This trend has continued into the non-NAFTA realm, as illustrated in *Genin v. Estonia*.[92] The tribunal in this case showed great sensitivity to regulatory control of the banking sector by an emerging market economy. It was reluctant to use the fair and equitable standard against Estonia, a standard that the plaintiff alleged was violated by the country's discriminatory measures. *Genin* may illustrate the proposition that subjective measures that an administration takes in response to specific situations in its economy should not be characterized by arbitral tribunals as unfair. Dicta in *ADF v. U.S.*[93] also seems to support such a proposition, which again reduces the scope for the fair and equitable standard.

But, despite *Genin*, it is uncertain whether tribunals will take the position under NAFTA that the fair and equitable standard is no more than what the customary international law minimum standard requires. It was used in some recent arbitrations, including, most importantly, *CMS v. Argentina*.[94] The tribunal there found that the measures taken by Argentina to curb the effects of the economic crisis were not fair and equitable.[95] Though the arbitrations against Argentina

---

89 41 ILM 1347 (2002).

90 The text of the Interpretive Statement is found in *UPS v. Canada*, Award on Jurisdiction, 22 November 2002, paras. 80–85.

91 The preliminary award in *UPS v. Canada*, para. 97, held that there was no independent existence for a fair and equitable standard outside the international minimum standard. A Canadian court, reviewing the award in *Metalclad*, held that lack of transparency could not be said to be a violation of the fair and equitable standard; 5 ICSID Rpts 236 (2001) (Supreme Court of British Columbia).

92 17 ICSID Rev. 395 (2001).

93 ICSID Case No. ARB (AF)/00/1 (2003).

94 ICSID Case No. ARB/01/8 (2005).

95 *CMS v. Argentina* suggested that when the legitimate expectations of a foreign investor are violated, liability could arise on the basis of the violation of the fair and equitable standard of treatment. The award does not demonstrate from where the concept of legitimate expectations is derived. There are suggestions in the literature that it is derived from English case law. If so, it must be taken into account that the doctrine is heavily constrained by competing doctrines, e.g., the principle that estoppel cannot run against the Crown. There appear to be no similar constraints on the notion of legitimate expectations by arbitral tribunals. The mode of converting the principle into a doctrine applicable at the international level has to be carefully explored.

that are pending may seek to focus on this standard as the basis of their awards, as *CMS v. Argentina* did, an award based on the standard does not stand on secure foundations. The standard is often used as a subsidiary justification for a holding based on expropriation. In *Middle East Shipping and Handling Co v. Egypt*,[96] an additional rationale for the holding against the respondent (Egypt) was that the seizure and auction of the property of the claimant without notification was a violation of the fair and equitable standard.

Expropriation

The expansionary trend in investment arbitration under treaties is most evident in the interpretation of the provisions on expropriation. The treaties themselves used expansive language, indicating that there were three categories of takings: direct, indirect and "anything tantamount to a taking."

The phrase "tantamount or equivalent to a taking" invites an expansion of the types of acts capable of being regarded as takings. The categories of direct and indirect takings have become more settled, with indirect takings coming to denote what is sometimes referred to as "creeping expropriation," in which the rights of foreign investors are progressively whittled away so that their investments diminish in value. This concept, too, is capable of significant expansion. Much of that expansion took place with the jurisprudence of the Iran–U.S. Claims Tribunal, which made an impact by unbundling rights of ownership and regarding interferences with each right of ownership as capable of being regarded as an expropriation.[97] But, that jurisprudence was based on a clear nexus between the conduct of the State and the right affected. Nevertheless, the ideas generated in these awards did play a role in later notions of takings.

In the context of NAFTA jurisprudence, these tendencies were extended further. The nature of the emerging NAFTA jurisprudence was such that, when the U.S. and Canada were involved, the tribunal would consist of members solely from developed countries. This permitted scope for the canvassing of expansive notions more easily. In the cases in which Mexico was involved, there does not appear to have been any desire on the part of Mexican arbitrators to

---

96 ICSID Case No. ARB/99/6 (2002), para.143.

97 For a survey of these awards, *see* George Aldrich, *The Jurisprudence of the Iran–U.S. Claims Tribunal* (Oxford University Press: 1996); and Charles Brower, *Iran–U.S. Claims Tribunal* (Kluwer: 1998).

stem this particular tide of expansion, the lead blocking position being taken more often by the United States upon becoming itself the target of the trend.

In *Metalclad*, an early NAFTA award, expropriation was defined as follows:[98]

> Expropriations under NAFTA includes not only open, deliberate and acknowledged takings of property, such as outright seizure or formal or obligatory transfer of title in favor of the host country, but also covert or incidental interference with the use of property which has the effect of depriving the owner, in whole or significant part, of the use or reasonably to be expected economic benefit of property even if not necessarily to the obvious benefit of the host country.[99]

Inherent in the definition of investment and other provisions in the investment treaties were notions that attracted creative interpretations. The definition of "investment" to include rights acquired under the law of the host country enabled the withdrawal of licences to operate by the administrative body to amount to expropriation. The bringing about of results that depreciated the value of the property was regarded as amounting to expropriation. The stage was set early in the arbitral case of *Ethyl*,[100] in which statements made by a Minister in the Canadian Parliament contemplating the ban of an allegedly carcinogenic substance produced by the claimant were said to bring about a fall in the value of shares in the claimant company, and therefore should qualify as expropriation. The current case by the Methanex corporation against the United States has features of *Ethyl*. It is being contested by the United States.

This expansionary trend has resulted from the indication in investment treaties that there is a third category of expropriations denoted by the phrase "tantamount to a taking." Given the effort to attribute meanings to this third category, Canada and the U.S. have sought to restrict the scope of the meaning of this phrase. In *Pope and Talbot v. Canada*,[101] the tribunal agreed with the Canadian argument that the phrase did not add anything to the existing categories of expropriation. It thus becomes a surplusage long in use in treaties

---

98 Para.103 of the award in *Metalclad*.

99 Justice Tysoe of the British Columbia Court, who reviewed the award, considered it to be "an extremely broad definition of expropriation."

100 The claim was settled with Canada, according to reports, paying around US$16 million to the Ethyl Corp.

101 41 ILM 1347 (2002).

against developing countries. One cannot avoid noticing this, if one is a developing country lawyer.

The third category, which is based on the view that "tantamount to property" does not exist, has now gained ground; the U.S. model treaty spells it out expressly. But, to the extent that it still remains stated in most treaties, the danger is that it will continue to be used. What has occurred is that there has been an attempt to promote theories of absolute property rights of foreign investors through investment treaties. In the 1990s and perhaps still today, there was a vigorous property rights movement in the U.S. It sought to insist on such rights within the United States. Investment treaties may be seen as an effort at the universalization of this notion of absolute property rights.[102] In fact, some U.S. and Canadian international lawyers argue that the property rights contained in NAFTA are in excess of those recognized by their respective domestic constitutional law systems.[103] The issue as to whether NAFTA creates greater property rights in a foreign investor and therefore violates the equality provisions of the Canadian Charter of Rights is being tested out before Canadian courts. The standard of protection for investors under NAFTA is discordant with Canada's own constitutional commitments. There is no direct property protection for Canadian citizens within Canada. Yet, it would appear that a foreign investor from Mexico or the U.S. is given such protection. This would be a problem for other Commonwealth countries as well where property rights are protected in a more attenuated fashion than they are in the United States.

Another area in which expansionary views on expropriation have caused concern relates to regulatory takings. When it came to regulatory takings made by developing countries, the matter did not become an issue; but when attempts at regulation by Canada and the U.S. were regarded as compensable takings, it became a matter of concern. There was a reluctance on the part of tribunals to regard regulatory takings, particularly environmental takings, as non-compensable. In *Santa Elena v. Costa Rica*,[104] the tribunal, faced with the

---

102 For an expansion of the view of the present writer on this proposition, *see* the Simon Reisman Lecture in International Trade Policy, Ottawa (2003), published in *Canadian Foreign Affairs* (http://www.carleton.ca/ctpl/conferences/index.html).

103 For Canada, *see* David Schneiderman, "Investment Rules and New Constitutionalism," 25 LAW AND SOCIAL INQUIRY 757 (2000); for the U.S., *see* Vicki Bean and Joel Beauvais, "The Global Fifth Amendment? NAFTA's Investment Protection and the Misguided Quest for an International Regulatory Takings Doctrine," 78 N.Y.U. L.REV 30 (2003).

104 15 ICSID Rev. 72 (2002); the passage cited was quoted and followed in *Técnicas Medioambientales Tecmed, S.A. v. United Mexican States*, ICSID Case No. ARB (AF)/00/2 (2003).

argument that the taking was effected in order to achieve environmental objectives, stated as follows:

> Expropriatory environmental measures—no matter how laudable and beneficial to society as a whole—are, in this respect, similar to any other expropriatory measures that a state may take in order to implement its policies: where property is expropriated, even for environmental purposes, whether domestic or international, the state's obligation to pay compensation remains.

The tribunal in *Tenicas Medioambientales Tecmed S.A. v. Mexico* found:[105]

> We find no principle stating that regulatory administrative actions are *per se* excluded from the scope of the Agreement (on investment protection), even if they are beneficial to society as a whole—such as environmental protection—particularly if the negative economic impact of such actions on the financial position of the investor is sufficient to neutralize in full the value, or economic or commercial use[,] of its investment without receiving any compensation whatsoever.[106]

Obviously, this would mean that a State that cannot afford to pay compensation has to desist from the environmental measure, "however laudable and beneficial to society as a whole." Since the environment or nature is viewed as a whole and as not belonging to a single state (the protection of the black puma which was involved in *Santa Elena* is not a matter for Costa Rica alone), views such as those expressed by the tribunal in *Santa Elena* are opposed by environmentalists. The same problems arise where cultural property is involved.[107]

The texts of new treaties evidence this. In the Singapore–U.S. FTA, the exchange of letters between the negotiators contains a letter that seeks to exempt regulatory takings from the treaty provision on expropriation. The same formula has now entered the text of the new model BIT of the U.S. The Canadian model BIT also seeks to preserve environmental takings from the scope of the

---

105 *Id.*

106 *Tecmed v. United Mexican States*, para 121.

107 *SPP v. Egypt* and the pending case, *Malaysian Historical Salvors, SDN, BHD v. Malaysia*, ICSID Case No. ARB/05/10 (2006), involved cultural property. The Great Barrier Reef was involved in an investment dispute involving Dillingham Moore and Australia.

provision on expropriation. (See Annex 8, *Novel Features in OECD Countries' Recent Investment Agreements.*)

But, problems remain. Even within domestic U.S. constitutional jurisprudence, the question of what amounts to a regulatory taking has not been fixed. There have been periodic shifts in defining what amounts to a non-compensable taking. This would be so in most societies, depending on factors such as political and economic ideology and stage of development. The U.S., during its early years of intensive infrastructure development, necessarily adopted a more expansive view of the government's power to enact regulatory takings without compensation. But, now, as the most advanced industrialized state, it takes a more restricted view, oftentimes even requiring that the depreciation in the value of a property be compensated. Not all societies can take such a position. There is a contrast between the view taken by the European Court on Human Rights, which may be said to give greater leeway to the public interests accompanying a State taking, and the view that is current in the U.S. Supreme Court, which is less amenable to infringements of property rights by the State. In this context, the resolution of the issue of what amounts to a regulatory taking would not meet with any acceptable solution. States may recognize the existence of such a category, but will not be able to agree on criteria with which to define its characteristics. But, nevertheless, the recognition of this distinct category is a change.

So, the pendulum keeps swinging between alternatives. Diverse forces shape the law at any given time. They may dictate the ascendancy of one set of ideas at one time, but a change in the configuration of these forces brings about corresponding changes in legal attitudes. We can witness these changes taking place in the field of foreign investment arbitration.

More specifically, in the field of regulatory expropriation, it could well be that a country like the U.S. may yet be forced into taking an expansionary view of takings at the domestic level, but curb such a view at the international level. As that country increasingly becomes enmeshed with foreign investment (it has been the largest recipient of foreign investment during the past several years), it can hardly maintain an international law that is levelled against it. With balance-of-payment difficulties and a favorable business climate, it is also a power that is witnessing the rapid economic rise of other countries eager to invest in its markets and purchase its companies.[108] Investment treaties help

---

[108] Witness the offer of China National Offshore Oil Corporation (CNOOC) to buy the U.S. oil and pipeline corporation Unocal.

such investments. Foreign MNCs can incorporate in Mexico and move investments into the U.S., securing NAFTA protection. The cases against the United States both within NAFTA and outside, through other investment treaties, will increase. When this happens, the U.S. may have to soften the international law of property protection that it has taken the lead in creating. Already, the defence that the United States is making in *Methanex* seems very familiar to developing country international lawyers.

Dramatic shifts may be in the offing, affecting also investment arbitration. It seems unfair that a system that has many positive features should have been diverted into uncharted waters, there to flounder and possibly diminish in vigor. It is necessary to fashion it in such a manner as to serve the interests of both host countries and foreign investors. This requires a restoration of the balance in the interests of foreign investors and host countries.

The Restoration of the Balance

Investment arbitration is in crisis.[109] The expansionary trends outlined above have brought about disenchantment with a system of undoubted value. The extent to which this has occurred bears repetition. In Argentina, the land of the Calvo Doctrine, the famous principle has been abandoned through the making of modern investment treaties, a development the country may be coming to regret. The inconsistent awards on the interpretation of the umbrella clauses have caused concern. Likewise, the inconsistent awards in *Lauder/CME v. Czech Republic*, which arose from the same facts, have similarly raised concern with the legitimacy of the system; these awards demonstrate that decisions seem to depend on the choice of the personnel to serve on arbitration panels. The potential for multiplicity of claims on the same set of facts also causes concern. The use of corporate nationality to facilitate a multiplicity of claims is another factor that needs to be assessed. The involvement of the same persons in the playing out of the events in the field has attracted the intervention of domestic courts.

Such occurrences, taken together, jeopardize the legitimacy of the system of investment arbitration. These consequences were quite unintended by States; they signed treaties in the hope of facilitating flows of investment, not in the

---

109 For another similar conclusion, *see* Susan Franck, "The Legitimacy Crisis in Investment Treaty Arbitration: Privatizing Public International Law Through Inconsistent Decisions," 73 Fordham L. Rev. 1521, 1537–1538 (2005).

expectation that they would have to face expensive arbitration with a potential for heavy damage. The very supposition of that bargain—that a surrender of sovereignty in an investment treaty will lead to greater flows of investment—now stands challenged. Unless a balance is brought about in the system of investment arbitration, it will suffer more and more from a crisis of credibility. The ways in which this balance can be restored need to be explored.

Preservation of Regulatory Space in Treaties

One avenue of escaping arbitration is to ensure that sufficient regulatory space is preserved in treaties to enable a State to exercise control over foreign investment so that each act of interference cannot be considered a treaty violation that leads to arbitration. It is interesting to compare the areas from which much of the new arbitrations have come. They are largely from Latin America, with the Argentinean economic crisis giving rise to the most claims against any single state, and secondly Eastern Europe. The Southeast Asian region has escaped from treaty arbitration to a significant extent. A comparison indicates that the investment treaties made in Southeast Asia are of a different type from those made in Latin American and Eastern Europe.[110] The spurt in the 1990s arose as a result of the turn to the market system in Eastern Europe, and Latin America, which was abandoning policies based on the *dependencia* thinking. The treaties those countries made account in a large measure for the spurt of treaties in the mid-1990s. They were largely liberalization treaties that tended to contain rights of establishment and secure standards of treatment and protection. Most of the expansionary trends identified above have also resulted from the treaties that were made during those times. In any event, these treaties did not conserve enough regulatory space because regulation was antithetical to free market notions. It would not be surprising if, in future years, these regions will rethink their foreign investment policies and investment treaties.

The Southeast Asian practice is much older and has evolved over the years. The conservation of regulatory space is a feature in all of these treaties, except for a few concluded recently. In this treaty practice, only "approved" investment is given treaty protection. In later years, the formula changed to give

---

110 In *Aguas del Tunari v. Bolivia*, an argument was attempted that the provision in the Netherlands–Bolivia treaty that admission was subject to laws and regulation of the State parties produced the result of subjecting the investment to local laws. This argument was rejected. The Asian treaties define "protected investment" as one made in accordance with the laws and regulations of the parties. The latter clause has a much broader jurisdictional scope than that in the *Aguas del Tunari* case.

protection only to those investments "made in accordance with the rules and regulations" of the host country. China, which has signed over 100 treaties, also uses the same formula. Some treaties, especially the older treaties made by Australia, contain an even more restrictive formula which requires that, for protection, the investment should have been made in accordance with "the laws and regulations from time to time in existence," indicating the continued subjection of the whole foreign investment process to the laws of the host country.

A comparison of the Asian economic crisis with the Argentinean crisis is instructive. Malaysia applied exchange controls as a solution to the crisis instead of following the prescriptions of the IMF like the other countries of the region; it escaped the crisis with less damage than other States, a fact later acknowledged by the IMF itself.[111] The country's exchange controls were in potential violation of the investment treaties Malaysia had made, as restrictions on capital flows and the repatriation of profits were prevented by exchange controls. This argument was tried out in *Grueslin v. Malaysia*, where the tribunal declined to exercise jurisdiction because there was no proof that the investment was an "approved" investment for purposes of protection.

The contrast with Argentina is clear. The manner in which each investment's protection is qualified, and the extent of the regulatory space conserved, have an impact on whether arbitration of claims is possible. In *Yaung Chi Oo Ltd v. Myanmar*, the same idea was stressed. The jurisdictional hurdles that have to be crossed in the Southeast Asian treaties are high, enabling the region to escape a proliferation of arbitrations. China, despite being the second largest recipient of foreign investment and a frequent participant in investment treaties, has escaped such arbitrations by adopting similar formulae and confining arbitration in its treaties to issues of expropriation only.

The conservation of regulatory space is attempted in liberalization treaties through the importation of techniques known from the field of international trade. Apart from the national security exception, an exception is made in a separate provision in the treaties for measures taken in order to protect public order. Such emergency clauses can also be found in liberalizing investment treaties. Such a clause was recently interpreted in *CMS v. Argentina*.[112] The issue was whether the Argentinean economic crisis was such an emergency as

---

111 5 ICSID Rpts 483 (2000).

112 Award, 12 May 2005 (http://ita.law.uvic.ca).

would justify the exemption under the provision.[113] The tribunal held that existence of the emergency was to be judged objectively and not by the respondent State. Had a subjective appreciation of the emergency been permissible, there would have been express words to this effect. After so holding, the tribunal found that, though the "crisis was severe, it did not result in total economic and social collapse." It would appear from the analysis of the tribunal that extraordinary circumstance of catastrophic proportions would be necessary for a State to invoke the exception relating to emergencies.

Hence, a technique of including exceptions based on emergencies may not be satisfactory unless it is couched in subjective terms, making the appreciation of the existence of an emergency a matter for conclusive decision by the state. The new model treaty of the U.S. includes such a subjective appreciation.

But emergencies are not the only issues that involve regulatory space. A State may, in the interests of its economic development, seek to change policies and laws so as to direct investment into appropriate areas. Such interferences could be interpreted as violating treatment or expropriation provisions. For this reason, the technique adopted in Southeast Asian treaties seems a better solution. There is nothing to show that the rate of investment flows into Southeast Asia has been slowed by conserving this bit of sovereign space. The conservation of such space is vital for channelling foreign investment into areas that a State thinks is appropriate, and it would be unwise to give up that space, quite apart from the fact that its conservation also helps to ensure that arbitration is not brought against it for frivolous reasons.

A State must consider the type of treaty that it wishes to sign, keeping in mind that the evidence to show that the existence is mixed as to the extent to which the existence of a treaty, in and of itself, increases flows of foreign investment. If it does feel that it is necessary to sign such treaties, then it must choose between the liberalization model and the other models that are available, knowing that the liberalization model may lead to the arbitration of disputes and will curb regulatory space.

It would appear that recent treaties, for example the Singapore–U.S. FTA, do not contain restrictions; but this may just be a surface appearance. On the

---

113 The provision, Article XI of the U.S.–Argentina treaty, read: "This Treaty shall not preclude the application by either Party of measures necessary for the maintenance of public order, the fulfillment of its obligations with respect to the maintenance or restoration of international peace or security, or the protection of its own essential security."

other hand, it could well be that there will be arbitrations made possible under it. Malaysia has also made an agreement with Japan which seems to be a liberalization agreement. Whether this will lead to changes in pattern of arbitration in Southeast Asia is yet to be seen. It could well be that the attraction of liberalization still dominates and will diminish only by further adverse experiences.

Other Measures

If States feel inclined to sign investment treaties, they must consider other means of fine tuning treaties in light of the recent experience relating to arbitrations. Corporate nationality provisions must be tightened to ensure that mere incorporation does not become an avenue for instituting arbitration so as to enable any company from a third country from utilizing the facilities of the treaty through incorporation. This would also ensure that the problem of round-tripping is solved. The exclusion of incorporation in islands of convenience should also be considered. A number of cases have arisen because companies find it convenient for a variety of reasons to incorporate in overseas territories of States with treaties. These treaties have application to these territories by way of extension. The prevention of such an extension should be considered.

The exhaustion of local remedies must be reintroduced as a rule as in customary international law. This enables the local courts to determine and define the issues. Besides, the local courts are the most convenient fora before which witnesses and documents can be conveniently presented. If there is a need to bypass the local remedies rule, this could be done through the negotiation of appropriate clauses in the foreign investment contract. There is no need why there must be a blanket approval for arbitration given to all comers. The State should be able to negotiate on the basis of the relative merits of the foreign investment as to whom should be given the right of arbitration, since, as is evident, it stands to lose part of its sovereignty. The Australia–U.S. FTA abolishes investor-State arbitration, leaving dispute resolution either to domestic courts or to the old mechanism of diplomatic protection. At the least, insistence on the use of local remedies before recourse to arbitration may provide an intermediate solution.

The suggested remedy of establishing an appeals system or systems will help only rich countries affected by arbitrations. The U.S. seems to seek such an appellate system within ICSID. It is not clear how developing countries stand to benefit, considering the heavy legal burden involved. Besides, the experience with annulment procedures shows that developing countries may lose out.

Appellate tribunals may arrogate to themselves the power to establish expansionary propositions more forcefully. If an appellate system is necessary, then why not allow the home country of the foreign investor to adopt the claims of the foreign investor and thus permit the matter of the non-enforcement of the award to be declared an inter-State dispute to be tested out before the International Court of Justice?

Confining Disputes to Purely Commercial Issues

The disputes that arise should be confined to purely commercial issues. If issues of international law are involved, there must be a requirement that persons qualified in that discipline should sit on the tribunals.[114] Commercial arbitrators may be inclined to come up with commercial solutions to problems that arise in investment arbitration without having regard to the concerns of the State.

Conclusions

This chapter set out to identify expansionary trends in investment arbitration in the hope that the identification of such trends will enable them to be controlled. As argued, unless such trends are controlled, investment arbitration will be resisted by States that have to bear the brunt of adverse decisions made on the basis of notions that they may not have contemplated when negotiating and concluding treaties. The legitimacy of awards will be adversely affected. It must also be remembered that the enforcement of an award that is not accepted by the relevant State is a long and tedious process. Available defences, for example sovereign immunity, come under greater strain, and there is a return to the realization that the sovereignty of States is the basis of the international order.

Investment treaties, as well as the system of arbitration they have set up, have in tandem supported a liberal vision and enhanced the protection that is provided by the law for MNCs. Developing countries, at different levels of development, should have the policy space to select and pursue their own priorities and adopt their own regulations in order to achieve their economic objectives.

---

114 The U.S. model treaty requires that persons qualified to decide issues arising from financial services alone should sit on such arbitrations. There is no reason why a requirement should not be competence in the area of international law so that the interests of countries and their sovereignty could have adequate reflection.

The approach to foreign investment will change. In 2004, the present author took the view that economic liberalism had begun to recede and that the ideological challenges to the basis of investment treaties as well to investment arbitration would increase. Two years down the road, one witnesses a situation in which this trend has gathered greater strength. It could well be that this new trend will continue and the older view that foreign investment is uniformly good and should receive uniform protection will recede. While there will continue to be a law that provides foreign investment protection, the conditions under which such protection will be afforded will come to be stated with greater clarity. The realm of foreign investment arbitration will have to respond by ensuring that enhanced protection for MNCs is balanced by giving greater weight to economic development and poverty reduction, environmental protection, fairness and justice.

CHAPTER 5

Variation in the Substantive Provisions and Interpretation of International Investment Agreements

*Patrick Juillard**

The Pros and Cons of Bilateral Investment Treaties: Commentary on M. Sornarajah's Views

M. Sornarajah has been critical of bilateral investment treaties (BITs) for an extended period, and the views which he expresses in his chapter in this volume should thus come as no surprise. His criticism, however, should not be taken lightly, if for no other reason than that it does reflect positions that are held in some circles, be it within developing countries, or within developed countries.

His criticism seems to be twofold. On the one hand, it deals with BITs, and on the other, it deals with the interpretation and application of BIT provisions through investor-State arbitration. This chapter is limited to the first aspect; i.e., the BITs themselves. The reason for this is that my contribution deals with the differences between the substantive provisions of international investment agreements (IIAs), including BITs.

Professor Sornarajah appears to focus upon four major concerns:

- BITs are imbalanced instruments, because they protect the rights of investors but not the rights of host countries. Indeed, this imbalance

---

* Professor Emeritus of International Law, University of Paris I (Panthéon-Sorbonne).

may pose a threat to the sovereignty of developing countries, whose basic interests may be jeopardized by the dispute settlement mechanism in BITs.

- Even though BITs are heavily tilted in favor of investors, they still miss their purpose, because they do not promote investment. Indeed, most BITs demonstrably do not create new flows of investment from North to South. Thus, while they may well be instruments of protection, they certainly are not instruments promoting vital Northern investment in the South.
- BITs, whatever their number, should not be considered monolithic. Increasing numbers of model BITs are now in existence, and they present significant differences vis-à-vis each other. Older model BITs had the primary purpose of protecting Northern investment in the South, whereas newer models focus on the free movement of investment in a globalized world. Treaties whose purpose and object differ so vastly from each other certainly cannot form a harmonized whole, able to provide a sound basis for the development of customary international law.
- BITs should not be overestimated or overrated as instruments of harmonization. Of course, one will find in each BIT the same provisions and even the same language. But although these provisions and language may be formally identical from one BIT to another, it may well be that they were never intended to carry the same substantive meaning. Thus, clauses that appear not to diverge one from each other may nevertheless lead to different interpretations. As a result, attempting to harmonize and standardize BITs would simply add disorder to disorder.

A few observations on each of these four points are warranted.

1. BITs are Imbalanced Instruments

BITs seem to be imbalanced instruments in the sense that they create rights for investors but not for host countries, and duties for the host countries but not for investors. This is the reason why investment disputes arising under BITs are most often introduced by investors: only investors have rights to vindicate.

The response to this argument is: so what? BITs were originally intended to restore a favorable climate for North-South investment. This could be done only by creating conditions that would encourage rather than discourage investors. BITs, therefore, rested upon a *quid pro quo* which certain commentators considered as imbalanced—though the adjective "asymmetric" would seem more appropriate. A host country offers favorable conditions of treatment and protection, while the country of origin undertakes to promote investment by its nationals into the host country. This *do ut des* does not involve investors. Investors, therefore, assume no responsibility, if for no other reason than that they were not parties to BITs, which is in the nature of a contract between sovereign States.

The contention that BITs create rights solely for investors and do not take into account the interests of host countries may however lose some of its accuracy. More and more BITs provide for the preservation of public interest against the vindication of private rights. The new 2004 U.S. model BIT clearly protects the rights of host countries to regulate foreign investment in the public interest, even though the object or effect of such regulations would fly in the face of some treaty rights accorded to foreign investors.

Indeed, the history of the 2004 U.S. model BIT shows that the federal government had to find some compromise between the positions of non-governmental organizations (NGOs), which were acting in defense of public interest causes, and the position of the business community, which was pushing for the highest degree of treaty protection in favor of investors. The business community in the U.S. seems to have taken a somewhat unfavorable view of the new model, on grounds that the standard of protection was higher in the old model than in the new one.

Such a development cannot be viewed as purely accidental. On the contrary, it reflects a long term tendency in the evolution of the BIT network. Hence, the contention that BITs will perpetuate an imbalanced system of rights and duties seems now open to question.

One additional factor must be stressed. BITs are treaties between States, and States enjoy sovereign equality. Therefore, as a matter of right, parties to a bilateral agreement are on an equal footage during the course of any negotiation. But, as a matter of fact, things were rather different in the 1970s and 1980s, at the time developed countries started to negotiate their BIT networks with developing countries. Typically, State A, a developed country, would send its model treaty to State B, a developing country, as a basis for negotiation, simultaneously requesting State B to suggest whatever modification it deemed suitable. Then, in a number of instances, nothing would happen, and State B would not even reply to State A. After a while, State A would try to revive the negotiation by again calling upon the developing country. State B would then answer by accepting the offer by means of formal adherence to the treaty. That is, no negotiation would ever take place.

The reason for this is not complex: until recently, many developing countries did not possess the capacity to analyze adequately the contents of complex model treaties. This, of course, could only accentuate the imbalance between North and South during the course of BIT negotiations.

However, that scenario is increasingly less common. Developing countries have begun to develop a knowledge of international economic law—and particularly investment law—and a capacity to apply it. A number of international institutions, especially the United Nations Conference on Trade and Development (UNCTAD), have played a key role in the process of capacity building.

Further, the old division between the capital-exporting North and capital-importing South is no longer as clear as in years past. Developing countries are exporting capital into Northern as well as Southern countries. As capital-exporting countries, they have developed their own model BITs, and have started building their own BITs networks. For instance, UNCTAD in recent years published models from even some of the poorest developing countries: the latest models originate from, among others, Benin, Bolivia, Burkina Faso, Burundi, Cambodia, Ghana, Guatemala, Kenya, Mongolia, Peru, Sri Lanka and Uganda. The kind of unilateralism that dominated the development of international investment law in the past is now an artifact of the past.

2. BITs Miss Their Point

Sornarajah claims that BITs are particularly nettlesome because their negatives are not compensated by sufficient positives—that is, they do not result in any increase of investment flows between contracting parties. Thus, the considerable efforts that States have devoted to the creation of their BIT networks are a waste of time and money, because investments covered by BITs would also have taken place in the absence of BITs. In the words of Article 31 of the Vienna Convention, BITs miss their "avowed object and purpose," the "promotion of investment."[1]

---

1 Vienna Convention on the Law of Treaties, 23 May 1969, http://www.worldtradelaw.net/misc/viennaconvention.pdf, Art. 31.

The argument raises complex questions particularly regarding the interpretation of the verb "promote." "Promoting," in the context of international investment law, is highly ambiguous. On the one hand, it may contemplate the establishment of conditions that will result in the increase of investment flows; on the other, it may contemplate solely the actual increase of investment flows between contracting parties. Thus, under the former interpretation, BITs would only create an "*obligation de moyens*" for contracting States, that is, an obligation to devise the legal means that would be necessary to stimulate additional investment flows. Under the latter interpretation, BITs would create an "*obligation de résultat,*" i.e., an obligation actually to stimulate additional investment flows.

BITs do not decide between both interpretations, a fact which, arguably, demonstrates that their purpose and object is not the promotion of investment, but the protection of investors. However, the preambles to the treaties, though appearing to be merely hortatory pieces of legal draftsmanship, shed some light on that question. Many of these preambles clearly state that the common interest of the contracting States is to establish favorable conditions in order to stimulate capital investment as between contracting parties—a statement that seems to point toward an *obligation de moyens* rather than an *obligation de résultat*, and which therefore may be in the best interest of capital-exporting countries rather than capital-importing countries.

BITs are legal instruments. As such, they create legal conditions, not economic conditions. In other words, the purpose and object of BITs is to eliminate legal obstacles to the promotion of investment. This may seem to be a modest role. Still, it might well be that this modest role could result in additional investment flows. In that vein, one should bear in mind that one of the most important consequences of the conclusion of a BIT is the gaining of eligibility to the national investment guarantee systems of importing countries by nationals of exporting countries. A simple comparison between the number of guarantees issued prior to and after the conclusion of a given BIT might provide a good indication of the effectiveness of the relevant treaty.

Furthermore, as Jeswald Salacuse and Sullivan have stressed in a recent article,[2] it is not impossible to show that recent BITs have a measurable effect on the flows of investment. A quantitative analysis, he asserts, would demonstrate

---

2 Jeswald Salacuse and Nicholas P. Sullivan, "Do BITs Really Work?: An Evaluation of Bilateral Investment Treaties and Their Grand Bargain," 46 HARV. INT'L. L. J. 67 (2005).

that most BITs have little if no visible effect on the increase in North-South investment flows; it does seem that BITs concluded by the U.S., however, would result in additional investment flows. A demonstration of that sort, obviously, is not an easy one to conduct. Not only must it be shown that the conclusion of a given BIT is concomitant with an increase in the flow of investment, but it must also be shown that this increase in the flow of investment would not have occurred if that BIT had not been concluded. Prudence is of the essence here.

3. There is no General Consensus on BITs

It is also submitted that the impact of BITs, both from the quantitative and qualitative standpoints, is not of such import as to reflect a general consensus between sovereign States. Much emphasis has been put on the actual number of BITs, which now is in excess of 2,500. Of course, this is a sizeable number. (See Annexes 6 and 7, *UNCTAD, IIA Monitors)*.But it still must be viewed in perspective. If each sovereign State were to conclude BITs with all other sovereign States, this would mean nearly 40,000 BITs. Thus, BITs are and are likely to remain a limited phenomenon.

The 2,500 figure simply indicates that developed countries, from which the most important flows of investment originate, have succeeded in building sizeable networks, each of which is in the range of 100 BITs. By itself, this suffices to account for the total number of 2,500. Further, as Sauvant indicated in the introduction to this volume, there seems to be a slowdown in the growth of BITs. This is easily explainable. Most Northern capital-exporting countries already have built their BITs networks, and thus the increase in number is now due to Southern capital exporters, which are building smaller networks and doing so at a slower pace.

These BITs, however, have been entered by and between sovereign States that represent each and every sector of the international community. From the geographical standpoint, BITs of the 1960s and 1970s were oriented North-South. But even at that time, one could witness the growth of West-East BITs. More recently, a number of BITs have been oriented South-South.

Tellingly, from the political standpoint, even those countries that had adopted an anti-investment stance, for various reasons, have now renounced that position and are doing their best to attract investment—primarily by concluding BITs. This is the case for such countries as Algeria and India, for example, the latter of which in recent years seems to be moving toward market capitalism and away from its traditional State-directed capitalism, replacing public investment with private investment. Even more significantly, this is true of Latin American countries. Traditionally, Central and South America have been staunch proponents of the Calvo Doctrine, and for that very reason were reluctant to accept the mechanisms for investor-State dispute settlement provided for in BITs. Similarly, they have until recently stayed away from the International Centre for Settlement of Investment Disputes (ICSID).

In short, the impetus seems to be there. Each and every capital-exporting or capital-importing country is now a party to a number of BITs. Can it be safely assumed, as a consequence, that State practice warrants the conclusion that BITs reflect a general consensus between sovereign States as to the promotion and protection of investment? Not everybody shares that opinion, and Sornarajah, for one, certainly does not.

The argument is as follows. Treaties must be interpreted in light of their purpose and object, such as agreed by the parties. The object and purpose of older BITs, such as those agreed between developed and developing countries, was the promotion and protection of investments. It may well be that BITs missed their purpose and object as instrument of promotion; but, by and large, they were successful as instruments of protection of Northern investment in Southern countries.

But newer BITs do not appear to focus solely on promotion and protection. Moreover, recent trade agreements also address investment issues. The purpose and object of these newer agreements has shifted to liberalization. This shift does not result from a general consensus between sovereign States; it just reflects a change in the orientation of economic policies in developed countries—particularly the U.S.

To be sure, the older U.S. models have always been preoccupied with liberalization. They included, unlike the European models, national treatment clauses that applied both to the pre-establishment and post-establishment phases, to ensure an open door policy for foreign investment. But the newer trade and investment agreements go one step further, in the sense that they link together the free movement of goods and services, on the one hand, and the free movement of capital, on the other.

The fact that the U.S. has embarked upon a policy of negotiating trade and investment agreements does not mean, however, that the world's largest economy has renounced its policy of negotiating BITs. Indeed, the U.S. released a new BIT model in 2004. One may assume that, if the U.S. has taken the time and effort to revise its old BIT model, it is presumably because it intends to continue expanding its BIT network. Thus, trade and investment agreements as well as investment agreements will co-exist in the future. Therefore, it cannot be said that there has been a shift from investment agreements to trade and investment agreements.

Investment agreements solely deal with investments, while trade and investment agreements purport to fill the vacuum resulting from the failure by the World Trade Organization (WTO) to conclude the Doha Round, by means of negotiating bilateral agreements with trade partners that share common positions with the U.S. But whatever the differences between the purposes of investment agreements on the one hand, and trade and investment agreements on the other, their provisions relating to investment are similar. Both types of agreements include the same establishment clauses, the same treatment and protection clauses, the same expropriation clauses, and the same dispute settlement clauses; thus, one is led to conclude that, so far as investment is concerned, there is no difference between the clauses in investment agreements and the clauses in trade and investment agreements. One will readily acknowledge that Chapter 11 of NAFTA, for instance, reads no differently from any other investment agreement.

4. BITs are not Instruments of Harmonization

Perhaps the most convincing argument submitted by Sornarajah, however, is that this massive body of BITs has not been successful in creating a public order of investment. This argument, however, seems, *prima facie*, to run against the weight of evidence. At first glance, all BITs incorporate the same set of principles and rules: fair and equitable treatment, full and entire protection and security, national treatment, most-favored-nation (MFN) treatment, adequate compensation in case of expropriation, etc. The reiteration of these principles and rules from one BIT to another BIT certainly suggests that we are presently witnessing a process of harmonization, and that the end result thereof can be no other than the creation of a unified public order of investment.

The present state of disorder that seems to characterize international investment law, however, raises serious questions about the soundness of that conclusion. This may be due to differences between languages. For instance, the general standard of treatment reads "fair and equitable treatment" in English, and "*traitement juste et équitable*" in French. (See Annex 8, *Novel*

Features in OECD Countries' Recent Investment Agreements.) It is assumed by most commentators that the two expressions are synonymous, but this remains open to question. "Fair" translates in French as "*loyal*," not "*juste*." It may well be that this is immaterial, but if it is not, the standard would not have the same meaning in English and in French. Furthermore, even if one were to assume that "fair and equitable treatment" and "*traitement juste et équitable*" are synonymous expressions, then the context of the U.S. model, on the one hand, and the French model, on the other hand, would clearly indicate that the drafters of these models did not share a common understanding of what that general standard actually means.

The U.S. model holds the view that the standard of "fair and equitable treatment" is just another denomination for the minimum standard of customary international law. Article 5, Sections 1–2 of the new 2004 U.S. model BIT clearly links the "fair and equitable treatment" standard to the minimum standard which is required by international customary law, and stresses that "fair and equitable treatment" does not require treatment that would go above or beyond the minimum standard of treatment.[3] This is not to say, however, that the standard is frozen in amber. Quite on the contrary, Annex A—international customary law—restates that customary international law may evolve, but that proof of that evolution must be given by showing what the contents of *consuetudo* are, and whether *opinio juris* attaches thereto. Article 5 and Annex A, taken together, issue a warning to arbitral tribunals: the latter will not be left free to decide, in their own discretion, what fair and equitable treatment means; they will have to look into the present state of development of international customary law in order to determine whether their findings are warranted under that law.

The French model also contains a "fair and equitable treatment" clause. Even if one assumes that the French wording and the English wording were equivalent to each other, the substance of the French clause still widely differs from the substance of the U.S. clause. To be sure, the opening clause in Article 4 of the French model states that fair and equitable treatment must be deemed to be a principle of international law, a statement that is not incompatible with the U.S. view. But Article 4 goes on to say that any and all obstacles that host countries put to the free use of energy and raw materials should be deemed in violation of fair and equitable treatment. Clearly, such an interpretation seems

---

3 U.S. Model Bilateral Investment Treaty (2004), Art. 5.1–2 (http://www.state.gov/documents/organization/38710.pdf).

totally disconnected from the minimum standard of international customary law. A host country may restrict the supply of energy to foreign investors because of shortages in the production of energy. Such a restriction might violate a number of treaty provisions, but it is highly debatable whether it should be deemed a violation of the fair and equitable treatment standard.

BITs were born out of a sense of emergency. Capital-exporting countries and capital-importing countries wanted to restore a favorable investment climate after the great wave of expropriation during the 1960s. This could only be done through an elaborate compromise. BITs reflect that compromise. They may not be perfect instruments. But they still have fulfilled, by and large, their avowed purpose, which was to dispel the enduring distrust between North and South. This success, however, was achieved at the cost of improvisation, and it may well be that we now are paying the price for this improvisation.

Responsibility for the Alleged Lack of Consistency

Does responsibility for the alleged lack of consistency in BITs rest with BITs themselves, or with the arbitral awards rendered under them?

A major issue of this volume is the lack of consistency seen in the interpretation and application of BIT clauses. To take only one example, there seems to be some shared understanding of the general meaning of MFN treatment. Indeed, the understanding of MFN treatment that the arbitral tribunals have expounded in *Maffezini*[4] and *Tecmed*[5] do not differ from each other, but still the results which the tribunals reached in both cases are completely at odds. Such an inconsistency, to say the least, does not favor legal security in the law of investment.

This lack of consistency may be attributed to two different causes, which can work jointly or severally. First, the inconsistency may result directly from the various clauses in the different BITs. There may be a shared understanding of what the general meaning of MFN treatment is. This does not mean, however, that the various MFN clauses in BITs are similar to each other. For instance, the extent of MFN treatment might vary from clause to clause. One of the issues with which arbitral tribunals have had to deal with is whether the

---

4 *Maffezini v. Kingdom of Spain*, ICSID Case No. ARB/97/7 (Fall 2001).

5 *Técnicas Medioambientales Tecmed, S.A. v. United Mexican States*, ICSID Case No.ARB (AF)/00/2 (2003).

dispute settlement mechanisms fall within the reach of the MFN clause. The answer to that question depends primarily on the wording of the MFN clause: does it include or does it exclude dispute settlement mechanisms?

Second, the inconsistency may result from differences in the interpretation of one clause by several arbitral tribunals. The so-called "umbrella clause" did not substantially differ between the Switzerland–Pakistan BIT and that between Switzerland and the Philippines; after all, both clauses derived from one sole model, i.e., the Swiss model. Still, the interpretations of that clause in *SGS Société Générale de Surveillance v. Pakistan*[6] and *SGS Société Générale de Surveillance v. Philippines*[7] seem irreconcilable, insofar as the question of the effect of the clause on obligations entered into by host countries vis-à-vis foreign investors is concerned. (See Annex 7, *UNCTAD, IIA Monitor, No. 4 (2006).*)

BITs are patterned on models. A sizeable number of these models have a common origin, which is the Abs-Shawcross draft, later embodied in the ill-fated Organisation for Economic Co-operation and Development (OECD) Draft Convention on the Protection of Foreign Property. Given that common origin, one might assume that these models, over the years, would have given rise to some general principles of international law governing the treatment and protection of foreign investment, and would therefore have contributed to the formation of international customary law in this area. The general framework of the BITs models, which appear to be identical from one to the other, can only confirm this conclusion.

The same clauses always seem to appear in the same order: definitions, admission of investment, standards of treatment and protection, expropriation and compensation, and then a dispute settlement mechanism or procedure. These seem to form the basic core of each and every model. Further, these clauses seem to rely upon the same basic notions: fair and equitable treatment; national treatment; MFN treatment; full and entire protection; basic requirements for expropriation and compensation; international arbitration of investor-host country disputes. This would appear to warrant the conclusion that there is not much dissimilarity between basic provisions from one model to another and, as a consequence, from one BIT to another.

---

6 *SGS Société Générale de Surveillance v. Pakistan*, Decision on Jurisdiction, ICSID Case No. ARB 01/13 (6 August 2003).

7 *SGS Société Générale de Surveillance v. Philippines*, ICSID Case No. ARB/02/6 (29 January 2004).

But appearances may be deceptive. One should be mindful that BIT models have undergone a process of differentiation. Not all are now patterned on the old Abs-Shawcross draft embodied in the doomed OECD project.

The OECD Convention was premised on investment protection, and, as a consequence, its clauses dealt with host country obligations with respect to the treatment of investment and rules governing expropriation and compensation. But new models have emerged over the years. The most elaborate certainly is the U.S. model, which widely differs from what had come to be known as the European model. The U.S. model is concerned with both free admission and full protection of U.S. investment in foreign countries, whereas the European model is more respectful of the sovereign right of host countries to admit or not to admit foreign investment. Thus, the European model has an admission clause, whereas the U.S. model, instead of an admission clause, has an establishment clause.

This entails a number of consequences. Both the European and U.S. models have national treatment and MFN clauses. Under the European model, these clauses will apply only during the post-establishment phase, whereas under the U.S. model, these clauses will apply during both the pre- and post-establishment phases. Thus, the significance of the national treatment and MFN clauses cannot be the same in the European model as in the U.S. model.

Furthermore, as discussed above, it may well be that the same concepts, taken in the same context, have different meanings from one model to another model, and, therefore, from one BIT to another BIT. For instance, the concept that underlies the umbrella clauses is that host countries will give full credit to commitments they enter vis-à-vis foreign investors. But what commitments? Do they include commitments resulting from applicable legislation or regulations? Or do they include contractual commitments and exclude all non-contractual commitments?

Minor differences in the wording of umbrella clauses may result in major differences with respect to arbitral interpretation of these clauses, as shown in the two S.G.S. cases. And what has just been said of the umbrella clause could also be said about a number of other clauses. The fair and equitable treatment clause has already been mentioned. There seems to be some common sense understanding of what constitutes fair and equitable treatment; but, still, if one ponders the U.S. and French models, which both contain that clause, the conceptions that are reflected therein are completely at odds. Under these conditions, how can we expect that one arbitral tribunal, called upon in order to interpret the U.S. clause, and another arbitral tribunal, called upon to interpret the French clause, would reach an identical result? It is true that several arbitral tribunals already had to pronounce on the U.S. clause, and that no arbitral tribunal has ever had to pronounce on the French clause, and that, as a result, inconsistency has so far been avoided. But inconsistent decisions are bound to be released.

Thus, the significant differences between the various clauses having the same purpose and object will necessarily result in significant differences between the interpretations delivered by various arbitral tribunals.

Arbitral Tribunals Usually Attempt to Reach Consistent Outcomes

One can therefore reasonably conclude from the previous discussion that, if there is any responsibility for the lack of consistency among arbitral awards, it does not rest entirely with arbitral tribunals. It is due, at least to some extent, to significant differences between substantive provisions of BITs that arbitral tribunals have the duty to interpret and apply.

But we can even go one step further. It seems that whenever arbitral tribunals are in a position to give a uniform interpretation of treaty provisions, however different in substance, they will not hesitate to do so—provided that some other applicable source of international law will afford them the necessary basis for that determination. This has been the case with the interpretation of the notion of "investment," which appears in each and every BIT, though its definition may vary from one treaty to another.

For example, Article 25 of the Washington Convention (the ICSID Convention) affords the basis that arbitral tribunals will use in order to reach a common definition of the word "investment" which will apply in each and every case, and whatever the differences, minor or major, among BITs.[8] There is something paradoxical to this approach, since Article 25 conspicuously avoids offering any definition of the word "investment." The Report of the drafters of the Convention shows that they intended to leave to arbitral tribunals the responsibility of defining the word "investment" on a case by case basis, and furnished them no explanation in order to reach a definition. But more and more often, ICSID tribunals are called upon to do so, at the request of foreign investors, in order

8 ICSID Convention, Regulation and Rules (ICSID & World Bank: Washington DC, 2006) (http://worldbank.com/icsid/basicdoc/basicdoc.htm).

to settle cases arising out of the alleged violation by host countries of some BIT provision. In the course of these proceedings, ICSID tribunals are frequently asked to pass upon preliminary objections to jurisdiction. In this respect, defendant States typically contend that the dispute is not within the jurisdiction of the tribunal, because it does not arise directly from an investment within the meaning of the Washington Convention. Thus, ICSID tribunals must decide whether the dispute involves an investment. In order to reach a decision on that issue, of course, they must define what constitutes an "investment."

The method that ICSID tribunals follow in order to resolve that question now seems well established. It is a two step process, in the sense that the arbitrators will conduct a double investigation. First, in order to define whether they have jurisdiction under the Washington Convention, they will ascertain whether the perquisites of Article 25 of that Convention are met. If this first question has been answered in the affirmative, the second step is to query whether the dispute relates to an investment within the meaning of the definitional section of the relevant BIT. If it does, then the arbitral tribunal will entertain jurisdiction over the case. This is the method that was followed in *Fedax*, *Salini*, *Dipenta* and *Joy Mining*.[9]

The language in the definitional section of the various BITs is so broad—as well as vague—that the second query is likely to be answered in the affirmative, and thus an ICSID tribunal will find in most instances that the dispute relates to an "investment." For instance, in almost all BITs, a subsection provides that "claims to money or to any rights to any performance having an economic value" shall be deemed to constitute an investment. Arbitral tribunals, however, and despite the broadness or vagueness of that definition, have issued repeated warnings to the effect that BITs do not cover everything. The arbitrators have even gone one step further in the *Joy Mining* case, and have held that bank guarantees could not be deemed to constitute an investment under Article 1(a)(iii) of the 1976 BIT between Egypt and the United Kingdom, which includes within the scope of investment "claims to money or to any performance under contact having a financial value."

The language in Article 25 of the Washington Convention, however, is even broader and vaguer than the one in the definitional section of the various

9 *Fedax v. Republic of Venezuela*, 37 ILM 1378 (1998); *Salini Costruttori S.p.A. and Italstrade S.p.A. v. The Hashemite Kingdom of Jordan*, ICSID Case No. ARB/02/13 (31 January 2006); Dipenta v. Algeria, ICSID Case No. ARB/03/8 (10 January 2005); *Joy Mining Machinery v. Egypt*, ICSID Case No. ARB/03/11 (2004).

BITs.[10] Indeed, the framers of the Convention deliberately avoided offering any definition of the term "investment," thereby leaving it to the ICSID tribunals to resolve the issue on a case by case basis. The paradox of the matter is that those tribunals have infused into Article 25 another definition of "investment," a definition that has been repeatedly used in a number of awards, and therefore seems now to be well-settled law. This arbitrator-made definition rests upon a combination of several elements, which ICSID tribunals have found inherent to the concept of investment, as used in Article 25: there can be no investment without (a) some contribution from the investor, (b) a certain duration closer to the long term than to the short-term and (c) the assumption of some risk by the investor.

A number of awards use these criteria in order to determine whether the case at hand relates to an investment. One of the best presentations of the arbitrator-made definition will be found in the *Dipenta* award. The panel (on which sat Emmanuel Gaillard, who participated in the Symposium which this book memorializes) held that:

> *Il paraît conforme à l'objectif auquel répond la Convention [de Washington] qu'un contrat, pour constituer un investissement au sens de la disposition [de l'Article 25], remplisse les trois conditions suivantes; il faut:*
>
> *a) que le contractant ait effectué un apport dans le pays concerné;*
>
> *b) que cet apport porte sur une certaine durée;*
>
> *c) qu'il comporte pour celui qui le fait un certain risque.*
>
> *Il ne paraît en revanche pas nécessaire qu'il réponde en plus spécialement á la promotion économique du pays, une condition de toute façon difficile á établir et implicitement couverte par les trois éléments retenus.*[11]

As the tribunal put it, there are objective criteria that will guarantee a minimal degree of *sécurité juridique*. This is corroborated by the *Joy Mining* award, mentioned above.

The *Joy Mining* award is one of the few cases that dismissed a claim on grounds of lack of jurisdiction, as it held that the dispute was not related to an investment. But in dismissing the claim, the ICSID tribunal made use of the very

---

10 ICSID Convention, Art. 25 (http://worldbank.com/icsid/basicdoc/basicdoc.htm).

11 *Dipenta v. Algeria*, ICSID. Case No. ARB/03/8 (10 January 2005).

same criteria that were cited by the arbitrators in *Dipenta* in order to affirm jurisdiction over that case. As the panel in the *Joy Mining* case wrote:

> Summarizing the elements that an activity must have in order to qualify as an investment, both the ICSID decisions mentioned above and the commentators thereon have indicated that the project in question should have a certain duration, a regularity of profit and return, an element of risk, a substantial commitment and that it should constitute a significant contribution to the host State's [*sic*] development. To what extent these criteria are met is of course specific to each particular case as they will normally depend upon circumstances of each case.[12]

Therefore, Article 25 of the Washington Convention, despite its flaws, has been used by ICSID tribunals to provide the legal basis that they need in order to determine, case by case, what constitutes or does not constitute an "investment." To be sure, the criteria to which they refer for the purpose of making that determination are nowhere expressed in Article 25. Rather, they have been drawn up by ICSID tribunals from previous awards and from the writings of legal scholars. This demonstrates, if anything, the willingness of ICSID tribunals to ensure legal stability—*sécurité juridique*, as the panel put it in the *Dipenta* case—by devising criteria that serve as a tool for harmonization. This shows that ICSID tribunals should be given credit for introducing a measure of consistency into a domain in which the number of applicable provisions, as well as differences among the languages in these provisions, might have led easily to a lack of consistency.

Such an approach is wholly consistent with international law and practice, specifically with the precept stated in Article 38(1) of the statute of the International Court of Justice (ICJ).[13] Article 25 expresses a rule: the dispute must relate to an "investment." ICSID tribunals ought to apply that rule. But Article 25 does not furnish any effective guidance in order for tribunals to determine whether the basis of the dispute is an "investment." ICSID tribunals therefore must look elsewhere to make that determination, and they indeed have turned to subsidiary means for ascertaining the contents of the Article 25 rule. Such subsidiary means, according to Article 38 of the Statute of the ICJ, are to be found in "judicial decisions and teaching of the most highly qualified

12 *Joy Mining Machinery v. Egypt*, ICSID Case No. ARB/03/11 (2004).

13 Statute of the International Court of Justice, Art. 38(1) (http://www.icj-cij.org/documents/index.php?p1=4&p2=2&p3=0).

publicists of the various nations." The arbitrators did nothing else in the *Dipenta* and *Joy Mining* cases.

Arbitral Awards May Still Conflict with Each Other

This still cannot obscure the fact that international investment law seems to suffer from some lack of consistency. A number of awards rendered by ICSID tribunals seem squarely to conflict with each other. Here again, however, appearances may be deceitful. Arbitral awards may be said to be in conflict only insofar as two ICSID tribunals, applying the same rule of law to two identical sets of facts, nevertheless reach decisions that cannot be reconciled.

This is merely to demonstrate that conflicts between ICSID awards are bound to remain quite exceptional. To be sure, an increasing number of disputes are now submitted to arbitration for their resolution—a factor that is likely to increase the number of conflicting decisions. But these disputes arise under different BITs, the provisions of which may be distinguishable; and they involve factual contexts that will necessarily vary one from the other, thereby calling for different solutions. These factual and legal differences call for a cautious use of the term "inconsistent." Inconsistent awards can be rendered only under comparable circumstances, both from factual and legal standpoints.

Why, then, has the feeling spread that legal stability is being jeopardized by an alleged lack of consistency among ICSID awards? Very simply stated, the reason for this is twofold. First, the state of the art has evolved, and newer BITs are now very different from what older BITs used to be. Their clauses are now much more sophisticated, and even replete with clarifications and explanations. But their ongoing evolution has caused a growing differentiation between the clauses in the various models. As noted above, the "fair and equitable treatment" clauses in the 2004 U.S. model and in the 1998 French model have very little in common, except for the use of the words "fair and equitable treatment." Arbitral tribunal cannot give uniform interpretations with respect to clauses that differ so vastly.

Second, arbitral tribunals most often can look nowhere for effective guidance. When it comes to the interpretation of such notions as "direct" or "indirect" expropriation, for instance, most BITs are of no help at all, and there are no subsidiary means for the determination of the law. Thus, ICSID tribunals are left alone to conduct their interpretative task.

The combination of these two factors is bound to result, from time to time, in apparent inconsistencies—even though these inconsistencies may be more apparent than real.

A good example of this is found in the two *S.G.S.* cases, which both deal with the interpretation of the so-called umbrella clause. In 2003, *S.G.S. v. Pakistan*[14] dealt with the umbrella clause in Article 11 of the Switzerland–Pakistan BIT, which provides that "Either Contracting Party shall constantly guarantee the observance of the commitments it has entered into with respect to the investments of the investors of the other Contracting Party."[15] The multinational firm, during the course of the proceedings, argued that the effect of the umbrella clause was to "elevate" breaches of a State contract under municipal law to the level of a breach of the BIT. The ICSID tribunal rejected the argument on the grounds that Article 11 would have to be more specifically worded before it could be read in the expansive manner submitted by Pakistan.[16]

The 2004 award in *S.G.S. v. Philippines* deals with the umbrella clause in Article X(2) of the Switzerland–Philippines BIT, which provides that "Each contracting Party shall observe any obligation it has assumed with regard to specific investments in its territory by investors of the other Contracting Party."[17] S.G.S. argued that failure by the Philippines to pay S.G.S. for services rendered under a State contract amounted to a breach of Article X(2) of the BIT.[18]

The two S.G.S. awards seem, *prima facie*, to be in conflict: the Pakistan award holds that breaches of contract cannot be regarded as amounting to breaches of the BIT, while the Philippines award holds that breaches of contract can be regarded as amounting to breaches of the BIT. This is all the more astonishing since both awards deal with an umbrella clause that is presumably borrowed from one sole model, i.e., the Swiss model.

It is therefore interesting to analyze the reasoning of the ICSID tribunal in the Philippines award in order to discover whether it was in any way influenced by the reasoning in the Pakistan decision. The reasoning of the Philippines tribunal was premised on two observations. First, the tribunal found that the wording of the umbrella clause was not the same in the Switzerland–Pakistan

---

14 ICSID Case No. ARB 01/13 (6 August 2003).

15 *Id.*, para. 163.

16 *Id.*, para. 171.

17 *Id.*, para. 115.

18 *Id.*, para. 128.

BIT and in the Switzerland–Philippines treaty—a finding that confirms that differences in the wording of treaty provisions may induce conflicts between awards, even though the provisions may have the same purpose and object. Second, the tribunal found that the reasoning in the Pakistan award was "unconvincing"—a finding that shows that arbitrators will not elude conflict whenever they come to believe that a decision was tainted by error.

The Philippines tribunal pointed at the differences in the wording of the two clauses. It started by recognizing that the position of Pakistan and the position of the Philippines, which were similar, were contradicted by the *S.G.S. v. Pakistan* award, the only other ICSID case which so far had directly ruled on the issue. But it also stressed that the umbrella clause in Article 11 of the BIT between Switzerland and Pakistan differed from the umbrella clause in Article X(2) of the BIT between Switzerland and the Philippines. The tribunal observed that, generally speaking, Article 11 was formulated in vaguer terms than Article X(2).

It also noted that the word "commitments" in Article 11 did not carry the same legal connotation as the word "obligations" in Article X(2), since these commitments could include unilateral commitments resulting from the legislation of either contracting party, whereas these obligations would include only contractual obligations assumed by either contracting party. Furthermore, the commitments that had been entered under Article 11 related to "the investments"; whereas the obligations that had been assumed under Article X(2) related to "specific investments" within the territory of either contracting party.

Of course, no one will take issue with this analysis, which presumably tends to show that Article X(2) is "considerably more specific" than Article 11—a showing that justifies distinguishing the decision in the Philippines case from that reached in the Pakistan tribunal. But this is precisely what seems questionable: the differences between the two clauses do not seem of such an import as to warrant different final resolutions.

But the tribunal in the Philippines case also ventured to say that it found the Pakistan decision "unconvincing." The arguments in support of that finding do not seem equally convincing. Perhaps the most interesting is the one at §122 of the award. The tribunal quotes with approval from the Pakistan award to stress its reliance on "general principles of international law." This would seem to indicate that general principles of international law might offer some guidance to arbitral tribunals whenever they are in the presence of treaty provisions of unclear significance.

The general principle of international law quoted here is the one according to which "violation of a contract entered into by a State with an investor of another State is not, by itself, a violation of international law." But the tribunal considers that the principle applies only in the absence of any umbrella clause, and that therefore it bears no relevance to the Philippines case, since the Switzerland–Philippines BIT embodies such an umbrella clause. Reliance on general principles of international law may nevertheless be helpful to avoid conflicting decision. Moreover, such reliance would be totally consonant with the provision in Article 42(1) of the ICSID Washington Convention. The lessons of the two S.G.S. cases, however, indicate that the risk of conflicting decisions remains real, and all the more so since arbitral tribunals will not always be prepared to overshadow differences between BIT provisions.

Analyses

It would be desirable, for the sake of a stable and predictable legal environment, to avoid inconsistency in arbitral awards. But since there is not one single cause for this lack of consistency, there probably is not one single method to avoid it.

Hypothesis #1: Inconsistency Is Caused by Tribunals

The lack of consistency may be attributable to different interpretations by different ICSID tribunals of one single BIT provision, or of several BIT provisions that would be similar in substance. ICSID, which is aware of the problem, has been trying to remedy the alleged lack of consistency by devising new procedures. From the procedural standpoint, this could arguably be done either by an amendment to the Washington Convention, pursuant to Articles 65–66, or by a decision of the Administrative Council, pursuant to Article 6(3).

None of these procedures seems appropriate. Amending a multilateral treaty is a long and cumbersome process, the outcome of which is always uncertain. Furthermore, resorting to a decision of the Administrative Council might be questioned as a matter of law, since such decisions are solely intended to "implement" the Convention, and not to ensure consistency through additional facilities entrusted with functions that might go beyond the delegation granted by Article 6(3).

ICSID has nevertheless made an attempt at investigating the feasibility of an additional facility that would have been created by a decision of the

Administrative Council, pursuant to Article 6(3) of the Convention. The purpose of that additional facility was to review ICSID awards, with a view to ensuring overall consistency among them. A number of member States seem not to have welcomed the proposal, which is now dormant. Whatever its future, it should be noted that the new 2004 U.S. model BIT provides for the creation of a review mechanism on the bilateral level, i.e., in each new BIT to be concluded by the U.S. As a consequence, a number of BITs recently entered into by the U.S. include such a review mechanism. No other model, however, appears to have followed that new path. (See Annexes 3 and 4, *ICSID Discussion and Proposal Papers*; Annex 1, *International Investment Instruments with Provisions Relating to an Appellate Review Mechanism*.)

Part of the consistency problem stems from the fact that awards are binding only *inter partes*. They have no force and effect *erga omnes*—no precedential value. Article 53 of the Washington Convention restates that basic rule by providing that "the award shall be binding on the parties"—which means, *a contrario*, that it shall not be binding upon third parties.

More recent model treaties reiterate that rule. For instance, Article 45(1) of the 2004 Canadian model provides that "an award made by a tribunal shall have no binding force except between the disputing parties and in respect of that particular case." In other words, as a matter of principle, an award does not possess the force that would normally attach to a precedent. Therefore, no arbitral tribunal will be bound by the decisions of earlier tribunals, which makes it difficult for a consistent *corpus juris* to emerge from ICSID awards.

Practice may however deviate from theory. More and more often ICSID tribunals give due deference to earlier ICSID awards. In *Dipenta*, quoted above, a number of earlier ICSID awards were cited in order to support the interpretation of the word "investment," as used in Article 25 of the Washington Convention. The exact signification of these citations, however, is not entirely clear. The arbitral tribunal mentioned the *Salini*[19] award, and observed that this award falls within a series of judicial decisions (*courant jurisprudentiel*) which comprises *C.S.O.B.*,[20] *Fedax*[21] and both *S.G.S.* cases. And then it goes on to say that some "objective criteria" may be drawn from these judicial

---

19 *Salini v. Jordan*, ICSID Case No. ARB/02/13 (31 January 2006).

20 *C.S.O.B. v. Slovak Republic*, ICSID CASE No. ARB/97/4.

21 *Fedax v. Republic of Venezuela*, 37 ILM 1378 (1998).

decisions in order to define the word "investment" as used in Article 25.[22] But the arbitral tribunal does not explain the legal value of this "series of judicial decisions." Should they be treated as elements of fact, which may be resorted to solely in order to ascertain the meaning of the word "investment?" Or should they be regarded as sources of law, having the force and value of precedents—despite the provisions of Article 53 of the Washington Convention?

Of course, to treat ICSID awards as sources of law—more specifically, as sources of international law—that might be resorted to by ICSID tribunals in order to settle disputes between foreign investors and host countries seems, *prima facie*, to run against the basic rule that arbitral awards are binding only on the parties. But one should also bear in mind the provision in Article 42(1) of the Washington Convention. This Article states that ICSID tribunals, in the absence of any choice of law, and in case the law of the contracting state would not govern, may apply such rules of international law as may be applicable. The question of whether rules of international law may result from judicial decisions is not one for discussion here. Suffice it to point again at Article 38(1)(d) of the statute of the ICJ, under which judicial decisions are not treated as sources of international law, but as subsidiary means for the determination of international law. But whatever the qualifications, international law ought to remain stable and foreseeable. This requires that judicial decisions be given an authority that goes beyond the relation between the parties.

To be sure, arbitral awards between foreign investors and host countries are not international decisions in the strict sense of the term. But this does not mean that these awards should not be treated as decisions of international tribunals from the standpoint of their force and effect. ICSID tribunals are in charge of interpreting and applying international agreements, i.e., BITs. In discharging this function, they are expounding international law. ICSID tribunals, in so doing, do not hesitate to borrow from all other sources of international law, including decisions from the ICJ, namely arbitral or judicial decisions that specifically deal with the law of investment, like the *E.L.S.I.*[23] decision.

Given the role that ICSID tribunals play in expounding international investment law, it would be highly desirable that their awards be given a force and effect that goes beyond the *inter partes* effect. Such a development would

---

22 ICSID Case No. ARB/03/8, paras 13–15.

23 *Elettronica Sicula S.p.A. (ELSI) (United States of America v. Italy)* (1989).

contribute to satisfy the requirement of continuity, which is vital for the stability of international law. It might not eliminate each and every inconsistency in international investment law. But it would help eliminate those inconsistencies in the law that result solely from conflicts between arbitral awards—as opposed to those that result from conflict between BIT provisions.

Hypothesis #2: Seemingly Identical BIT Provisions Actually Vary in Substance

Another possibility is that the seeming lack of consistency is primarily attributable to application, by ICSID tribunals, of BIT provisions which, though they have the same purpose and object in various treaties, nevertheless vary in substance.

BITs are patterned on different models, which have been developed by States and, sometimes, international organizations. These models may differ from each other; and their clauses, even though their purposes and objects would be the same, may vary from BIT to BIT. Differences among the wording in these clauses, even though seemingly of minor significance, may give rise to arbitral awards that will be in open conflict with each other. The responsibility for these inconsistencies cannot be said to rest primarily with ICSID tribunals. It must be traced to the lack of consistency in the wording of various BIT provisions.

Here again, it would be highly desirable, for the sake of legal stability, to eliminate these differences among BIT provisions. But such a step could be achieved only by switching from bilateralism to multilateralism—i.e., by substituting one multilateral convention for the various BITs. This is no easy task, obviously. There have been a number of attempts at drafting a multilateral treaty, and none of them has been successful.

The two latest efforts—the failed Multilateral Agreement on Investment (MAI) drafted by the OECD and the aborted multilateral framework on investment contemplated by the Doha Declaration—raised the question of whether such an instrument would be feasible at all. But time has passed. Whatever the difficulties, it might well be that the time has come to launch a new effort. Circumstances now may be more favorable than they ever have been. The opportunity should not be lost on policymakers.

CHAPTER 6

Explanations for the Increased Recourse to Treaty-Based Investment Dispute Settlement: Resolving the Struggle of Life Against Form?

*Jeswald W. Salacuse**

A. Background

As international investment gained momentum in the immediate post-World War II era, foreign investors seeking the protection of international investment law found an ephemeral structure consisting largely of scattered treaty provisions, a few contested customs and some questionable general principles of law. As late as 1970, the International Court of Justice in *Barcelona Traction* found it "surprising" that the evolution of international investment law had not gone further and that no generally accepted rules had yet

* Henry J. Braker Professor of Law, Fletcher School of Law and Diplomacy, Tufts University. Email: jeswald.salacuse@tufts.edu.

crystallized in light of the growth of foreign investment and the expansion of international activities by corporations in the preceding half-century.[1]

For investors at the time, the international legal structure was seriously deficient in at least four respects. First, it was incomplete, for it failed to take account of contemporary investment practices and address important issues of investor concern, such as their rights to make monetary transfers from the host country. Second, the principles that did exist were often vague and subject to varying interpretations. Indeed, as recently as 2004, one scholar, discussing the role of customary international law applicable to international investments, found that "there are few customs in this sense in the field of foreign investment."[2]

Third, the content of international investment law was contested, particularly between industrialized countries and newly decolonized developing countries that, in the 1970s, began to demand a "new international economic order" to take account of their particular needs.[3] Finally, existing international law offered foreign investors no effective enforcement mechanism to pursue their claims against host countries that had injured or seized investments or refused to respect contractual obligations. Aggrieved foreign investors who were unable to negotiate a satisfactory settlement, secure an arbitration agreement with a host government or find satisfaction in the local courts had few options other than to seek espousal of their claims by their home country governments, a process that by its very nature was more political than legal.

As a result of these four deficiencies, investors had no assurance that investment contracts and arrangements made with host country governments would not be subject to unilateral change by those governments at some later time. Foreign investments, particularly in developing countries, were, in the words of Raymond Vernon, "obsolescing bargains" between the investor and the host country, as commitments made became subject to renegotiation and cancellation later on.[4] Years earlier, in his exploration of the role of contract in the social

---

1 *Barcelona Traction, Light and Power Company, Limited* (*Belgium v. Spain*) (New Application: 1962), Judgment of 5 February 1970, 1970 I.C.J. Reports 3.

2 M. Sornarajah, *The International Law on Foreign Investment* 89, 2nd Edition (Cambridge University Press: 2004).

3 Jeffrey A. Hart, *The New International Economic Order* (St. Martin's Press: 1983).

4 Raymond Vernon, *Sovereignty at Bay: The Multinational Spread of U.S. Enterprises* 46 (Basic Books: 1971).

order, Karl Llewellyn, a noted U.S. legal scholar, had captured more poetically this same tension between negotiated agreements and subsequent reality when he likened it to a Greek tragedy: "Life struggling against form …."[5] In the post colonial era of nationalizations and contract renegotiations, the political and economic facts of life in host countries struggled hard against the form of various legal commitments made to foreign investors. In that struggle, life usually triumphed over form.

B. The Movement Toward Treatification

To change the dynamics of this struggle and protect the interests of their companies and investors, developed countries began a process of negotiating international investment treaties that, to the extent possible, would be: 1) complete, 2) clear and specific, 3) uncontestable, and 4) enforceable. These treaty efforts took place at both the bilateral and multilateral levels, which, though separate, tended to inform and reinforce each other.[6]

The bilateral efforts, in particular, bore fruit. Beginning in 1959, individual developed countries, negotiating on the basis of predetermined models and prototypes, concluded bilateral investment treaties (BITs) with specific developing countries in order to protect their investors in those countries by 1) subjecting host countries to a set of international legal rules that they had to respect in dealing with foreign investors and their investments, and 2) giving investors themselves the right to bring a claim in international arbitration against host country governments that violated those rules.[7] The BITs' intent was to restrain host country actions against the rights of investors—in other words, to enable the form of legal commitments made to investor to resist the forces of change often demanded by the political and economic life in host countries. By the end of 2005, nearly 2,500 BITs affecting more than 170 countries had been negotiated, and other important treaties containing similar investment provisions, such as the North American Free Trade

---

5 Karl N. Llewellyn, "What Price Contract? An Essay in Perspective," 40 YALE L. J. 704–751, 751 (1931).

6 *See, e.g.*, Thomas W. Walde, *Introductory Note*, European Energy Conference: Final Act, Energy Charter Treaty, Decisions, and Energy Charter Protocol on Energy Efficiency and Related Environmental Aspects, 34 ILM 360 (1995) (noting the strong influence of BITs on the trade provisions of a multilateral energy treaty); Patrick Juillard, "Le Réseau Français des Conventions Bilatérales d'Investissement: á la Recherche d'un Droit Perdu?," 13 DROIT ET PRATIQUE DU COMMERCE INTERNATIONALE 9, 16 (1987) (noting that France based its model BIT on the 1967 Organisation for Economic Co-operation and Development [OECD] Draft Convention on the Protection of Foreign Property).

7 Jeswald W. Salacuse, "BIT by BIT: The Growth of Bilateral Investment Treaties and Their Impact on Foreign Investment in Developing Countries," 24 INT'L LAW 655 (1990).

Agreement (NAFTA) and the Energy Charter Treaty, had been concluded. As a result of this process, a widespread treatification of international investment law had taken place in a relatively short time. (See Annex 6, *UNCTAD, II Monitor, No. 4 (2005)*.) An important support for this new architecture has been the International Centre for Settlement of Investment Disputes (ICSID), formally established in 1965 as an affiliate of the World Bank to resolve disputes between host countries and foreign private investors. Although ICSID did not hear its first case until 1972, it was destined to become an important institution for international investment dispute resolution.

Today, unlike the situation that prevailed in the immediate post-World War II era, foreign investors in many parts of the world are protected primarily by international treaties, rather than by customary international law alone. For all practical purposes, treaties have become the fundamental source of international law in the area of foreign investment.[8] This shift has been anything but theoretical. For one thing, it has imposed a discipline on host country treatment of foreign investors. In those cases in which host governments failed to abide by their commitments to investors, governments have found themselves as respondents in international arbitration proceedings, and in many cases they have been held liable to pay injured investors substantial damage awards. Today, increasingly in the international investment domain, legal form seems to be winning out in its struggle with life.

C. Investor-State Dispute Settlement

What explains the increased recourse to treaty-based investment dispute settlement? At the outset, it should be pointed out that many investment treaties provide for up to *four* dispute settlement processes to which foreign investors may have recourse in the event of a conflict with a host country: local courts, negotiation, conciliation, and international arbitration. Some, but not all, treaties require the aggrieved investor to seek a remedy in local courts of the host country for a fixed period of time before invoking other specified processes. Virtually all treaties require the aggrieved investor to engage in negotiations with the host country to resolve their conflict before having recourse to arbitration. There is little evidence on the use of negotiations to resolve disputes, their success or failure and how treaty provisions are employed in the process. Certainly, an interesting question is whether the prospect of

---

8 Patrick Juillard, "L'Evolution des Sources du Droit des Investissements," 250 RECUEIL DES COURS DE L'ACADÉMIE DE DROIT INTERNATIONAL 74, 74 (1994).

investor-State arbitration has impeded or facilitated negotiated settlements. Sometimes investment treaties also require the investor and the host country to engage in mediation or conciliation through the intervention of a third party, the results of which are nonbinding.

But the concern today about dispute settlement in international investment law is not about the efficacy or fairness of local courts, negotiation or conciliation in the resolution of investment disputes. Rather, the concern over the dispute settlement mechanism created by investment treaties centers almost exclusively on international arbitration. The remainder of this chapter will therefore focus on investor-State arbitration as a method of investment dispute settlement.

One of the most significant developments in contemporary international investment law, as compared to the situation as recently as ten years ago, has been the growth of investor-State arbitration to settle investment disputes. According to UNCTAD's 2006 *World Investment Report*, during the period 1987–2005 a total of 226 investor-State treaty arbitrations had been brought, virtually all of which involved private investors as claimants and States as respondents. This number, however, is only an estimate of the number of investor-State arbitrations, because the cloak of confidentiality that covers many such proceedings prevents gathering precise, comprehensive data on this form of investment dispute settlement. It is safe to assume that the total number of investor-State arbitrations is somewhat larger, but probably not substantially so. Of this number, 136 were brought before ICSID and 90 at other arbitral institutions, including the International Chamber of Commerce (ICC), the Stockholm Chamber of Commerce and *ad hoc* arbitrations under UNCITRAL rules.[9] The growth in the number of cases has not been even and gradual over the 18 years under study. About two-thirds of these 226 cases have been filed since the beginning of 2002 alone. Investor-State arbitration has experienced a sharp increase in recent years, with over 40 treaty-based arbitration cases being commenced in each of 2003, 2004 and 2005. Thus, in the realm of international investment, investor-State arbitration has become increasingly common and arbitral awards interpreting and applying investment treaty provisions have become increasingly numerous. For international law firms, investor-State arbitration, once an arcane field of interest only to a

---

9 UNCTAD, *World Investment Report 2006: FDI from Developing and Transition Economies: Implications for Development* (United Nations Publication: 2006) [Hereinafter UNCTAD 2006], p. 27.

few scholars and specialists, has become an established and presumably lucrative area of legal practice employing hundreds of lawyers.

Granting a private party the right to bring an action in an international tribunal against a sovereign State with respect to an investment dispute is a revolutionary innovation that now seems to be taken for granted. Prior to the treatification of international investment law, investor-State arbitration claims were relatively rare events that required specific agreements by the parties to arbitrate disputes arising from specific investments.[10] What most investment treaties accomplish is to provide an open-ended promise to investors by the host country to arbitrate all claims relating to any investment covered by the treaty's provisions.

Despite its growing prevalence, the uniqueness and power of investor-State arbitration should not be overlooked. For one thing, investor-State arbitrations are not simple commercial disputes that affect only the parties immediately involved. Since most investor-State arbitrations judge the legality of governmental measures, such as those concerning taxation, environmental standards and pricing rules, the resulting arbitration decisions have significant public policy consequences relating to the ability of sovereign governments to regulate enterprises within their territories. Because of these public policy consequences, one scholar has characterized investor-State arbitration as a method of "transnational governance" since an international tribunal is judging the legality of public policy measures of a specific country.[11] Moreover, there are few instances in international law in which a private party may compel a sovereign State to defend the legality of that State's actions in an international forum and, if it fails to defend itself successfully, pay substantial damages for the injury caused to the private party by such action. The field of international trade law, for example, contains no similar procedure. Violations of trade law, even though they strike at the economic interests of private parties, are matters resolved directly and solely by States. The World Trade Organization (WTO) does not give a remedy to private persons injured by trade law violations.[12]

---

10 For a discussion of one of the first investor-State arbitration cases, *see* V. Veeder, "The Lena Goldfields Arbitration: The Historical Roots of Three Ideas," INT'L & COMP. L.Q. 747 (1998).

11 Gus Van Harten, "Private Authority and Transnational Governance: The Contours of the International System of Investor State Protection," REVIEW OF INT'L POLITICAL ECONOMY Vol. 12, No. 4, 600–623 (2005).

12 Glen T. Schleyer, "Power to the People: Allowing Private Parties to Raise Claims Before the WTO Dispute Resolution System," 65 FORDHAM L. REV. 2275, 2277 (1997).

It should also be noted that investment treaties usually grant aggrieved investors the right to prosecute their claims autonomously, without regard to the concerns and interests of their home countries. It is this mechanism that gives important and practical significance to international investment agreements, a mechanism that truly enables these treaties to afford protection to foreign investment. Without the possibility of enforcement when host countries violate treaty provisions, international investment treaties would be mere statements of good will by signatory States, devoid of real legal content.

In almost all investor-State arbitrations, it is the investor who is the claimant and the host country that is the respondent. Two reasons may explain why States rarely initiate arbitration cases against investors. First, host countries generally consider their internal legal processes, namely their regulatory powers and their judicial functions, sufficient to handle their claims against investors in the event of dispute. Second, bilateral investment treaties grant investors rights but rarely impose obligations that host countries may enforce through arbitration. Thus, among all ICSID cases, only two (*Tanzania Electric Supply Company Limited v. Independent Power Tanzania Limited*[13] and *Gabon v. Société Serte*[14]) were initiated by States, and jurisdiction in both cases was based on contracts with the investor, not investment treaties.

D. Reasons for the Growth of Investor-State Arbitration

One can identify at least six reasons for increased recourse to investor-State arbitration: 1) the growing availability of arbitration as a remedy; 2) the lack of satisfactory alternatives for aggrieved investors; 3) the politics of investor-State disputes; 4) the occurrence of major crises; 5) the transformation of the global investment climate; and 6) the development of facilitating factors. Let us examine each of these reasons in turn.

1. Growing Availability of Arbitration as a Remedy

A simple explanation for the growth of investor-State arbitration is that a rapidly increasing number of investment treaties, most of which have been signed since the early 1990s, have given a rapidly growing number of investors a remedy that they never had before to deal with perceived violations of

13 ICSID Case No. ARB/98/8.

14 ICSID Case No. ARB/76/1.

their rights. Whereas only 309 BITs had been concluded by the end of 1988,[15] the total number of BITs had reached nearly 2,500 by the end of 2005,[16] in addition to other important treaties, such as NAFTA, the Energy Charter Treaty, and various free trade agreements which also provide for investor-State arbitration—surely a substantial feat of international law-making in so short a period of time. The result of this effort has been the creation of an increasingly dense BIT network linking approximately 180 countries. That network is destined to become even denser in the years ahead. For example, as of May 2006, 67 other international investment agreements involving 106 countries were in the process of negotiation.[17] At the end of 2005, the total stock of international investment amounted to approximately US$11 trillion and involved at least 77,000 multinational corporations (MNCs) and their 770,000 affiliates.[18] In view of the vast size of international investment, the large and growing number of international investors, the inevitability of some degree of conflict in any investment relationship, and the fact that a foreign direct investment is by its nature a long-term transaction that may be adversely affected by changes in circumstances, it is not surprising that some investors would experience disappointed expectations and that they would attribute that disappointment to governmental actions that violate investment treaties. It is also not surprising that a percentage of these disappointed investors would ultimately have recourse to investor-State arbitration to seek redress for their grievances.

No one likes to be sued. Indeed, any defendant in a lawsuit usually considers that lawsuit as an outrage, a perversion of justice, an unjust attack that has been orchestrated by nefarious forces including lawyers of questionable morality. So it is natural for governments, many of which have never been challenged in a judicial forum of any kind, to object to being forced to defend their actions in an international arbitral proceeding. It also natural for such governments to point to the growing number of investor-State investment cases as a litigation explosion that has gotten out of hand and to assert that the system that allows it is seriously defective.

But are an estimated total of 226 investor-State arbitration cases over a period of 18 years a sign of a litigation explosion and a defective system of investment dispute resolution? It is difficult to determine the appropriate standard to be

---

15 Athena J. Pappas, "References on Bilateral Investment Treaties," 4 ICSID REVIEW—FOREIGN INVESTMENT LAW JOURNAL 189, 194–203 (1989).

16 UNCTAD 2006, p. 28.

17 *Id.*, p. 28.

18 *Id.*, pp. 9-10.

used in answering that question. Given the trillions of dollars of international investments made during that time, the great number of investment projects undertaken, and the many investors involved, one could say that 226 cases, when compared to litigation rates in domestic courts, are really not terribly significant and that such a small number of litigated cases indicates that investor-State relationships on a global basis are surprisingly harmonious. But, as indicated above, investor-State arbitrations are not ordinary commercial cases like those that fill the dockets of domestic courts. They concern public policy questions of far-reaching significance. Even bearing their special nature in mind, one can still ask whether 226 public policy cases over 18 years are too many.

In short, is the concern over the growth of investor-State arbitration due more to the national and political sensitivities of State respondents than to the reality of the situation? Do the protests of respondent governments justify a criticism of the investor-State arbitration systems established by treaties or is it the natural reaction of any defendant in a law suit—a State or private party—to blame the system rather than the conduct that prompted the lawsuit in the first place? In evaluating the statistics on the number of investor-State arbitrations lodged, one must also remember than many of these cases are ultimately settled through negotiations. Thus for example, of the 31 BIT cases concluded under ICSID auspices during the period 1987–2003, 13 were concluded by negotiated settlement of the parties and only 18 by award of the tribunal.[19]

On the other hand, these general statistics may fail to capture the financial and other hardships that individual cases may impose on particular countries, particularly poor developing countries. The potential costs of an investor-State arbitration proceeding are basically threefold. First, a host country faces the risk of having to pay a substantial award, whose amount in relation to its budget and financial resources may prove staggering. Whereas the average award in an ordinary commercial arbitration is less than a million dollars, an award in an investor state arbitration is usually many times that amount.[20] For example, arbitral tribunals rendered awards of US$270 million, plus substantial interest, against the Czech Republic, US$71 million against Ecuador, US$824 against Slovakia, and US$133.2 million against Argentina, to mention only a few.

---

19 The International Bank for Reconstruction and Development, *World Development Report 2005: A Better Investment Climate for Every One* (World Bank: 2004), p. 181.

20 Noah Rubin, "The Allocation of Costs and Attorney's Fees in Investor-State Arbitration," 18 ICSID Review—Foreign Investment Law Journal 109–129 (2003).

Second, the host country must bear the substantial costs of conducting the arbitration itself. This cost usually consists of two elements: the expenses of its legal representation and its share of the costs of administering the arbitration. The costs of legal representation in a lengthy arbitration proceeding can be extremely heavy. For example, the Czech Republic in the case mentioned above reportedly spent US$10 million on its legal defense. The average costs of defending an investor-State arbitration is US$1–2 million. In addition, the host country must bear its share of the administrative costs, including the fees of the arbitrators. This element on average is between US$400,000 and US$500,000. The case of *International Thunderbird Gaming Corporation v. United Mexican States,* a NAFTA case under UNCITRAL rules decided in January 2006, is illustrative. The total costs of the proceeding were US$3,170,692, consisting of US$405,620 in arbitrators fees; US$99,632 in various administrative expenses; US$1,502,065 in Mexico's legal representation costs; and US$1,163,375 in Thunderbird's costs of representation.[21] It is possible for a host country that wins a case to recoup some of these costs from the investor who commenced the case; however, the rules on apportionment of costs among the parties vary and in any case are subject to significant discretion by the tribunal. Moreover, if a host country loses the case, it may itself be required to pay a portion of the claimant investor's costs.

The third hardship imposed on host countries by investor-State arbitrations are the "policy costs." Often the host country has adopted the measure subsequently challenged in arbitration for reasons that it considers necessary to advance public welfare. An investor-State arbitration proceeding that puts in question the legality of such measures and ultimately judges them illegal may not only result in a substantial award to the investor concerned but may also lead to the repeal of modification of such measures for the country as a whole.

2. Lack of Other Satisfactory Remedies

An investor-State arbitration proceeding is a costly, risky and time consuming process that usually has the effect of destroying whatever business relationships remain between the aggrieved investor and the host country. One can therefore assume that a rational investor will not lightly have recourse to this dispute settlement process and will, moreover, examine other options for

21 *International Thunderbird Gaming Corporation v. United Mexican States* (26 January 2006) (*available at* http://www.naftaclaims.com).

redress of its grievance before doing so. A second reason for increased recourse to investor-arbitration therefore may be that aggrieved investors, having undertaken that search for other options, have concluded that they have no better cost effective, reliable remedies for the settlement of disputes than investor-State arbitration. This lack of other effective remedies has the effect of encouraging investors to have recourse to international arbitration.

Aside from recourse to international arbitration, an investor aggrieved by the actions or inaction of a host government has basically four options: 1) acceptance of governmental action by absorbing or off-setting the costs of alleged wrongful governmental action or inaction; 2) negotiation of a settlement of the dispute with the host government; 3) mediation, conciliation or other alternative dispute resolution methods involving the help of a third party; and 4) recourse to the courts or other judicial institutions of the host country. Let us evaluate each of these options.[22]

a. Acceptance and Internal Adjustment

Not all alleged violations of investment treaties result in litigation. Depending on the costs of alleged wrongful governmental action, an investor may merely decide to absorb or find ways of off-setting the costs of that action. The investor makes that decision essentially on the basis of an evaluation of the costs and benefits of other actions in comparison to acceptance. In making that calculation, the investor will often evaluate the long-term benefits of continuing productive relations with the host country government and the local business community against the costs to be incurred by taking some other action. The decision will also be influenced by the investor's ability to absorb the additional costs or to shift those costs to other persons.

On the other hand, while host country governments always assume that the investor can and should take this acceptance option, there are powerful forces driving against it. The shareholders, creditors, financing institutions, and other stakeholders of corporate investors expect corporate management to maximize profits for the corporation so as to benefit those stakeholders. If, as a result of a governmental action violating an investment treaty, a corporate investor has a substantial claim under international law against the host country, corporate management may have an obligation to pursue that claim vigorously.

22 *See* Susan Franck, Chapter 9.

Failure to do so may be viewed under the law applicable to the corporation or its contract with stakeholders as a violation by management or the board of directors of their legal duties to shareholders and other stakeholders. A substantial claim under international law against a host country is a corporate asset, and the investor therefore may have a legal obligation not to abandon it, particularly if that claim may have a material impact on the operations of the investor.

A further argument against doing nothing in the face of an alleged investment treaty violation is that it may encourage other violations in the future. If an investor does nothing in response to a host country violation, it may become more vulnerable to other violations in the future by the host country in question or other host countries where it has other investments. If the investment treaty is truly to serve as a discipline on host country government behavior, individual investors must be willing to challenge that behavior by invoking a treaty's provisions.

On the other hand, it must be acknowledged that any system of litigation entails the risk of frivolous lawsuits, and investor-State arbitrations are no exception. Investors may bring baseless arbitrations either because they honestly have misevaluated the strength of their claims, because they view the arbitration as a means to pressure a negotiated settlement from the host country or because they believe they have relatively little to lose and the potential to gain a great deal. One way for arbitrators to dissuade such frivolous cases is to allocate all or a substantial portion of the arbitration costs to such claimants if they lose their case.

b. Negotiation

Many disputes between foreign investors and host countries are resolved through negotiation. Indeed, it is safe to say that virtually all such disputes go through a period of negotiation before reaching settlement or advancing to the stage of formal investor-State arbitration. Accurate, comprehensive statistics on negotiated settlements of investor-State conflicts are not available, but one would suppose that, over the last 18 years, such settlements vastly outnumber the estimated 226 investor-State arbitrations that have been lodged.

Various factors will determine whether a particular investor-State negotiation will be successful, so it is difficult to generalize. For example, in 1993, Enron, a U.S. corporation, and the Maharashtra State Electricity Board (MSEB) in India signed a contract whereby a consortium led by Enron would build the Dabhol Power Project, a US$2 billion investment, and the MSEB agreed to buy the electricity produced over the following 20 years. When a new government came to power in Maharashtra, as a result of elections, it cancelled the contract, alleging that the power tariff was too high and that the contract was not in Maharashtra's best interests. Negotiations between Maharashtra and Enron ensued, resulting in modification of the contract, a reduction in power tariffs and the continuation of the project. One factor that led to this result was that Enron's business strategy in India at the time contemplated undertaking numerous energy projects throughout India in the years ahead. Enron judged those potential future investment relationships to be worth more than winning an arbitration award in a case that would certainly be a long protracted struggle and that might ultimately destroy its opportunities to undertake other power projects in the country. It therefore constantly remained open to a negotiated settlement throughout its conflict with Maharashtra.

Maharashtra's subsequent reevaluation of its own interests also led it to become more open to a negotiated settlement. When the Maharashtra government cancelled the electricity supply agreement, it assumed that its action would entail relatively little cost. It also assumed that other investors would be willing to step into the shoes vacated by Enron or that the government would be able to find indigenous solutions to its power shortage. Once those assumptions proved false and Enron had begun an arbitration case in London with a claim of US$300 million, Maharashtra became considerably more open to renegotiation than it was at the time it cancelled the contract.[23] Thus it would appear that in some cases at least the existence of an investor-State arbitration remedy for the investor may encourage flexibility and create an incentive for host governments to negotiate a settlement. So it may well be, when examining the totality of investor-State negotiations, that the prospect of investor-State arbitrations is a factor inducing negotiated settlements of investor-State disputes.

On the other hand, a variety of factors can prevent the achievement of a negotiated settlement. A host country government's belief that vital national interests are at stake, an investor's perception that its crucial economic interests are in play, the political dynamics of the host country, the inability of

---

23 Jeswald W. Salacuse, *The Global Negotiator: Making, Managing, and Mending Deals Around the World in the Twenty-first Century* (Palgrave Macmillan: 2003) [Hereinafter Salacuse 2003], pp. 236–247.

the investor to mitigate its loss by other means and the appointment of incompetent or dysfunctional negotiators to represent the parties are just some of the factors that can inhibit the negotiation process and often stop it dead in its tracks.

Unrealistic expectations of the parties are a further obstacle to successful negotiations. The alternative to a successful negotiation in most cases is arbitration in which the investor will be the claimant and the State refusing that claim the respondent. International investor-State arbitration has risks and costs for both sides, and it is important that both sides understand them thoroughly as they approach the negotiation process so they can accurately evaluate the worth of any proposal put forward. When the investor overvalues the strength of its claim and the host country undervalues the worth of the claimant's case, opportunities for a successful negotiated settlement decline. Various factors may lead to this miscalculation, including the failure of their lawyers to give their clients a realistic and brutally frank assessment of the strength of their respective cases and the likelihood of prevailing in arbitration.

c. Mediation, Conciliation and Other Forms of Voluntary Third-party Intervention

Often, third persons—sometimes called mediators, conciliators or facilitators—can help the parties to a dispute resolve their conflict when they themselves are unable to do so. Mediation and its variations are age-old conflict resolution techniques that can be found in all societies, from rural villages to international diplomacy, from urban neighborhoods to legislative corridors. Mediation is essentially the intervention of a third person into a dispute in order to help the disputants achieve a voluntary agreement about the matters in conflict. It is of course a constant in international political disputes from the Middle East to Northern Ireland. A party is able to help the disputants move toward resolution of their dispute because the third-party brings to the situation skills and resources that the parties themselves lack. The intervener's communication skills, objectivity, knowledge, creativity, stature, and positive relationships with the disputants are some of the key resources that may help settle the conflict.

Traditionally, companies engaged in an international business dispute have not actively sought the help of mediators. They have first tried to resolve the matter themselves through negotiation, but when they judged that to have failed they have immediately proceeded to arbitration or litigation. Various factors explain their failure to try mediation and other forms of voluntary third party intervention: lack of knowledge about these processes and the institutions that may provide them, the fact that companies tend to give control of their disputes to lawyers whose professional inclination is to litigate, and the belief that mediation is merely a stalling tactic that only delays the inevitability of an arbitration proceeding.[24]

With increasing recognition of the disadvantages of arbitration, some companies are beginning to turn to more explicit forms of mediation to resolve business disputes. Increasingly, when a dispute can be quantified—for example, the extent of damage to an asset by a partner's action or the amount of a royalty fee owed to a licensor—the parties will engage an independent third party such as an international accounting or consulting firm to examine the matter and give an opinion. The opinion is not binding on the parties, but it has the effect of allowing them to make a more realistic prediction of what may happen in an arbitration proceeding.

One type of voluntary third-party intervention that has particular relevance for investor-State conflicts is *conciliation*. Many arbitration institutions, such as ICSID and the International Chamber of Commerce, offer a service known as conciliation, which is normally governed by a set of rules. Generally, in institutional conciliation, a party to a dispute may address a request for conciliation to the institution. If the institution concerned secures the agreement of the other disputant, it will appoint a conciliator. While the conciliator has broad discretion to conduct the process, in practice he or she will invite both sides to state their views of the dispute and will then make a report proposing an appropriate settlement. The parties may reject the report and proceed to arbitration, or they may accept it. In many cases, they will use it as a basis for a negotiated settlement. Conciliation is thus a kind of non-binding arbitration. Its function is predictive. It tends to be rights-based in its approach, affording the parties a third person's evaluation of their respective rights and obligations. Conciliators do not usually adopt a problem-solving or relationship building approach to resolving the dispute between the parties. The process is confidential and completely voluntary. Either party may withdraw from conciliation at any time.

---

24 Jeswald W. Salacuse, "Mediation in International Business," *in* Jacob Bercovitch, ed., *Studies in International Mediation* (Palgrave Macmillan: 2002), pp. 213–228.

Since conciliation is confidential, public information on the process itself is scant. One of the few published accounts concerns the first conciliation conducted under ICSID auspices, in which a retired English judge, Lord Wilberforce, successfully acted in 1984–1985 as a conciliator to help resolve a dispute involving the distribution of US$143 million in profits between Tesoro Petroleum Corporation and the country of Trinidad and Tobago. The conciliation lasted under two years and cost a mere US$11,000.[25] Despite the success of this first ICSID conciliation, this form of dispute settlement has not become widely used in resolving investor-State disputes. For example, whereas by 2006 ICSID had received 192 requests for arbitration since its creation, it had only received 5 requests for conciliation. Similarly, from 1988 to 1993, a period in which over 2,000 arbitration cases were filed at the International Chamber of Commerce, the ICC received only 54 requests for conciliation. Of that number, the other party in the dispute agreed to conciliation in only 16 cases; however, the ICC appointed only ten conciliators, since the parties settled the dispute or withdrew the request in six cases. Of the ten conciliations, nine had been completed by 1994, five resulting in complete settlement.[26]

The reasons why parties in investor-State investment disputes have not chosen to have recourse to conciliation and other forms of voluntary third-party intervention more frequently are not clear, but it is certainly a subject of study that institutions such as ICSID, the ICC and other organizations concerned about the increase in investor-State arbitration should address. The development of more effective forms of mediation and conciliation in which both investors and States have confidence may serve to create an attractive alternative to international arbitration and thereby reduce recourse to this costly form of dispute settlement.

d. Local Courts

A final alternative to investor-State arbitration for aggrieved investors is recourse to the courts of the host country. Depending on the country involved, this option, which some BITs require as a step preliminary to arbitration, poses a variety of problems for foreign investors. First, local courts may suffer from a lack of judicial independence and be subject to the political control of the

---

25 Lester Nurick and Stephen J. Schnably, "The First ICSID Conciliation: *Tesoro Petroleum Corporation v. Trinidad and Tobago*," 1 ICSID REVIEW—FOREIGN INVESTMENT LAW JOURNAL 340–353 (1986).

26 Eric Schwartz, "International Conciliation and the ICC," 10 ICSID REVIEW—FOREIGN INVESTMENT LAW JOURNAL 98 (1995).

host government, thus depriving the investor of a neutral forum. Second, even if the judiciary is independent, it may nonetheless harbor prejudice toward foreign investors, as the courts of the U.S. state of Mississippi demonstrated in the local trial analyzed by the ICSID arbitration *Loewen Group v. United States*.[27] Third, many local courts may not have the expertise to apply complex principles of international law to complicated foreign investment transactions. And finally, local courts often strain under a heavy backlog of cases and inefficient procedures that deny expeditious justice and make the prospect of any final judicial determination of a conflict illusory. For these reasons, investors do not generally consider local courts an effective option to international arbitration of their disputes, and thus generally seek to avoid them.

3. The Politics of Investor-State Disputes

Investor-State disputes are not only legal in nature, they are also political. Indeed, it is the political dimensions of such conflicts that primarily preoccupy host country government officials. Within individual host countries, the public, political groups and the media often take positions on such disputes, and the nature and tenacity of their views can influence how host country officials deal with the investor and the dispute. This factor, for example, may make it difficult for host country officials to negotiate a settlement of a dispute since any negotiated settlement can be challenged by political opponents and the media as "selling out to foreigners," weakness or the product of corruption. Not only do the politics of investor-State dispute settlement inhibit a negotiated settlement, they may actually encourage and prolong arbitration since host country officials can blame any unfavorable result on three foreign arbitrators, thereby shifting responsibility away from the government.

This dynamic was apparently at work in the famous "Pyramids Case," which pitted a group of foreign property developers against the government of Egypt with respect to a proposed "destination resort" to be constructed near the Giza Pyramids. The Egyptian government had initially approved the project, but under public pressure ultimately cancelled it. At one point in the history of this case, which continued over 15 years, a tentative settlement of US$10 million was negotiated. When the proposed settlement was presented to the Prime Minister for his approval, he asked what the alternative was. When told that the alternative was for Egypt to continue to defend itself in arbitration,

---

27 ICSID Case No. ARB(AF) 98/3.

he found that option to be preferable since an agreement to settle the case for US$10 million would open him to attack by opponents and the media. Ultimately, in 1993, after the case wound through ICC arbitration, the courts of France and ICSID arbitration (resulting in an award of US$27.6 million, plus US$5 million in costs, which was then challenged in annulment proceeding), Egypt and the investors agreed to a negotiated settlement of US$17.5 million. This result might have been avoided if Egypt and the investors had agreed to intervention at an earlier stage by a distinguished conciliator who would have provided an expert opinion on a fair settlement of the conflict, and thus given the prime minister the political cover that he felt he needed. In any event, methods aimed at resolving investor-State disputes must find ways to accommodate the political dimensions of those disputes.

4. The Occurrence of Economic Crises

Domestic litigators know that economic recessions and crises provoke lawsuits as various claimants fight over their share of a shrinking pie. The same phenomenon is at work in international investment. Major financial crises often lead to conflict and those conflicts ultimately find their way to arbitration tribunals. The financial crises in Argentina, Russia and East and Southeast Asia have all led to increased recourse to arbitration. For example, of the approximately 110 registered cases at ICSID in March 2006, 36 cases involve Argentina as a respondent. All of these cases have arisen as a result of the country's financial crisis at the beginning of this century.

5. The Transformation of the Global Investment Climate

A more remote but nonetheless important cause for the increase in investor-State disputes has been the transformation of the global investment environment that has taken place during the past 20 years. Beginning in the post-World War II era, virtually all developing countries rejected the liberal economic model and believed that their governments had the primary responsibility for bringing about national economic development. As a result, their systems were characterized by: 1) state planning and public ordering of their economies and societies; 2) reliance on state enterprises as economic actors; 3) restriction and regulation of the private sector; and 4) governmental limitation and control of international economic transactions, especially foreign investment. Indeed, many countries had serious reservations about the role of foreign direct investment in their development and therefore adopted measure to control and limit it. By the mid-1980s, this approach to development began to lose its hold on the minds and actions of policy makers, aid agencies and international financial institutions. Seeking to transform themselves into "emerging markets," developing countries increasingly privatized their state enterprises, engaged in deregulation, opened their economies, instituted markets to allocate resources and began aggressively to encourage foreign direct investment.[28]

The efforts at foreign investment promotion took a variety of forms, including legislation to liberalize the economies, incentives to attract foreign investors, road shows, public relations campaigns and, of course, the conclusion of BITs with capital exporting States. Thus, within a short time, the position of foreign investors in many countries was transformed from that of a dubious presence at the sufferance of the government to that of an eagerly sought after and much courted guest. The result of this transformation may have led foreign investors to undertake their investments with high and perhaps unrealistic expectations about their importance to the country and their status in it. Having been eagerly courted by host country governments, investors may have come to believe that they were investing not at the sufferance of the government but as of right. When the results of their investments did not accord with what they believed they had been promised by the host country, their disappointment led them to sue governments in arbitration, rather than to accept meekly any losses caused by government actions.

6. Facilitating Factors

Investor-State arbitration was once a rare and arcane international process, the province of a few experts. That is no longer the case. As a result of its growth, various factors have developed that encourage recourse to this form of dispute settlement process. In a sense, these factors are a result of the growth in international arbitration, but they may also be a cause for increased recourse. First, the growing number of cases and awards, some of which have been covered in the media, have led to an increased understanding of this dispute settlement process and heightened ability to predict the results of future cases. International investors and their lawyers have no doubt used this knowledge in deciding whether or not to invoke arbitration in individual disputes.

---

28 Jeswald W. Salacuse, "From Developing Countries to Emerging Markets: A New Role for Law in the Third World," 33 THE INTERNATIONAL LAWYER 875–890 (1999).

The elaboration by arbitral tribunals of various international legal principles affirming the protection of investor rights, as well as the award of substantial damages and their subsequent payment by host country governments, have also encouraged a move toward arbitration. Second, the growth of law firms with expertise in what had previously been an arcane area of the law has meant that investors have an important resource to assist them in deciding whether or not to arbitrate, and then in actually carrying forward the arbitration. At the same time, having made substantial investments in developing investor-State arbitration capabilities, these same law firms also have an incentive to encourage clients to have recourse to this form of dispute-settlement. Finally, in a relatively short period of time, tribunals and law firms have refined the technology and processes of investor-State arbitration, thereby facilitating the handling of cases and perhaps as a result encouraging other aggrieved investors to invoke this process.

E. Conclusion

Inherent in investor-State relationships is a constant struggle of life against form, a continuing tension between economic and political forces in host countries and the legal commitments previously made to foreign investors by host governments. If that struggle, to use Llewellyn's metaphor, is a Greek tragedy, then investor-State arbitration has become an increasingly important stage on which that drama is played. This chapter has tried to explain the development of that phenomenon in terms of certain structural characteristics: 1) the increased availability of investor-State arbitration as a remedy for aggrieved investors; 2) the perceived inadequacy of other remedies; 3) the politics of host countries; 4) the outbreak of severe economic crises; 5) the transformation of the global investment environment; and 6) the evolution of certain facilitating factors.

Following the example of certain research on litigiousness in domestic courts,[29] one might also seek explanations for the increased recourse to investor-State arbitration in the nature and identity of the parties themselves. Just as scholars have found that certain persons are more likely to sue in a domestic setting than are others, it may well be that certain investors—by virtue of their nationality, industry, financial structure or type of project—are more likely than other investors to have recourse to investor-State arbitration.

---

29 *See e.g.*, Theodore Eisenberg and Henry S. Farber, "The Litigious Plaintiff Hypothesis: Case Selection and Resolution," 28 RAND Journ. of Economics S92–S112 (1997).

Similarly, certain States, by virtue of their type of government or political system, may be more likely to resist settlement of claims and therefore may be more likely than other States to find themselves as respondents in arbitration cases. This approach suggests a potentially rich area for further research; however, scholars wishing to undertake it face a perhaps insurmountable obstacle to obtaining necessary data because of the cloak of confidentiality that covers most investor-State arbitration cases.

Regardless of the need for more research on, and a better understanding of, investor-State disputes and the processes for their settlement, one may expect investor-State arbitration to grow in quantity and importance in the years ahead. Conflict between host country governments and foreign investors is an inherent risk of the foreign investment process. The six factors that have facilitated recourse to investor-State arbitration will remain in place and continue favoring recourse to it by disappointed investors. More importantly, BITs, in their function as instruments of international law, have granted apparently durable rights to present and future investors and have established durable structures for their enforcement. Disappointed investors continue to be able to invoke those rights and employ those structures relatively easily when, for one reason or another, they believe that their legitimate expectations have been unjustifiably frustrated by host country government actions. One detects no sentiment for movement by developing country governments to undertake the potentially costly task of revising those rights, structures and treaties to diminish the likelihood of investor-State arbitration in the future.

CHAPTER 7

The Proliferation of BITs: Conflicts of Treaties, Proceedings and Awards

*Giorgio Sacerdoti**

Commentary

The considerable number of bilateral investment treaties (BITs) in force has given rise to conflicts when, in relation to the same subject matter, a right of action exits for a given investor (or related investors) under different BITs. In fact, two recent international disputes, the *CME v. Czech Republic* and *Lauder v. Czech Republic* arbitrations, have attracted widespread attention as the first example in which this situation has arisen.

The same acts by the Czech Republic were subject to two separate arbitrations conducted concurrently. The two cases, however, underwent conflicting procedures, were dealt with under conflicting governing treaty provisions and resulted in seemingly conflicting awards. This situation has highlighted the risks inherent in the current international investment regime of intricate, non-coordinated networks of BITs. The fundamental risk is that this glaring inconsistency could potentially bring a backlash against international investment.[1] On the other hand, the speedy completion of all litigation in the

* Professor of International and European Law, Bocconi University, Milan, Italy; Member of the Appellate Body, World Trade Organization, Geneva, Switzerland. Email: giorgio.sacerdoti@unibocconi.it.

1 I have focused on different aspects of the cases than those dealt with here in my article "Investment Arbitration under ICSID and UNCITRAL Rules: Prerequisites, Applicable Law, Review of Awards," 19 ICSID Review—Foreign Investment Law Journal 1–48 (2004).

Czech cases (including full payment by the State concerned), notwithstanding these complexities, indicates that international commercial arbitration (rather than institutional frameworks providing for remedies such as consolidation of proceedings) may effectively resolve disputes, with full respect given to substantive law and due process.

The *CME* and *Lauder* arbitrations were possibly the first publicly known disputes, under a BIT, decided through international commercial arbitration proceedings in accordance with the UNCITRAL rules instead of within the International Centre for Settlement of Investment Disputes (ICSID). The national courts of the country where the award was rendered, Sweden, had to rule on the challenge, brought in accordance with the local arbitration statute, by the losing State, in which the Czech Republic argued to set aside the awards based on the alleged conflict of the two proceedings and resulting awards.

The disputes arose from the interference in 1996–1999 by the Media Council, an agency of the Czech government, with the contractual scheme under which "CME Czech Republic BV," a Dutch company controlled by the U.S. businessman Ronald Lauder, was operating in partnership with a local investor, TV Nova, the most successful commercial television in the Czech Republic. The interference brought about the exclusion of CME and the destruction of its investment.

CME began arbitration against the Czech Republic in 2000 in accordance with the provisions of Article 8 of the 1991 BIT between the Netherlands and Czechoslovakia, claiming unfair treatment and expropriation without compensation. This article provides that disputes between a contracting State and an investor of the other contracting State concerning an investment of the latter shall be submitted to an *ad hoc* arbitral tribunal, which shall determine its own procedure "applying the arbitration rules of the U.N. Commission for International Trade Law (UNCITRAL)." The article also includes a clause on applicable law and a reference to the Stockholm Chamber of Commerce; based on this link, arbitration took place in Stockholm.

The proceedings and the award between Lauder (a U.S. citizen) and the Czech Republic were likewise the result of UNCITRAL arbitration, initiated in 1999 and carried out (in London) in conformity with similar provisions found in Article 6 of the 1991 BIT between the U.S. and Czechoslovakia. This arbitration was based on the fact that CME's investment was "controlled directly or indirectly by Mr. Lauder" and that the BIT covered also "indirect investments" in Art.I.1(a). In contrast to the Dutch BIT, the U.S.–Czech BIT gave the investor the alternative option to resort to ICSID, but Lauder chose UNCITRAL arbitration.

In its award of 3 September 2001, the London tribunal found no injury, although it concluded that the Czech government had acted unfairly in some respect. The Stockholm tribunal, however, in a partial award of 13 September 2001, found that the Czechs had violated several articles of the BIT, behavior amounting to *de facto* expropriation of CME's investment.

The Czech government challenged this award before the competent Court of Appeal of Stockholm according to the Swedish Arbitration Act of 1999,[2] claiming *inter alia* major procedural errors and lack of jurisdiction, in that the arbitrators had disregarded the principles of *lis pendens* and *res judicata* in light of the London proceedings and award. The Court of Appeal rejected all challenges against the Stockholm award. Shortly thereafter the tribunal concluded the *quantum* phase of the arbitration, awarding about US$ 250 million in damages to CME.[3]

Argument

First, we must note that this situation is not as extraordinary as it would first appear. The possibility of such conflicts due to parallel or multiple proceedings is inherent in a world with different sovereignties, uncoordinated politically or, even less, judicially.

We see this situation also as to private litigation and inter-State litigation. For the former, even at the regional level, under the Brussels Convention (replaced in 2002 by EC Regulation 44/2001), which coordinates jurisdiction within the European Community, there are loopholes and situations in which more than one country may take jurisdiction. The European Court of Justice has acknowledged this situation, notably in case of tort actions.[4]

---

2 An English translation of the Act is reprinted *in* 17 ARB. INT'L 425 (2001); *see especially* Arts. 33 and 34 on invalidity and the setting aside of awards.

3 For the text of the *Lauder* award of 3 September 2001, *see* 14 WORLD TRADE AND ARBITRATION MATERIALS 35 (2002); for the *CME* partial award of 13 September 2001, *see ibid*, 109 (2002); for the final award of 14 March 2003, *see ibid*, Vol. 15, 83 (2003). For the Court of Appeals of Stockholm decision of 15 May 2003, *see* 42 ILM 919 (2003). All the decisions are available at (http://www.cetv-net.com).

4 ECJ, 30 November 2006, 21/76 *Bier v. Mines de Potasse d'Alsace;* 7 March 1995, C-68/93, *Fiona Shevill v. Presse Alliance;* 19 September 1995, C-364/93, *Marinari v. Lloyds Bank plc & Zubaidi Trading Co.*

At the global level, the negotiations at The Hague Conference on Private International Law aimed at concluding a world convention on jurisdiction and recognition of judgments; it dragged on unsuccessfully for many years before being abandoned for a more modest objective. One of the reasons was that many States were and are unwilling to limit *a priori* their courts' jurisdiction even in instances where a closer link with another country is generally recognized.[5] Thus, contrary to the initial optimistic expectations, legislators and diplomats are not willing to, or capable of, establishing, through multilateral treaties, a level of coordination matching and reflecting the globalization of commercial relations and the quest for legal security by businesspersons and investors.

Regarding international commercial arbitration, interference between arbitral proceedings and litigation before national courts has not been eliminated as completely as hoped by either domestic statutes on arbitration or by the New York Convention on Recognition and Enforcement of Foreign Arbitral Awards. Parallel proceedings may sometimes develop, and the solution of a conflict is often uncertain in a given case.[6]

As to international relations, the multiplication of international courts has been a mixed blessing. On the one hand, the international system has considerably evolved. It is not any more characterized by a general absence of judicial organs endowed with the competence to adjudicate disputes pursuant to an *ex parte* application, thus leaving them unresolved in the hands of the parties. On the other hand, the lack of coordination has rendered all those involved attentive to the risk that a multiplication of courts may mean conflicts of jurisdictions,[7] and that a danger of fragmentation of applicable international law may result.[8] (See Annex 6, *UNCTAD, IIA Monitor, No. 4 (2005)*.)

---

5 *See The Hague Preliminary Draft Convention on Jurisdiction and Judgments*, Fausto Pocar and Costanza Honorati, eds. (Cedam: 2005). A "Choice of Court" Convention was adopted by the Conference in 2005, instead.

6 For an updated review of the issue, *see* Bernardo Cremades and Julian Lew, eds., *Parallel State and Arbitral Procedures in International Arbitration*, ICC Dossiers (2005). A further area of conflicts result from the possibility that an award annulled in the country where it was rendered will still be recognized as valid in another jurisdiction pursuant to the New York Convention under the well-known *Hillarion—Chromalloy* doctrine.

7 *See* "The Proliferation of International Tribunals: Piercing Together the Puzzle," 31 NYU J. INT'L L. & POL. (Symposium Issue), at 679 (1999); and Charles N. Brower and Jeremy Sharpe, "The Coming Crisis in the Global Adjudication System," 19 ARB. INT'L 313 (2003).

8 See the International Law Commission Study, *Fragmentation of International Law: Difficulties Arising From the Diversification and Expansion of International Law*, Doc. A/CN.4/L.682 of 13 April 2006.

Specifically, the operation of the dispute settlement system of the World Trade Organization, notwithstanding its unique exclusivity and compulsory nature (or possibly because of these features), has witnessed instances in which conflicts with other international jurisdictions have been at least hinted at. The softwood lumber dispute between Canada and the U.S., for instance, has been brought in different aspects to several WTO panels (some of whose decisions have been appealed) and also to NAFTA panels. Thus, while one of these cases was pending at the WTO,[9] a NAFTA panel dealt with the same subject matter. The later panel, however, applied domestic U.S. law to countervailing duties rather than the WTO Agreement on Subsidies and Countervailing Measures (SCM), in conformity with the NAFTA provisions on review of certain domestic decisions by bi-national NAFTA panels. Neither country claimed in either forum that one proceeding should be stayed for fear of a conflict; but one could envisage that a domestic statute applied within the NAFTA dispute might be found not in compliance with a WTO agreement in Geneva, or vice versa.

The WTO dispute in the case *Mexico—Tax Measures on Soft Drinks and Other Beverages*[10] presented more directly the possibility of overlapping or interference by a treaty regime with another. Here, Mexico invoked an alleged breached by the U.S. of NAFTA, specifically of its dispute settlement provisions, in order to justify its non-compliance with certain GATT provisions. Mexico, however, did not rely on the general principles of State responsibility allowing countermeasures.[11] Rather, it sought to justify its position by relying on Art. XX(d) of GATT, claiming that the measures it was maintaining were necessary to "secure compliance" by the U.S. of its obligations under NAFTA. The Appellate Body distinguished the question of jurisdiction from those of the merits, stating that it had no competence to decide a dispute arising under NAFTA.[12] As to the merits, the Appellate Body evaluated the claim under Art. XX(d). It concluded that the conditions for its application were in any case not met, since the terms necessary to "secure compliance with laws and regulations" in Art. XX(d) of the GATT 1994 did not encompass WTO-inconsistent measures applied

---

9 *See United States—Final Countervailing Duty Determination with Respect to Certain Softwood Lumber from Canada*, Report of the Appellate Body, WT/DS257/AB/R, 19 January 2004.

10 *Mexico—Tax Measures on Soft Drinks and Other Beverages*, Report of the Appellate Body, WT/DS308/AB/R, 6 March 2006.

11 Art. 49, ILC Draft Articles on State Responsibility. Annex to the UN General Assembly doc A/RES/56/83, 28 January 2002.

12 *See* WT/DS308/AB/R, Para. 56.

by a WTO member to secure compliance with another WTO member's obligations under an international agreement.[13]

Lawyers are familiar with these types of situations.[14] This type of conflict may also affect investment disputes, actual or potential, because BITs have increased immensely in number and in coverage, both as to the definition of investment (*ratione materiae*) and as to the definition of investor (*ratione personae*). Recourse by investors (with the assistance of an ever larger bar of international investment lawyers) has made use of these developments, so that actual arbitrations and awards have dramatically increased.

Until recently, BITs were resorted to for a direct solution of disputes between foreign investors and countries in isolated cases, mainly in instances of blatant expropriation. BITs, and more generally BIT arbitration, were taken into account as the "depoliticized" judicial alternative to diplomatic protection, an instrument that had led in the past to political conflicts but rarely actual remedies for the aggrieved investor.[15] The legal community has now become fully aware of the possibilities offered to aggrieved investors by BITs. BIT arbitration is not the only option when the dispute with the host country concerns an operating investment. While BIT arbitration is—in the first place—an alternative to domestic litigation, it sometimes may be resorted to in parallel with domestic litigation,[16] or after the exhaustion of domestic remedies, even when this is not a requirement.

The well-known issue of the relationship between contract claims under domestic law (not to speak of umbrella clauses) and treaty-based investment claims is a part of this broader picture.[17]

---

13 *Id.*, Para. 68, 77, 79.

14 *See* Cesare Romano, "The Americanization of International Litigation," 19 OHIO STATE J. DISPUTE RESOLUTIONS, at 89 (2003); Sarah Kellog, "Towards an International Legal System," WASHINGTON LAWYER, September 2006, at 23.

15 I have focused on this issue in a previous paper, "Bilateral Treaties and Multilateral Instruments on Investment Protection," HAGUE COLLECTED COURSES 269, 255–460 (1997).

16 This is a possibility or a risk when the relevant BIT does not provide for "the fork in the road" obligation to opt between arbitration and domestic litigation (as is the case for U.S. BITs).

17 *See* Christian Schreuer, "Investment Treaty Arbitration and Jurisdiction over Contract Claims—The *Vivendi-I Case* Considered," *in* Todd Weiler, ed., *International Investment Law and Arbitration* (Cameron May: 2004), p. 281; Emmanuel Gaillard, "Investment Treaty Arbitration and Jurisdiction over Contract Claims—The SGS Cases Considered," *in* Todd Weiler, ed., *International Investment Law and Arbitration* (Cameron May: 2004), p. 325.

Something similar is not unknown at the WTO. In dumping disputes, a case is sometimes brought by a government challenging the WTO-consistency of an antidumping duty imposed on a given enterprise by the defendant State's authorities. The litigation is State-State, as it always necessarily is at the WTO: in such an international proceeding, the sovereign claimant challenges the international validity or legality of domestic legislation or its application in light of treaty obligations, with a view to protecting the company affected, as in a traditional diplomatic protection case. This is not a bar, however, to the company affected pursuing at the same time a challenge against the antidumping measure before the domestic courts of the importing country under local law.[18]

In the *CME/Lauder* cases, the foreign investor could resort to forum shopping and initiate two parallel arbitrations because the U.S.–Czech BIT allows claims by an "indirect investor," a provision found also in BITs of many other countries, notably including those of Switzerland. To enhance protection, BITs cover not only direct ownership but also indirect control in an investment carried out through a company established in a third country, as was the case in the CME operation. This wider coverage was a reaction to the *Barcelona Traction* case, in which diplomatic protection by the country of shareholders was denied.[19] In that case, the World Court referenced the more complete protection that *ad hoc* treaties would afford, and that "invitation" did not fall on deaf ears. Thus, an indirect investor, such as Lauder, may invoke (and has invoked) the protection afforded by the U.S. treaty, notwithstanding the fact that his investment through CME was also protected by another treaty, in this case the BIT between the Netherlands and Czechoslovakia (and its successor State, the Czech Republic).[20]

---

18 Thus in *European Communities—Antidumping Duties on Malleable Cast Iron Tube or Pipe Fittings from Brazil*, Report of the Appellate Body, WT/DS219/AB/R, 22 July 2003, Brazil challenged various procedural steps and determinations by the EC antidumping authorities in a given procedure (Council Reg. EC No 1784/2000) as it had affected a Brazilian exporter subject to that investigation. A separate challenge to the European Court of Justice might have been envisaged. Indeed, in more than one case, while the governments of affected exporters were challenging the application of the U.S. antidumping provisions at the WTO, challenges under U.S. law against those same measures were pending before the U.S. Court of International Trade; *see US—Countervailing Duties on Certain Corrosion-Resistant Carbon Steel Flat Products from Germany*, Report of the Appellate Body, WT/DS 213/AB/R, 28 November 2002, p. 141.

19 *Barcelona Traction, Light and Power Company, Limited (Belgium v. Spain)* (New Application: 1962), Judgment of 5 February 1970, 1970 I.C.J. Reports 3.

20 Another example could be that of different investors in the same joint venture company suing separately the host country under different BITs, based on their different nationality. Minority shareholders, and not just the controlling shareholders, are indeed protected under most BITs.

In such a case, the attractiveness of forum shopping is increased by the different protection, both as to substance and procedure, that BITs may grant; BITs, though often similar, are by no means identical. The notion of "investor" and of "investment" is not uniform in all treaties. The issue further arises in practice because the kinds of disputes that can be brought to arbitration may differ. For instance, the BITs of the U.S. are rather more restrictive in that they protect only against breaches of the treaty itself,[21] while under other BITs contractual breaches under domestic law or other violations may also be covered.[22]

Conclusions

To conclude, what are the instruments available to prevent, sort out and resolve conflicts between separate proceedings, and awards, involving the same or connected investment disputes? Various distinctions have to be made in order to provide an answer, even if schematic.

1. A first distinction is between disputes concerning the same host country measure challenged under the same BIT, brought either (a) by different investors, or (b) by substantially the same or related investors. The first case (1.a) is rather frequent: the claims are separate. A factual relation is that the first decision in time (whether the measure is or is not in breach of the BIT) may influence the decisions of later cases, as a non-binding but possibly persuasive precedent. NAFTA investment disputes have given rise to the first situation, while the *CME/Lauder* situation is an example of the latter (1.b).

2. The solution depends also on the forum and its procedural rules on parallel proceedings, if any. Only NAFTA (now followed by the latest U.S. model BIT and some free trade agreements of the U.S.[23]) provides for consolidation of proceedings in both cases (1.a) and (1.b) above.[24] ICSID does not provide for consolidation, nor is its annulment proceeding of relevance to sort out

---

21 This is mentioned without taking into account any possible extension based on the "umbrella clause."

22 *See Salini & Italstrade v. Morocco*, Award on Jurisdiction, ICSID Case No. ARB/00/4, 23 July 2001.

23 *See* Barton Legum, "Lessons Learned from the NAFTA: The New Generation of US Investment Treaty Arbitration Provisions," 19 ICSID REVIEW—FOREIGN INVESTMENT LAW JOURNAL 344 (2004).

24 Art. 1126. A tribunal established under this Article may consolidate pending arbitral proceedings when it is satisfied that claims submitted to arbitration under Article 1120 have a question of law or fact in common and this is "in the interest of fair and efficient resolution of the claims." Consolidation has been invoked in some cases by host country defendants, but has generally been resisted by claimants. It has been denied in one instance, involving U.S. investors against Mexico, and granted in another (Canadian investors against the U.S.), both in 2005. For an evaluation, *see* John Knox, "The 2005 Activity of the NAFTA Tribunals," 100 AJIL 429 at 432–433 (2006).

conflicts between proceedings and awards such as those at issue here. In international commercial arbitration, in any cases conducted under different rules and in different countries, only voluntary consolidation is possible.[25] The exception of *lis pendens* is well known in domestic legal systems, where it is used to prevent the same litigation (based on identity of parties, issues and claims) being brought before different courts or being reopened. It may be available within one jurisdiction also to solve possible conflicts between proceedings introduced and pending at the same time before a court and an arbitral tribunal, or before different arbitral tribunals.[26]

International commercial arbitration is not, however, connected to a single legal system; its very transnational setting precludes a superior authority that could settle in a binding way with worldwide effect any conflict.[27] Even in public international law, as mentioned previously (though for partially different reasons), conflicts between different conventional fora cannot be settled by recourse to some hierarchic organ or mechanism if not agreed between the parties.[28] The conflict between arbitral and judicial proceedings can result in interference by state courts with arbitration: anti-suit injunctions by one judicial authority against another, judicial or arbitral, are not unknown, but may be ineffective or counterproductive. They may increase litigation instead of streamlining it.[29]

3. A further distinction has to be made between parallel proceedings, where the *lis pendens* principle has a limited application as mentioned above, and conflicts between awards. A real conflict may arise only when the parties in two cases are the same or closely connected, and the issue and claims are the same. There is a lack of authoritative mechanisms to solve conflicts both between awards

---

25 Consolidation had been proposed in the *Lauder* arbitration but rejected by the Czech Republic. This circumstance was raised against the host country when the Czech Republic challenged the later CME award in Stockholm as having been rendered against the principle of *lis pendens*.

26 In case of connected parties (such a parent company and a subsidiary), a conflict may be prevented if the principle that an arbitration clause of the parent may bind also the subsidiary is found to be applicable. *See* Marc Blessing, *Extension of the Scope of an Arbitration Clause to Non-Signatories*, ASA Series No 6, p. 151 (1994).

27 *See* Hans van Houtte, "Parallel Proceedings before State Courts and Arbitration Tribunals: Is there a Transnational 'lis alibi pendens' Exception in Arbitration or Jurisdiction Conventions?," *in Arbitral Tribunals or State Courts: Who Must Defer to Whom*, ASA Special Series No15, January 2001.

28 *See* Patrizia Vigni, "The Overlapping of Dispute Settlement Regimes: An Emerging Issue of International Law," 11 ITALIAN YEARBOOK INT'L L. 139 (2001).

29 *See* the ICSID Decision on jurisdiction in *SGS v. Pakistan*, ARB 01/13, 6 August 2003, following a final decision by the Supreme Court of Pakistan restraining SGS from pursuing the ICSID arbitration; *Cf.* M. Lau, "SGS SA v. Pakistan," 19 INT'L ARB. 179 (2003).

rendered in different settings (for instance, between ICSID and UNCITRAL awards) and different UNCITRAL awards.[30] It is up to domestic authorities of a given country, when asked to recognize conflicting awards, to solve the conflict between conflicting private awards applying appropriate domestic legal rules. These vary, but generally prevent at least double recovery.

30 Due respect must be paid, however, to Art. 54 of the ICSID Convention, which provides for "automatic" recognition of ICSID awards in all States parties to the Washington Convention.

CHAPTER 8

The Growing Diversity and Inconsistency in the IIA System

*Anna Joubin-Bret**

Commentary

My comments concern the substantive provisions of international investment agreements and the increased recourse to treaty-based investment dispute settlement.

Patrick Juillard highlights the issue of lack of coherence between awards rendered by international arbitral tribunals and explained it with the lack of coherence among the investment treaties that are at the basis of interpretation and application in investor-State dispute settlement cases. He specifically mentions the different approaches taken by the United States and Canada on the one hand and European countries on the other hand. Illustrations of this explanation can be found in the study on *Bilateral Investment Treaties 1995–2006: Trends in International Rule-making.*[1]

Since the 1990s, the number of bilateral investment treaties (BITs) negotiated has risen significantly, with 2,495 BITs completed by the end of 2005.[2] There is

---

* Senior Legal Advisor and Training and Technical Assistance Coordinator, International Arrangements Section, Division on Investment, Technology and Enterprise Development, UNCTAD. Email: anna.joubin-bret@unctad.org.

1 UNCTAD, *Bilateral Investment Treaties 1995–2006: Trends in International Rule-making* (United Nations Publication: 2006).

2 *See, e.g.*, UNCTAD, *Recent Developments in International Investment Agreements*, IIA Monitor, No. 2 (2006), (http://www.unctad.org/en/docs/webiteiia20067_en.pdf).

a trend toward increased sophistication and complexity in these BITs, in order to define better some key provisions and the dispute settlement mechanism; but this trend illustrates the treaty practice of few countries, mainly the United States, Canada and recently some other countries in the Western Hemisphere.

As Juillard pointed out, there is a difference in approach between the U.S. and Canada and the European countries that illustrates the lack of coherence in treaty practice. But the vast majority of BITs negotiated during the past decade have been patterned on the classical post-establishment investment protection model, and there has been very little evolution in their substantive content.

However—and here comes the interesting part—a detailed analysis of at least 500 of these treaties shows a clear lack of consistency among them, a lack of clarity in the provisions themselves and a different level of protection afforded to foreign investors, depending on the treaty.

Let me give an example:

The "fair and equitable treatment" standard is used in very different manners in BITs of the past decade, thereby creating major differences in its interpretation.

- Some BITs do not provide for fair and equitable treatment to investors.
- Some provide for fair and equitable treatment, full stop.
- Some refer to fair and equitable treatment in accordance with principles of international law, while others refer to international customary law.
- Some treaties refer to fair and equitable treatment as a part of the international minimum standard of the treatment of aliens.
- Others (quite a large number, actually) combine fair and equitable treatment with national treatment and most-favored-nation (MFN) treatment, mixing an absolute standard with two relative standards and referring to the relative standards as the comparators to assess whether an investor has been treated in a fair and equitable manner.

The same differences in approaches to—and hence in the substantive content of—provisions can be found as far as other substantive provisions are concerned, with very different wording indicating different understanding. (See Annex 8, *Novel Features in OECD Countries' Recent Investment Agreements.*)

An additional comment concerns the level of protection afforded by so-called "South-South" BITs, BITs concluded between two developing countries. During the past decade, there has been a significant increase in such BITs; but from a qualitative point of view, there has been very little evolution. In fact, South-South BITs tend to use more general language, allow for expansive interpretations (sometimes beyond what the contracting parties may have envisaged), and with some limitations in the level of protection that are not used by the same countries when negotiating in a North-South context.

Some countries use different approaches in their treaties concluded during the past ten years, depending on the respective treaty partners. This can create interesting MFN effects—and it explains, in my view, differences in interpretation by arbitral tribunals.

This situation requires that each arbitral award needs to stay within the strict limits of the facts of the case and particularly of the wording of the underlying treaty.

As regards the dramatic growth of investor-State disputes discussed by Karl P. Sauvant in his introductory chapter and in detail by Jeswald Salacuse, I would like to refer to *International Investment Agreements Monitors* published by the UNCTAD Secretariat in 2004 and November 2005. These document the increase in disputes and describe some responses; for example, a pilot course on managing investment disputes has been conducted by the UNCTAD Secretariat in October 2005 in cooperation with the OAS Secretariat and the Washington College of Law at American University. Further, two sessions of an Advanced Training Course on Managing Investment Disputes were held in Latin American countries in 2005 and 2006.[3]

---

3 For more information and to download IIA Monitors on investor-State dispute settlement, *see* website of UNCTAD (http://www.unctad.org/iia).

PART III

Promoting Consistency and Coherence

CHAPTER 9

Challenges Facing Investment Disputes: Reconsidering Dispute Resolution in International Investment Agreements

*Susan D. Franck**

Henry Ward Beecher once observed, "[l]aws and institutions are constantly tending to gravitate … [and] [l]ike clocks, they must be occasionally cleansed and wound up, and set to true time."[1] Beecher's comments reflect that, as law, societies and governments evolve, there are inevitably challenging transitional periods that require a re-examination of the foundations upon which a system was founded. Dispute resolution systems are no different. When they undergo fundamental growth, a re-consideration of the system's efficacy and utility can promote both its integrity and legitimacy to ensure it provides appropriate services to its stakeholders.[2]

International investment law has experienced a particular growth. While the number of bilateral investment treaties (BITs) expanded in the past four decades,[3]

---

* Assistant Professor of Law, University of Nebraska College of Law. Email: sfranck2@unl.edu.

1 Henry Beecher, *Life Thoughts, Gathered from the Extemporaneous Discourses of Henry Ward Beecher* (Philips, Sampson and Company: 1858), p. 129.

2 For the purposes of this chapter, the word "stakeholder" is intended to refer to those persons or entities either directly or indirectly affected by investment-related conflicts. Stakeholders most commonly take the form of home countries, host countries, investors and the citizens of host countries.

3 "Bilateral Investment Treaties in the mid-1990s," UNCTAD/ITE/IIT/7, Sales No. E.98.II.D.8 (1998) [Hereinafter UNCTAD 1998].

there has also been a more recent growth of disputes arising under these agreements.[4] Unsurprisingly, the escalation in the availability and use of the dispute resolution process has led to a teething period. The boundaries of States' previously untested international law obligations are being sketched; and parties and non-parties have both cheered and jeered the efficacy, efficiency and fairness of the system for resolving investment disputes. Given these developments, the system may have evolved to the point where it would be useful to clean the proverbial clock.

This chapter explores, on a preliminary basis, how "dispute systems design" could aid the dispute resolution process in investment treaties and permit stakeholders to make a more informed choice about their dispute resolution options. In other words, it considers whether the resolution of investment-treaty disputes might be re-designed to minimize the cost of conflict and maximize its beneficial byproducts. It first discusses the role of conflict and the design of dispute resolution systems. Given the potential insights from dispute systems design, it next assesses the unexplored or under-explored utility of dispute resolution options along the dispute resolution continuum. The chapter concludes by suggesting that a systematic greater consideration of dispute systems design is needed in order to diagnose accurately what the system requires and generate a set of principles to guide the design process. The hope of such an endeavor would be to develop an effective, efficient, fair and legitimate process for resolving investment treaty conflict.

Conflict, Dispute Systems Design and Investment Treaties

Reconsidering Conflict

In the classic formulation, conflict is like water. It occurs naturally and, although its structure can be transformed, it will continue to exist. Despite its social connotation, conflict is not *per se* good or evil. Rather, it is necessary for institutions to survive, thrive and develop. Nevertheless, extreme circumstances—whether a flood or a drought—can have serious repercussions on effective development.[5]

---

4 "Research Developments in International Investment Agreements," UNCTAD Research Notes, UNCTAD/WEB/ITE/IIT/2005/1, 30 August 2005 (http://www.unctad.org/sections/dite_dir/docs/webiteiit20051_en.pdf) [Hereinafter UNCTAD 2005a], pp. 1–3, 13–15; and "Investor-State Disputes Arising from Investment Treaties: A Review," UNCTAD/ITE/IIT/2005/4, (http://www.unctad.org/en/docs/iteiit20054_en.pdf) [Hereinafter UNCTAD 2005b], pp. 4–6.

5 Cathy Costantino and Christina Sickles Merchant, *Designing Conflict Management Systems: A Guide to Creating Productive and Healthy Organizations* (Jossey-Bass: 1996) [Hereinafter Costantino and Merchant 1996].

This applies with equal force in the context of international investment.[6] Conflict between investors and host country governments can occur when there is dissatisfaction with an interaction, process or result. Conflict can be a positive force, however. For investors, it can create opportunities for commercial innovations, and governments can use it as an occasion to adapt how they legislate and regulate those they govern.

When conflicts do arise, they can often be addressed informally without the threat of legal sanctions—often because of personal relationships, the ability to adapt business models or regulatory discretion that permits parties to address their underlying needs and interests. These informal processes can fail, however, and conflict can crystallize as a formal dispute. At either the formal or informal stage of conflict management, having a properly designed dispute resolution system can constructively draw conflict to the surface, channel its productive forces and avoid potentially more destructive by-products.

Approaches to Dispute Resolution

There is a robust literature dedicated to designing disputing systems to manage conflict.[7] This systematic approach to dispute resolution has been surprisingly effective in reducing the negative by-products of conflict. Part of using dispute systems design effectively, however, is to understand the different approaches to dispute resolution.

In their pioneering work on dispute systems design, Ury, Brett and Goldberg articulated a systematic way of looking at dispute resolution procedures. It identified three fundamental approaches parties can use to resolve disputes: (1) using *power* (in the form of violence, war, strikes) to impose a solution; (2) relying on *legal rights* to determine the merits of parties' positions; and (3) focusing on parties underlying *interests* to create mutually acceptable

---

6 J.G. Merrills, *International Dispute Settlement*, 4th Edition (Cambridge University Press: 2005) [Hereinafter Merrills 2005], p. 1.

7 Costantino and Merchant, 1996; Allan J. Stitt, *Alternative Dispute Resolution for Organizations: How to Design a System for Effective Conflict Resolution* (Wiley: 1998) [Hereinafter Stitt 1998]; William L. Ury, Jeanne M. Brett and Stephen B. Goldberg, *Getting Disputes Resolved: Designing Systems to Cut the Costs of Conflict* (Jossey-Bass: 1988) [Hereinafter Ury et al. 1988]; *see also* Susan D. Franck, "Integrating Investment Treaty Conflict and Dispute Systems Design," 92 MINN. L. REV. 161 (2007) (http://papers.ssrn.com/sol3/papers.cfm?abstract_id=969252) [Hereinafter Franck 2007].

solutions that meet parties' needs. Ury et al. expressed a general preference for interest-based dispute resolution as it tends to reduce transaction costs, improve satisfaction with the result and decrease the probability that disputes will recur. Nevertheless, they acknowledged that there are circumstances when resolving disputes on the basis of rights or power may be necessary—or simply desirable—particularly where uncertainty about the boundaries of parties' legal rights inhibits negotiation, or when a fundamental societal value is at stake.[8] Later scholars have suggested that many dispute resolution systems might start with power-based dispute resolution methods, but they eventually move toward a more rights-based methodology and ultimately evolve to interest-based conflict management.[9]

Having articulated these primary approaches to resolving disputes, Ury and his colleagues suggested that institutions create effective conflict management systems by engaging in: (1) diagnosis of the current system, (2) creation of a dispute resolution system according to practical principles,[10] (3) implementation

---

8 Ury et al. 1988, pp. 4–17.

9 Costantino and Merchant 1996, pp. 49–54.

10 Originally, Ury et al.'s principles related to: (1) focusing on interests to encourage the use of interest-based dispute resolution, (2) providing loop-backs to make procedures available that allow parties to return to lower-cost dispute resolution methods, (3) providing low-cost interest-based rights and power or rights-based procedures if the interest-based ones fail, (4) building in consultation before and after disputes, (5) arranging the procedures in a low-to-high cost sequence, and (6) providing the motivation, skills and resources necessary to ensure that the procedures are supported (Ury et al. 1988). Others have since developed different, but related, principles.

Costantino and Merchant, for example, use six different guiding principles including: (1) developing guidelines for whether ADR is appropriate, (2) tailoring the ADR process to the particular problem, (3) building-in preventative methods of ADR, (4) making sure that disputants have the necessary knowledge and skill to choose and use ADR, (5) creating ADR systems that are simple and easy to use and resolve the disputes early, at the lowest organizational level, with the least bureaucracy, and (5) allowing disputants to retain maximum control over choice of ADR method and the selection of a neutral. (Costantino and Merchant, 1996).

Shariff has continued this analysis in an international context and suggests analyzing issues of membership, scope, centralization, control and flexibility. He suggests these issues should be considered in conjunction with the following principles, namely that institutions should: (1) strive for inclusiveness by incorporating into their structure all stakeholders likely to be affected by the institution's work, (2) seek broad coverage of many related issues of interest to the institutional membership rather than being limited to a specific or narrow issue area, (3) seek depth of jurisdiction on individual issues areas such that they are empowered to take many kinds of action on issues within their mandate, (4) seek to build central sources of information gathering and dissemination, (5) decentralize and proliferate discussions and conversations among institutional members in multiple forums and forms, (6) vest control over decisions in those most interested and affected by them, and (7) embed opportunities for regular review of principal design decisions in order to integrate learning from experience (Khalil Z. Shariff, "Designing Institutions to Manage Conflict: Principles for the Problem Solving Organization," 8 HARV. NEGOT. L. REV. 113 (2003) [Hereinafter Shariff 2003]).

and approval of the new design, and (4) evaluation of the design and diffusion of the procedures to the rest of the institution.[11] Using these tools, Ury and his colleagues transformed distressed dispute systems—where parties resolved small conflicts by immediate resort to power struggles—into healthier systems. Their efforts focused on designing dispute systems that permit interest-based dispute resolution and, should these efforts fail, relied upon rights-based adjudication—and only used power as a last resort. This remodeling of the dispute resolution architecture had significant benefits. Not only was there an improvement in the result, institutional integrity and ongoing relationships, but there were also reduced transaction costs in terms of lost time, money, emotional investments and opportunities.[12]

Investment Treaties and Dispute Resolution Options

Given its success, Ury's conception of dispute systems design has grown beyond its original use in U.S. domestic law.[13] Commercial entities and government institutions increasingly resort to conflict management to establish a web of dispute settlement methods to meet the particular needs of the parties' and the dispute.[14] Even with its success in these other contexts, there has been surprisingly little literature that considers the utility of dispute resolution design for investment disputes arising from or related to bilateral investment treaties.

There does appear, however, to be a need for a more systematic consideration of dispute resolution options. Commentators question whether the dispute

11 Costantino and Merchant have a similar approach. They recommend first identifying and involving the appropriate stakeholders and then finding an appropriate dispute systems designer to conduct an organizational assessment. Next, create a design architecture to consider where, when and how to use ADR on the basis of identified principles. After training and educating the stakeholders on the use of the system, the program can then be implemented, evaluated and revised as necessary (Costantino and Merchant 1996).

12 Ury et al. 1988.

13 Lisa Bingham, "Mediation at Work: Transforming Workplace Conflict at the United States Postal Service," IBM Center for the Business of Government (2003) [Hereinafter Bingham 2003]; Peter Robinson, Arthur Pearlstein and Bernard Mayer, "DyADS: Encouraging 'Dynamic Adaptive Dispute Systems' in the Organized Workplace," 10 HARV. NEGOT. L. REV. 339 (2005) [Hereinafter Robinson et al. 2005].

14 Francisco Orrego Vicuña, "Arbitration in a New International Alternative Dispute Resolution System," 18(2) News from ICSID (2001) (http://www.worldbank.org/icsid/news/n-18-2-1.htm) [Hereinafter Vicuña 2001]; Shariff 2003.

resolution system is in crisis,[15] while UNCTAD suggests concerns "could be addressed by improving the dispute settlement procedures" and ICSID revises its arbitration procedures.[16] Presumably changes might reduce financial exposure (of investors and host countries), improve public perception of how investment disputes are managed and possibly prevent future disputes. Irrespective of whether change is needed or implemented, if the re-evaluation is done in a transparent and co-operative manner, the process of evaluating has the potential to strengthen the credibility and institutional legitimacy of the process of resolving investment disputes.

This section will first consider the historical roots and current dispute resolution systems embossed in investment. It will then consider various dispute resolution options and evaluate their unique costs and benefits. Thereafter, the future of managing investment treaty conflict can be assessed in light of the current structure and other potential options.

a. The Evolution of Investment Dispute Resolution

Recall how conflict scholars suggest that dispute systems evolved. Costantino and Merchant suggested early systems focus on power dynamics; but as they transform, there is a focus on judicialization and rights-based adjudication; and ultimately systems evolve toward a more interest-based conflict management system.[17] Likewise, Ury et al. observed that systems are often distressed where they resort to the use of force or power as a matter of course to resolve disputes; but when systems focus on rights and interests, they become more effective and efficient.[18] This is not dissimilar from the evolution of the resolution of investment treaty conflict.

---

15 Susan D. Franck, "The Legitimacy Crisis in Investment Treaty Arbitration: Privatizing Public International Law Through Inconsistent Decisions," 73 Fordham L. Rev. 1521 (2005) [Hereinafter Franck 2005a]; Charles H. Brower, II, "Structure, Legitimacy and NAFTA's Investment Chapter," 36 Vand. J. Transnat'l L. 37 (2003) [Hereinafter Brower 2003]; Ari Afilalo, "Towards a Common Law of International Investment: How NAFTA Chapter 11 Panels Should Solve Their Legitimacy Crisis," 17 Geo. Int'l Envtl. L. Rev. 51, 88 (2004) [Hereinafter Afilalo 2004].

16 UNCTAD 2005b, pp. 53–54; ICSID, "Possible Improvements of the Framework for ICSID Arbitration," (22 October 2004), (http://www.worldbank.org/icsid/highlights/improve-arb.pdf) [Hereinafter ICSID 2004]; ICSID "Suggested Changes to the ICSID Rules and Regulations: Working Paper of the ICSID Secretariat," (12 May 2005) (http://worldbank.org/icsid/highlights/052405-sgmanual.pdf) [Hereinafter ICSID 2005]; ICSID Convention Rules and Regulations, ICSID/15 (April 2006) (http://worldbank.org/icsid/basicdoc/basicdoc.htm) [Hereinafter ICSID Basic Documents 2006].

17 Costantino and Merchant 1996, pp. 49–54.

18 Ury et al. 1988.

Governments historically relied on the use of force and "gunboat diplomacy" to resolve investment disputes. Given the costs—and the failure of this process to encourage foreign investment—States evolved away from this model. Instead, they shifted to a focus on rights. In an effort to promote foreign investment and instill confidence in the stability of the investment environment, States promulgated treaties that created substantive obligations.[19] These efforts primarily began with so-called "Treaties of Friendship, Commerce and Navigation," and ultimately developed into more structured investment agreements (such as BITs) or other investment agreements (such as multilateral agreements, for example the North American Free Trade Agreement [NAFTA] and the Energy Charter Treaty [ECT]).[20] The treatification of rights and obligations marked a shift away from power-based dispute resolution and a move toward the development of a rights-based system of neutral adjudication. This sea change affected two main areas of international investment law. First, it offered a new, mutually agreed set of substantive rights to foreign investors for rights, including expropriation, national treatment and fair and equitable treatment.[21] Second, for the first time, States offered foreign investors a dispute resolution system that permitted investors to enforce directly their new substantive rights against a host government.[22]

This second aspect is noteworthy. It meant that investors were not simply granted an illusory promise—they were also granted a forum for redressing violations of their substantive rights. Prior to this development, when government conduct adversely affected their investment, investors were relegated to a series of somewhat unappealing dispute resolution options. These options often left investors to the political mercies of either their own or the host country government in deciding how (if at all) to address an investor's complaints. Specifically, investors might attempt to negotiate directly with government officials—but they would often be ignored. Likewise, they might lobby government officials in their home jurisdiction to either engage in diplomatic negotiations with the host country government or espouse a claim before the International Court of Justice—and they would often be ignored.

---

19 Franck 2005a, pp. 1525–1526; Kenneth J. Vandevelde, *United States Investment Treaties: Policy and Practice* (Kluwer: 1992), pp. 7–22.

20 M. Sornarajah, *International Law on Foreign Investment* (Cambridge University Press: 1994) [Hereinafter Sornarajah 1994], pp. 231–237; Guillermo A. Alvarez and William W. Park, "The New Face of Investment Arbitration: NAFTA Chapter 11," 28 Yale J. Int'l L. 365 (2003), pp. 366–367.

21 Giorgio Sacerdoti, "Bilateral Treaties and Multilateral Instruments on Investment Protection," *in Recueil Des Cours*, vol. 269 (Brill Academic: 1997) [Hereinafter Sacerdoti 1997].

22 Franck, 2005a, pp. 1541–1545.

Investors also might consider suing host country governments in their home country courts—but this was often fruitless where host countries had recourse to the defense of sovereign immunity.[23] In other cases, investors might have to address the conflict unilaterally. They might simply absorb the cost of adverse government action by either doing nothing or making a claim under their political risk insurance.[24] In extreme cases, investors might consider resorting to physical violence as a self-help remedy.[25]

The "arbitration addition" was revolutionary. It gave investors direct—and nearly unfettered—access to host country governments, which promised to resolve claims arising under investment treaties through what amounted to a sophisticated choice of forum clause.[26] Although there may be preconditions to arbitration,[27] once the conditions are satisfied, treaties typically give investors the right to make an election amongst pre-determined dispute resolution options to resolve a dispute.[28] Once an investor makes the election, the host country government must resolve the matter under the investor's preferred methodology. For example, investment treaties permit investors to choose among: (1) litigating disputes before the host country government's national courts, (2) arbitrating disputes before ICSID or (3) arbitrating disputes before an *ad hoc* tribunal that is bound by the UNCITRAL Arbitration Rules.[29]

Part of this "judicialization" of managing investment treaty conflict may be due in part to an evolution in the use of and expectations about international

---

23 Ian Brownlie, *Principles of Public International Law*, 6th Edition (Oxford University Press: 2003), pp. 677–715; Sacerdoti 1997, pp. 412–415.

24 Jeswald W. Salacuse, "Explanations for the Increased Recourse to Treaty-Based Investment Dispute Settlement: Resolving the Struggle of Life Against Form?" *in* Karl Sauvant, ed., *Coherence and Consistency in International Investment Law* (Oxford University Press: 2007); Franck 2005a, pp. 620–621.

25 The BBC has reported on a British-owned gold mining company in Ghana that allegedly engaged in a practice of shooting illegal miners on sight. Angus Stickler, *Ghana's Ruthless Corporate Gold Rush* (18 July 2006) (http://news.bbc.co.uk/1/hi/programmes/file_on_4/5190588.stm). The story does not indicate whether this action was part of the company's normal commercial operation or was, perhaps, a result of the government's failure to provide full protection and security.

26 Susan D. Franck, "The Nature and Enforcement of Investor Rights Under Investment Treaties: Do Investment Treaties Have A Bright Future?" 12 U.C. Davis J. Int'l L. & Pol'y 47 (2005) [Hereinafter Franck 2005b].

27 *See infra* section A(3)(b) for a discussion of the current system of resolving investment disputes, including the use of non-binding dispute resolution and other preconditions to arbitration.

28 Christopher Schreuer, "Traveling the BIT Route: Of Waiting Periods, Umbrella Clauses and Forks in the Road," 5 J. World Invest. and Trade 231 (2004) [Hereinafter Schreuer 2004].

29 This is one area in which investor-State and State-to-State dispute resolution diverge. State-to-State arbitration does not generally permit a government to make an election as to the final dispute resolution method.

arbitration. Historically, arbitration was not a forum where decision-makers were prized for their impartiality; rather, arbitrators' value came in their exercise of expert professional discretion, facility to create unique solutions, ability to recommend settlement terms to parties, capacity to act as an internal partisan during deliberations, or some combination of these factors.[30] Under these conditions, the popularity of international arbitration waxed and waned over time.[31] As it has evolved in an international context, however, arbitration has shifted away from a group of "grand old men" dispensing discretionary wisdom. Instead, in the twentieth century, the process has blossomed. Today, international arbitration technocrats focus on creating a fair and impartial process that results in an award based upon the factual record and independent legal analysis.[32]

Part of this judicialization may account for arbitration's success in the resolution of public and private international disputes. In the private international law context, as international trade has flourished, arbitration has become the primary vehicle for the resolution of international commercial disputes. Its popularity and success can be attributed to a variety of sources including its neutrality, speed, cost, confidentiality, ability to select an expert adjudicator and the ease of enforcement under the New York Convention for the Enforcement of Foreign Arbitral Awards.[33]

In the public international context, arbitration has also found fertile ground. It has caused politicians such as Benjamin Franklin to remark "When will mankind be convinced and agree to settle their difficulties by arbitration?"[34] and motivated William Jennings Bryan to attempt to prevent World War I by promoting treaties to foster the resolution of disputes by arbitration.[35] In the investment context, treaties such as the Jay Treaty (1794)[36] and Treaty of

---

30 Yves Dezalay and Bryant G. Garth, *Dealing in Virtue: International Commercial Arbitration and the Construction of Transnational Legal Order* (University of Chicago Press: 1996) [Hereinafter Dezalay and Garth 1996]; Laura J. Cooper, "*The Process of Process: The Historical Development of Procedure in Labor Arbitration*," *in Arbitration 2005: The Evolving World of Work*, Proceedings of the Fifty-Eighth Annual Meeting, National Academy of Arbitrators, Bureau of National Affairs, vol. 99 (2006).

31 David J. Bederman, *International Law Frameworks* (Foundation Press: 2001), p. 238.

32 Dezalay and Garth 1996; Catherine Rogers, "Fit and Function in Legal Ethics: Developing a Code of Conduct for International Arbitration," 23 Mich. J. Int'l L. 347, 353 (2002) [Hereinafter Rogers 2002].

33 Jan Paulsson, "Dispute Resolution," *in* Robert Pritchard, ed., *Economic Development, Foreign Investment, and the Law* (Kluwer: 1996), pp. 211–212 [Hereinafter Paulsson 1996].

34 Brainy Quotes (http://www.brainyquote.com/quotes/quotes/b/benjaminfr169230.html).

35 Michael Kazin, *A Godly Hero: The Life of William Jennings Bryan* (Knopf: 2006).

36 Treaty of Amity, Commerce, and Navigation, Nov. 19, 1794, U.S.–Gr. Brit., 8 Stat. 116 [hereinafter Jay Treaty].

Ghent (1814) began using arbitration for resolving investment-related disputes by giving creditors access to an international commission to press their claims. Article VI of the Jay Treaty, for example, provided British creditors with the right to adjudicate claims for compensation; and Article VII granted U.S. creditors similar rights against the British government.[37]

Where tribunals adhered to articulated rules and engaged in reasoned legal analysis, arbitration tended to be successful. Cases such as the *Alabama Claims* case, which involved Britain's responsibilities as a neutral during the U.S. Civil War, marked a watershed in the development of international arbitration. The U.S. and British governments established a five-member tribunal composed of nationals from the U.S., Britain, Italy, Switzerland and Brazil. Following a strict juridical procedure and the parties' agreed *lex specialis*, the tribunal issued a reasoned award against Britain, which was paid.[38] Nevertheless, where early "arbitrations" were not pure applications of the rule of law but a blend of juridical and diplomatic considerations, there were concerns that arbitration was an extension of gunboat diplomacy and/or imperialism.[39]

b. The Status Quo for Resolving Disputes

At present, treaties are individually negotiated between and among sovereign governments. Without a multilateral agreement on investment, there is no uniform treatment of dispute resolution methods in investment treaties.[40] Although there are exceptions, there does appear to be a general trend, however. In particular, the resolution of investor-State treaty claims occurs primarily through some type of non-binding dispute resolution and/or arbitration. State-to-State dispute resolution exhibits a similar pattern.[41]

---

37 Merrills, however, has suggested that this was not arbitration in its modern conception. Rather, it was "supposed to blend juridical with diplomatic considerations to produce (in effect) a negotiated settlement." (Merrills 2005, p. 92).

38 *Id.*, pp. 94, 105.

39 *Id.*, pp. 92–93; Bederman 2001, p. 238; Barton Legum, "The Innovation of Investor-State Arbitration under NAFTA," 43 Harv. Int'l L.J. 531, 534–535 (2002) [Hereinafter Legum 2002].

40 Scholarship in related to dispute resolution design could benefit from an empirical analysis of the most common dispute resolution systems (and most prominent exceptions) provided in BITs. It is, however, very difficult to analyze these matters. *See, e.g.*, Jason W. Yackee, *Conceptual Difficulties in the Empirical Study of Bilateral Investment Treaties* (May 2006) (http://papers.ssrn.com/sol3/papers.cfm?abstract_id=903680). Nevertheless, this chapter relies upon publicly available discussions about the content and scope of dispute resolution provisions.

41 At present, investment treaties contain a unique combination of both State-to-State dispute resolution and investor-State dispute resolution (Franck 2005b). While this chapter focuses primarily on investor-State

In the investor-State context, BITs generally call for the "amicable resolution" of disputes. Commentators suggest that this provision is intended to refer to the use of non-binding dispute resolution mechanisms such as negotiation, mediation or conciliation to resolve disputes.[42] NAFTA is slightly more precise, requiring that "disputing parties should first attempt to settle a claim through consultation or negotiation."[43] Nevertheless, while the ambiguity may have been intended to preserve flexibility and the informality of the dispute resolution process, the lack of guidance creates difficulties. The meaning of these obligations is not explained; particularly for legal cultures with different dispute resolution traditions, it fails to articulate mutual expectations about how the parties should begin to attempt to resolve their dispute. Moreover, there are no mandates particularizing what the process should entail and how it should be accomplished. This lack of a clear consent to procedural parameters and the lack of substantive obligations leave the "amiable resolution" methodology with little force. It is unclear what effect these provisions have had on the resolution of investment disputes.

Irrespective of whether this unparticularized form of dispute resolution is required or simply recommended,[44] there is usually a time limit on how long it must continue. Treaties generally require, for example, that after submitting a notice of dispute investors wait three or six months before filing an official request for arbitration. This suggests the waiting period is primarily intended to provide more of a "cooling off" period to permit parties to gather resources and develop an internal strategy for dispute resolution prior to the commencement of adjudication. By way of example, Schreuer observed that Article 11 of the German model BIT provides "Divergencies [sic] concerning investments ... should as far as possible be settled amicably .... If the divergency cannot be

---

arbitration, to complete a thorough analysis of the system, both aspects of the system deserve serious and individual consideration. (United Nations Centre on Transnational Corporations 1988, pp. 66–70; UNCTAD 1998, pp. 92–96; Rudolf Dolzer and Margrete Stevens, Bilateral Investment Treaties (Martinus Nihjoff Publishers: 1994) [Hereinafter Dolzer and Stevens 1994], pp. 119–120; "Dispute Settlement: General Topics, Dispute Settlement: Investor-State," UNCTAD/ITE/IIT/30 (2005). (http://www.unctad.org/en/docs/iteiit30_en.pdf) [Hereinafter UNCTAD 2003b], pp. 12–14.

42 Noah Rubins, "Comments to Jack C. Coe, Jr.'s Article on Conciliation," 21(4) Mealy's Int'l Arb. Rep. 21 (2006) [Hereinafter Rubins 2006]; Schreuer 2004.

43 NAFTA Art. 1118.

44 Generally, BITs do not require mandatory non-binding dispute resolution, such as conciliation or mediation. Where conciliation is present, it may be offered under established procedures (such as the UNCITRAL, ICSID Conciliation Rules or ICSID Additional Facility Conciliation Rules). Particularly in investor-State disputes, it is typically an option offered either prior to or instead of arbitration (Rubins 2006).

settled within six months of the date when it has been raised by one of the parties in dispute, it shall ... be submitted for arbitration."[45]

Beyond the question of whether or not BITs provide for non-particularized "amicable settlement" or conciliation, most BITs do provide that arbitration is the final method for resolving treaty-based claims. Given the textual prevalence of arbitration provisions in BITs—and the absence of less systematic reliance on other forms of dispute resolution—it appears that arbitration has historically been the presumed "best" mechanism for resolving investment disputes.[46] There has, unfortunately, been little (if any) systematic or empirical enquiry into whether this assumption is correct—and whether that assumption is equally applicable to investor-State and State-to-State dispute resolution. It is, for example, generally unclear whether drafters of model BITs or individual treaties analyzed the utility of "cooling off" periods, or whether arbitration is the appropriate default dispute resolution mechanism.[47] (See Annex 8, *Novel Features in OECD Countries' Recent Investment Agreements*.)

c. Understanding the Choice for Arbitration

In explaining the shift toward arbitration and the judicialization of treaty disputes, some suggest the phenomenon occurred because an "increasing number of capital importing countries came to realize that their self-interest was served by agreeing to arbitrate investment disputes."[48] There has, however, been little explanation or documentation of this phenomenon or why arbitration might also be in the interest of capital exporting countries. Moreover, there has not been a coherent explanation of why other dispute resolution systems were less desirable.

During the initial phase of BIT negotiation during the late 1950s and 1960s, there does not appear to have been a systematic analysis of why arbitration might be preferable to other dispute resolution options—either binding or

---

45 Schreuer 2004, p. 232.

46 Dolzer and Stevens 1994, pp. 119–122, 129–136.

47 The Australia–United States Free Trade Agreement, which did provide for State-to-State dispute resolution but failed to provide investors with a direct right to arbitrate disputes, is a notable exception to this general trend (Dodge 2006).

48 Alvarez and Park 2003, pp. 366–368.

non-binding.[49] Thus, an over-reliance on arbitration is hardly surprising. The "alternative dispute resolution revolution" did not start in the United States until the late 1970s and did not gain significant prominence until the 1980s and 1990s; and the dispute systems design movement was in its infancy during the late 1980s and early 1990s.[50] It has taken even longer for the benefits of alternative dispute resolution and dispute resolution design to find a home across the Atlantic.[51] It is curious, however, that even during the surge of treaty drafting during the 1990s—after these two movements had gained significant ground—there was little (if any) consideration for why arbitration was still the preferred—let alone appropriate—method for resolving disputes.

There are undoubtedly a variety of explanations for this phenomenon. First, as the system of resolving investment treaty claims remained relatively untested during this time, there was little need to re-evaluate the status quo. In other words, changes were unnecessary as there was no visible evidence of dysfunction. Second, as countries continued to draft model BITs and negotiate BITs on that basis, there was likely institutional momentum to stick to the traditionally approved format. Revisions or re-negotiation would require explanations at various levels of government. Expending energy to make changes may not have been worth the effort, particularly where treaties appeared to proffer the promised rewards—namely foreign investment—and the disuse of the arbitration system meant there were minimal costs. Third, practical considerations may have played a role. Although the business community may have started to use interest-based mechanisms to resolve business to business disputes, they may have been unwilling to endorse interest-based dispute resolution models in the investor-State context without evidence of their successful implementation. Similarly, to the extent that non-binding, interest-based dispute resolution mechanisms like mediation and negotiation might exclude the public, non-governmental organizations may not have been interested in advocating for these dispute resolution processes.

Perhaps more importantly, treaty drafters may have used arbitration because it was associated with tried and tested institutions. It was seen as working well

---

49 UNCTAD 1998; Dolzer and Stevens 1994.

50 Jean R. Sternlight, "ADR is Here: Preliminary Reflections on Where it Fits in a System of Justice," 3 NEV. L. J. 289 (2003) [Hereinafter Sternlight 2003].

51 David J.A. Cairns, "Mediating International Commercial Disputes: Differences in U.S. and European Approaches," 60 OCT. DISP. RESOL. J. 62 (2005) [Hereinafter Cairns 2005]; Vicuña 2001.

and had the patina of international legitimacy. Thomas Franck[52] has explained that international institutions can become legitimate by affiliating with the proven institutions of international law's past.[53] The Iran–U.S. Claims Tribunal was able to resolve disputes between foreign investors and host governments using a process that adhered to the rule of law and—with one exception[54]—did not require stakeholders to resort to physical violence to settle complaints.[55] Meanwhile, the ICSID Convention created an institution designed to resolve disputes through arbitration. More importantly, international commercial arbitration was gaining steam with success of the New York Convention and many countries adopting progressive arbitration laws based upon the 1985 UNCITRAL Model Law on International Commercial Arbitration. Arbitration seemed to be working. In contrast to cases resolved at the International Court of Justice,[56] investment disputes were getting resolved efficiently. Sophisticated counsel was available to make effective arguments. Parties were complying with awards, and streamlined enforcement mechanisms were readily available. In these circumstances, it was not unreasonable to desire the continuation of a process that appeared to have some success in achieving practical results.

Beyond the institutional legitimacy, there are practical reasons that arbitration was seen as effective. International commercial arbitration has certain systematic efficiencies in its model that could be grafted onto the investment treaty model. For instance, the neutrality of international arbitration permits the independent and impartial resolution of disputes. It escapes the perception of unfair local advantage or outright partiality of the court system in favor of the host government. In addition, rather than engaging in lengthy litigation before a national or international court, arbitration was presumed to save time, money and other internal resources. Although they outsource authority to resolve the dispute, parties retain a degree of control over the process of resolving

---

52 The author of this essay is unrelated to Professor Franck.

53 Thomas M. Franck, *The Power of Legitimacy Among Nations* (Oxford University Press: 1990).

54 Memorandum Re: Challenge to Arbitrators Kashani and Shafeifei by the Government of the United States of America, 7 IRAN U.S.-CL. TRIB. REP. 281, 292 (1986). One Iranian judge was quoted as saying: "If Mangard ever dares to enter the tribunal chamber again, either his corpse or my corpse will leave it rolling down the stairs." *Iranian Judge Threatens A Swede at The Hague*, N.Y. TIMES, Sept. 7, 1984, at A5. Subsequently, the Tribunal's President suspended all tribunal proceedings. *U.S.-Iran Arbitration Suspended at The Hague*, N.Y. TIMES, Sept. 20, 1984, at A9.

55 Charles N. Brower, *The Iran- United States Claims Tribunal* (Springer: 1998).

56 *See generally* F. A. Mann, "Foreign Investment in the International Court of Justice: the ELSI Case," 86 AM. J. INT'L L. 92 (1992); Case Concerning Eletronica Sicula, S.p.A (ELSI), *United States of America v. Italy*, 1989, I.C.J. Reports 4.

the conflict. Not only can they select their decision-makers, but they can also tailor the arbitration process to meet their needs and the peculiarities of a specific investment dispute. There were other unique aspects of arbitration that made it a desirable alternative to litigation before national or international courts. In particular, arbitration was confidential and would permit parties to preserve sensitive commercial data, prevent adverse publicity and preserve ongoing relationships. Arbitration also had a streamlined enforcement mechanism, which made it preferable to having to enforce a judgment through the U.N. Security Council or needing to engage in time-consuming national court litigation to enforce foreign court judgments.[57] Ultimately, investment treaty arbitration has been seen to resolve disputes and, after exhausting contested awards through the normal legal process, parties have generally paid awards.

Nevertheless, one wonders whether a different dispute resolution system would be more efficient, effective and better address concerns of stakeholders. It would, however, be imprudent to presume a different system would be superior to the current framework without a diagnosis of the system, consideration of the dispute design and an assessment of the costs and benefits. The implications are not insignificant. While there have been concerns about transparency, consistency, fairness and regulatory authority, choosing a different system for resolving disputes may ameliorate the problems or perhaps simply lead the issues to manifest themselves in a different fashion. The goal should be to purify the waters of investment-related conflict rather than contaminating the water supply.

The use of dispute systems design to diagnose and assess the current system's dispute resolution needs may be one way to begin this process. Future work can and should consider the specific application of dispute systems design for the resolution of investment treaty conflict. It might, for example, consider how to do a conflict assessment, analyze existing patterns of disputing and consider what are the appropriate principles upon which a system should be based.[58] In connection with this, this chapter turns to a systematic consideration of different options for resolving investment treaty conflict and how they are used (if at all) to manage conflict effectively.

---

57 Recently, however, there has been concern as to the enforceability of investment treaty awards, particularly in the context of the claims against Argentina; *see, e.g.*, Osvaldo J. Marzoti, "Enforcement of Treaty Awards and National Constitutions (the *Argentinean Cases*)," 7 Bus. L. Int'l 226 (2006).

58 Franck 2007.

The Range of Options: Appropriate Dispute Resolution and the Dispute Resolution Continuum

It is essential to place the resolution of investment disputes in its wider context. "The settlement of any dispute, not just investment disputes, requires the adoption of the most speedy, informal, amicable and inexpensive method available."[59] Finding the most "appropriate" mechanism for resolving specific categories of types of investment disputes, however, can be challenging. Nevertheless, there are decided benefits to tailoring a design to the unique needs of the particular system. These benefits might include the promotion of democratic values, minimizing resources exerted on dispute resolution, increasing productivity, increasing satisfaction with outcomes, decreasing the recurrence of disputes and improving public relations.[60] Finding the appropriate dispute resolution is therefore a matter of some importance.

Historically, the term "ADR" has been viewed as "alternative dispute resolution." There has, unfortunately, been confusion about what that term means. In a domestic context, "alternative dispute resolution" has tended to mean any dispute resolution process that occurs outside national courts; but because of its prevalence in the international context, there has been some debate as to whether arbitration was truly "alternative" dispute resolution.[61] While this is an interesting intellectual debate, it is a distraction from the fundamental need to provide for the appropriate and effective resolution of investment disputes. Therefore, for present purposes, "ADR" is defined as an *appropriate* dispute resolution mechanism. In an effort to facilitate the creation of a dispute resolution system that functions effectively and meets systemic needs for managing conflict, the purpose of this section is to consider the spectrum of mechanisms—whether non-binding, binding or hybrids—that are available to stakeholders for resolving investment disputes.

Beyond the problem of defining ADR, there is also a confusion that persists in many jurisdictions and different cultures as to the meaning of specific ADR alternatives. This lack of a common understanding and mutual expectations

---

59 UNCTAD 2003b, p. 11.

60 Richard C. Reuben, "Democracy and Dispute Resolution: Systems Design and the New Workplace," 10 Harv. Negot. L. Rev. 11 (2005) [Hereinafter Rueben 2005]; CPR Institute for Dispute Resolution, *Resource Book For Managing Employment Disputes* (2004); Ury et al. 1998.

61 Paulsson 1996, p. 210; Vicuña 2001; Ucheora Onwuamaegbu, "The Role of ADR in Investor-State Dispute Settlement: The ICSID Experience," 2(2) *News from ICSID*, 12 (2005) (http://www.worldbank.org/icsid/news/news_22-2.pdf) [Hereinafter Onwuamaegbu 2005].

has significant implications.[62] For example, Amy Cohen eloquently explains: "Mediation changes as it travels; its instantiation anywhere is subject to local variation and intervention as it makes contact with state and customary law, politics, and social struggles."[63] Given different cultural understandings and the potential for mismatched expectations at a sensitive juncture in the dispute resolution process, it is vital to create a common lexicon. Establishing this framework will assist in framing future analysis and debate, foster an appreciation for variations in the approaches and permit stakeholders to make informed choices.

Theoretically, there are a variety of options for resolving investment treated disputes. The classic formulation in dispute resolution circles is that the "forum [should] fit the fuss."[64] In order to make an informed choice of the appropriate of the design of a dispute resolution system, it is useful to consider the options along the dispute resolution continuum that might be employed individually or in combination to resolve investment-related disputes. Once the spectrum of choices is clear, designing dispute systems is more efficient.[65]

Stressing that "arbitration is only one of many ADR choices," Costantino and Merchant identify six broad categories of ADR options: preventative, negotiated, facilitative, fact-finding, advisory and imposed ADR.[66] Each category involves varying levels of third-party intervention, with their own distinct costs and benefits; and each category can be implemented at different junctures. In an effort to create a common framework for discussing ADR in the context of investment law, this chapter adopts Costantino and Merchant's categories for understanding ADR mechanisms.[67] The breadth and generality of the categories promote understanding of the primary nature of the mechanism without being hindered by the particularities of the distinct mechanisms within the categories. Once the fundamental character of the process is defined,

---

62 Roger Fisher and William Ury, *Getting to Yes: Negotiating Agreement Without Giving In* (Houghton Mifflin Company: 1981), p. 34.

63 Amy J. Cohen, "Debating the Globalization of U.S. Mediation: Politics, Power, and Practice in Nepal," 11 Harv. Negot. L. Rev. 295, 296 (2006).

64 Frank E.A. Sander and Stephen Goldberg, "Fitting the Forum to the Fuss: A User-Friendly Guide to Selecting an ADR Procedure," 10 Negot. J. 49 (1994) [Hereinafter Sander and Goldberg 1994].

65 Costantino and Merchant 1996; Ury et al. 1988.

66 Costantino and Merchant 1996, pp. 37–41.

67 In Ury et al.'s conception of interest, rights and power-based dispute design system, the first five methods are likely to be more interest-based and Imposed ADR is likely to involve rights-based adjudication. Power-based resolution, as previously defined, can take the form of war, violence, strikes, or physical aggression (Ury et al. 1988).

it then identifies primary dispute resolution processes in the category. The description of the various processes is by no means exhaustive. While there will be variations and permutations, articulating the common framework—and beginning to assess the costs and benefits of its elements—is a useful place from which to start.

Preventative ADR

Preventative ADR mechanisms are designed to preempt disputes. Recognizing that conflict is an inevitable aspect of human interactions, preventative ADR methods do not try to stop conflict from arising; rather they channel potential areas of disagreements into a problem-solving arena in order to avoid the crystallization and escalation of disputes. In the context of investment disputes, this might take various forms, such as negotiated rule making, the use of good offices to engage in peer-review of the dispute or the use of an ombudsperson.[68]

a. The Benefits of Negotiated Rulemaking and Good Offices

Encouraging host country governments to participate in negotiated rulemaking in domestic administrative law can mitigate potential international law conflicts at the outset rather than waiting until the harmful effects of the regulation are apparent. There is a rich literature considering the value of negotiated rule making in the United States.[69] Undoubtedly, there would be up-front costs related to the process of creating consensus, selecting the right types of areas for negotiated rulemaking and addressing concerns about degree of public participation. Nevertheless, proactively using negotiated rulemaking to prevent disputes could have significant benefits. For instance, it could lead to: the prevention of subsequent disputes, the modeling good government, an improvement in the quality of government regulation, the promotion of democratic values and the enhancement of governmental legitimacy.[70]

---

68 There are also other forms of preventative ADR partnering and joint problem solving. These, however, may work best in a more commercial context.

69 Cary Conglianese, "Assessing Consensus: The Promise and Performance of Negotiated Rulemaking," 46 DUKE L.J. 1255 (1997) [Hereinafter Conglianese 1997]; Lawrence Susskind and Gerard McMahon, "The Theory and Practice of Negotiated Rulemaking," 3 YALE J. ON REG. 133 (1985) [Hereinafter Susskind and McMahon 1985].

70 Jody Freeman and Laura I. Langbein, "Regulatory Negotiation and the Legitimacy Benefit," 9 N.Y.U. ENVTL L.J. 60 (2000) [Hereinafter Freeman and Langbein 2000].

Likewise, using "good offices" might have merit. In this instance, a person in a position of authority and prestige could facilitate communications between the parties and provide peer-review to prevent disputes from arising or escalating.[71] Although such preventive diplomacy has achieved mixed results in the public international law context, it remains a potential tool in the toolbox for governments seeking to maximize the utility of the design of their dispute resolution system. UNCTAD has referenced the possibility of using "good offices," although it has not analyzed the issue systematically.[72] Interestingly, UNCTAD appears to view "good offices" as a step to be taken only after negotiated ADR mechanisms fail; but this should not prevent it from being used as a preventative mechanism to check the escalation of disputes and improve communication *ex ante*.

b. Opportunities with Ombuds

Ombuds might also be used to manage conflict and prevent the escalation of disputes. Ombuds have their roots in China, Egypt and Germanic tribes, but were used most prominently in connection with democratic governance in Sweden, where they provided a bridge between private individuals and the government. More recently, ombuds have been used successfully in the United Kingdom, United States and the European Union, as well as in corporate contexts.[73]

An ombudsperson is an official, appointed either by a public or private institution, whose fundamental function is to remain impartial and receive complaints and questions from a defined constituency about issues within the ombuds' express jurisdiction. The ombuds' mandate is to resolve complaints at an early stage. To carry out this method, ombudspersons have many tools. They might direct constituents to other processes or opportunities that may resolve the issues, or, they may raise the problem at an appropriate level within the organization.[74] In its classic definition, the ombudsperson is an "officer appointed by the legislature to handle complaints against administrative and

---

71 Linda C. Reif, "Conciliation as a Mechanism for the Resolution of International Economic and Business Disputes," 14 Fordham Int'l L.J. 578 (1991) [Hereinafter Reif 1991]; Bederman 2001, p. 236.

72 UNCTAD 2003b, pp. 11–12.

73 Harold J. Krent, "Federal Agency Ombuds: The Costs, Benefits and Countenance of Confidentiality," 52 Admin. L. Rev. 17 (2000) [Hereinafter Krent 2000]; Vicuña 2001; Philip J. Harter, "Ombuds—A Voice for the People," Disp. Resol. Mag. (Winter 2005), p. 5 [Hereinafter Harter 2005].

74 Ombuds may also have authority to mediate disputes. By and large, they resolve conflict through a hybrid process of investigation and conciliation in order to prevent the escalation of disputes.

judicial action," serving as a watchdog over those actions while exercising independence, expertise, impartiality, accessibility, and powers of persuasion rather than control.[75] While they generally lack the power to make binding decisions, order administrative conduct or reverse administrative action, their capacity to make recommendations and to publicize their findings has an impact. An ombudsperson's "authority and influence derive from the fact that he is appointed by and reports to one of the principal organs of state, usually either the parliament or the chief executive."[76] Ultimately, an ombudpersons' mandate is not to protect the organization's reputation. Rather, his or her objective is to promote reasoned, fair and ethical conduct in the organization and to take a view based upon integrity, legality and principle.[77]

The use of ombuds has a level of built-in acceptance and confidence in both the governmental and the corporate context. They first have the benefit of history and a legacy of authority. Because ombuds are associated with a practice that has a long, multi-cultural tradition that has been effective in many contexts, this pedigree promotes symbolic validation, which lends the process legitimacy.[78] Ombuds offices have the benefit of equality, where those who are affected by a conflict have a place to give voice to their concerns. Unlike an investor's unilateral right to bring claims under a treaty, investors, citizens and governmental officials could have theoretical access to the ombuds office for the filing of complaints.[79]

Beyond these more theoretical benefits, there are also practical benefits of using ombudspersons to prevent disputes. For parties with investment-related concerns, an ombuds office offers a clear line of authority for receiving complaints and lowers the cost of raising issues. This has the benefit of permitting smaller investors or parties with smaller conflicts to have their concerns heard and addressed. In essence, it facilitates access to justice and decreases the stigma of announcing and quickly resolving disputes. While theoretically it could increase the number of recorded disputes, presumably this would not mean the number of disputes actually increased but, rather, there would be an increase in reporting problems. Commentators have noted that "submitting an investment dispute to arbitration under a treaty can decrease the chances of

---

75 Shirley A. Wiegland, "A Just and Lasting Peace: Supplanting Mediation with the Ombuds Model," 12 OHIO ST. J. ON DISP. RESOL. 95, 96 (1996) [Hereinafter Wiegland 1996].

76 Krent 2000.

77 Wiegland 1996.

78 Franck 1990, pp. 91–110.

79 Wiegland 1996.

amicable resolution of the dispute because settlement of a treaty claim requires approval of additional decision-makers in the government and therefore complicates any resolution."[80] Ombuds are a natural antidote to this. Rather than letting problems fester and reach the boiling point, an ombudsperson provides an early opportunity to intervene and improve the situation. In other words, there is a formal process that allows parties to address issues informally before ratcheting up the costs and formality of conflict resolution.

As there is often too little information and problems with disbursing the available information at the beginning of a conflict, commentators have suggested that the prospects of early settlement are often "dim"—particularly when multiple agencies are involved.[81] Ombuds, however, could provide an antidote to this problem. Because an ombudsperson is an independent part of the host country government, the office would be in a position to know the agencies, entities or people whose involvement would be needed to resolve matters.

The requirement, for example in an investment treaty, to establish an ombuds office would require governments to determine in advance who would have institutional responsibility for resolving investment-based disputes and with whom ombuds should liaise. Using ombudspersons as an information conduit would create an opportunity to manage conflicts more effectively when they do arise and minimize the information vacuum in order to clear the way for early (or easier) dispute resolution. As "the best chance to resolve a dispute between a foreign investor and a government agency is likely before the investment dispute becomes a dispute under an investment treaty,"[82] ombuds provide a unique opportunity to catch and resolve conflict before a dispute is crystallized. This is a useful alternative to making a formal claim and dedicating institutional resources to win and/or litigate to the end, irrespective of the cost.

An ombuds office could also serve as a conflict barometer. It would alert governments to where they are most likely to encounter difficulties; with that information, they would be in a position to make more informed and rational

---

80 Barton Legum, "The Difficulties of Conciliation on Investment Treaty Cases: A Comment on Professor Jack C. Coe's 'Towards a Complementary Use of Conciliation in Investor-State Disputes—A Preliminary Sketch,'" 21(4) Mealy's Int'l Arb. Rep. 23 (2006) [Hereinafter Legum 2006]; Jack J. Coe, Jr., "Toward a Complementary Use of Conciliation in Investor-State Disputes—A Preliminary Sketch," 12 U.S. Davis J. Int'l L. and Pol'y 7 (2005) [Hereinafter Coe 2005].

81 Legum 2006.

82 Legum 2006.

legislative and regulatory choices. Moreover, ombuds can enhance the image and legitimacy of government agencies. While it could not make or change policy, the presence of an ombuds office can encourage government officials to support their decisions with sufficient reasoning. In addition, providing the regulated public with a direct form of communication and feedback can promote democratic values and institutional legitimacy.[83]

c. *Challenges with Preventative Dispute Resolution*

The same benefits, however, could create problems for governments, investors and other interested parties. All of these types of Preventative ADR will share common difficulties. Because they are not as frequently used, parties may be hesitant to try them. In the case of negotiated rulemaking or good offices, stakeholders may be unwilling to consider these options until a "mutually hurting stalemate" exists. In other words, until the difficulties with the existing system reach a point that is unbearable for all stakeholders, the system may not be ripe for the use of these options.[84]

Similarly, governments may be unfamiliar with the process of using ombudspersons. Some governments may find it alien and undesirable. Beyond the inertia of continuing with the status quo, governments may be unwilling to expend the resources necessary to create such an office. They may believe, for example, that there are an insufficient number of investment-related conflicts to justify the establishment of an office. Moreover, the creation of an ombuds office would front-load the process of managing disputes by requiring the creation of structures. Should governments fail to see the down-stream, long-term benefits of the creation of an ombuds office, they may decide the cost is not worth the benefit.

There may also be other difficulties. As ombudspersons' persuasive authority comes from autonomy, expertise, neutrality and status, the office's effectiveness can be diminished when any of these essential characters are lacking or impaired. Should an ombuds' affiliation with the government be perceived to compromise independence, people may be less willing to seek his or her assistance.

---

83 Krent 2000.

84 Andrea Schneider, "The Day After Tomorrow: What Happens Once A Middle East Peace Treaty Is Signed?" 6 Nev. L.J. 401 (2006); I. William Zartman, "Timing and Ripeness," *in* Andrea Kupfer Schneider and Christopher Honeyman, eds., *The Negotiator's Fieldbook: The Desk Reference For The Experienced Negotiator* (ABA Section of Dispute Resolution: 2006).

Ombuds should not be a mouthpiece of the government that institutionalizes the status quo while ignoring the concerns of other stakeholders.[85] In the past, this has been one of the primary obstacles to using ombuds effectively.[86] To ensure proper neutrality and the ability to perform their core functions, any ombuds office would need physical as well as fiscal independence from any one constituency to minimize the appearance of bias.[87]

There may also be challenges related to confidentiality. There are disagreements about whether communications to ombuds are privileged and whether confidentiality is appropriate. Certain stakeholders may assert that the transparency of the ombuds process is critical to promote settlements that are in the public interest. Meanwhile, other stakeholders might suggest confidentiality is fundamental to an effective process. A lack of confidentiality may create difficulties in maintaining the perception of an ombud's neutrality; and it may also inhibit the full and frank disclosure of problems, which might chill the use of the ombuds and frustrate a primary reason for its creation. One can imagine an investor with a long-term regulatory relationship with a government who would be concerned about government reprisals for the reporting of problems.[88]

These possible concerns are not trivial. Consideration should be given to ways to address and neutralize these concerns to strike an appropriate balance. Although the devil would undoubtedly be in the details, the promise of an ombuds office should not be overlooked. The flexibility, distinct capacities and institutional position provides a unique opportunity to constructively resolve conflict. Ultimately, these preventative ADR methods hold the important promise of preventing disputes from crystallizing and allowing parties to allocate their resources effectively.

Negotiated ADR

Negotiated ADR involves communications between the parties to a conflict; the result of such discussions will be either to create a mutually acceptable resolution or terminate the process, presumably to pursue other ADR methods.

---

85 Wiegland 1996.

86 *Id.*

87 If an ombud serves at the whim of a government with little job security, for example, he or she may be tempted to forgo well-deserved criticism of administrative actions.

88 Krent 2000.

All negotiations are not the same, however. Even if one agrees to negotiate, parties can use different approaches to negotiation, which creates variations in the negotiation process. Parties tend to adversarial bargaining,[89] interest-based bargaining,[90] or a combination of these approaches[91] during the negotiation process. In adversarial bargaining, parties focus on legal rights, tactical positions, gaming the process, and the use of power to distribute limited resources. Typically, this means a party will make extreme offers, offer few concessions, make threats, and distort information in an effort to be the "winner" in what is typically a win-lose scenario.[92] In the interest-based approach, parties focus on meeting their underlying needs and objectives in order to create joint solutions that fairly address their mutual interests. This approach tends to require parties to separate people from the problem, focus on underlying interests, generating a variety of options before deciding what to do, and making decisions based upon objective criteria.[93]

Irrespective of their theoretical approach, in the context of investment disputes parties might use different types of negotiated ADR. The parties to the dispute may use, for example, either direct or indirect forms of negotiation.

a. The Utility of Indirect Negotiation

Diplomacy is a form of indirect negotiation. In this process, investors might encourage their home government to engage in private diplomatic discussions with the host country to resolve their underlying complaints about host government behavior. These government-to-government negotiations may increase investors' leverage. Having their home government to advocate on their behalf brings political clout to the dispute resolution table and emphasizes

---

89 This process has also been referred to in the literature as distributional or positional bargaining (Carrie J. Menkel-Meadow, Lela Porter Love and Andrea Kupfer Schneider, *Mediation: Practice, Policy and Ethics* (2006) [Hereinafter Menkel-Meadow et al. 2006], pp. 39–51).

90 This process is also referred to as problem-solving, integrative bargaining or principled bargaining; *Id.*

91 There is a broad literature on negotiation style. *See, e.g.*, G. Richard Shell, *Bargaining for Advantage: Negotiation Strategies for Reasonable People* (Penguin: 1999); Martin A. Rogoff, "The Obligation to Negotiate in International Law: Rules and Realities," 16 Mich. J. Int'l L. 141 (1994) [Hereinafter Rogoff 1994]; Chris Guthrie, "Panacea or Pandora's Box?: The Cost of Options in Negotiation," 88 Iowa L. Rev. 601 (2003) [Hereinafter Guthrie 2003]. As a thorough discussion of this important point is beyond the scope of this project, this chapter only provides a cursory overview of the literature.

92 Russell Korobkin, "A Positive Theory of Legal Negotiation," 88 Geo. L.J. 1789 (2000) [Hereinafter Korobkin 2000].

93 Fisher and Ury 1981; Carrie J. Menkel-Meadow, "Toward Another View of Legal Negotiation: The Structure of Problem Solving," 31 UCLA L. Rev. 754 (1984) [Hereinafter Menkel-Meadow 1984].

the importance of the claim. Such an approach may also expand the range of potential solutions by introducing the resources of another party into the dispute resolution process. Nevertheless, there are drawbacks. First, an investor's home government may have little interest in pursuing an investor's claim; and investors will have expended resources for a minimal return. Between 1960 and 1974, for example, the United Nations identified 875 distinct governmental takings of foreign property in 62 countries, but it unclear whether investors' home governments ever pursued these claims.[94] Second, should a government decide to espouse an investor's claim, investors run the risk of having their disputes inextricably intertwined with larger inter-governmental objectives. As a result, little may come from the negotiation. Third, even if negotiations prove successful, investors may find themselves subject to a unsatisfactory resolution over which they had little input or control and which does not address their needs. Fourth, there may be difficulties with enforcement of any diplomatic agreement.

b. The Benefits of Direct Negotiation

An investor also might engage in direct negotiations with a host country government. This option gives more direct control over the process, management and result of the dispute resolution process. It also provides an opportunity to create a solution that is most likely to address the parties' unique needs and interests. Investors and the host country government may find negotiation useful in the case of infrastructure projects, in which protracted dispute resolution may create alienation in a critical on-going relationship; or where there is a desire to minimize the time and cost allocated to resolving small conflicts.

In the context of disputes being resolved primarily by arbitration, there is some anecdotal evidence suggesting that parties have used direct negotiations successfully. ICSID's website suggests that several ICSID cases concluded with settlement agreements. Some of these are BIT claims, such as *AES Summit Generation v. Hungary*; and at least two BIT-based claims, *Lemire v. Ukraine* and *Goetz v. Burundi*, have awards embodying settlement agreements.[95] Interestingly, several of these cases have resulted in settlement after a jurisdictional decision.[96] Meanwhile, counsel for ICSID has also noted that

94 Jeswald W. Salacuse, "BIT by BIT: The Growth of Bilateral Investment Treaties and Their Impact on Foreign Investment in Developing Countries," 24 Int'l Law. 655, 659 (1990) [Hereinafter Salacuse 1990].

95 ICSID List of Pending and Concluded Cases 2006 (http://www.icsid.org).

96 ICSID does not have a publicly available list of investment treaty cases that have resulted in settlement. A cursory analysis of ICSID's website and other publicly available awards, however, indicates that, after a

there are an "increasing percentage of ICSID [arbitration] cases that are discontinued following settlement."[97] There have also been negotiated settlements in the context of *ad hoc* arbitration, such as in *Ethyl Corp. v. Canada*, which also settled after a jurisdictional award.[98]

While this anecdotal evidence suggests negotiation has some promise for resolving investment treaty conflict, there are several limitations. First, there is little empirical evidence systematically analyzing the role that direct or indirect negotiation plays in the resolution of investment disputes. It is therefore unclear to what extent this anecdotal information is generalizable to a larger population of investment disputes. Indeed, there may be a sample bias. Those cases settling after the invocation of the ICSID arbitration mechanism may be systematically different than those negotiated settlements arising in different contexts. Likewise, because investment disputes are confidential (either because they are not registered through the ICSID system or have not yet escalated to become public knowledge), there may be fundamental variances between confidential settlements and those cases for which there is public information. Second, although it is clear that some cases are settling, the confidential nature of the settlement means that it is impossible to analyze how the negotiations occur and what factors affect parties' willingness and ability to settle. Third, because the settlements are confidential, it is difficult to evaluate longitudinally compliance with the settlement, parties' satisfaction with the substantive result and the recurrence of later investment-related disputes. It would, therefore, be useful to obtain empirical evidence to analyze the potential benefits of negotiation.

c. The Common Challenges for Negotiated ADR

Despite its strengths, negotiated ADR inevitably has certain pitfalls. As a non-binding and consensual mechanism, there are challenges related to

---

decision on jurisdiction, several BIT-based cases have settled, including: (1) *Impregilo S.p.A. v. Islamic Republic of Pakistan*, ICSID Case No. ARB/03/3, (2) *IBM World Trade Corp. v. Republic of Ecuador*, ICSID Case No. ARB/02/10, (3) *Aguas del Tunari S.A. v. Republic of Bolivia*, ICSID Case No. ARB/02/3, and (4) *SGS Société Générale de Surveillance S.A. v. Islamic Republic of Pakistan*, ICSID Case No. ARB/01/13. (ICSID List of Pending and Concluded Cases 2006; ICIS List of Online Decisions 2006; Investment Treaty Arbitration, Chronological Listing of Awards [as of 11 August 2006] [http://ita.law.uvic.ca/chronological_list.htm]).

97 Onwuamaegbu 2005.

98 Coe 2005, pp. 29–30; ITA Awards 2006.

securing consent to negotiate, how negotiations occur, the enforceability of the agreement and the public nature of the rights.

Obtaining host country government consent to negotiate may prove challenging. Particularly where governments are not required to negotiate, host country governments might reject or ignore requests for consultation.[99] There may also be difficulties engaging in negotiation where there is intra-government conflict. Governments may find it difficult to use negotiation when: (1) the government is unaware one of its subdivisions, agencies or instrumentalities has engaged in conduct that has led to a dispute, (2) it is unclear what agency is responsible for dispute resolution, (3) a responsible agency does not have authority to settle the dispute, or (4) there may be no governmental resources or funds appropriated to resolve the conflict. Particularly in a novel, complex and inconsistent area like investment treaty law, settling disputes through negotiation can be challenging because of the need for a clear record showing the facts and the law that justify a settlement.[100]

Governments may also actively wish to avoid an investor's approach for negotiation when binding, rights-based adjudication is preferable. Parties may believe adjudication will produce a substantially better result. Parties may also wish to avoid the political fallout for not exhausting all of their legal rights or agreeing to settle a politically sensitive dispute. In some cases it may be more politically expedient to have a third-party impose a decision, rather than having a compromise be seen as a betrayal of national interests.[101] Beyond this, parties may wish to pursue adjudication initially if is likely to create a more favorable opportunities to negotiate a settlement in the future.

The negotiation process itself contains a series of challenges. Because it is non-binding, parties need not pursue negotiation once it starts. Should parties use negotiation to manipulate or delay the proceedings in pursuit of other objectives, this can complicate the dispute resolution process. Negotiation can also be ineffective if the parties' positions are far apart and there are few common interests to create a zone of possible agreement.[102] Particularly for parties using adversarial bargaining, the lack of certainty about the parties' legal rights means parties become entrenched in their reasonable beliefs that

---

99 Merrills 2005, pp. 23–24.

100 Rubins 2006; Legum 2006.

101 Rubins 2006.

102 *Id.*

their case is stronger as a matter of law. This can translate into a belief that compromise is unnecessary, which makes negotiation difficult.

The process can also be complicated by a "stakeholder problem," where it is unclear who must or should be present at the negotiation table. This can manifest itself in different ways. For example, having inappropriate people involved in negotiations can create difficulties. There may be challenges identifying the right persons who can negotiate effectively on behalf of a government and commit the host country government to a settlement.[103] This can create challenges when a critical branch of government, a key government representative or private entity is absent. Likewise, failure to include other critical stakeholders—such as groups directly affected by the settlement—may create problems. In any of these scenarios, this prevents the forging of a consensus; or, even if an agreement is reached, the negotiated solution may not properly resolve the underlying dispute. The end result is that negotiation that is not handled properly is the breeding ground for future disputes.

Even if negotiations lead to a settlement, there may still be problems with enforcement of settlement agreements. One can only imagine a change in government or corporate leadership that leads a party to abandon the settlement agreement—at which point parties may need again to consider the ADR implications.

Finally there may also be a category of concerns related to the public nature of these rights. Investment treaty rights arise from public international law obligations and tend to implicate public issues.[104] Particularly given the state of the case law in this area, at least one scholar has articulated a concern that such private resolution "is one less reasoned adjudication than might otherwise have been available to contribute" to the development of the jurisprudence.[105] Although written in the context of domestic dispute resolution, the work of Owen Fiss suggests that any loss of the public adjudication of public rights is likely to have an adverse affect on adjudicator's capacity to redress power imbalances and trivialize the remedial effects of claims designed to redress public wrongs. To the extent that more formal and public adjudication are lost, it runs the risk of imposing profound social costs.[106]

---

103 Onwuamaegbu 2005.

104 Franck 2005b, pp. 70–77.

105 Coe 2006, p. 25.

106 Owen M. Fiss, "Against Settlement," 93 YALE L.J. 1073 (1984) [Hereinafter Fiss 1984].

There is no doubt that these are important considerations in choosing how to resolve disputes, but this does not mean that the benefits of negotiation should be overlooked. The opportunity to create tailor-made resolutions in a cost-effective manner is a fundamental attribute. The goal should be to use dispute systems design to help determine if, when and under what circumstances should cases be negotiated.[107]

Facilitated ADR

Like its negotiated ADR counterpart, the goal of facilitated ADR is to harmonize parties' expectations, refine claims, clarify the issues, encourage settlement, and thereby decrease transaction costs, improve satisfaction with the result and prevent the recurrence of future disputes. It differs, however, in the process by which these goals are achieved. Facilitated ADR involves a neutral third-party assisting the disputants to reach a satisfactory resolution. This typically involves some form of conciliation or mediation. It might also involve the use of an ombudsperson.

a. Distinguishing Mediation and Conciliation

In the international context, commentators suggest conciliation and mediation are often used interchangeably.[108] Doubtless, this is because both processes involve a neutral third party assisting the parties to reach a solution of their own accord.[109] Employing the services of a third-party neutral to resolve disputes peacefully is precisely why both mechanisms are a form of facilitated ADR.

---

[107] Carrie J. Menkel-Meadow, "Whose Dispute Is it Anyway?: A Philosophical and Democratic Defense of Settlement (In Some Cases)," 83 Geo. L.J. 2663 (1995) [Hereinafter Menkel-Meadow 1995].

[108] UNCTAD 2003b, p. 21; Coe 2005; Rubins 2006; Alan Redfern and Martin Hunter, *Law and Practice of International Commercial Arbitration*, 4th Edition (Sweet and Maxwell: 2004). Redfern and Hunter nevertheless suggest at pp. 37–38 that a distinction might be appropriate. They note that a mediator "will listen to an outline of the dispute and then meet each party separately—often 'shuttling' between them—and try to persuade the parties to moderate their respective positions". On the other hand, "a conciliator was seen as someone who went a step further than the mediator, so to speak, in that the conciliator would draw up and propose the terms of an agreement that he or she considered represented a fair settlement."

[109] Onwuamaegbu 2005; Luis Miguel Diaz and Nancy J. Oretskin, "Mediation Furthers the Principles of Transparency and Cooperation to Solve Disputes in the NAFTA Free Trade Area," 30 Denv. J. Int'l L. and Pol'y 73 (2001) [Hereinafter Diaz and Oretskin 2001].

Nevertheless, for the purposes of clarity, managing the expectations and creating a common framework for discussion, this chapter draws a distinction between the two concepts. The key difference between mediation and conciliation is the degree and formality of the process.

Mediation is an informal process in which mediators tend to focus on identifying interests, reframing representations and canvassing a range of possible solutions to move the parties toward agreement.[110] There are many forms of mediation, which might involve anything from a mediator serving as information conduit or creating an atmosphere to loosen tension, to engaging in "shuttle diplomacy" to trying to transform the parties' relationship.[111] Mediation is not about using a series of rules or legal rights to resolve disputes. Rather, it uses a process-based model to bring two parties closer together toward agreement. Although there are variations, most mediation tends to focus on stages of dispute resolution including: (1) agreeing to mediate; (2) understanding the problem by identifying issues and interests; (3) generating options; (4) reaching agreement; and (5) implementing the agreement.[112] What happens in the individual dispute is largely a function of the parties, the nature of the dispute and the orientation and approach of the mediator.

In contrast, given its historical roots in public international law, conciliation tends to provide a more structured process.[113] Rather than relying on general guidelines, it is replete with formal rules related to jurisdictional objections, potential pleadings, the gathering of evidence and issuing written recommendations for settlement.[114] This makes the process more institutionalized, in a manner akin to formal adjudication. Arbitration commentators acknowledge this and describe conciliation as part of a "rules system" where the procedural formalities are articulated in advance—like civil procedure or evidentiary rules—to indicate how the process will operate and on what basis a neutral will make his or her determination.[115] In this sense, the formality of the process makes conciliation looks more like non-binding arbitration.[116] Nevertheless, as conciliation is aimed

---

110 Merrills 2005; Reif 1991.

111 Menkel-Meadow et al. 2006.

112 Leonard L. Riskin, *Mediation Training Guide* (2004) [Hereinafter Riskin 2004]; Kathleen Severens, *Basic Mediation Training Manual*, 5th Edition (International Institute for Negotiation and Conflict Management: 2005) [Hereinafter Severens 2005]; Diaz and Oretskin 2001, pp. 84–86.

113 Mary Ellen O'Connell, ed., *International Dispute Settlement* (Ashgate Dartmouth: 2003), p. xvi.

114 Merrills 2005; Reif 1991.

115 Rubins 2006.

116 Onwuamaegbu 2005.

at settlement from the outset, parties may be more likely to reach agreement than they would if participating in a full-scale adversary proceeding.[117]

Irrespective of whether it occurs in the context of mediation or conciliation, third-party neutrals can vary in their orientation and approach.[118] There are a variety of different models of facilitative ADR. The approach of Len Riskin's famous "Grid System" asks neutrals to consider whether: (1) the parties wish to define their dispute broadly or narrowly, and (2) the neutral should adopt either an evaluative or facilitative orientation to problem-solving. In an "evaluative" approach, neutrals may find themselves focusing more on evaluating the relative strengths and weaknesses of the merits of parties' factual and legal contentions in order to push settlement in a particular direction. In contrast, a "facilitative" approach may ask involved parties and the neutral party to focus more on identifying creative "win-win" strategies.[119]

Gary Friedman and Jack Himmelstein have also developed an "understanding-based" model of mediation in which parties resolve their conflicts through understanding their adversary's perspectives, priorities and concerns.[120] Other scholars use transformative mediation as a means of transforming the relationship between disputing parties.[121] Still others may find themselves moving between different styles at different points in the process.[122] Nevertheless, regardless of the approach a particular neutral has, parties generally control selection of the neutral(s) and—as part of the appointment process—may condition appointment on using a particular set of tactics or approach during the facilitative ADR process. Particularly given the multiplicity of definitions available for both mediation and conciliation, setting expectations about what to expect from the neutral and the dispute resolution process is useful.

---

117 Lester Nurick and Stephen J. Schnably, *The First ICSID Conciliation: Tesoro Petroleum Corp. v. Trinidad and Tobago*, 1 ICSID Review—Foreign Investment Law Journal 340, 349 (1986) [Hereinafter Nurick and Schnably 1986].

118 Diaz and Oretskin 2001, pp. 86–87.

119 Leonard L. Riskin, "Understanding Mediators' Orientations, Strategies and Techniques: A Guide for the Perplexed," 1 Harv. Negot. L. Rev. 7 (1996) [Hereinafter Riskin 1996]; Leonard L. Riskin, "Decision-Making in Mediation: The New Old Grid and the New New Grid System," 79 Notre Dame L. Rev. 1 (2003) [Hereinafter Riskin 2003].

120 Gary J. Friedman and Jack Himmelstein, "Resolving Conflict Together: The Understanding-Based Approach to Mediation," 4 J. Am. Arb. (2005) [Hereinafter Friedman and Himmelstein 2006].

121 Robert A. Baruch Bush and Joseph Folger, *The Promise of Mediation: The Transformative Approach to Conflict*, Rev. ed. (Jossey-Bass: 2005).

122 E. Patrick McDermott and Ruth Obar, "What's Going On In Mediation: An Empirical Analysis of the Influence of a Mediator's Style on Party Satisfaction and Monetary Benefit," 9 Harv. Negot. L. Rev. 75, 108–109 (2004) [Hereinafter McDermott and Obar 2004].

b. Using Mediation to Resolve Investment Disputes

UNCTAD has commented favorably about the creating of mediation as a pre-arbitration means of settling disputes, explaining "mediation may be a more useful means of reaching an amicable settlement than the use of comparatively formal conciliation proceedings."[123] Nevertheless, at present, ICSID does not provide mediation services. ICSID has expressed interest in establishing a mediation facility to allow parties to resolve disputes on a more informal, voluntary and confidential basis—possibly even with a neutral who does not have subject matter expertise.[124] This approach may serve to facilitate communication, decrease the risk that settlement will cause a party to lose face, and narrow the issues in a dispute in order to achieve cost and time savings.[125] While there have been some suggestions about what the process might entail, the future of ICSID's efforts to create a mediation facility is uncertain.[126]

Policymakers wanting to provide for mediation would need to address various structural matters such as: (1) should mediation be mandatory, (2) would or could it occur independently or concurrently with an imposed ADR process, or (3) whether it would be institutional or *ad hoc*. There might also be concerns about procedural issues, including the process of selecting mediators, the language and location of the mediation and the rules regarding confidentiality.[127]

c. Using Conciliation to Resolve Investment Disputes

ICSID does have a facilitative ADR system for resolving investment disputes. Observing that there is a "particular importance to the availability of facilities for international conciliation," the ICSID Convention establishes a process for making a request for conciliation, constituting a Conciliation Commission and defining the duties of the conciliators.[128] The Convention requires a Commission "to clarify the issues in dispute between the parties and to endeavor to bring about agreement between them upon mutually acceptable

---

123 UNCTAD 2005b, pp. 53–54.

124 ICSID 2004, p. 4; Onwuamaegbu 2005.

125 Onwuamaegbu 2005.

126 There was a suggestion that mediation should be without prejudice to the rights of parties in other forms of dispute resolution. Similarly, it was suggested that mediation be conducted alongside arbitration proceedings so that a settlement agreement might ultimately be incorporated into an award pursuant to ICSID Arbitration Rules 43(2). *Id.*

127 Diaz and Oretskin 2001, p. 8.

128 ICSID 2006, pp. 19–21.

terms [and]... may at any stage of the proceedings and from time to time recommend terms of settlement to the parties". Meanwhile, it obligates the parties to "cooperate in good faith ...[and] give their most serious consideration to [the Commission's] recommendations."[129]

While the ICSID's Conciliation Rules do not articulate how the Commission and the parties should carry out their respective mandates, the Rules suggest the Commission may wish to take a more evaluative approach[130] Rule 22 permits the Commission at any time (either orally or in writing) to "recommend that the parties accept specific terms of settlement or that they refrain ... from specific acts that might aggravate the dispute [and] point out to the parties the arguments in favor of its recommendations." In keeping with the more formal nature of conciliation, the Conciliation Rules also let the Commission request written statements from the parties, rule on its own jurisdiction, rule on requests to disqualify conciliators, hold hearings, and take evidence in the form of documents or witness testimony and issue a report at the closure of the proceedings.[131] Despite these suggested formalities, neither the ICSID Convention nor the Conciliation Rules suggest that conciliators are prohibited from engaging in less formal or facilitative actions; this implicitly suggests conciliators retain discretion to fashion the "forum to the fuss."

The Convention and Conciliation Rules require the Conciliation Commission to prepare a report. If the conciliation was successful, the report notes the issues in dispute and records that the parties have reached agreement. If, on the other hand, it appears to the Commission at any time during the process that there is no likelihood of agreement, the Commission's report must simply note the submission of the dispute to conciliation and record the parties' inability to reach agreement.[132]

In its effort to promote conciliation and provide investment-related dispute resolution services, ICSID also has Additional Facility Conciliation Rules for investor-State disputes where the parties have consented to conciliation. The formal procedures for Additional Facility Conciliation are similar to the conciliation procedures occurring under the ICSID Convention, including

---

129 *Id.*, Art. 34(1), p. 21. This is not dissimilar from the UNCITRAL Conciliation Rules that permit the conciliator, at any stage of the proceedings, to make proposals for the settlement of a dispute (Nassib G. Ziadé, "ICSID Conciliation," 13(2) News from ICSID, 3 (1996) [Hereinafter Ziadé 1996], p. 6).

130 Nurick and Schnably 1986, p. 348.

131 ICSID 2006, pp. 89–97.

132 ICSID 2006, pp. 21, 97–98; Onwuamaegbu 2005.

requesting written statements from the parties, challenges to jurisdiction and disqualification of conciliators, taking of evidence and issuing a report.[133]

As of 2006, ICSID's website reflects that it has only had five cases registered for conciliation: *SEDITEX Engineering Beratungsgesellschaft für die Textilindustrie m.b.H. v. Madagascar* (ICSID Case No. CONC/82/1); *Tesoro Petroleum Corp. v. Trinidad and Tobago* (ICSID Case No. CONC/83/1); *SEDITEX Engineering Beratungsgesellschaft für die Textilindustrie m.b.H. v. Madagascar* (ICSID Case No. CONC/94/1); *TG World Petroleum Ltd. v. Niger* (ICSID Case No. CONC/03/1); and *Togo Electricité v. Republic of Togo* (ICSID Case No. CONC/05/1).[134] It is not apparent whether all these are all investment treaty cases, as substantive information about these conciliations is not publicly accessible. But to the extent that all ICSID cases involve investment conflict, the available information suggests that conciliation can be effective in fostering settlement. In two cases, *TG World* and the first *SEDITEX* conciliation, the parties reached a settlement soon after the request for conciliation was registered and before a Commission was established. In a third case—in which Lord Wilberforce acted as sole conciliator—*Tesoro* ended with a successful settlement that caused counsel for the host country to write "use of ICSID's conciliation facilities deserves serious consideration in every case."[135] The second *SEDITEX* case appears not to have been subject to further dispute resolution and was not registered for ICSID arbitration. In only one case, *Togo Electricité*, conciliation efforts appear to have been unsuccessful, and ICSID registered a request for arbitration in the four days after the conciliation proceedings closed.[136]

Although limited in number, these cases suggest that certain types of cases may be well-suited for conciliation. Noting that arbitration may be too adversarial in some cases, counsel from ICSID explains that conciliation can be most effective in "cases in which the parties are engaged in an ongoing long-term project, involving significant amounts in sunk costs, where it is necessary to resolve disputes while the project is continuing. Disputes in oil and gas exploration projects, particularly, come to mind—as do mining and long-term

---

133 ICSID, ICSID Additional Facility Rules, ICSID/11 (Apr. 2006) (http://www.worldbank.org/icsid/facility/AFR_English-final.pdf) [Hereinafter ICSID Additional Facility Rules 2006], pp. 27–42.

134 ICSID, List of Pending Cases (as of 26 July 2006) (http://www.worldbank.org/icsid/cases/pending.htm) and List of Concluded Cases (as of 26 July 2006) (http://www.worldbank.org/icsid/cases/conclude.htm) [Hereinafter ICSID Pending and Concluded Cases 2006]; Onwuamaegbu 2005.

135 Nurick and Schnably 1986, p. 344.

136 ICSID Pending and Concluded Cases 2006.

infrastructure projects."[137] Overall, the general anecdotal evidence suggests that conciliation can be used directly (as in *Tesoro*) or indirectly (as in *TG World* and *SEDITEX*) to facilitate settlement.

d. Challenges for Facilitative ADR

Despite this rosy picture, there are limitations to facilitative dispute resolution. Both mediation and conciliation can only be as effective as the parties wish it to be; and this factor may be governed by the parties' immediate circumstances and the nature of the dispute.[138] Beyond this, there are difficulties generalizing about the efficacy of mediation and conciliation on the basis of ICSID's conciliation data. There is a risk that the small and limited set of data from ICSID suffers from sample bias. First, it is not clear whether the cases in which parties opted to conciliate are representative of the broader class of investment disputes, let alone treaty-based investment disputes. If the five cases were atypical, then there would be doubt as to the generalizability of conciliation's utility in other situations. Second, the data only relate to conciliation at ICSID and do not address mediation or conciliation that occurs on an *ad hoc* basis or through a different institution. Given the unique nature of the ICSID Convention and ICSID Conciliation, it is possible that mediation or conciliation occurring under different auspices may be less (or possibly more) successful. It would be helpful to analyze how investment disputes might be resolved, for example, under the UNCITRAL Conciliation Rules. Third, the success of mediation or conciliation may depend heavily upon the identity of the third-party neutral. Where the parties have greater confidence in the neutral, the recommendations are likely to carry greater weight and positively influence settlement.[139] Likewise, if parties appoint neutrals with an insufficient degree of respect from both parties, they may be less successful.

With only five conciliation cases against 132 arbitration cases registered at ICSID in 2005,[140] the sheer numbers suggest that ICSID Conciliation is a disfavored dispute resolution mechanism. Various factors may have led to this phenomenon. It may be caused by a lack of awareness of its existence. Counsel at ICSID has commented that "the Centre has recently begun to remind

137 Onwuamaegbu 2005.
138 Merrills 2005, pp. 41–44, 88–90.
139 Nurick and Schnably 1986, p. 345.
140 UNCTAD 2005b, pp. 4–5.

parties of the existence of the [conciliation] mechanism."[141] This can cause downstream problems, as parties may be hesitant to use a dispute resolution mechanism viewed as untried and untested.

The lack of use may also be a function of the ready availability of arbitration in BITs and parties' preference for binding adjudication. Parties may view such non-binding dispute resolution as little more than a needless and time-consuming exercise, as it can involve as much time as, and comparable expenses to, binding dispute resolution. Particularly, investors that have already experienced "protracted correspondence, negotiation, and perhaps even administrative battles with the State" may believe "the time has come for more forceful steps. Likewise, State parties may be unwilling to participate in a process that will not yield a solution imposed from the outside, for bureaucratic and political reasons."[142] Nevertheless, in certain cases, the "prospect of a binding award may be necessary to motivate one party or the other to bargain seriously" in conciliation.[143]

Negotiated and facilitated ADR share common difficulties. Like its negotiated counterpart, facilitated ADR experiences challenges in obtaining party consent. Part of the problem may be a lack of an express consent to a facilitative ADR method in a BIT. Even with pre-existing consent, parties may not elect to use it or may choose to use it in a dilatory manner. Muthucumaraswamy Sornarajah has suggested that conciliation can "be frustrated by the adoption of dilatory tactics."[144] In addition, there can be challenges with including the appropriate stakeholders and securing enforcement. In the public international law context, one need only consider the *Rainbow Warrior* situation, where France failed to abide by the terms of its mediated settlement and a binding dispute resolution was ultimately required.[145]

Facilitative ADR experiences other unique issues. As a neutral is involved in the facilitation process, it is vital to ensure that the neutral is both perceived to be and actually is independent and impartial. Decision-facilitators that lack these qualities may have an adverse impact on the legitimacy of the dispute resolution process. Another concern is that, given recent concerns about transparency, governments may be disinclined to be involved in non-transparent

---

141 Onwuamaegbu 2005.

142 Rubins 2006.

143 Nurick and Schnably 1986, p. 349.

144 Sornarajah 1994, p. 266.

145 Bederman 2001, pp. 236–237.

dispute resolution mechanisms. Since facilitative ADR usually occurs in private and is often subject to confidentiality obligations, this may run counter toward the trend toward increased governmental openness.[146] However, facilitated ADR mechanisms are different from imposed ADR mechanisms that provide a public function by adjudicating public rights. Facilitative ADR is not rights-based adjudication and the creation of legal norms, as it is primarily concerned with interest-based dispute resolution. Unlike fact-finding or imposed ADR, in which confidentiality inhibits a full and informed discussion of the disputes, confidentiality in facilitated ADR is necessary to promote a forthright and effective discussion about the parties' mutual interests and concerns. Without confidentiality, the system functions inefficiently; it creates discomfort that inhibits the full and frank discussions that can lead to the articulation of party interests and mutually satisfactory resolutions.[147] If parties were concerned that comments would be used against them later, this would inhibit the discussion necessary to create opportunities for a win-win settlement.[148]

Consideration of these concerns is vital. Nevertheless, "the unprecedented number of pending investor-State cases and the rate at which new cases are filed would seem to warrant a renewed dose of 'serious consideration' with a view to more fully institutionalizing" some sort of facilitated ADR regime.[149] Using dispute systems design to diagnose and appropriately adapt the system could integrate the strengths of a facilitative process while minimizing the risks of the challenges.

Fact-Finding ADR

Rather than a formal adjudication of substantive rights, fact-finding ADR mechanisms involve identifying a neutral expert or special master to engage in basic fact-finding in a dispute. This mechanism is similar to an expert determination where a neutral fact-finder, presumably with subject matter expertise, finally resolves fundamental—yet contested—issues.[150]

---

146 Onwuamaegbu 2005.

147 Article 35 of the ICSID Convention provides for confidentiality in conciliation proceedings. Interestingly, although parties are prevented from relying on views expressed by the other party or Commission reports or recommendations, there are no provisions as to the confidentiality obligations of Conciliators or non-parties affiliated with the process. *See* ICSID 2006, p. 21.

148 Ziadé 1996, pp. 3–4.

149 Coe 2005, p. 44.

150 Merrills 2005, pp. 45–48; O'Connell 2003, pp. 26, 105–119.

a. The Benefits of Fact-Finding

Fact-finding has the potential to narrow the matters in dispute and create common ground between the parties. Particularly where there is a discrete issue—such as asset valuation—that can be definitively resolved at an earlier stage, this might lead to a quick resolution of a dispute. Put in more commercial terms, using fact-finding to determine the scope of damages before liability may permit parties to bargain more effectively once the scope of precise liability is defined. Using fact-finding could save time and costs, permit investors to concentrate on their core business and let host countries focus on the more pressing duties of government. Likewise, narrowing the scope of a potential dispute provides an opportunity to decrease the risk of escalating or exacerbating a dispute, which may be important when there is an ongoing relationship. Beyond this, a fact-finding body can construct a historical record that—much like the work of truth and reconciliation commissions—may produce benefits for both the parties and society at large.[151]

Unfortunately, the practical utility of using fact-finding to resolve investment disputes is under-explored. Theoretically, as neither the Convention nor the Rules expressly prohibit such actions, an ICSID Conciliation Commission might be able to engage in fact-finding as part of its mandate for recommending settlement terms. ICSID Conciliation Rule 22(2) implies that fact-finding may be a critical facility as, when it issues recommendations, the Commission "shall point out to the parties the arguments in favor of its recommendations."[152] Given the confidentiality limitations of ICSID Conciliation, there is little information on how neutral experts or panels resolve disputed factual issues through a conciliation facility.

Luckily, in 1978 ICSID created provisions for Additional Facility Fact-Finding. Aaron Broches, ICSID's Secretary-General when the Fact Finding Rules were introduced, observed that the processes would provide parties with an impartial assessment of facts to prevent disputes on specific factual issues and the escalation of disputes.[153]

Unlike conciliation and arbitration, ICSID's Fact-Finding Rules do not require at least one party be an ICSID member. Rather, provided both parties agree,

---

151 Martha Minnow, *Between Vengeance and Forgiveness: Facing History after Genocide and Mass Violence* (Beacon Press: 1998).

152 ICSID 2006, p. 94.

153 Onwuamaegbu 2005.

any investor or government can initiate a fact finding proceeding. The Fact-Finding Rules provide that an independent committee—comprised of a sole or uneven number of commissioners—will examine the disputed facts and provide the parties with an impartial assessment.[154] The Rules envisage that there will be oral proceedings, written submissions, evidence and witness testimony. The Fact-Finding proceedings end with a Report that "shall be limited to findings of fact. The Report shall not contain any recommendations to the parties nor shall it have the character of an award," and the parties will be "entirely free as to the effect to be given to the Report."[155] Although the parties could agree otherwise, it is, in other words, primarily a form of non-binding dispute resolution.

As originally conceived, Additional Facility Fact-Finding was intended to be "a process for preventing, rather than settling legal disputes as a result of a perceived need for fact-finding proceedings in the 'pre-dispute' stage."[156] Nevertheless, in nearly 30 years, no cases have ever been brought under this Facility.[157] This may be due to many of the same problems facing ICSID Conciliation. People may be unaware of the existence of the Fact-Finding Facility. Moreover, the lack of a critical mass of cases establishing it as a tried and tested method of dispute resolution may inhibit parties from using it. The default, non-binding nature of the fact-finding may also make it inappropriate for some cases.[158]

Although the Fact-Finding Facility has suffered from non-use, fact-finding deserves renewed consideration. There are minimal institutional costs to maintaining the current facility. Reconsidering its structure and finding ways to make it more acceptable to stakeholders might actually increase the utility of the process.

In the public international law context, fact-finding bodies, such as the "inquiry" process at the Permanent Court of Arbitration, have been useful in making an impartial investigation of disputed facts. The *Dogger Bank* incident

---

154 ICSID, ICSID Additional Facility for the Administration of Conciliation, Arbitration and Fact-Finding Proceedings (January 2003) (http://worldbank.com/icsid/facility-archive/facility-en.htm) [Hereinafter ICSID Additional Facility for the Administration of Conciliation, Arbitration and Fact-Finding 2003], p. vi.

155 ICSID Additional Facility Rules 2006, pp. 20–22.

156 ICSID Additional Facility for the Administration of Conciliation, Arbitration and Fact-Finding 2003, p. vi.

157 Onwuamaegbu 2005.

158 One wonders whether ICSID Fact-Finding would be more effective if the Additional Facility rules were amended to provide binding dispute resolution.

is a classic example. In *Dogger Bank*, a Russian fleet on its way through the North Sea fired on English commercial fishing trawlers; one vessel was sunk, the remaining two ships were seriously damaged, and there were two dead and six wounded among the civilian crew. The Russians claimed they were attacked by Japanese torpedo boats mingling with the trawlers; if this were true, it would have justified the Russian action. The parties submitted this disputed factual issue to an International Commission of Inquiry. The inquiry found "there was no torpedo boat either among the trawlers nor on the spot, [and] the fire opened by Admiral Rozhdestvensky was not justifiable." After this single fact was established, the conflict was resolved and Russia gave the United Kingdom an indemnity of £65,000.[159] Cases such as this suggest that there is hidden utility in this methodology that deserves further exploration.

b. The Challenges of Using Fact-Finding to Resolve Investment Conflict

There are various difficulties associated with using Fact-Finding ADR. *Dogger Bank* is only one of five fact-finding commissions at the Permanent Court of Arbitration, which suggests fact-finding processes may not be suitable for broad types of dispute resolution.[160] Moreover, as investment disputes often involve disputes of fact, law and mixed questions of fact and law, many cases may not be suitable for fact-finding. Pure fact-finding commissions might complicate—rather than streamline—the dispute resolution process. As fact-finding does not generally appear as a dispute resolution option in investment treaties, it may prove difficult to get party consent. After a dispute has arisen, it may be challenging to secure party agreement on the use of fact-finding.

There may be other difficulties. Both the investor and State must be willing to accept that a fact-finding body—possibly in public[161]—may show that their

159 Merrills 2005, pp. 47–48.

160 "Dispute Settlement: General Topics—1.3," UNCTAD, Permanent Court of Arbitration, UNCTAD/EDM/Misc.232/Add.26 (2003) (http://www.unctad.org/en/docs/edmmisc232add26_en.pdf) [Hereinafter UNCTAD 2003a], p. 12.

161 The confidentiality of ICSID's Fact Finding Additional Facility is uncertain. The Commission certainly has confidentiality obligations, which were "aimed at fostering an environment of free and uninhibited negotiations…[where] either party would not be restrained by the fear of prejudicing itself should the conciliation prove fruitless" (Ziadé 1996, p. 4). Article 8 requires commissioners to declare they "shall keep confidential all information coming into my knowledge as a result of my participation in the proceeding as well as contents of any report drawn up by the committee"; and Article 9 provides that that the "sessions of the Committee shall not be public" (ICSID Additional Facility Rules 2006, pp. 19–20). Likewise, Article 4(5) of the Additional Facility Rules requires the Secretary-General to "keep confidential any or all information furnished to him" (*Id.*, p. 12). Nevertheless, the rules are silent as to whether the

version of the facts is wrong. As a practical matter, parties may be unwilling to subject themselves to the scrutiny and potential embarrassment. There is some evidence that States may be particularly sensitive to a risk of loss, particularly when it involves reputational harm.[162] Finally, there may be enforcement difficulties, particularly where parties have not agreed to be bound by the factual determinations. While noteworthy, these concerns should not mean investors and States reject this option out of hand. Rather, parties may wish to consider creating a system that incorporates fact-finding facilities at an appropriate juncture for appropriate disputes.

Advisory ADR

Advisory ADR might be used to evaluate and "reality-test" the parties' respective claims so that they can make more informed decisions as to the utility of pursuing formal adjudication. This might involve engaging in some sort of early evaluation by a neutral, a mini-trial or some form of non-binding arbitration.

a. Opportunities for Advisory ADR

In early neutral evaluation, parties may choose a third party to provide an opinion on a legal issue in dispute. In the U.S. domestic context, early neutral evaluation has been used successfully to resolve claims. One empirical study indicates that 80% of lawyers who were required by a court to go through this process later reported they were satisfied with the process and would voluntarily use early neutral evaluation in the future. The same study also suggested that the key predictor to having a successful early neutral evaluation was the attitude and skills of the neutral evaluator.[163]

A mini-trial typically involves attorneys for each side presenting the major aspects of their case to a tribunal composed of their respective clients as well as a presiding neutral who can then advise about a probable outcome and

---

parties have a duty of confidentiality or whether the public is prevented from attending those hearings that are not committee sessions, which are related to the proceeding.

162 Andrew T. Guzman, "The Cost of Credibility: Explaining Resistance to Interstate Dispute Resolution Mechanisms," 31 J. Legal Stud. 303 (2002).

163 Joshua D. Rosenberg and H. Jay Folberg, "Alternative Dispute Resolution: An Empirical Analysis," 46 Stan. L. Rev. 1847 (1994) [Hereinafter Rosenberg and Folberg 1994].

work with the clients to facilitate settlement.[164] Corporate entities have used mini-trials successfully to promote the free exchange of information and focus the minds of top management on the strengths and weaknesses of their respective cases. The private nature of this process has the potential to minimize costs and time allocated to dispute resolution, preserve an on-going relationship and avoid potential public embarrassment.

Little work has been done to consider how these procedures might apply in the context of investment disputes. This may be due to the challenges that these forms of dispute resolution are likely to face. Presumably some of the benefits of early neutral evaluation might be captured by formats such as ICSID Conciliation or ICSID Additional Facility Conciliation. Moreover, there is an argument that ICSID Conciliation already essentially is non-binding arbitration. There may be critical benefits to working within an existing institution, such as ICSID. Provided it is not inconsistent with the ICSID Convention, it may be possible to modify the nature of the dispute resolution services—or the parties' expectations in how they will be utilized—in order to capture benefits from other ADR formats.

b. Challenges Related to Advisory ADR

Despite the benefits, there are inevitably potential costs. Mini-trial and non-binding arbitration have challenges similar to those experienced by imposed ADR—namely they arguably have all of the costs and none of the benefits of reaching a binding decision. Moreover, to the extent that these non-binding proceedings have the look and feel of binding dispute resolution but are nevertheless private, there may still be concerns related to the public interest and a lack of transparency. Particularly in the context of a mini-trial, non-governmental organizations may wish to participate in the process; and there may be repercussions for exclusion. One also wonders, however, whether States have the same cost-benefit calculus as investors. Presumably foreign investors are rationale actors motivated by the need for profit and would be willing to settle under the acceptable commercial conditions; nevertheless, this may not always be the case and investors may not be able to use the process effectively. Meanwhile, host country governments—who may be influenced by commercial realities—may be more motivated by political objectives. They may also lack the flexibility to settle on purely commercial terms.

[164] Costantino and Merchant 1996, p. 40.

Other factors such as clear authority to settle, the availability of funds, the legal risk and the likelihood of recovery may affect a government's ability to accept the result of early neutral evaluation or a mini-trial. Nevertheless, it is possible that certain disputes might benefit from the availability of this process, and thus this issue is worthy of more systematic consideration.

Imposed ADR

Imposed ADR is at the most formal end of the dispute resolution continuum. Imposed ADR procedures typically involve an adjudicatory body making a final and binding decision. In this context, adjudicators are typically neutral and may base their decisions upon legal principles.[165] In the international context, the precise format of imposed ADR can vary. The adjudicators might be either arbitrators or judges; and judges may either come from national courts or international judicial bodies. The adjudication process may occur at a mixed claims commission, a claims tribunal akin to the Iran–U.S. Claims Tribunal, a series of independent *ad hoc* arbitral tribunals, or litigation under the auspices of the International Court of Justice (ICJ). It might also take the form of international litigation before a national court. Under each of these approaches, the adjudicators will be bound to follow different set of rules and regulations during the process of resolving the parties' dispute.

a. The Benefits of Imposed ADR

This chapter has already alluded to a variety of benefits to using an imposed ADR option. The nature of imposed ADR makes its availability critical to promote the final and binding adjudication—and permit bargaining in its proverbial shadow. Many (but not all) imposed ADR methods—particularly arbitration and national court judgments—have the benefit of efficient international enforceability. Imposed ADR has also experienced an increased push toward transparency, which promotes democratic values. Admittedly, imposed ADR varies in its commitment to transparency. The proceedings before the ICJ and the Iran–U.S. Claims Tribunal are typically open to the public. Many—but not all—national courts are transparent. Meanwhile, there is an increasing trend toward transparency in investment treaty arbitration.[166]

165 Merrills 2005, pp. 91–92.

166 Franck 2005a; Franck 2005b.

Specific forms of imposed ADR may have unique benefits. Arbitration and mixed claims commissions have the added benefit of being able to tailor the procedural framework to the issues in the particular dispute. They also offer the benefit of limited opportunities to attack the adjudicator's decision, which further streamlines the dispute resolution procedure. Presumably, such tailoring is likely to create disputes that may be faster and less expensive than their counterparts in national court litigation. Beyond this, there may be utility in being able to "blame any unfavorable result on three foreign arbitrators" and shift responsibility away from the parties.[167]

b. The Costs of Imposed ADR

Nevertheless, not all of these theoretical benefits are realized. Arbitration has particular risks.

i. Lost Time and Money

Cases can take years to arbitrate and cost more than litigation or other forms of dispute resolution.[168] Anecdotal evidence in the investment context suggests a similar phenomenon, which suggests that—rather than focusing on their core commercial or governmental objectives—parties expend significant resources on dispute resolution. Even investors that have successfully claimed under investment suggest that investment arbitration is simply "too slow, too costly and too indeterminate."[169] Increased fiscal costs for resolving disputes implicate other hidden costs, which may limit parties' access to justice. A smaller corporate investor, particularly with a small dispute, may be unable to pursue arbitration because of the extensive costs—even though the investor is being deprived of investment rights. The situation is more pronounced when a group of small companies are each experiencing distinct deprivations, but have no commercial choice but to absorb the cost of the violation of their legal rights.[170] Likewise, a host country government with limited financial resources may experience a similar phenomenon when it must defend itself on an inadequate budget. Ultimately, the financial cost of imposed ADR may,

---

167 Jeswald Salacuse, *Alternative Methods of Treaty-Based, Investor-State Dispute Resolution* (2006), p. 14 [copy on file with author].

168 Christian Bühring-Uhle, *Arbitration and Mediation in International Business* (Kluwer: 1996), pp. 140–148.

169 Coe 2005, p. 9.

170 Vicuña 2001.

as a practical matter, limit those who have access to the forum. This suggests that the stakeholders may be benefited from a system that provides a broader set of ADR mechanisms.

ii. Arbitrator Neutrality

There are also concerns that arbitrators are not perceived to be neutral in their adjudication. While there are opportunities to challenge arbitrators who lack impartiality or independence, there are nonetheless continuing reasons for parties' negative perceptions of the fairness and integrity of the dispute resolution process. There may, for example, be difficulties related to an arbitrator's potential "issue conflicts," where the same person serves as arbitrator and counsel in two separate cases with related legal issues and has the capacity to create legal authority as an arbitrator that may be of benefit to a client in his or her role as counsel.[171] Similarly, arbitrators may act as non-neutrals or advocates; there is also the possibility of "toxic" arbitrators who may disrupt or delay proceedings to the advantage of one party.[172]

iii. Party Control Over Outcome

Although control of the dispute resolution process is also a benefit, this may be illusory. Investment treaties typically present investors with pre-determined options for where and how their disputes can be resolved through arbitration. Although having one option is better than none, one wonders, for example, why countries would want to close the door to their local courthouses or other forms of imposed ADR. For example, although Mexico is willing to entertain NAFTA-based investment litigation, domestic legislation in the United States and Canada appears to prevent foreign investors from bringing NAFTA claims in their respective national courts.[173] Likewise, one wonders whether Argentina would have been happier with an option to create a mixed claims commission to deal with the universe of claims it received as a result of its currency crisis. Beyond a simple choice of forum, requiring arbitration presupposes the use of procedural rules that investors had little opportunity to negotiate; and while

---

171 Judith Levine, "Dealing With Arbitrator 'Issue Conflicts' in International Arbitration," 61 Apr. Disp. Resol. J. 60 (2006) [Hereinafter Levine 2006].

172 James H. Carter, "Improving Life with the Party-Appointed Arbitrator: Clearer Conduct Guidelines for 'Nonneutrals,'" 11 Am. Rev. Int'l Arb. 295 (2000) [Hereinafter Carter 2000]; Susan D. Franck, "The Role of the International Arbitrator," 12 ILSA J. Int'l and Comp. L. 499 (2006) [Hereinafter Franck 2006].

173 Franck 2005b.

parties can attempt to agree to variations after the fact, as a practical matter this may prove challenging once a dispute has arisen.

iv. Transposing Benefits into Costs: Confidentiality and Discretion

In the context of treaty arbitration, some of the benefits of arbitration can become costs. Confidentiality and discretion are two key examples. Confidentiality was historically extolled as a reason to opt for arbitration. Nevertheless, the lack of transparency of the awards and the process of resolving investment disputes has costs. Investment treaties are public documents that articulate public law rights, which are fundamentally different from private commercial rights in at least two ways.

First, treaty disputes have considerable third-party implications that implicate the public interest.[174] Beyond the effect experienced by a foreign investor or its shareholders, investment arbitration affects taxpayers of the host government as well as entities impacted by its legislative and regulatory choices.[175] Excluding those impacted by the resolution of the investment dispute can foster a sense of unfairness and a lack of procedural justice. Particularly for democratic institutions with a tradition of giving the governed a voice in the process of government, this can lead to a backlash with financial and political costs. As a result, it is unsurprising that governments such as those of the United States and Canada have worked to redress this procedural difficulty by making access to awards, pleadings and hearings more open.[176] What is more surprising, however, is the failure of other countries with democratic institutions to follow this lead.

Second, because these awards interpret new international investment rights, keeping treaty claims confidential prevents the efficient and consistent development of a coherent and considered legal doctrine. Unlike commercial law where there is a developed body of law and precedent, investment treaty law is relatively new. As a result, there is a dearth of established legal doctrine. The awards in recent cases that are publicly available have only just begun to sketch the boundaries of legal rights, and the academic literature is still in its formative years. While making awards public arguably increases the cost of arbitration—as tribunals and parties must address them—this overlooks fundamental costs

---

174 OECD, "Transparency and Third Party Participation in Investor-State Dispute Settlement Procedures: Statement by the OECD Investment Committee" (11 June 2005) (http://www.oecd.org/dataoecd/25/3/34786913.pdf).

175 Franck 2005b.

176 *Id.*

of confidentiality. The availability of analogous cases, legal reasoning or *amicus* submissions can increase the efficiency of a tribunal's determinations and improve the quality of the tribunal's reasoning. In addition, by signaling that like cases will be treated alike, it promotes perceptions of fairness and supports the legitimacy of the process.

Confidentiality also leads to uncertainty for both investors and host governments attempting, respectively, to organize their investments, make governmental policy and determine dispute resolution strategy. Without a sense of how the law will be applied—and access to the awards making those determinations—there can be little justified reliance. While investment arbitration awards are not *de jure* precedent, tribunals and parties treat them as *de facto* authority and rely upon them. Keeping cases confidential deprives tribunals of useful reasoning, prevents tribunals from treating like cases alike and also denies investors and governments a reasonable opportunity to organize their respective affairs in accordance with articulated legal standards.

It seems that governments originally thought that confidentiality was appropriate. Presumably this may have been because they anticipated that there would only be a small number of claims and there was no need to publicize the possibility of government liability; governments may also have been less concerned about inconsistencies in the decisions because, with confidentiality, there would be blissful ignorance of potential inconsistencies. Recent history, however, demonstrates the fallacy of both these propositions. The number of claims has increased; and as arbitrators search for authority to inform their own reasoning when faced with novel legal rights, they have sought out similar awards. Because of the critical nature of the issues raised in investment disputes, awards have found their way into the public domain. As the historical benefit becomes a liability, the future challenge will be how best to manage the need for confidentiality against the desirability of public access.

The use of arbitrators' open-textured discretion to adjudicate cases has also created unexpected costs.[177] In some contexts, parties may need arbitrators to exercise more discretion to issue awards quickly with minimal legal reasoning. This might be desirable in certain circumstances. For example, in labor arbitration there is a preference for final discretionary awards that need not be consistent; this can help prevent labor unrest. Nevertheless, in the context of

---

[177] Coe 2005; Michael A. Scodro, "Deterrence and Implied Limits on Arbitral Power," 55 Duke L.J. 547 (2005).

investment treaty claims, unreasoned and quick awards may be undesirable. It can create confusion. Unexplained decisions create difficulties for parties and arbitrators in understanding the scope of substantive investor protections and what circumstances should constitute liability-creating events. It can also increase litigation risk where tribunals make procedural determinations with an outcome-determinative effect. If, for example, tribunals exercise discretion to shift arbitration costs under the applicable rules—but they do not explain either the legal authority for or their rationale for making a decision—parties may question the fairness and basis of the determination. Likewise, if arbitrators do not shift costs, and still do not explain why, investors and governments are again left in the same precarious situations wondering what factors justify the determination. Perhaps more importantly, investors and host governments involved in future disputes will have minimal information available to them to predict how future tribunals might evaluate costs-related measures, which may not be an insignificant aspect in the case. In *Aguas Del Tunari v. Bolivia*, while the investor claimed at least US$25,000,000 in damages, the settlement ultimately made Bolivia responsible for US$1,600,000 in legal fees—well over 5% of the claimed compensation.[178] As parties bargain in the shadow of the law, relying on arbitrator discretion—without information about how rules, standards, practice, and precedence will influence the exercise of that discretion—prevents parties from negotiating effectively. Without reliable and predictable information about the potential costs of the arbitration procedure, there could be an adverse impact on parties' capacity to engage in an accurate and clear cost-benefit calculus.

c. Moving Beyond Investment Treaty Arbitration

Ultimately, investment treaty arbitration may not be everything its creators wished it to be. There are a variety of factors that suggest the theoretical benefits of arbitration may not materialize and purported benefits can transform into costs. This ultimately suggests that it is unwise to focus unduly on arbitration as an all-purpose paradigm.

It does suggest that the time is right to consider proactively how to use other imposed ADR mechanisms—such as a claims commission—to resolve disputes with finality. There have been some suggestions, for instance, that this

---

178 Paul Harris, *Company Drops Demand over Water Contract Canceling*, SAN FRANCISCO CHRONICLE (19 January 2006) p. A–3.

format might address concerns related both to transparency and consistency.[179] Likewise, it suggests that it may be useful to think systematically about the range of ADR mechanisms. As this chapter suggests, other processes—particularly underutilized facilities at ICSID and with ombuds—are promising options. The challenge will be to determine the right blend of party autonomy, efficiency and due process for a wide range of circumstances.

There has been some scholarship that has begun to consider how specific aspects of the ADR continuum, namely mediation and conciliation, might usefully improve the system.[180] Coe has made significant strides in thinking systematically about how and when to use facilitated ADR in connection with imposed ADR. Nevertheless, one wonders whether this conception of the problem is overly narrow. The challenge may be to expand one's conception of conflict management to think more broadly about how to diagnose the difficulties the system is facing, critique the existing process and provide principles to guide the creation of effective and legitimate dispute resolution systems.

Challenges for the Future

The challenge for the future is how to think seriously about the value of designing comprehensive dispute resolution mechanisms to resolve investment disputes. Being systematic in the approach to conflict management could provide a unique opportunity to capitalize on the efficiency of various processes across the ADR continuum. It also provides an opportunity to increase satisfaction both with the process and the ultimate result, as well as promoting integrity of the dispute resolution system. Nevertheless, there will be challenges as different governments perhaps make different assessments of the utility of engaging in this level of conflict management.

We are at a unique historical juncture in the evolution of resolving investment-related disputes. We have an opportunity not just to ask how to improve the arbitration system by focusing on issues such as transparency, consistency and coherence; rather we can and should consider how to manage conflict related to investment treaties in a systematic manner. Arbitration is no doubt part of that puzzle. But as the review of the dispute resolution continuum suggests, there are other opportunities worthy of ongoing consideration.

---

179 W. Michael Reisman, "Control Mechanisms in International Dispute Resolution," 2 U.S.-Mex. L.J. 129, 136–137 (1994); Franck 2005b, pp. 81–82.

180 Coe 2006; Rubins 2006; Legum 2005; Onwuamaegbu 2006.

The opportunity to decrease costs, increase efficiency and interject procedural fairness in the system should not be discounted. The evaluation of the structure can provide a reasoned explanation for the status quo and give stakeholders affected by the outcome of disputes a chance to participate in the system's creation. Ultimately, such an analysis has the unique benefit of strengthening the legitimacy of the dispute resolution process and giving stakeholders confidence in the system's capacity to protect their rights and produce just results.

CHAPTER 10

Transparency in International Dispute Settlement Proceedings on Trade and Investment

*Hugo Perezcano Díaz**

Although international dispute settlement proceedings involving trade and investment agreements are not new, concerns about transparency are somewhat recent. The first GATT dispute settlement case was filed in 1950. During the life of the GATT, a total of 53 cases were submitted to dispute settlement—a small number by today's standards, but a large one considering the origins and evolution of the system. Investor-State dispute settlement proceedings date back to the early 1960s, when they were first incorporated into bilateral investment treaties (BITs) and subsequently developed in the Washington Convention of 1965 that established the International Centre for Settlement of Investment Disputes (ICSID). Prior to 1997, when the first NAFTA Chapter 11 case was filed, 38 cases had been initiated under the ICSID Convention rules.

Yet, concerns about the transparency of such proceedings, the possibility of third party participation and the method of appointing arbitrators and their accountability were first voiced only in 1997, shortly after the first few NAFTA Chapter 11 cases were filed. Similar concerns were raised in respect of the WTO dispute settlement proceedings at nearly the same time.

---

* Head of the International Trade Practices Unit of the Secretariat of the Economy in Mexico; formerly General Counsel for International Trade Negotiations. Email: hperezca@economia.gob.mx.

There is no single answer that explains why transparency is such a recent demand. Many factors are involved. The first and most obvious one is that there has been increased awareness in civil society of international trade and investment topics, which has led to its greater involvement in this arena. This, in turn, has been the result of the history and evolution of the international agreements containing such mechanisms and of the proceedings themselves.

International Dispute Settlement Proceedings: The GATT and the WTO

Historical Context

The GATT was to be a part of a larger international agreement that would have established the International Trade Organization, but the latter part of the project never came to fruition. Because of political complications surrounding the establishment of such an organization and given that the U.S. President only had congressional authority to negotiate an agreement that was narrower in scope, the original Contracting Parties decided to adopt the GATT as a provisional agreement, which would be substituted by the ITO Charter once domestic approval had been obtained.

Interest in the U.S. for the broader ITO agreement began to wane in the years following adoption of the GATT. The President failed to secure domestic support, and in the 1950s he gave up completely in the efforts to obtain congressional approval for the ITO Charter. With the U.S. dropping out, other countries desisted as well in their own domestic efforts. They felt that it was not worth setting up the ITO if the U.S., which had been the driving force behind its creation and was the most important player in world trade in the post-war era, was not to be part of the institutional framework. The GATT thus remained a provisional agreement until the WTO Agreement succeeded it almost 50 years later.

This had important implications for dispute settlement. The ITO Charter was to contain detailed dispute settlement rules, and provided for the assistance of the International Court of Justice. In contrast, the GATT dispute settlement mechanism is anchored in Articles XXII and XXIII, which in general provide for consultations between the disputing parties and the intervention of the GATT Contracting Parties upon referral of the matter to them.

The complex and detailed WTO dispute settlement mechanism that we know today slowly evolved from those two articles, and developed from a practice of international trade negotiations. The first disputes were submitted to the Contracting Parties as a whole, through their permanent representatives in Geneva, who had been original GATT negotiators. The Contracting Parties later decided to address the cases in working groups composed of three or five representatives charged with hearing the disputing parties, investigating the circumstances of the case and issuing a report, which was then submitted to all the Contracting Parties for their consideration, adoption or rejection. Working groups evolved into panels and certain rules began to emerge. GATT practice was first codified in 1966 at the behest of developing countries. This initial codification eventually led to the Tokyo Round *Understanding regarding Notification, Consultation, Dispute Settlement and Surveillance* of 1979 (the "Tokyo Round DSU").

Transparency concerns were very different at the outset from what they are now. The Contracting Parties were concerned with the public availability of relevant laws, regulations and other measures of general application, as well as the availability of domestic administrative, judicial or arbitral tribunals with jurisdiction over customs and similar matters. Thus, the GATT transparency obligations (Article X) were limited to publishing such measures so that trading firms and governments could become acquainted with them, and having independent tribunals with jurisdiction to review the practice of administrative agencies responsible for trade matters. The Tokyo Round DSU added an obligation to notify other Contracting Parties of the adoption of trade measures that affected the operation of the GATT.

Dispute settlement proceedings themselves were confidential. The Tokyo Round DSU provided that written memoranda submitted to panels were considered confidential, but were made available to the parties to the dispute. Hearings were held with the parties concerned, and panels would also hear the views on any other Contracting Party that had a substantial interest in the matter.

Increased Transparency

Access to Documents

The WTO Agreement incorporated the 1947 GATT unchanged, and together with certain protocols, understandings and decisions of the GATT Contracting Parties, named it GATT 1994. WTO Members affirmed their adherence to the principles for the management of disputes applied under Articles XXII and XXIII of GATT 1947, and the rules and procedures as further elaborated and modified by the WTO *Understanding on Rules and Procedures Governing the Settlement of Disputes* (the DSU).

The DSU codified the GATT practice of keeping proceedings confidential. The areas where this applies are: consultations; proceedings involving good offices, conciliation and mediation and specifically the positions taken by the parties to the dispute; panel proceedings; and those of the Appellate Body (see articles 4, 5, 17 and 18 of the DSU). An exception marked the first small steps toward increased transparency in these proceedings. Article 18(2) provides as follows:

> Written submissions to the panel or the Appellate Body shall be treated as confidential, but shall be made available to the parties to the dispute. Nothing in this Understanding shall preclude a party to a dispute from disclosing statements of its own positions to the public. Members shall treat as confidential information submitted by another Member to the panel or the Appellate Body which that Member has designated as confidential. A party to a dispute shall also, upon request of a Member, provide a non-confidential summary of the information contained in its written submissions that could be disclosed to the public.

Thus, the DSU provided that a disputing party may disclose statements of its own position to the public and that it shall deliver a non-confidential summary of its submissions for public disclosure at the request of any WTO Member.

Non-disputing Party Participation (amicus curiae)

In mid-1997, several non-governmental organizations (NGOs) made submissions to the WTO panel in the *U.S.-Shrimp* case.[1] The complaining parties—India, Malaysia, Pakistan, Thailand—objected to this participation by NGOs and requested the panel to reject the submissions, arguing that it had no authority to accept and consider them. The panel concluded that it would be incompatible with the provisions of the DSU to accept the submissions, but allowed any party to incorporate them as their own into their briefs. The U.S. did so. The complaining parties challenged this determination by the

1 *United States—Import Prohibition of Certain Shrimp and Shrimp Products*, Report of the Appellate Body, WT/DS58/AB/R, 12 October 1998.

panel before the Appellate Body, which concluded that the panel had erred in its determination that it would be incompatible with the DSU to accept *amicus curiae* submissions. It stated that the DSU gave panels and the Appellate Body a broad right to seek information, which included the discretion to accept information from non-disputing parties, even if it was unsolicited. In the *EC-Asbestos* case,[2] the Appellate Body anticipated that it might receive a large number of *amicus curiae* submissions and adopted specific rules for dealing with them. However, the Appellate Body limited the application of such arguments to that specific case.

These decisions by the panel and the Appellate Body—especially the latter—triggered a heated debate within the WTO. The issue was taken up by the WTO General Council, in which a majority of the WTO Members expressed their objection.

The Appellate Body has confirmed its decision to accept non-disputing party submissions (from private parties, NGOs and non-participating WTO Members), but in light of the debate, it has treaded carefully and has in practice never considered unsolicited submissions.

As of 2006, the issue was the subject of negotiations of the DSU in the context of the Doha Round, but progress has been stalled given the suspension of the Round.

International Dispute Settlement Proceedings: NAFTA

Chapter 20: State-State Dispute Settlement Mechanism

NAFTA was negotiated between the end of 1991 and the summer of 1992, when the Uruguay Round negotiations were still underway and far from being concluded. NAFTA Chapter 20, which contains the Agreement's general dispute settlement mechanism, was modeled on the dispute settlement provisions of the Canada–U.S. Free Trade Agreement of 1988 and the Dispute Settlement Understanding contained in the so-called "Dunkel Text"[3] that was being negotiated at the time in the Uruguay Round.

---

2 *European Communities—Measures Affecting Asbestos and Asbestos-Containing Products*, Report of the Appellate Body, WT/DS135/AB/R, 12 March 2001.

3 Arthur Dunkel, who was the Director General of the GATT Secretariat during the Uruguay Round negotiations, compiled and arranged all the texts that were being negotiated and produced a single document that made it easier for negotiations to proceed. The document was called the Dunkel Text.

NAFTA article 2012 provides as follows:

> 1. The Commission shall establish by January 1, 1994 Model Rules of Procedure, in accordance with the following principles:
>
> . . .
>
> (b) [T]he panel's hearings, deliberations and initial report, and all written submissions to and communications with the panel shall be confidential.

The Model Rules of Procedure provide:

> 35. The Parties shall maintain the confidentiality of the panel's hearings, deliberations and initial report, and all written submissions to and communications with the panel, in accordance with such procedures as may be agreed from time to time between representatives of the Parties.

However, in 1995 the NAFTA Parties agreed to begin opening proceedings to the public, consistent with—and even going a bit further than—the WTO (which had entered into force on January 1, 1995). In July 1995 the NAFTA Parties exchanged letters that allowed each to make its own submissions and those of the other Parties available to the public, subject to redaction of information that could properly be classified in order to protect personal privacy or a Party's essential confidentiality concerns. The letters also provided that the transcripts of the hearing could be released to the public 15 days after the publication of the panel's final report.

While the NAFTA Parties have developed rules for non-disputing party participation and agreed to provide for open hearings, this transpired in the context of investor-State arbitration, which was accepted as well in Chapter 20 proceedings. Therefore, it will be addressed below.

Chapter 11: NAFTA's Investor-State Dispute Settlement Mechanism

Investor-State dispute settlement procedures have a different history. The ICSID Convention of 1965 provides a cohesive set of fairly detailed rules that have not changed much over four decades of operation. As in the case of the GATT and the WTO, transparency in the context of investor-State proceedings is a somewhat recent concern. Investor-State dispute settlement proceedings have long been around, but in their origins and for much of their history, they went rather unnoticed. Their widespread use began in 1997 and has increased dramatically since. Of the 226 cases registered by UNCTAD through the end of 2005, 70% were initiated since the beginning of 2002.[4] (See Annex 6, *UNCTAD, IIA Monitor, No. 4 (2005).*)

The sharp increase in the number of cases; the fact that investor-State proceedings involve claims for damages directed against governments[5] and thus entail the expenditure of public funds in case of adverse awards (in some cases for quite large amounts); and the fact that some cases have involved investments in sensitive sectors of particular interest to environmental NGOs, such as *Ethyl Corporation v. the Government of Canada* (gasoline additives), *Methanex Corporation v. The United States of America* (gasoline additives) or *Metalclad Corporation v. The United Mexican States* (ICSID Case No. ARB(AF)/97/1) (toxic waste landfill), have all contributed to raise civil society's level of awareness and boost its arguments for greater transparency.

Some countries have taken steps toward increasing transparency, but fragmentation poses a serious challenge—according to UNCTAD, by the end of 2005 the total number of IIAs exceeded 5,200, and some countries are renegotiating existing agreements[6]—and efforts to develop multilateral rules on investment have thus far failed.

Efforts to provide for greater transparency have been limited to the NAFTA and some more recent agreements entered into by the NAFTA Parties, especially the United States.

In 2001, the NAFTA Free Trade Commission, comprised of the three countries' trade ministers, issued a declaration that clarified that nothing in the NAFTA imposes a general duty of confidentiality on disputing parties in Chapter 11 arbitrations, and agreed to make public in a timely fashion all documents submitted to, or issued by, an arbitral tribunal, subject to protection of confidential business information and other types of information protected by law. All three NAFTA Parties publish on their respective web sites the key documents in all arbitrations: submissions of the parties, procedural orders,

---

4 *See* UNCTAD, *World Investment Report 2006: FDI from Developing and Transition Economies: Implications for Development* (United Nations Publication: 2006).

5 This is not necessarily the case under the ICSID Convention, but, as noted by UNCTAD, of the cases initiated since 2002, only one was initiated by a government. (*Id.*)

6 "Systemic Issues in International Investment Agreements (IIAs)," UNCTAD IIA Monitor No. 1 (2006). Footnote 1 states: "The IIAs universe is composed of bilateral treaties for the promotion and protection of investment (or bilateral investment treaties), treaties for the avoidance of double taxation (or double taxation treaties), other bilateral and regional trade and investment agreements as well as various multilateral agreements that contain a commitment to liberalize, protect and/or promote investment."

hearing transcripts and awards. Other documents could be available on request.

Consistent with the developments in the WTO, in 2003 the NAFTA Parties clarified as well that it was within Chapter 11 tribunals' discretion to accept submissions by non-disputing parties and that nothing in the NAFTA limited that discretion. They recognized, however, that participation of non-disputing parties could affect the orderly course of arbitral proceedings, and thus developed specific rules modeled on those adopted by the WTO Appellate Body.

More recently, in 2004, the NAFTA Parties agreed to support open hearings; Canada and the U.S. had previously agreed to do so, but Mexico had lagged behind in light of its different legal culture and the more recent adoption of its Transparency Law.[7] They agreed to develop specific rules governing open hearings—the NAFTA Parties have not yet done so[8]—and to apply the same degree of openness to Chapter 20 proceedings.

Conclusions

In recent years, some steps have been taken toward greater openness in international dispute settlement proceedings. Efforts can and should redouble. Yet, transparency, while important, should not be regarded as an historical imperative or inevitability. It is, in fact, a rather recent claim in the international arena. While in countries such as the United States or Canada transparency laws have been in force for many years, others are only now initiating domestic processes toward increased transparency, and others have not even begun to consider the issue. Mexico's Transparency Law dates back to 2002, and it is still in the process of implementation. Also, Mexico's law applies merely at the federal level; states still lag behind.

Globalization will certainly play a key role in fostering change, but in the WTO, with 150 members with different legal systems and different cultures, it is not surprising to find some countries reluctant to embrace greater openness. In investor-State proceedings, with a hugely fragmented network of treaties, achieving transparency will be a major task. Perhaps it is time to re-think the prospect of multilateral rules.

---

7 The Federal Law on Transparency and Access to Public Governmental Information of 11 June 2002.

8 This commitment was also tied to an agreement to resolve certain Chapter 20 issues, which has not happened either.

CHAPTER 11

Provisions in the New Generation of U.S. Investment Agreements to Achieve Transparency and Coherence in Investor-State Dispute Settlement

*Michael K. Tracton**

Modern U.S. investment agreements contain a number of provisions that further the objectives of transparency and coherence in international investor-State dispute settlement. These include, but are not limited to, consideration of a possible appellate or similar mechanism to review arbitral awards. (See Annex 1, *International Investment Instrument with Provisions to an Appellate Review Mechanism.*)

In 2004, the United States concluded a rewrite of its model bilateral investment treaty (BIT), which was used as the basis for the BIT signed by the United States and Uruguay in 2005.[1] The United States seeks to achieve overall consistency between its BITs and free trade agreement (FTA)

---

* Bilateral Investment Treaty Coordinator, Office of Investment Affairs, U.S. Department of State. The views presented here are expressed in the author's personal capacity and do not necessarily reflect those of the Department of State or the U.S. Government. Email: TractonMK@state.gov.

1 Treaty Concerning the Encouragement and Reciprocal Protection of Investment, 4 November 2005, U.S.–Uruguay (http://www.state.gov/e/eeb/tpp/c16209.htm). This treaty entered into force on November 1, 2006.

investment provisions, so nearly identical language is found in the investment chapters of FTAs the United States has negotiated since the enactment of the Bipartisan Trade Promotion Authority Act of 2002 (TPA Act),[2] including those with Chile, Colombia, the Dominican Republic and five Central American countries (Costa Rica, El Salvador, Guatemala, Honduras, Nicaragua) (CAFTA-DR), Morocco, Oman, Peru, and Singapore.

These agreements draw from long-standing U.S. BIT principles, the U.S. experience with investor-State arbitrations under the North American Free Trade Agreement (NAFTA) and the negotiating objectives on foreign investment in the TPA Act. One of the negotiating objectives of the TPA Act is to improve mechanisms used to resolve investor-State disputes, including "providing for an appellate body or similar mechanism to provide coherence to the interpretations of investment provisions in trade agreements ..."[3]. The TPA Act also calls for transparency in the dispute settlement process to the fullest extent possible, the expeditious disposition of claims, the deterrence of frivolous claims, as well as other objectives.[4]

Potential for an Appellate Mechanism

Recent U.S. agreements do not establish an appellate mechanism for investment arbitrations; rather, they contemplate the potential for creating one in the future. The agreements mentioned above, except for the CAFTA-DR, contain both of the following commitments:

- First, to "consider whether to establish a bilateral appellate body or similar mechanism" within three years after the agreement enters into force.[5]

The U.S. model BIT is available on the website of the U.S. Department of State (http://www.state.gov/documents/organization/38710.pdf).

2 Bipartisan Trade Promotion Authority Act of 2002, Pub. L. 107–210, § 2101(a) et seq. (2002) (codified at 19 U.S.C. § 3801 et seq.).

3 *Id.* at § 2102(b)(3)(G).

4 *Id.* at § 2102(b)(3)(G), 2102(b)(3)(H).

5 *See, e.g.*, Free Trade Agreement, U.S.–Chile, 6 June 2003, Annex 10-H (http://www.ustr.gov/assets/Trade_Agreements/Bilateral/Chile_FTA/Final_Texts/asset_upload_file1_4004.pdf) [hereinafter U.S.–Chile FTA]. Provisions of the U.S.–Chile FTA are cited as examples in the notes that follow. Identical or similar provisions are contained in the U.S.–Uruguay BIT and modern U.S. FTAs, including CAFTA-DR and agreements with Chile, Colombia, Morocco, Oman, Peru, and Singapore.

- Second, to "strive to reach an agreement" to permit a multilateral appellate body to review awards under the agreement if the mechanism for such an appellate body is established under a separate multilateral agreement.[6]

The CAFTA-DR contains the second of these commitments, and calls for the establishment of a working group to study the appellate issue and to provide a draft appellate amendment.[7] The CAFTA-DR also includes an illustrative list of issues for the working group to consider, including the applicable standard of review, the composition of an appellate panel, its relation to underlying arbitration agreements and laws on the recognition and enforcement of arbitral awards, and the effect of decisions by the appellate body or similar mechanism.[8]

Other Provisions Designed to Achieve Transparency and Consistency

There are a number of other provisions in the U.S. model BIT and recent U.S. agreements that help to further the interests of transparency and consistency. Some of these provisions are also reflected in NAFTA or have been the subject of debate in NAFTA investor-State cases.

First, a provision that is new to recent U.S. agreements provides for "interim review" of draft decisions or awards; if one of the disputing parties requests, the tribunal shall circulate a draft decision or award to the disputing parties and to the non-disputing government party, in which case the disputing parties have an opportunity to provide written comments.[9] The purpose is to provide an additional check against errors. As these agreements provide, this review procedure does not operate if an appeal is available through a future appellate mechanism.[10]

One can imagine situations in which this provision could be helpful. For instance, a disputing party may feel that a draft award mischaracterizes arguments that it made in a hearing or written submission, has made a basic error of fact (e.g., computation of damages) or has made an error of law.

---

6 *See, e.g.*, U.S.–Chile FTA Art. 10.19(10).

7 Central American Free Trade Agreement, 5 August 2004, Costa Rica–Dom. Rep.–El Salv.–Guat.–Hond.–Nica.–U.S., Art. 10.20(10), Annex 10-F (http://www.ustr.gov/assets/Trade_Agreements/Bilateral/CAFTA/CAFTA-DR_Final_Texts/asset_upload_file328_4718.pdf).

8 *See Id.* at Annex 10-F.

9 *See, e.g.*, U.S.–Chile FTA, Art. 10.19(9)(a).

10 *See, e.g.*, *Id.* at Art. 10.19(9)(b).

A respondent government might propose changes related to the legal reasoning of a decision, even if it does not change the outcome in that particular case, because of the government's interest in how future tribunals may perceive the decision in considering the same or a similar issue. The tribunal may ultimately disagree with the comments it receives under the interim review provision, but the tribunal must consider them before issuing its decision or award on liability.

Second, recent U.S. agreements provide the government parties with the opportunity jointly to make binding interpretations of the agreement, and any decision or award must be consistent with the joint declaration.[11] NAFTA also contains such a provision, which has been used, for example, to clarify the parties' interpretation of the minimum standard of treatment article. In the earlier phases of NAFTA Chapter 11 arbitration, some tribunals misinterpreted that article.[12] In July 2001, the NAFTA Parties issued a binding interpretation clarifying, among other things, that NAFTA Article 1105(1) prescribes the customary international law minimum standard of treatment of aliens.[13]

Third, recent U.S. agreements, like NAFTA, provide the non-disputing government the right to make submissions to the tribunal regarding the interpretation of the agreement.[14] When the government parties take a common

---

11 *See, e.g., Id.* at Art. 10.21(3).

12 For example, the tribunal in *Pope & Talbot* found the standard of "fair and equitable treatment" to be "*additive* to the requirements of international law." *See Pope & Talbot, Inc. v. Canada*, para. 110 (Award) (10 April 2001) (emphasis in original). The tribunal in *Pope & Talbot* "exceeded its authority by interpreting a general 'fairness' obligation to be 'additive' of the minimum standard of treatment contained in Article 1105(1), even though it recognized that 'the language of Article 1105 suggests otherwise.' The NAFTA Free Trade Commission expressly rejected that interpretation, stating that '[t]he concepts of "fair and equitable treatment" and "full protection and security" do not require treatment in addition to or beyond that which is required by the customary international law minimum standard of treatment of aliens.'" *See* Counter-Memorial of the United States of America, *Glamis Gold Ltd. v. United States of America* (19 September 2006), p. 229.

13 *See* paragraph B of the 31 July 2001 interpretation of the NAFTA Free Trade Commission of Certain Chapter 11 provisions, which is available at the website of the U.S. Department of State (http://www.state.gov/documents/organization/38790.pdf). This interpretation has been applied in subsequent NAFTA Chapter 11 awards. *See, e.g.*, the tribunal's award in *Loewen*: "the effect of the Commission's interpretation is that 'fair and equitable treatment' and 'full protection and security' are not free-standing obligations. They constitute obligations only to the extent that they are recognized by customary international law. Likewise, a breach of Article 1105(1) is not established by a breach of another provision of NAFTA. To the extent, if at all, that NAFTA Tribunals in *Metalclad Corp v. United Mexican States* ICSID Case No. ARB(AF)/97/1 (Aug 30, 2000), *S.D. Myers, Inc. v. Canada*, (13 November 2000), and *Pope & Talbot, Inc. v. Canada*, Award on the Merits, Phase 2, (10 April 2001) may have expressed contrary views, those views must be disregarded" (*Loewen Group, Inc. and Raymond L. Loewen v. United States of America*, ICSID Case No. ARB(AF)/98/3, para. 128 (Award) (26 June 2003)).

14 *See, e.g.*, U.S.-Chile FTA, Art. 10.19(2).

position in their submissions, the United States has argued it constitutes a "subsequent practice in the application of the treaty which establishes the agreement of the parties regarding its interpretation" within the meaning of customary international law as reflected by the Vienna Convention on the Law of Treaties, which a tribunal must take into account.[15] Like joint interpretations under the governing law article, this mechanism helps guard against fragmentation in the jurisprudence.

Fourth, recent U.S. agreements provide for full transparency. They mandate that written submissions be made available to the public in a timely fashion.[16] Hearings are to be open to the general public, subject to appropriate logistical arrangements.[17] Rules are provided to safeguard business confidential or other protected information. [18]

Many of these transparency measures have already been put into practice in the NAFTA context. In the early stages of NAFTA Chapter 11 cases, there was considerable public criticism of "secret NAFTA tribunals." Since then, progress on transparency has been rapid and wide-ranging. Consistent with the 2001 NAFTA interpretation (which provided that NAFTA does not impose a general duty of confidentiality),[19] pleadings and other documents in the proceedings have been posted on the websites of all three NAFTA Parties, including the website of the State Department's Office of the Legal Adviser.[20] Hearings have been opened to the public through closed circuit television cameras at the World Bank.

Transparency in investor-State proceedings serves a number of policy objectives, such as coherence and consistency. For example, a tribunal's rulings on the substantive and procedural issues before it can provide persuasive guidance for other tribunals addressing the same or similar issues.

---

15 See the Counter-Memorial on Competence and Liability of Respondent United States of America, *Mondev International Ltd. v. United States* (1 June 2001), p. 34, which finds the agreement of the three NAFTA parties regarding the minimum standard of treatment provision as confirmed in submissions to various Chapter 11 tribunals to be authoritative. *See* Vienna Convention on the Law of Treaties, 23 May 1969, Art. 31(3)(b),1155 U.N.T.S. 331: "There shall be taken into account ... any subsequent practice in the application of the treaty which establishes the agreement of the parties regarding its interpretation...."

16 *See, e.g.*, U.S.–Chile FTA, Art. 10.20(1).

17 *See, e.g., Id.* at Art. 10.20(2).

18 *See, e.g., Id.* at Art. 10.20(3)–(5).

19 *See* paragraph A of the 31 July 2001 interpretation of the NAFTA Free Trade Commission (referred to in note 13).

20 *See* the website of the U.S. Department of State (http://www.state.gov/s/l/c3439.htm).

Fifth, since NAFTA, modern U.S. agreements contain a provision for consolidating claims in investor-State proceedings.[21] In general there is nothing preventing disputing parties from mutually agreeing to consolidate their investor-State cases under the agreement. However, if there is a difference over whether to do so, the consolidation article provides a mechanism for a tribunal to decide whether consolidation of all or part of the claims is warranted, based on whether there are questions of law or fact in common that arise out of the same events or circumstances, and whether consolidation would be in the interest of fair and efficient resolution of the claims. NAFTA contains a similar consolidation provision that was invoked for the first time in 2005, first in cases against Mexico (arising out of Mexican regulations on high fructose corn syrup in soft drinks), and then in cases brought against the United States (concerning the United States' imposition of duties on softwood lumber from Canada). In the high fructose corn syrup case, the consolidation tribunal denied Mexico's consolidation request.[22] In the softwood lumber case, the consolidation tribunal consolidated the claims in their entirety.[23]

The provisions referred to above are procedural in nature, but modern U.S. agreements also contain language to clarify certain substantive protections. The U.S. model BIT and recent agreements clarify that the minimum standard of treatment provision prescribes the customary international law minimum standard of treatment, using phrasing also found in the 2001 NAFTA interpretation.[24] An annex on expropriation provides guidance to tribunals on factors to consider in deciding whether an indirect expropriation has occurred.[25] A separate annex clarifies how customary international law is formed.[26] Such clarifications provide added assurance that tribunals will take a consistent and coherent approach on these questions that is consistent with the intent of the parties.

---

21 *See, e.g.*, U.S.–Chile FTA, Art. 10.24.

22 *See Corn Products International, Inc. v. United Mexican States*, ICSID Case No. ARB(AF)/04/1, Order of the Consolidation Tribunal (20 May 2005).

23 *See* A Request for Consolidation by the United States of America of the Claims in: *Canfor Corporation v. United States of America, Tembec et al. v. United States of America, Terminal Forest Products Ltd. v. United States of America*, Order of the Consolidation Tribunal (7 September 2005). On 7 December 2005, Tembec et al. petitioned the United States District Court for the District of Columbia to vacate the Consolidation Order.

24 *See, e.g.*, U.S.–Chile FTA, Art. 10.4(1)–(3).

25 *See, e.g.*, *Id.* at Annex 10-D.

26 *See, e.g.*, *Id.* at Annex 10-A.

CHAPTER 12

Preliminary Rulings in Investment Arbitration

*Christoph Schreuer**

Coherence and consistency of the case law in international investment arbitration has become a matter of concern. Apart from the odd instances of conflicting decisions concerning the same sets of facts,[1] there are now several areas in international investment law that have developed diverse lines of authority. This is despite the fact that most tribunals carefully examine previous decisions and follow precedents most of the time.[2]

Two examples may suffice to illustrate the danger of conflicting case law and the disorientation that follows in its wake. One concerns so-called "umbrella clauses." An umbrella clause is a provision in a treaty under which the States parties undertake to observe obligations they may have entered into with respect to investments. In other words, contractual obligations and other undertakings are put under the treaty's protective umbrella. It is widely accepted that, under the regime of an umbrella clause, violations of a contract between the host State and the investor are treaty violations.[3] It would seem to

---

* Professor of Law at the University of Vienna. Email: christoph.schreuer@univie.ac.at.

1 *See especially Ronald S. Lauder v. The Czech Republic*, Final Award, 9 ICSID Rpts 66 (3 September 2001), and *CME v The Czech Republic*, Partial Award, 9 ICSID Rpts 121 (13 September 2001). But *see also CMS Gas Transmission Company v. Argentina*, Award, 44 ILM 1205 (12 May 2005), and *LG&E Energy Corp., LG&E Capital Corp., LG&E International Inc. v. Argentina*, Decision on Liability (3 October 2006) (reaching conflicting decisions on closely related facts).

2 *See* Christoph Schreuer, "Diversity and Harmonization of Treaty Interpretation in Investment Arbitration," 2(3) Transanational Dispute Management (April 2006); Christoph Schreuer and Matthew Weiniger, "Conversations Across Cases—Is there a Doctrine of Precedent in Investment Arbitration?," in *Oxford Handbook of International Investment Law* (forthcoming 2008).

3 François Rigaux, "Les situations juridiques individuelles dans un système de relativité générale," 213 Recueil des Cours 229–230 (1989–I); I.F.I. Shihata, "Applicable Law in International Arbitration: Specific Aspects in the Case of the Involvement of State Parties," *in The World Bank in a Changing World*, vol. II

follow that a provision in a bilateral investment treaty (BIT) offering consent to arbitration for violations of the BIT extends to contract violations covered by the umbrella clause. (See Annex 7, *UNCTAD, IIA Monitor, No. 4 (2006).*)

But the meaning and consequences of clauses of this kind have turned out to be among the most controversial in international investment law. Some tribunals have given umbrella clauses their full effect.[4] Others have doubted the effect of such clauses and have held that they cannot be meant to extend the protection of an investment treaty to ordinary commercial contracts.[5]

Another example concerns the applicability of most-favored-nation (MFN) clauses in investment treaties to the provisions on dispute settlement in these treaties. Some tribunals have held that MFN status enables the claimant to select the more favourable arrangements on dispute settlement in treaties between the respondent State and third States.[6] Others have vigorously denied the applicability of MFN clauses to dispute settlement.[7]

(Martinus Nijhoff: 1995), p. 601; P. Weil, "Problèmes relatifs aux contrats passés entre un Etat et un particulier," 128 Recueil des Cours 130 (1969-III); F. A. Mann, "British Treaties for the Promotion and Protection of Investments," 52 *British Year Book of International Law* (Oxford University Press: 1981), p. 246; Rudolf Dolzer and Margrete Stevens, *Bilateral Investment Treaties* (Martinus Nihjoff Publishers: 1994); Kenneth Vandevelde, *United States Investment Treaties: Policy and Practice* (Kluwer Law and Taxation Publishers: 1992), p. 78; J. Karl, "The Promotion and Protection of German Foreign Investment Abroad," 11 ICSID REVIEW—FOREIGN INVESTMENT LAW JOURNAL 1, 23 (1996); Thomas Wälde, "Energy Charter Treaty-based Investment Arbitration," 5 JOURNAL OF WORLD INVESTMENT AND TRADE 373, 393 (2004); S. Alexandrov, "Breaches of Contract and Breaches of Treaty," 5 JOURNAL OF WORLD INVESTMENT AND TRADE 555, 565–567 (2004); A. Sinclair, "The Origins of the Umbrella Clause in the International Law of Investment Protection," 20 ARBITRATION INTERNATIONAL 411 (2004).

4 *SGS v. Philippines*, ICSID Case No. ARB/02/06, Decision on Jurisdiction (29 January 2004), paras. 125, 128; *CMS Gas Transmission Company v. Argentina*, Award, 44 ILM 1205 (12 May 2005), paras. 296-303; *Eureko v. Poland*, Partial Award (19 August 2005), paras. 244–260; *Noble Ventures v. Romania*, Award (12 October 2005), paras. 42–62; *Siemens v. Argentina*, Award (6 February 2007), para. 206.

5 *SGS v. Pakistan*, Decision on Jurisdiction, ICSID Case No. ARB /02/06 (2003), at paras. 163–173; *Joy Mining Machinery v. Egypt*, ICSID Case No. ARB/03/11 (2004), para. 81; *El Paso v. Argentina*, Decision on Jurisdiction, ICSID Case No. ARB/03/15 (27 April 2006), paras. 66–86; *Pan American Energy v. Argentina*, Decision on Preliminary Objections, ICSID Case No. ARB/03/13 (27 July 2006), paras. 92–115.

6 *Maffezini v. Kingdom of Spain*, Decision on Jurisdiction, ICSID Case No. ARB/97/7, paras. 38–64; *Siemens v. Argentina*, Decision on Jurisdiction (3 August 2004), paras. 32–110; *Gas Natural v. Argentina*, Decision on Jurisdiction (17 June 2005), paras. 24–31, 41–49; *Suez, Sociedad General de Aguas de Barcelona S.A., and InterAguas Servicios Integrales del Agua S.A. v. Argentina*, Decision on Jurisdiction (16 May 2006), paras. 52–66; *National Grid PCL v. Argentina*, Decision on Jurisdiction (20 June 2006), paras. 53–94; *Suez, Sociedad General de Aguas de Barcelona S.A., and Vivendi Universal S.A. v. Argentina and AWG Group Ltd. v. Argentina*, Decision on Jurisdiction (3 August 2006), paras. 52–68.

7 *Salini v. Jordan*, Decision on Jurisdiction (29 November 2004), para. 119; *Plama v. Bulgaria*, Decision on Jurisdiction, 44 ILM 721 (8 February 2005), paras. 183, 184, 223, 227; *Telenor v. Hungary*, Award (13 September 2006), paras. 90–100.

It is evident that a system that operates with a large number of differently composed tribunals is vulnerable to discrepancies of this kind. Even well meaning and competent arbitrators are unlikely to agree on all points all the time. Courts with a permanent composition are more likely to produce a consistent case law. But a permanent court for investment disputes is an unlikely goal, at least for the time being.

There are several conceivable methods to achieve a measure of harmonization in the decisions of tribunals. An appeals procedure would be one possibility. But appeals procedures carry obvious disadvantages, and their establishment would encounter a number of obstacles—only one of which is Article 53(1) of the ICSID Convention.[8] Article 53(1) would have to be either amended (a near impossible task) or circumvented, which is awkward to say the least. (See Annex 2, ICSID Convention excerpts.)

The most effective way to achieve judicial coherence and consistency is not necessarily to submit decisions to review and reversal. An appeal presupposes a decision that has been made already, that will be attacked for a perceived flaw and that may be revised and repaired.

Rather than remedy the damage after it has occurred, it is more sensible to address the problem of inconsistency through preventive action. A method to secure the coherence of case law that has been remarkably successful is to allow for preliminary rulings while the original proceedings are still pending.[9] Under such a system, a tribunal would suspend proceedings and request a ruling on a question of law from a body established for that purpose.

This procedure has been applied with a large measure of success in the framework of European Community law.[10] It effectively secures the uniform application

---

8 Article 53(1) of the ICSID Convention provides: "The award shall be binding on the parties and shall not be subject to any appeal or to any other remedy except those provided for in this Convention."

9 The idea was put forward before: *see* Gabrielle Kaufmann-Kohler, "Annulment of ICSID Awards in Contract and Treaty Arbitrations: Are there Differences?," *in* Emmanuel Gaillard and Yas Banifatemi, eds., *Annulment of ICSID Awards* 289 (Juris Publishing: 2004). *See also* Gabrielle Kaufmann-Kohler, "In Search of Transparency and Consistency: ICSID Reform Proposal," 2(5) Transanational Dispute Management (2005), p. 8.

10 *See especially* Paul Craig and Grainne De Búrca, *EU Law: Text, Cases and Materials*, 3rd Edition (Oxford University Press: 2003), pp. 432–481; Mads Andenas, ed., *Article 177 References to the European Court—Policy and Practice* (Butterworths: 1994); David Anderson, *References to the European Court* (Sweet & Maxwell: 1995); Allen Dashwood and Angus Johnston, eds., *The Future of the Judicial System of the European Union* (Hart Publishing: 2001); Gráinne de Búrca and J.H.H. Weiler, eds., *The European Court*

of European law by domestic courts in all member States through preliminary rulings of the Court of Justice of the European Communities (European Court). Article 234 (formerly Article 177) of the Treaty establishing the European Community (TEC) provides:

> The Court of Justice shall have jurisdiction to give preliminary rulings concerning:
>
> (a) the interpretation of this Treaty;
>
> (b) the validity and interpretation of acts of the institutions of the Community and of the ECB;
>
> (c) the interpretation of the statutes of bodies established by an act of the Council, where those statutes so provide.
>
> Where such a question is raised before any court or tribunal of a Member State, that court or tribunal may, if it considers that a decision on the question is necessary to enable it to give judgment, request the Court of Justice to give a ruling thereon.
>
> Where any such question is raised in a case pending before a court or tribunal of a Member State against whose decisions there is no judicial remedy under national law, that court or tribunal shall bring the matter before the Court of Justice.

Under Article 234 TEC, any national court or tribunal of a member State may decide to refer a question with regard to the interpretation (or validity) of European Community law to the European Court, when a decision on that question is necessary to enable the national court to give a judgment. Where such a question is raised before a court of last instance, the court is under an obligation to request a preliminary ruling from the European Court.

Article 234 TEC ensures that questions regarding the interpretation of Community law are referred to the European Court before the judgment is rendered. Article 234 TEC establishes the "interpretative monopoly" of the European Court with regard to Community law and assures its uniform interpretation by national courts. Preliminary rulings help to avoid divergent interpretations and further the efficient application of community law *ex ante.*

---

of Justice (Oxford University Press: 2001); H. Schermers, C. Timmermans, A. Kellerman and J. Stewart Watson, *Article 177 EEC: Experiences and Problems* (North Holland: 1987).

They are preferable to the frequently cumbersome appellate mechanisms that are engaged *ex post*.

The preliminary rulings procedure is based on the close cooperation between national courts and the European Court. It is widely accepted in practice and frequently used by national courts. Proceedings for preliminary rulings are always initiated by a national court and not by one of the parties.

The parties to the original proceedings as well as Community organs have the opportunity to submit observations in these proceedings. There is also a hearing. The preliminary ruling is rendered in the form of a judgment. The decision binds the domestic court that requested the ruling as well as any courts that may have to decide the same case in appeal. Preliminary rulings also have a strong impact on national courts in other cases dealing with the same or similar questions.

This procedure promotes the uniform interpretation and application of Community law even before the judgment of the domestic court is rendered. Article 234 has turned out to be of seminal importance for the development of Community law. It is through preliminary rulings that the European Court has developed some of the most central concepts and principles of Community law. Specifically, Article 234 has been the principal means through which the relationship between the national and Community legal systems has been developed.

Adapted to investment arbitration, this method could provide for an interim procedure whenever a tribunal is faced with an important question. Such an important question may be described as a fundamental issue of investment treaty application, a situation in which a tribunal wants to depart from a "precedent" or where there are conflicting previous decisions. In such a situation, the tribunal might be required to suspend proceedings and request a ruling. Once that ruling has been forthcoming, the original tribunal would resume its proceedings and reach an award on the basis of the guidance it has received through the preliminary ruling. This method could become a successful means to ward off inconsistency and fragmentation.

A mechanism of this kind would require the establishment of a central and permanent body that would be authorized to give preliminary rulings. A permanent body of this kind would be less ambitious than a permanent court for the adjudication of investment disputes. It would not do away with the basic structure of current investment arbitration consisting of a multitude of individual tribunals. But, if successfully used, it could guarantee a large measure of harmonization without depriving the tribunals of their basic competence to adjudicate the cases submitted to them.

Preliminary rulings would leave Article 53 of the ICSID Convention untouched. A mechanism of this kind would not provide an appeal or remedy against awards contrary to the ICSID Convention. Preliminary rulings would not affect the principle of finality. The delay caused by a request for a preliminary ruling would be much more limited than an appeals procedure that sets in only after the original proceedings have resulted in an award. Whereas an appeals procedure might reach a measure of consistency through a costly and time consuming repair mechanism, preliminary rulings could help to prevent the development of inconsistencies in the first place.

A number of details would have to be worked out. One is under what circumstances a tribunal would request a preliminary ruling and whether it would be under an obligation to do so. Another question would be whether these rulings would bind the tribunal or would merely constitute recommendations. Not least, the composition of a body charged with giving preliminary rulings would require detailed discussion.

CHAPTER 13

Transparency and Consistency in International Investment Law: Can the Problems be Fixed by Tinkering?

*Howard Mann**

Commentary

The issues of transparency and consistency in international investment law today raise fundamental questions of regime building.

The international investment law regime has essentially grown as an ad hoc, institutionally deprived regime. To be sure, some institutions are involved, but they are fragmented in their roles, have no mandate over the overall regime's development process and lack any processes for ongoing review of the evolution of this area of law. The International Centre for Settlement of Investment Disputes (ICSID) provides an institutional home to much arbitration, but it has no mandate to review and develop the substantive laws upon which its tribunals rule. UNCITRAL provides rules for investor-State disputes, but does not even catalog the cases that take place under them. The United Nations Conference on Trade and Development (UNCTAD) has a role in looking at the substantive side, but it is limited in scope and analytical in nature: it has no

* Howard Mann, Ph.D., is the Senior International Law Advisor to the International Institute for Sustainable Development, and a practicing international lawyer in Ottawa, Canada. Email: h.mann@sympatico.ca.

functional role in relation to any international investment agreements (IIAs) and no mandate to convene or promote negotiations on such agreements. The Organisation for Economic Co-operation and Development (OECD) regards itself a leader in the field, but its promotion of a Multilateral Agreement on Investment ended in disarray and disrepute, a situation from which it has yet to recover in terms of building a forward looking role. The World Trade Organization (WTO) was properly rejected in 2003–2004 as a forum for multilateral investment negotiations.

The thesis posed here is that the institutional void is linked to the lack of conception of international investment law in a regime context. This encourages the continued proliferation of bilateral and regional agreements, dispute settlement that takes place in secrecy and conflicts of interests in the tribunal process; and more, it impacts the transparency and consistency of the regime. It also presents challenges to the credibility of the regime that continue to jeopardize its opportunities for new growth.

This situation arises today even though international investment law is not in its infancy. Over 2,500 existing bilateral investment agreements and more than 220 investor-State disputes exist. A simple comparison to the WTO is useful here. In 1994, the GATT embarked on a process of transparency building and consistency enhancement through the specific institutionalization of its dispute settlement process in the successor WTO. The establishment of a binding dispute settlement system and an overseeing Appellate Body addressed critical issues at the foundation of trade law, and moved the dispute settlement process to a rule of law model instead of simply an ad-hoc dispute resolution process.

In short, the international investment law system to date actually has been designed as a non-institutionalized system. Dispute settlement has been left not to an institutional home but to the marketplace of arbitrators, lawyers and public and private sector arbitration bodies, whose inherent self-interest in the status quo is manifest. Negotiations remain ad hoc, often distorted by power imbalances between rich and poor countries (capital exporters and capital importers). Transparency and accountability at all levels are limited, if not simply absent. And proposals to fix the system are limited in nature and scope. With all this, can tinkering accomplish anything useful, or is more fundamental change required?

Muthucumaraswamy Sornarajah's chapter notes, with his customary panache, that one cannot simply layer an appellate body onto an otherwise rotting foundation and expect all will be well. Nor, I would suggest, can one simply consider picking the lowest-hanging transparency fruit as a solution. Rather, let us look for a moment at some of the issues that need to be addressed in a comprehensive way, but from a legal regime perspective as opposed to being bound by where the failing system currently is.

Conflicts of Interest

There are two types of conflict of interest that are now problematic from the viewpoint of transparency and consistency, and even more so from the viewpoint of public accountability. The first has often been discussed in recent years, and been the subject of at least one court case. This concerns the circumstance of lawyers who represent an investor or State in one arbitration while at the same time sitting as arbitrator in another case.[1] Many in the international arbitration bar continue to argue that this is acceptable and part of the normal course of conducting business. Indeed, some support for this may have been more reasonable when the system was producing one or two cases every few years and these were kept largely confidential. But neither of those premises hold true anymore: now, there are 50 or more cases being initiated every year, and the awards are specifically touted as part of the law that future cases are decided upon. (We will return to these issues below.)

Other observers see this double booking as a gross conflict of interest. The one court case, heard in Amsterdam, that appears to have addressed this issue specifically arose out of an investor-State arbitration at The Hague Permanent Court of Arbitration; the court there found a conflict of interest and ordered the arbitrator/lawyer involved to desist from one of the two roles.[2]

Although this is obviously one of the examples of low-hanging fruit for the attention of potential reformers, it remains problematic. It is readily evident, looking through the lists of lawyers and arbitrators that are active on a number of arbitrations, that multiple such situations are ongoing today, and more can be expected in the future. Anecdotal information also suggests that some lawyers who sit as arbitrators are now "hiding" their related legal advisory work by acting as advisors to counsel rather than as named counsel. The court case in Amsterdam has done nothing, it appears, to stop this practice, and it is

---

1 The issue is precisely the same if a lawyer sitting as an arbitrator has partners or associates who act as lawyers in other arbitrations. The interest of one partner is the interest of all partners here.

2 *Republic of Ghana v. Telekom Malaysia Berhard*, District Court of The Hague, 18 October 2004, Challenge No. 13/2004; Petition No. HA/RK 2004.667; and Challenge No. 17/2004, Petition No. HA/RK/2004/778, 5 November 2004 (http://www.transnational-dispute-management.com/).

now painfully obvious that the tribunals will not self-govern in keeping with the court decision in this regard. It is not that the case is unknown, rather that it is simply ignored. The issue also does not appear to be part of any required disclosure forms in any express manner.

Viewed from a legal system or regime perspective, this type of conflict of interest—acting for clients on the same issues one is judging in another context—clearly merits addressing. The rise in importance of arbitral awards as precedents for future awards makes this issue even more critical. While some legal systems do allow such crossovers at lower legal levels, crossovers are not allowed in any democratically designed system at levels where final decisions on major issues are involved. There is a rationale for this: whether real or apparent, the average person cannot expect someone to be unbiased as an arbitrator when he or she must advocate a specific position on the same issues in a separate context. Put more starkly, the average person cannot expect an arbitrator to rule against the very arguments he or she is making in a second case on the same issues, knowing that his or her participation in such a decision will undercut his or her client's interest in the other arbitration. It is this test of real or apparent conflict of interest that governed the court in Amsterdam, and it is this test that governs in all major legal systems of the world, where legitimacy, transparency and accountability are all important factors.

The same can be said of the second type of conflict of interest, to which scant attention has been paid to date. This is the use as arbitrators of lawyers who come from major law firms that generally represent large corporations who are themselves foreign investors. In this circumstance, it is readily arguable that the arbitrators have clients that have a specific interest in the expansion of the scope of investor protections. Would the average observer be surprised, in this context, by the expansive interpretations that have been given to concepts such as fair and equitable treatment in recent years? Or, would the average observer have expected this in view of the number of arbitrators attached to law firms with major corporate client bases? No conspiracy theory is needed here, just some recognition of the interests and predilections of the lawyers participating in the system, even those with the purest of intentions.

Once again, from a legal regime perspective, almost all legal systems preclude judges from continuing to practice as lawyers in order to prevent exactly this kind of real and apparent conflict of interest. The international investment law system—or rather non-system—needs to address this issue.

Resolutions for both types of conflict of interest are readily available: standing rosters of arbitrators who are not active in law firms, increased use of professors, disclosure requirements for involvement in other arbitrations, a greater role for recently retired lawyers who "graduate" to arbitrator, etc. The idea, floated recently by the former Secretary General of ICSID, Roberto Danino, that changes in this regard can be accomplished by self regulation appears stillborn in the face of the ongoing disregard for the Amsterdam court decision to date by tribunals.[3] As long as the arbitration system remains the private preserve of the legal community, and not part of public international law's investment regime in a palpable way, it will not be able to reform itself.

Transparency: the Publication of Documents and Access to Hearings

Transparency issues begin with negotiations and end with the dispute settlement process. To date, neither is vested with a significant degree of transparency, understood as public access to documents or the actual proceedings.

Almost all investment negotiations today are conducted in secrecy. In most cases, the public will not even be aware of such negotiations. Yet, we have seen in several recent contexts that public awareness, where it does exist, can have a major political impact. Witness two recent examples. First, negotiations on a proposed South Africa–U.S. free trade agreement that included an investment chapter were stopped by South Africa for reasons that included a number of concerns with the proposed investment chapter. Second, U.S.-Pakistan negotiations on an investment agreement were similarly halted by the smaller country when the U.S. refused to make changes to its model investment agreement.[4] The latter was even the subject of an international conference in London to debate the key issues. In both cases, public awareness has changed the course of otherwise expected events.

On the dispute settlement end, only the investor-State arbitrations under the North American Free Trade Agreement (NAFTA) and more recent agreements involving the U.S. are fully subject to notice to the public (the first step in transparency), timely publication of all arbitration documents and

---

3 Roberto Danino, "Making the Most of International Investment Agreements: A Common Agenda," TRANSNATIONAL DISPUTE MANAGEMENT, January 2006 (http://www.transnational-dispute-management.com).

4 Very recent press reports suggest they may be about to resume, based on certain U.S. concessions.

decisions, an expectation of open hearings and opportunities for civil society participation through *amicus* briefs. Outside of this select circle of agreements, only ICSID requires the listing of all pending and completed cases. UNCITRAL cases, unless registered at ICSID for the conduct of the arbitration, are not revealed to the public in any systematic way.[5] Cases at the International Chamber of Commerce and the Stockholm and London international arbitration centers are routinely not revealed to the public. Even their decisions may never be released.

Public access to hearings follows more or less the same pattern. Only under NAFTA and more recent U.S. investment agreements is there a guarantee or even an expectation of open hearings.[6] Tribunal decisions under the ICSID and UNCITRAL rules have precluded allowing open hearings at the discretion of the tribunal, requiring both sides to agree to public access for this to occur.[7] In some cases, both sides have agreed, but this appears to be rare.[8] The point is, however, that when this has occurred it has been on the initiative of the arbitrating parties, not due to the right of the public to witness the process. Outside the NAFTA context, little progress has been made to date on this issue of public access to hearings.

On a related question, the acceptance of *amicus curiae* briefs in investor-State arbitrations, progress has been made by means of rulings, under the UNCITRAL and ICSID rules, that tribunals have the jurisdiction to accept such briefs even if the arbitrating parties disagree.[9] These positive decisions have opened up

---

5 The UNCITRAL arbitration rules have just recently been opened for review in what is expected to be a 1.5–2 year process. This and other issues will arise in that context.

6 Under NAFTA, a non-legally binding statement from the U.S. and Canada sets out an expectation of open hearings, but Mexico has not participated in making this statement. However, more recent U.S. agreements ensure that public access to hearings is guaranteed.

7 The most recent changes to the ICSID Rules of Arbitration allow a tribunal to decide to open the hearings, subject to a veto by either party. This is a subtle change. In the first known case where this was tested, the disputing investor-party objected to the open hearing. *Biwater Gauff Tanzania Ltd v. Tanzania*, ICSID Case No. ARB/05/22, Procedural Order No. 5, 2 February 2007.

8 Public hearings were held, for example, in the case of *Methanex Corporation v. United States of America*, under NAFTA and the UNCITRAL rules and hosted by ICSID. However, this took two requests by concerned civil society groups. The first was rejected when Methanex refused, while the second was accepted when Methanex changed its mind.

9 Some examples include, Decision of the Tribunal From Petitions of Third Persons to Intervene as *"Amicus Curiae," Methanex Corporation v. United States of America*, 15 January 2001 ("Amicus decision") (http://naftaclaims.com/Disputes/USA/Methanex/MethanexDecisionReAuthority*Amicus*.pdf); *United Parcel Service of America Inc. v. Government of Canada*, Decision of the Tribunal on Petitions for Intervention and Participation as *Amici Curiae*, 17 October 2001 (http://naftaclaims.com/Disputes/Canada/UPS/UPS DecisionReParticipationAmiciCuriae.pdf); *Aguas del Tunari v. Republic of Bolivia*, ICSID Arbitration

some of the process. However, they have not always been accompanied by orders allowing access to the arbitration pleadings, making informed participation by civil society much more difficult and potentially uninformed and thus irrelevant on key issues.[10] In addition, only under NAFTA is there a set of rules to be applied for *amicus* brief purposes, leaving other tribunals without any specific guidance.[11]

The primary rule of any legal system in a democratic context is very simple: for justice to be done it must be seen to be done. Yet this most basic rule is flouted by ongoing demands for secrecy in matters often central to public policy decision-making, where the conflict is not just about private sector money, but about the balance between the public welfare and private interests. Secrecy in many cases as to the very existence of an arbitration, lack of access to documents, closed hearings, and, in many cases, no public release of the final or interim decisions make a mockery of this basic principle. There is no indication this is about to change quickly, or broadly. Again, a systemic approach to investment law as part of the international law of globalization, and an appropriately transparent institutional structure, provide a practical and principled approach to addressing this issue.

The matter can be summed up quite simply: the absence of notification of arbitrations to the public, the absence of public documents and closed arbitral proceedings force us to confront the question of how we can know we have a system of law, and be operating under that system, when one cannot even see the system operating.

Appellate System

Consistency and the issue of an appellate system for investor-State arbitrations are often seen as related issues. While some argue that arbitral awards are becoming more and more consistent, the present commentator does not see things this way. Indeed, it seems to me that on almost every major legal standard

---

ARB/02/03, where a provisional decision to consider *amicus* submissions was made but never advanced due to the settlement of the case; and *Aguas Argentinas v. Argentina*, *Amicus Curiae* Decision, ICSID Case No. ARB/03/19; Order in Response to a petition for Transparency and participation as *Amicus Curiae*, 19 May 2005.

10 For a salient example, *see* Procedural Order No. 5 in *Biwater v. Tanzania*, for an example of the complexities and difficulties that lack of transparency and access to the arbitration materials create in the *amicus curiae* context.

11 Statement of the Free Trade Commission on Non-Disputing Party Participation, 7 October 2003 (http://www.dfait-maeci.gc.ca/nafta-alena/Nondisputing-en.pdf).

common to investment agreements (national treatment, most-favored-nation [MFN] treatment, fair and equitable treatment, expropriation) the full body of awards present us with irreconcilable views and approaches today. That UNCTAD has recently suggested a similar concern is worth noting here, given UNCTAD's support for these agreements.[12]

The result is that the final decision in an investor-State case hinges perhaps just as much on a clear understanding of the scope of the law to be applied as it does on a clear understanding of the predilections of the chosen arbitrators in relation to the scope of the rules. This takes us right back to the issue of conflict of interest in the choice of arbitrators. Indeed, it is becoming increasingly clear that some major law firms have a chosen group of arbitrators they like to draw from, while others choose people they know have rather fixed views of the law, or what the law should be. Either way, the appointment of arbitrators is now becoming a significant issue that only adds to the uncertainty of the outcome and state of the law as law, and thus to the ongoing risks of inconsistency in awards.

Introducing an appellate level would, as a consequence, have the impact of imposing consistency, and thus greater clarity, for both host countries and investors. It would also have the effect of ending the ad hoc revision and review processes currently in use through ICSID or domestic courts. In addition, much as the WTO Appellate Body has instilled consistency in the WTO law, it has also instilled a layer of accountability for WTO Panels that did not exist before the Appellate Body was formed. This has also achieved a much higher degree of public acceptability of the final results.

This is not low-hanging fruit, however. It requires full consideration of international investment law as a legal regime, requiring consistency and clarity, rather than simply resolution of any one-off dispute. With well over 200 arbitrations now in existence or finished, and the precedential role of individual awards increasing, such a regime-based view would seem rather easy to endorse. However, an appellate body has been rejected in the recent revision of the ICSID rules, and no existing IIA has provision for an operational appellate mechanism.[13] (See Annex 1, *International Investment Instruments with Provisions Relating to an Appellate Review Mechanism.*)

---

12 UNCTAD, *Investor-State Disputes Arising From Investment Treaties: A Review* (United Nations Publication: 2005).

13 However, several recent U.S. agreements have included a provision to reconsider this issue in a designated period of time after the agreement comes into force. This is the most advanced statement on this issue to date.

Conclusions: Investor-State Arbitration and the Rule of Law

So where do these individual issues take us? What is important, it is submitted, is conceptualizing the application of the rule of law to the international investment law field itself. This includes clear rules on conflict of interest, public accountability and transparency, a system that ensures consistent approaches to the meaning of substantive and procedural rules, and a system of regime-based oversight like most other public international law fields have developed over the past decades. This requires replacing ad hoc negotiations and dispute settlement processes with a regime-based approach. The GATT did this in full measure with the creation of the WTO in 1995. In the area of international investment law, it is no longer sufficient simply to advocate the use of international investment agreements as a vehicle for promoting the rule of law by others, when the conduct of the system itself so clearly lacks for the application of the rule of law to itself.

Yet such a step, indeed a very large step, cannot be taken when the proponents of the current regime are unwilling to accept the need to develop a regime-based approach to the future development of the system. Reliance on ad hoc systems and self-governance in the face of the control of the dispute settlement process by a relatively small and still largely homogeneous group of lawyers does not constitute a system under law. However, this status quo will not work from the longer term perspective of the role of international investment law as part of the international law of globalization. Those who fail to see the need for such a systemic, regime-oriented viewpoint doom the existing system to a continuous draining of public credibility and acceptability.

Fundamental to issues of both transparency and consistency—both intimately connected with regime legitimacy—is the notion that the regime itself must also be subject to the rule of law. For the international investment regime to establish itself as that, the goal must move beyond the promotion of the rule of law for others to include the promotion of the rule of law within the regime itself.

CHAPTER 14

Improving the System of Investor-State Dispute Settlement: The OECD Governments' Perspective

*Katia Yannaca-Small**

This commentary focuses on the reaction of the Organisation for Economic Co-operation and Development (OECD) governments to proposals and ideas for change to the current system of investor-State dispute settlement. We will first look at the discussion related to the possibility of introducing an appeal mechanism and continue with the discussion on transparency and third party participation and other measures, such as consolidation of claims, to reduce potential inconsistencies among arbitral awards.

I. Discussion of the Appeal Mechanism

The introduction by the United States in its bilateral investment treaties and Free Trade Agreements of the possibility of establishing an appellate mechanism to review investment disputes stirred up an interest in the OECD Investment Committee, which started exploring the feasibility and usefulness of such a mechanism.[1] (See Annex 1, *International Investment Instruments with*

---

* Legal Advisor on International Investment, Investment Division, Directorate for Financial and Enterprise Affairs, OECD. This chapter reflects comments presented at the Columbia Program on International Investment Symposium, April 2006. It represents the personal views of the author. Email: catherine.yannaca-small@oecd.org.

1 *See* OECD, "Improving the System of Investor-State Dispute Settlement: An Overview," *in International Investment Perspectives* (2006), Chapter 7.

Provisions Relating to an Appellate Review Mechanism.) At the same time, the International Centre for Settlement of Investment Disputes (ICSID) made concrete proposals toward establishing such a mechanism. Joint OECD/ICSID consultations with arbitrators, counsel and government experts raised both advantages and disadvantages of this undertaking:

Advantages

Consistency

One of the main advantages advanced was the avoidance of inconsistent decisions, with the example of the Czech cases prominent. The notion of consistency was viewed from three angles:

- Avoiding conflicting opinions or different conclusions when two tribunals constituted under different agreements deal with the same set of facts.
- Fostering coherent interpretations of basic principles that may underlie differently worded provisions in various agreements, thereby enhancing the development of a more consistent international investment law.
- Achieving uniformity in the challenging of awards.

This last objective might be furthered if traditional bases for annulment were incorporated in an appeal mechanism that became the exclusive means to challenge an award.

Rectification of Legal Errors and, Possibly, Serious Errors of Facts

The possibility of rectification might help allay public concern that awards affecting important public policy issues and interests could be enforced despite serious error.

Review Confined to a Neutral Tribunal versus National Courts

The advantage of review by a neutral tribunal, a feature of the ICSID system, does not yet exist for review of non-ICSID awards. Those awards are indeed subject to review, though usually one limited in scope, by domestic courts that may have a local bias or be subject to governmental influences.

Effective Enforcement

It was suggested that the creation of an appeal mechanism might enhance the expeditious and effective enforcement of awards if a respondent filing an appeal were required to post a bond in the amount of the award and if appeal decisions were excluded from domestic court review.

Disadvantages

Against the Principle of Finality

Finality has traditionally been seen as one of the major advantages of arbitration over judicial settlement. There was, however, a view that the public-interest issues at stake in investment arbitration might make the acceptance of the risk of flawed or erroneous decisions in this field less justifiable in the name of finality than it would be in commercial arbitration.

Could Result in Additional Delays, Costs and Caseload

There was a view that these problems could be greater than those already associated with proceedings under the "set-aside" national court systems, which can take years before they conclude.

One remedy to the time concern could be setting specific time limits in the appellate process. A second suggestion is that, by limiting the scope of review to pure questions of law and excluding any error of fact, cost and time might be saved.

Also, there was a concern that there would be a tendency to appeal in every case, which would result in decreased confidence in the main body of decisions. The requirement of a bond to secure the award and the cost of the proceedings was mentioned as a disincentive to appeal.

Politicization of the System

Finally, there was a concern that the de-politicization of investment disputes, considered one of the achievements of investor-State arbitration, could be undermined by having governments appealing on every case they lose, in order to please their constituencies. In addition, it was argued that if the choice of the appellate arbitrators were to be made by the States only, there would be a risk of bias against investors. Counter-arguments were also advanced, for instance about the benefits investors could also draw from the appeal, and different solutions might be envisaged for the choice of arbitrators to ensure neutrality of the system.

Conclusions as to the Appeal Mechanism

The discussion did not produce any positive results for the appeal proposal. With the exception of the NAFTA governments, the majority of the OECD did not seem to consider the issue urgent enough to embark on a radical system change. Further, they did not even evidence any sense of being directly concerned, which may be attributable to the fact that the majority have never been respondents to a case and continue to view the subject from an exclusively "home country" perspective.

However, OECD governments saw an interest in making an effort to improve the system and in considering other ways for doing so. They looked at a number of ideas,[2] such as:

- Transposing to investment arbitration the International Chamber of Commerce mechanism for scrutiny of awards by adding an extra layer of control before the awards are sent to the parties. This would require, in addition to a trained Secretariat, an independent permanent judicial body to mirror the ICC Court of Arbitration. This idea was dismissed as too radical, as it would require an important systemic change.
- The establishment of an Additional Annulment Facility to mirror ICSID's Additional Facility Rules so that non-ICSID members would also have access to the self-contained ICSID system of annulment. This idea raised a number of questions, including whether an arbitral award would be effectively shielded from set-aside procedures without a treaty, and was finally dismissed as well.

---

2 *Id.*

II. The Discussion on Transparency

An area in which the OECD governments thought progress could be made was the strengthening of transparency. There was a feeling that easy, quick and tangible results could be obtained by supporting the systematic publication of awards and expressing encouragement for third party participation in the proceedings.[3]

They saw particular value in the systematic publication of awards because:

- There is a growing number of arbitration decisions and awards that are likely to influence future cases;
- It enhances the equality of the parties, giving both sides access to all opinions and decisions; and
- It would contribute to the further development of a public body of jurisprudence that would allow investors and host countries to understand how investment agreements are interpreted and applied and ultimately contribute to a more predictable and consistent system.

Third party participation, including submissions and access to hearings, met a more qualified reaction. Although the governments saw merit in this opening, they considered it preferable that it be subject to specific rules and guidelines and close monitoring.

These discussions gave rise to the following public statement adopted by the OECD Investment Committee in June 2005, favoring additional transparency:

> There is a general understanding among the Members of the Investment Committee that additional transparency, in particular in relation to the publication of arbitral awards, subject to necessary safeguards for the protection of confidential business and governmental information, is desirable to enhance effectiveness and public acceptance of international investment arbitration, as well as contributing to the further development of a public body of jurisprudence. Members of the Investment Committee generally share the view that, especially insofar as proceedings raise important issues of public interest, it may also be desirable to allow third party participation, subject however to clear and specific guidelines.

---

3 OECD, "Transparency and Third Party Participation in Investor-State Dispute Settlement Procedures," *in International Investment Law: A Changing Landscape, a Companion Volume of the International Investment Perspectives* (2005).

III. Discussion on Consolidation of Claims

The multiplication of investment agreements with investor-State dispute settlement provisions has raised the risk of multiple and conflicting awards, as essentially the same disputed situation can lead to awards under different treaty regimes as well as under different contracts. Investors are sometimes able to claim breaches of different BITs and to seek relief through different arbitration proceedings under each of the invoked treaties in respect of a single investment and regarding the same facts. The "Czech cases" (*CME/Lauder v. the Czech Republic*)[4] and the approximately 40 cases currently pending against Argentina and arising from the same events, demonstrate the increasing complexity of such situations.

Although the experience up to now does not show major inconsistencies among arbitral awards, some decisions considered inconsistent by certain parties and the evolving landscape in investment arbitration led to discussions within the OECD Investment Committee. This discussion was based on a paper examining the advantages and disadvantages of consolidation drawing from the experience in the commercial arbitration context.[5]

However, although there was acknowledgment in the Committee that consolidation of claims emanating from the same state measure and based on similar factual and legal elements could protect against such a risk, there was no consensus that the advantages of consolidation provisions in investment agreements exceed its disadvantages. The consent of the parties as a prerequisite for a request for consolidation and concerns about confidentiality still weighed strongly against the advantages of this measure.

A few treaties presently provide for consolidation. In the absence of such provision, the disputing parties wishing to do so can ask for consolidation or "de facto" consolidation, and arbitral institutions such as ICSID could facilitate the latter process by appointing the same panel of arbitrators. This has already been done in some of the cases against Argentina.

---

4 *CME Czech Republic B.V. v. Czech Republic*, Partial Award (13 September 2001), (http://mfcr.cz/Arbitraz/en/PartialAward.doc) and *Lauder v. Czech Republic*, Final Award (3 September 2001) (http://www.mfcr.cz/scripts/hpe/default.asp).

5 For a more detailed discussion of this issue *see* "Consolidation of Claims: A Promising Avenue for Investment Arbitration?" *in International Investment Perspectives* (OECD 2006) Chapter 8.

PART IV

Critical Views on an Appellate Mechanism in Investment Disputes

CHAPTER 15

Options to Establish an Appellate Mechanism for Investment Disputes

*Barton Legum**

This chapter explores options to establish an appellate mechanism for investment disputes. First, I will review the options that have been tabled for establishing such an investment mechanism. This section can be summarized in four words: there are no options.

Second, I will examine why, despite the substantial discussion of this topic over the past four years, there are no options on the table. In this part of the chapter, I will show that the current investment law environment is not well suited to an appellate mechanism. I will then explore whether a compelling need for such a mechanism has been established, and finally argue that the cure in this case could well be worse than the disease.

The chapter concludes with a few general observations on the prospect of an appellate mechanism and the way forward.

Options to Establish an Appellate Mechanism

The discussion of an appellate mechanism for investment disputes moved into the mainstream during the second half of 2002, when the United States

* Counsel, Debevoise & Plimpton LLP, Paris. From 2000–2004, Mr. Legum served as the Chief of the NAFTA Arbitration Division, Office of the Legal Adviser, United States Department of State. Email: blegum@debevoise.com.

Congress enacted the Bipartisan Trade Promotion Authority Act.[1] The Act identified for U.S. free trade agreements a negotiating objective of "providing for an appellate body or similar mechanism to provide coherence to the interpretations of investment provisions in trade agreements."[2]

Bilateral free trade agreements negotiated in 2003 and later between the U.S. and Chile, Singapore, Morocco and others contained a type of provision that negotiators called a "socket": the agreements acknowledged the possibility of an appellate mechanism being established, and set forth, in the event such a mechanism materialized, an "agreement to agree" to have that mechanism apply to the free trade agreement.[3] The agreements also provided that, within a certain period of time after entry into force, the contracting States would "consider whether to establish a bilateral appellate body or similar mechanism."[4] (See Annex 1, *International Investment Instruments with Provisions Relating to an Appellate Review Mechanism.*)

These provisions went one step further in the Central American Free Trade Agreement, signed in August 2004. The CAFTA required establishment of "a Negotiating Group to develop an appellate body or similar mechanism to review awards rendered by tribunals" within three months of the agreement's entry into force.[5] It further required the contracting States to "direct the Negotiating Group to provide to the Commission, within one year of

---

1 *See* Trade Act of 2002, P.L. No. 107 –210, 116 Stat. 933 (2002). The negotiating objective under discussion appears in Title XXI of Division B of the Trade Act of 2002, known as the Bipartisan Trade Promotion Authority Act of 2002, which has been codified at 19 U.S.C. §§ 3801 et seq. *See* Trade Act of 2002, P.L. No. 107–210, sec. 2101(a), 116 Stat. 993 (2002) (codified at 19 U.S.C. § 3801(a)).

2 19 U.S.C. § 3802(b)(3)(G)(iv).

3 *See, e.g.*, Free Trade Agreement, Chile–U.S., 6 June 2003, Art. 10.19(10). This states: "If a separate multilateral agreement enters into force as between the Parties that establishes an appellate body for purposes of reviewing awards rendered by tribunals constituted pursuant to international trade or investment agreements to hear investment disputes, the Parties shall strive to reach an agreement that would have such appellate body review awards rendered under Article 10.25 in arbitrations commenced after the appellate body's establishment." (http://www.ustr.gov/assets/Trade_Agreements/Bilateral/Chile_FTA/Final_Texts/asset_upload_file1_4004.pdf).

4 *See, e.g., id.* annex 10-H: "Within three years after the date of entry into force of this Agreement, the Parties shall consider whether to establish a bilateral appellate body or similar mechanism to review awards rendered under Article 10.25 in arbitrations commenced after they establish the appellate body or similar mechanism."

5 Central American Free Trade Agreement, 5 August 2004, Costa Rica–Dom. Rep.–El Salv.–Guat.–Hond. Nica.–U.S., Annex 10-F (http://www.ustr.gov/assets/Trade_Agreements/Bilateral/CAFTA/CAFTA-DR_Final_Texts/asset_upload_file328_4718.pdf).

establishment of the Negotiating Group, a draft amendment to the Agreement that establishes an appellate body or similar mechanism."[6]

In October 2004, the International Centre for Settlement of Investment Disputes (ICSID) added momentum to discussions of an appellate mechanism by releasing a working paper that floated the idea of a new ICSID "Appeals Facility."[7] ICSID held a series of meetings with member States, non-governmental organizations, the international arbitration community and others to solicit views on the wisdom of such a facility.[8] The result of those wide and intensive consultations was a conclusion in May 2005 that "it would be premature to attempt to establish such an ICSID mechanism at this stage, particularly in view of the difficult technical and policy issues raised" by such a mechanism.[9] No text on appeals was tabled and no reference to an appeals facility appears in the recently adopted amendments to the ICSID rules.[10]

So where do efforts to establish an appellate mechanism stand? The prospect of a multilateral appeals mechanism under ICSID's auspices is off the table. There are now signed free trade agreements and investment treaties between the U.S. and 13 other countries that expressly contemplate the possibility of an appellate mechanism.[11] But no negotiations to establish an appellate mechanism have been announced, and no text is on the table anywhere. There are, despite

---

6 *Id.*

7 ICSID Secretariat, "Possible Improvements of the Framework for ICSID Arbitration 14-16" (22 October 2004) (http://www.worldbank.org/icsid/highlights/DiscussionPaper.pdf). (This article is reproduced in Annex 3.)

8 *See* ICSID Secretariat, "Suggested Changes to the ICSID Rules and Regulations 3" (12 May 2005): "In addition to sending the Discussion Paper to members of the Administrative Council for their comments, the Secretariat of the Centre sought comments on the Paper from business and civil society groups and from arbitration experts and institutions around the world. The present Working Paper outlines the results of this extensive consultation and makes several follow up suggestions." (*http://www.worldbank.org/icsid/highlights/052405-sgmanual.pdf*). (This article is reproduced in Annex 4.)

9 *Id.* at 4: "The members of the Administrative Council and others who provided comments on the Discussion Paper expressed appreciation for the initiative to review the framework for ICSID arbitration and identify possible improvements. There was general agreement that, if international appellate procedures were to be introduced for investment treaty arbitrations, then this might best be done through a single ICSID mechanism rather than by different mechanisms established under each treaty concerned. Most, however, considered that it would be premature to attempt to establish such an ICSID mechanism at this stage, particularly in view of the difficult technical and policy issues raised in the Discussion Paper. The Secretariat will continue to study such issues to assist member countries when and if it is decided to proceed towards the establishment of an ICSID appeal mechanism."

10 *See* Barton Legum, "La réforme du CIRDI: vers une juridictionnalisation de l'arbitrage transnational?" *in* Ferhat Horchani, ed., *Où va le droit de l'investissement?* (A. Pedone: 2006).

11 The countries in question are Chile, Colombia, Costa Rica, Dominican Republic, El Salvador, Guatemala, Honduras, Morocco, Nicaragua, Oman, Peru, Singapore and Uruguay.

the fanfare surrounding this issue two or three years ago, no options currently in play to establish an appellate mechanism for investment disputes.

Why Are There No Options?

Why, indeed, are there no options? I believe that three reasons, broadly put, explain the lack of concrete proposals at this time.

The Current Investment Law Environment is Ill-adapted

The first and perhaps most important reason is a structural one: the current environment of international investment law is ill-suited to appeals. As the other scholars and commentators have noted many times in this volume, international investment law is defined by some 2,500 bilateral investment treaties (BITs) negotiated over a half-century by hundreds of different combinations of countries. As might be expected, the provisions of these treaties are different from each other in important respects, although their text is also similar—sometimes deceptively similar—in many respects.

An example: the most-favored-nation (MFN) provision in the investment chapter of the recently signed U.S.–Peru free trade agreement requires MFN treatment "with respect to the establishment, acquisition, expansion, management, conduct, operation, and sale or other disposition of investments."[12] The MFN provision in the recently signed Angola–U.K. BIT requires MFN treatment "as regards [the] management, maintenance, use, enjoyment or disposal of … investments."[13] The texts of the two provisions are certainly similar.

But the contextual bases of the two provisions vary in a critical respect. The Peru–U.S. free trade agreement explains, in a footnote to the MFN provision, that the provision's text "does not encompass dispute resolution mechanisms."[14]

---

12 Free Trade Agreement, U.S.–Peru, 7 December 2005, Art. 10.4 (http://www.ustr.gov/assets/Trade_Agreements/Bilateral/Peru_TPA/Final_Texts/asset_upload_file925_8697.pdf).

13 Investment Promotion and Protection Agreement, 4 July 2001, Angola–U.K., Art. 3(2) (http://www.fco.gov.uk/Files/kfile/Print%20Angola%205525,0.pdf).

14 *See* Free Trade Agreement, U.S.–Peru, 7 December 2005, Art. 10.4 n.2: "For greater certainty, treatment 'with respect to the establishment, acquisition, expansion, management, conduct, operation, and sale or other disposition of investments' referred to in paragraphs 1 and 2 of Article 10.4 does not encompass dispute resolution mechanisms, such as those in Section B, that are provided for in international investment treaties or trade agreements" (http://www.ustr.gov/assets/Trade_Agreements/Bilateral/Peru_TPA/Final_Texts/asset_upload_file925_8697.pdf).

The Angola–U.K. BIT, by contrast, explicitly confirms that the obligation of MFN treatment *will* apply to dispute resolution mechanisms.[15] Thus, these two treaties use remarkably similar language to remarkably different ends: in one instance to expressly reject *Maffezini* and in the other instance expressly to embrace the result in *Maffezini*.[16]

This example drives home the observation made by the tribunal in the *OSPAR Convention* case:

> "The application of international law rules on interpretation of treaties to identical or similar provisions of different treaties may not yield the same results, having regard to, *inter alia*, differences in the respective contexts, objects and purposes, subsequent practice of parties and *travaux préparatoires*."[17]

While international investment agreements may have similar or identical texts, because they were negotiated at widely varying times between diverse States with varying intentions, different content will be, and should be, given to that text by tribunals applying established principles of treaty interpretation. The goal of achieving consistency and coherence across the full body of international investment law today, therefore, is chimerical. The diversity of texts and contexts across the 2,500 treaties is such that a truly consistent and coherent interpretation of them is neither possible nor permissible under accepted rules of treaty interpretation.

It is noteworthy that the great majority of standing international tribunals—including the rare international appellate bodies—have issued from a single underlying multilateral agreement with very broad participation negotiated at a single point in time. The International Court of Justice emerged from the negotiations that led to the creation of the United Nations; the International

---

15 *See* Investment Promotion and Protection Agreement, 4 July 2001, Angola–U.K., Art 3(3): "For avoidance of doubt it is confirmed that the treatment provided for in paragraphs (1) and (2) above shall apply to the provisions of Article 1 to 11 of this Agreement." (http://www.fco.gov.uk/Files/kfile/Print%20Angola%205525,0.pdf). Article 8 sets forth the investor-State dispute resolution procedure, and Article 9 sets forth the State-to-State mechanism.

16 *Cf. Maffezini v. Kingdom of Spain*, ICSID Case No. ARB/97/7, 16 ICSID Review—Foreign Investment Law Journal 1, 14–25 (Decision on Jurisdiction of 25 January 2000).

17 Dispute Concerning Access to Information under Article 9 of the OSPAR Convention (*Ireland v. U.K.*), para. 141 (Final Award of 2 July 2003) (http://www.pca-cpa.org/ENGLISH/RPC/OSPAR/OSPAR%20final%20award%20revised.pdf) (quoting ITLOS Order of 3 December 2001).

Tribunal on the Law of the Sea from the U.N. Convention on the Law of the Sea; and the WTO Appellate Body from the Uruguay Round. These international tribunals generally have as their primary function to decide cases arising under the agreement or set of agreements that were negotiated at the time they were established. The WTO Appellate Body addresses cases arising under the WTO agreements; the International Tribunal for the Law of the Sea addresses cases arising under the U.N. Law of the Sea Convention; the International Court of Justice was established as the principal judicial organ of the United Nations.

By contrast, as we have just seen, an appellate system for investment treaty arbitration would not have as its task the interpretation of a single agreement or set of agreements to which all of its members are party. It would have as subjects for decision hundreds of BITs negotiated at different times between different countries with differing provisions.

This structural difference between the current international investment law environment—consisting of a multitude of different treaties—and the environment that typically accompanies the birth of standing international tribunals—a single multilateral agreement with a single set of provisions to be consistently construed—is fundamental. As long as the investment law environment has these characteristics, I submit, the argument for an appellate mechanism based on consistency of results will have little traction. And indeed, it is significant that the IISD Model International Agreement on Investment for Sustainable Development proposes an appellate mechanism only in the more nurturing context of a single, multilateral agreement on investment.[18]

The Need Has Not Yet Been Established

The second broad reason why there are no options for an appellate mechanism now on the table is that the need for greater consistency and coherence has not compellingly been established.

---

18 *International Institute for Sustainable Development, IISD International Agreement on Investment for Sustainable Development* vii (2005) ("Viewed as a multilateral approach, the Model Agreement also provides a single window approach to addressing the defects in the now over 2,000 bilateral and regional agreements, all of which more or less share the same type of model. Thus, IISD believes that a multilateral approach offers significant advantages over further proliferation of bilateral agreements and regional agreements.") (http://www.iisd.org/publications/pub.aspx?id=685); *id.* at 21 (outlining appellate body for investment disputes).

First, we are still in the early days of investment treaty jurisprudence. The cumulative docket of 200-some investment treaty disputes over the past 40 years is less than that handled by a single judge in a New York domestic court in a single year; it is similarly insignificant compared, say, to the 10,000 cases decided by the Mixed Claims Commissions after World War I. The empirical case for a need for greater consistency and coherence lacks a statistically significant data set.

Second, the anecdotal problems identified would not necessarily be fixed by an appellate system in any event. The poster child for lack of consistency in investment arbitration is the pair of decisions in *Lauder v. Czech Republic* and *CME v. Czech Republic*. The tribunals in those two cases did indeed reach different decisions based on the same factual record and arguments by the same counsel for the same or closely related parties. But the different decisions stemmed from a contrasting appreciation of the facts of the case, not from a fundamentally different understanding of the applicable law. Under the model of appellate review adopted by the few international appellate bodies in existence today, this difference in appreciation of the facts would be corrected on appeal only if no reasonable arbitrator could have possibly so understood the facts of the case.[19] I do not believe that either *Lauder* or *CME* would be subject to correction on appeal under such a standard of appellate review.[20]

Finally, as any professional advocate will note, a certain level of inconsistency is inevitable in any system of administration of justice. Reasonable judges and juries can reasonably reach different results based on the same facts. And advocacy—how a case is argued and presented—really does make a difference. That is why the bar exists and why clients are willing to pay lawyers to

---

19 *See Prosecutor v. Vasiljevic*, Case No. IT-98-32-A, Judgment of 25 Feb 2004, at 2-3 (I.C.T.Y. App. Chamber): "Regarding errors of fact, the Appeals Chamber will only substitute the Trial Chamber's finding for its own when no reasonable trier of fact could have made the original finding. Further, it is not any error of fact that will cause the Appeals Chamber to overturn a decision by a Trial Chamber, but one which has led to a miscarriage of justice, which has been defined as 'a grossly unfair outcome in judicial proceedings, as when a defendant is convicted despite a lack of evidence on an essential element of a crime'" (http://www.un.org/icty/vasiljevic/appeal/judgement/val-aj040225e.pdf) (footnotes omitted); *see also EC—Measures Concerning Meat and Meat Products (Hormones)*, Report of the Appellate Body, WT/DS26/AB/R, WT/DS48/AB/R, 16 January 1998, para. 132: "[w]hether or not a panel has made an objective assessment of the facts before it, as required by Article 11 of the DSU, is...a legal question which, if properly raised on appeal, would fall within the scope of appellate review."

20 For full disclosure, attorneys with my law firm (Debevoise & Plimpton LLP) represented the claimants in the *Lauder* and *CME* cases, although I myself was not associated with the firm at the time the cases were litigated.

represent them. The fact that advocacy makes a difference means that a result that a great advocate might achieve might be different from the result that a lesser advocate might obtain with the same file. Every legal system in which judges are human and cases are presented by lawyers has a certain built-in tolerance for inconsistency. The argument that the inconsistency seen in the few investment awards to date exceeds the usual tolerance levels has not yet been supported.

Is the Cure Worse than the Disease?

The third and final reason why there are no options on the table for an appellate mechanism is that the cure here could be far worse than the disease. The wrong sort of appellate body for investment disputes could do a tremendous amount of damage. Imagine an appellate body that considered its role as a sort of constitutional court in investment matters, and consistently took an activist stand in favor of the investors/claimants in every case to come before it. This could be an economic disaster for developing countries, a political disaster for developed countries, and a generalized disaster for the future of international investment law.

Consider the same scenario, but with an appellate body whose members were decided exclusively by the developing countries that controlled the majority of votes by contracting States, and which routinely upheld the States' arguments. A similarly disastrous outcome would ensue.

Because the stakes for an appellate mechanism are so high, States are understandably reluctant to tackle the problem before the problem is compellingly shown to exist. This, as noted above, is not the case.

Conclusions

In conclusion, I am pessimistic about the near-term prospects of a unitary appellate mechanism with broad jurisdiction to review awards in investment disputes. As long as the environment of international investment law is characterized by a multitude of bilateral treaties, the case that an appellate mechanism could ensure consistency and coherence is not a compelling one. As someone who spent much time while at the U.S. State Department working on a proposal for an appellate mechanism, this conclusion fills me with some regret—but strikes me as the most realistic assessment of the situation.

The structural issues I have identified apply with much less force to the subset of free trade agreement investment chapters and investment treaties negotiated by the United States over the past three years. The texts of these treaties are highly consistent, and the presence of one common party to each treaty adds a certain stability. It will be interesting to see whether, in the near term, a more modest appellate mechanism limited to these agreements will emerge.

CHAPTER 16

Avoiding Unintended Consequences

*Jan Paulsson**

What issues of coherence? There is no reason to be alarmed about inconsistent *obiter dicta*. Irreconcilable differences in *rationes decidendi* have been far rarer than supposed. From a practitioner's viewpoint, there is no crisis of unpredictability. The structural cures imagined were conceived in haste and would have engendered vast disruption, out of all proportion to the familiar task of establishing jurisprudence in new areas of law. Normative hesitations are likely to be resolved in usual and legitimate ways. The demands for greater transparency, on the other hand, should be viewed with sympathy. They hold a realistic promise of leading to better law. The debate was stimulating and worthwhile. It enabled us to determine that on balance there was no balance. One big idea was bad, the other good.

Debate is healthy, and often constructive. It is most likely to be constructive when those who engage in the dialog are scrupulous about fact and transparent in motive.

Some may well believe that representatives of capital-importing States were mistaken on hundreds of occasions when they signed BITs, and that their interests are in fact adversely affected by such treaties. But if those who hold such views participate in a debate on the ostensible subject of reforming international legal processes relating to investment with the undisclosed determination that anything which stifles the emerging systems of investor protection is good, they are guilty of false pretences. Whether one should dismantle the current system is another debate. It is perfectly legitimate, but should not be

* Partner, Freshfields Bruckhaus Deringer. E-mail: jan.paulsson@freshfields.com.

addressed in camouflage; it is perverse to pretend to reform what one would rather destroy.[1]

The editors have asked me for a practitioner's evaluation of the suggestions that surfaced in 2005 concerning imaginable corrective features in investment arbitration. One of the attractions of this volume is precisely that it is dominated by undogmatic contributions, at once sophisticated and dispassionate.[2] Proposals for a universal appellate mechanism, it seems, have little realistic future, while the cry for greater transparency has been muted for the opposite reason: ready acceptance. (Implementation is another matter.) And yet this collection of papers will remain a valuable record of the two debates which concluded the first significant decade of modern investment arbitration.[3]

Disclosures and Premises

I have participated in a significant number of investment arbitrations—nearly 30 under the ICSID Rules alone. I have served as advocate and arbitrator. (Under what conditions that should be allowed is yet another legitimate debate,[4] but not one to be addressed in this contribution.) As an advocate, I have represented investors and states alike, somewhat more often the latter than the former. I have acted for the same African State in 14 international arbitrations, reporting to a succession of ministers who over the course of 20 years apparently saw the value of the professional defence of that State's interests. It is not so that whatever is good for lawyers is good for

---

1 Dr. Mann writes, in Chapter 13, that the international investment law regime is "institutionally deprived," explaining that the few relevant institutions "are fragmented in their roles, have no mandate over the overall regime's development process and lack any processes for ongoing review of the evolution of this area of the law." This is of course a fundamental insight about international law, which, it must also be said, has revealed itself to a multitude of international scholars since well before the days of Grotius. If Dr. Mann believes that the development of investment protection should be put on hold until this inconvenience is repaired, perhaps by a truly representative global conclave in which states—whose treaty practice so far has only maintained the "rotting foundation" of a system whose participants have a "manifest self-interest in the status quo"—would not have a decisive voice, he is in fact standing in the way of progress.

2 I have little hesitation in recommending that the reader start with Chapter 14, one of a series of remarkable "working papers" prepared by the Investment Division of the OECD. Authored by Katia Yannaca-Small, these studies provide lucid, informative, and thoughtful descriptions of actual developments unencumbered by personal visions *de lege ferenda*. The last of these virtues cannot be claimed by the present author.

3 To use the words of Professor Franck, when "dispute resolution systems ... undergo fundamental growth, a re-consideration of the system's efficacy and utility can promote both its integration and legitimacy" (Chapter 9).

4 With respect to which one should accept without hesitation that Dr. Mann's pertinent criticism must be answered.

the world. Nor indeed does the prosperity of corporate entities (or that of governments) have any *raison d'être* except as a means to a good end. But I believe the prospect of legal protection of investors to be valuable, to be preserved and enhanced. I might add that I see no paradox in the concept that investor protection would be enhanced by the expansion and clearer articulation of the *obligations of investors.*[5]

I do not choose to defend this position by insisting that foreign investment is a good thing. It is enough that this is the view taken by the representatives of sovereign States everywhere. Nor do I insist that treaty protections measurably increase investment volumes. The data are inconclusive; the methodology of studies of this proposition—and yes, sometimes their motivation—is suspect. What attracts me to the objective of investor protection are above all two positive effects.

First, a good international regime of investor protection holds out the promise over time of reducing the profit margins that investors demand. This is a matter of singular macro-economic importance. Some resource-rich developing countries can afford the legal-risk premium which results from governance by fiat, but for the poorer countries it is an oppressive burden. It will take a long time before investors are willing to put their capital into Sierra Leone in the expectation of as low a rate of return, and over as long a term, as they are happy to accept in Switzerland. Yet there can be little doubt that moving in this direction is in Sierra Leone's interest.

The second effect leads to more immediate benefits: I am encouraged by what I have seen when government officials—like their corporate counterparts—become conscious of the fact that they may have to justify their acts or omissions before neutral international tribunals. This has a way of modifying their conduct in a way which seems to have a positive effect on internal governance. Perhaps through a phenomenon which some sociologists call *compliance pull,* they begin to distance themselves from old habits of opacity, arbitrariness, clientilism. They begin to embrace better practices more consonant with their self-image as modern leaders attached to their country's prestige. They come to demand it of their colleagues. Nor should one forget the positive feedback associated with the ever more frequent successes

---

5 See in this connection Professor Juillard's comments about recent developments under his first—and hypothetical—subheading, "BITs are Imbalanced Instruments" (Chapter 5).

encountered by developing countries in international fora.[6] Such satisfactions reinforce behaviour that leads to those gratifying results.

With that background, I propose a series of observations. The first, under the heading "Incoherences of the Incoherence Complaint," is a hard look at the problem purportedly identified by critics of investment arbitration. One can hardly fault investment awards for failing to do the impossible. A failure to understand the notion of *precedent* will lead to unhelpful exaggerations. Any significant legal evolution is a dialog between law-givers (read *BIT drafters*) and law-appliers (read *investment arbitrators*) which perforce takes some time to yield dialectic conclusions—even more so in an international context. The second set of observations describes "Natural Corrections" which I predict will yield satisfactory results and should be allowed to produce their benefits. Next, the section entitled "The Illusion of Cure" examines the decisive drawbacks of proposed structural transformations. Finally, I explain my ready acceptance of the need for greater transparency, and how it relates to the search for coherence and consistency.

Incoherences of the Incoherence Complaint

Why have psychologists over the centuries been unable to develop a workable formula to achieve harmony among human beings? Perhaps for the same reason that international arbitrators in the course of a decade of a flurry of investment arbitrations have not been able to develop a workable formula for determining when a commonwealth should compensate an individual for detriment caused by a new policy designed to benefit society as a whole.

Some questions are eternal. To take the issue of compensable regulatory measures—or those of abuse of power, minimum standards of fairness, denial of justice, or discrimination—they are simply immune to resolution by abstraction. Looking backward, it is plain that no national system has reached the promised land of the Answer. Incoherence abounds. (To take the example of a highly respectable and sophisticated legal system and a particular issue which has been the subject of infinite and powerful academic efforts, I have had the occasion to experience the essential truth of a disabused comment that if you ask six German lawyers for an explanation of unjust enrichment,

6 To mention three notable successes on the part of respondents from three continents, all decided within three months of each other roughly one year after the April 2006 Symposium: *Ahmonseto, Inc. et al. v. Egypt*, 18 June 2007; *MCI Power Group L.C. and New Turbine, Inc. v. Ecuador*, 31 July 2007; and *Fraport AG Frankfurt Airport Services Worldwide v. Philippines*, 16 August 2007.

you will get a dozen answers.) Looking into what I hope is a counterfactual crystal ball, I perceive that the same irreductible indeterminateness would be generated by appellate investment adjudicators.

So let us not beat about the bush. When critics of international arbitration bemoan the lack of consistency and coherence, they are blaming the process for failing to achieve the impossible—and proposing solutions which would fare no better. Once again, the hidden agenda needs to come out: what is being questioned is the very concept of neutral international adjudication and its necessary constraint on sovereignty. Adjudication of matters of public law is everywhere a constraint on collective sovereignty. Such is its nature and function.

States have good reason to accept the international rule of law, and the binding adjudications of international arbitrators, because it gives them the power to make meaningful promises.[7] That power is valuable; it makes economic transactions less expensive as the legal-risk premium decreases.

But since there has been so much talk of incoherence, let us consider that debate on its own terms—as if there were no hidden agenda.

It is imperative to sense the difference between the rationale of a case and incidental observations. The decision-making function is exercised when a tribunal upholds or denies a claim. The normative basis of that decision is of particular interest because that is where judges or arbitrators assume their responsibility. If a claim is rejected because the plaintiff has failed to take an obvious step to avert prejudice, we have a clear precedent for the proposition that there is a duty to mitigate. But if a claim is upheld, the basis is a finding of liability. An incidental statement to the effect that "recovery to claimants may be compromised if they fail to mitigate damages, but no proof of such failure was presented here" is *not* the basis for the decision. It may be persuasive of the existence of the norm, but it is of lesser weight.

---

7 As the Permanent Court of International Justice put it in *The SS Wimbledon* (Merits), Series A, No. 1 (1923) at 25:

> "The Court declines to see in the conclusion of any Treaty by which a State undertakes to perform or refrain from performing a particular act an abandonment of its sovereignty. No doubt any convention creating an obligation of this kind places a restriction upon the exercise of the sovereign rights of the State, in the sense that it requires them to be exercised in a certain way. But the right of entering into international engagements is an attribute of State sovereignty."

To take another example: an investment award may say that claimants must cumulatively satisfy the ICSID Convention definition as well as any BIT definition of the notion of "investment," but that is not necessarily the holding of the decision if the tribunal decides that both definitions are satisfied. The holding is simply that both definitions are in fact satisfied; it is not necessary to rule on the consequences of a contrary hypothesis. Unless the tribunal says something more, the proposition that both *must* be satisfied is properly understood as a holding only in a case where a claimant is sent packing because it failed under one definition, and the tribunal said it did not matter if it could have succeeded under the second.

Why would anyone care? Is this pedantry? Let me answer with rhetorical questions.

Is there not a world of difference between saying that parachuting is a wonderful sport, and actually stepping out of a plane at 3,000 feet? Between expressing conviction that gold will once again reign supreme and converting all one's savings into it? Between saying that something must be done to conserve energy and actually signing a public proposal for a ban of popular but wasteful automobiles? The point is obvious: to create *precedents* for the prevalence of sky-jumping, or investments in gold, or public commitment to unpopular reform, talk is not enough.

Arbitrators' opinions are no more or less interesting than those of any commentators. What we really want to know is the reason which they said led them to the outcome for which they have taken personal responsibility. That is where, we may reasonably surmise, they exhibit particular care.

In the *SGS v. Pakistan* case, I assisted Pakistan. Naturally I was very interested in the parallel case of *SGS v. Philippines*. What happened in my case was that the ICSID tribunal refused to rule on a claim of contractual debt because the contract called for arbitration in Islamabad, not ICSID arbitration. In the Filipino case, a second ICSID tribunal refused to rule on a claim of contractual debt because the contract called for litigation in Makati. There is no difference between those two precedents. The local press in Karachi and Manila were equally jubilant upon the announcements of the respective awards. But did not the *Philippines* arbitrators state that they declined to follow the Pakistan case? True enough, and I have chided one of them in public—in his presence—for having been too discursive. (He appeared to take it in stride.) The only thing wrong with their award was that it *said* that it was different from *SGS v. Pakistan*—setting a thousand tongues wagging about "inconsistent" ICSID decisions. But do not ask them to explain just how the decisions are irreconcilable unless you are a stalwart of scholasticism.

As for the conflict between the Lauder group and the Czech Republic, it is true that two different UNCITRAL tribunals appreciated the same conduct of the Czech Government in different ways, with radically opposed financial consequences.[8] That may or may not satisfy the participants in that case (it depends on one's views of hedging as a litigation strategy). But as *precedents*—as indicators to be used by parties and practitioners to understand legal criteria by which future conduct will be assessed—the two awards are not at all incompatible. Their understanding of the relevant legal standards, including causation, were perfectly congruent; their findings of fact were not. That is untidy, but no catastrophe, nor indeed surprising: such things happen when a story is told in different ways on different occasions to different people. (The Czech Republic surely rues its initial rejection of the claimants' offer of consolidation of the two cases before the tribunal which awarded nil damages.)

Sensible messages may be perceived by drafters and readers of awards. To a drafter: eschew lectures about issues unnecessary to the disposition of the case. To a reader: if the drafter has yielded to the temptation to digress, treat the thing with a good dose of benign neglect.

As arbitral practice expands, and as the field of international law itself expands in breadth of coverage and complexity, the calibre of awards is liable to greater unevenness. Some awards are influential, others best forgotten. There are awards which have been annulled and awards which have resisted annulment applications. There are awards which have not been tested at all. There are awards signed by panels of renowned jurists and awards rendered by sole arbitrators whose reputations are yet to be made. There are awards rendered by eminent persons careful of their reputation in the field and awards rendered by one-time arbitrators. There are awards rendered by a majority and awards rendered unanimously. Some awards record the merest indication of disagreement, while others are accompanied by an impressive dissent. Some dissents are powerful and elegant and make the majority look fragile; others are partisan diatribes with quite the opposite effect. Some awards are linguistically deficient; others are models of drafting. Some are highly disciplined texts;

---

8 Discussed *inter alia* by Professor. Schreuer and Mr. Legum in Chapters 12 and 15.

others are discursive to the point of self-indulgence. There are awards which seem to be the product of inexorable reasoning, and others which seem nothing but the result of a vote. There are awards signed by arbitrators who maintain impressive consistency from one case to the next, and—I hope in no more than two instances—awards signed by arbitrators who seem not to remember what they put their names to the previous year. Even Homer nods, so arbitrators entitled to the greatest respect occasionally find themselves in cases where the matter at hand seems to defeat their acumen and their patience.

The reality of investment arbitration is that the quality of advocacy varies greatly from case to case. Some speculative claims are prosecuted on a wing and a prayer by inexperienced pleaders, perhaps more in the hope of creating pressure than with the intent of developing a sustained and cogent case before an international tribunal. Such parties—claimants or respondents—may find themselves confronting knotty and fundamental issues which they do not have the resources to deal with. There are limits to *jura novit curia*. Silk purses are not readily produced from sow's ears. And so major issues may be decided in the context of a mediocre debate. Once the decision is handed down, the disappointed party may lose heart and decline to pursue available means of recourse, such as the ICSID ad hoc committee mechanism. What is left may be a decision by a sole arbitrator handicapped by artless pleadings. This is a matter of reality which commentators often ignore when they express concerns about perceived inconsistencies of awards. Arbitrators do not answer exam questions tidily articulated by the finest academics; they decide cases as they are presented, whatever the imperfections of the pleadings and the spottiness of the factual record.

This may be a good place to note that there is something peculiar about the investment arbitration issues which have generated the most debate. What are these issues? One is certainly the scope of most-favored-nation (MFN) provisions. Another is quite clearly the effect of so-called umbrella clauses (containing the undertaking to respect agreements). A third relates to difficulties arising out of the coexistence of contract claims and treaty claims. A fourth is to assess whether a dispute actually arises out of an investment and therefore qualifies for treaty protection. These four categories of issues have something in common which cannot fail to strike the practitioner: the fact that a respondent state loses a debate concerning MFN clauses, umbrella clauses, or the preclusion of contract claims does not in and of itself cost the state a single penny. They all concern the claimant's access to investment arbitration. That battle can be a Pyrrhic victory for the investor, who is enabled to proceed but may ultimately lose on the merits and come to regret having embarked upon a costly and losing campaign.

This leads me to whimsical interrogation. What is the opposite of a Pyrrhic victory? Perhaps an Elysian defeat? Surely there must be some expression to describe a bitter disappointment which turns out to be the unique gateway to great satisfaction.

Losing jurisdictional battles can be just such things. The joy of winning dismissal is often ephemeral, as reality sets in—the dispute remains. The simple point is made in a rhetorical question: what is better, prevailing on a jurisdictional objection or losing it—and then winning on the merits?

A good example was the border dispute between Bahrain and Qatar, which Bahrain considered to have been settled in 1939. Qatar disagreed, and over the years kept raising claims to something on the order of one-third of Bahrain, principally the Hawar Islands. This was a problem which simply refused to go away, and marred relations between the brother States for three generations. Finally Qatar brought its case before the International Court of Justice on the foundation of a protocol which Bahrain believed did not create international jurisdiction. This issue was decided against Bahrain, by a narrow majority over vehement dissenting opinions. It was a very annoying defeat for Bahrain, which as the party in possession had no desire for a debate in an international forum whether it should abandon what it considered its territory. Yet six years later, in 2001, having pursued its case vigorously, Bahrain prevailed on the merits and the Hawar Islands remain Bahrain's. The historical problem was resolved. The two countries could move to talk of cooperation instead of confrontation—and so they have.

Similarly, in investment cases many states focus on the objective of avoiding the international forum, only to discover that it was not fully a success; that the problem will not go away.[9] Consider the parties' posture in

---

9 Professor Sornarajah (Chapter 4), true to form, seems to consider that for a state to have to participate in an investment arbitration is in and of itself a calamity. Yet many states have found it highly satisfactory to be able to address and resolve a poisonous difficulty before a neutral tribunal. Nor is it only in winning that a state shows its reliability; several states have shown that they can be good losers, and I would argue that it is money well spent. Poor countries routinely find it possible to buy gleaming but realistically unusable military hardware for eight-figure amounts in hard currency. If they are unwilling to spend a fraction of such sums as a measure of their adherence to the rule of law, one may conclude that this has more to do with unwise priorities than with impoverishment. (In considering the stakes of this discussion,

the aftermath of the *Lucchetti v. Peru* ICSID award, which the tribunal described thus:

> Given that the present Award is responsive to a jurisdictional objection, the factual and legal propositions at the heart of Lucchetti's substantive case have naturally not been tested. Lucchetti contends that it was invited to invest in Peru, made its investment properly, expended tens of millions of dollars in building the most advanced industrial installations in the country, and established a model of operational success, employing a substantial workforce and making good, competitive products with export potential. Lucchetti also stresses that it has not been alleged (let alone proved) that its establishment in Peru as an investor was procured by irregular means. It is therefore in a fundamentally different position than someone whose initial agreement is said to have been procured by fraud or corruption. Most of all, it claims that its assets have been spoliated in a purely arbitrary and pretextual fashion....
>
> The only question entertained by this Tribunal is precisely whether the claim brought by Lucchetti falls within the scope of Peru's consent to international adjudication under the BIT. Lucchetti has not satisfied the Tribunal that this is the case, and thus finds itself in the same situation as it would have been if the BIT had not come into existence. Its substantive contentions remain as they were, to be advanced, negotiated, or adjudicated in such a manner and before such instances as it may find available.[10]

How much better, one surmises, to be in the position of Ukraine, having lost the infamous jurisdictional battle in *Tokios Tokelés* only to prevail on the merits.[11] The list of similarly situated respondent States is rather quickly lengthening.[12]

A distorting factor in the debate about investment arbitration is often overlooked despite its seeming obviousness. BITs and other instruments of investment protection establish obligations on the part of states. The respondents are therefore nearly invariably states. Like most parties who are sued, they are

---

is it irrelevant to point out that the UN World Investment Report 2007 announced that foreign direct investment in Africa had doubled over two years to US$36 billion, and credited a better business environment?)

10 7 February 2005, paras. 60 and 62. The author was a member of that tribunal.

11 ICSID, 26 July 2007 (Merits).

12 The last, as this is written, being *Parkerings Compagniet v. Lithuania*, ICSID, 11 September 2007.

not disposed to accept that they have a case to answer. As a consequence, a chorus of affected states complains that there is something wrong with the system. (In time it will be seen that investors are also likely to find fault with the system as they come to the costly realization that it is not a cure-all to their business problems.) Even states which have traditionally favoured investment protection and have not been exposed to adverse decisions—like the United States, still undefeated in modern investment arbitration practice despite high-profile attempts in cases like *Loewen*, *Mondev*, and *Methanex*—appear discomfited by the very prospect of having to justify their conduct.

Yet the international rule of law necessarily involves restrictions on the freedom to act. They are not inherently inimical, but to be accepted as a matter of enlightened long-term self-interest.

Here another distorting factor comes into play. In a manner reminiscent of the strident debates more than a quarter of a century ago about the short-lived New International Economic Order, challenges to investment arbitration seem to reflect group-think at the seats of international organizations, involving delegations representing anyone but the Ministries of Finance or Commerce, rather than the positions of ministries having primary responsibility for economic policy.

One particularly annoying manifestation of this distortion is the recurrence of purportedly humorous remarks on the theme that developing countries sign BITs without a clue as to their content. When one does not know what else to do in order to proclaim achievement at the end of an uneventful state visit, so the story goes, why not sign a protocol on cultural cooperation—or a BIT? This is preposterous. It may well be that persons who find themselves at international gatherings find it tempting to "defend their countries" by complaining that bad bargains were foisted upon unnamed colleagues by sinister outside forces—even if the objectors had no role in the formulation of policy or in the negotiation of the instruments in question.

This stale joke suffers from the radical defects of being offensive and wrong. Life in many developing countries is extremely challenging, and individual capacity for discernment is often far higher than that required for success in developed systems of governance where it is sufficient merely to master and follow the rules. Norms relevant to investment protection are not complicated in principle: they establish that the government shall not confiscate, discriminate, or abuse its power in unfair ways. Not only do these three great normative categories tend to be uncontroversial; they represent the ardent desires even in societies sceptical of capitalist models. This, and not ignorance, fecklessness, or manipulation, explains why BITs tend to be so textually compact—and so readily accepted.

Of course there is a fourth category of norms which is of a very different genus: the *procedural* innovation of international arbitration entitling an investor to seek redress. This is the sole cause of the debates reflected in this volume, and it is of course a sea change. The first three substantive categories of norms, grand though they may sound, amount to very little if they are to be applied by courts who are subservient to the very officials who may have violated one of the three. What about foreigners lacking local influence? Should they be given access to neutral, international justice?

BITs readily answer this question in the affirmative. Critics of investment protection have suggested that this reflects an imposition by capital-exporting powers.

How then can they explain that these four pillars of investment protection—three prescriptive, one remedial—were precisely the ones at play in the first modern investment arbitration, namely the case of *SPP v. Egypt*, where the protective instrument was not a treaty at all, but an investment protection law conceived in 1974 by no one but the Egyptian Government itself?

Moving to the present, Ms. Joubin-Bret's valuable review of recent practice (as a Senior Advisor at UNCTAD) leads her to comment not only on the "significant increase" in South-South BITs in the decade 1995–2005, but that these show "very little evolution from a qualitative point of view" and indeed "tend to use more general language" and "allow for expansive interpretation."[13]

It is very difficult to imagine any retort to these observations that does not imply further insult to negotiators from developing countries.

Natural Corrections

In 1995, I predicted that there might be "an epochal extension of compulsory arbitral jurisdiction over States, at the behest of private litigants who wish to rely on governmental undertakings even though they have not contracted for a forum."[14] Something like that seems to have happened. I also wrote that the

---

13 Chapter 8.

14 "Arbitration Without Privity," 10 ICSID Review 232, at p. 256.

prospects for investment arbitration may "depend on the degree of sophistication shown by arbitrators when called upon to pass judgment on governmental actions."[15]

If I may now venture a new prediction, it is that after a sustained flurry of decisions over the past decade we are already likely to see a second wave, or rather a second generation, of investment awards. Its principal characteristics will be the consolidation of dominant trends; the continued isolation of perplexing outliers among awards; and thus, quite simply, more consistent awards.

This process of natural correction is anything but surprising; it is an expected feature of any maturing system.

In the interest of brevity, let us consider three illustrative tendencies in the recognition of norms inherent in the area of State responsibility to foreign investors. Each of them reinforces the defences of respondent States. They may be described as parts of a pendulum swinging the other way, after an initial movement toward the attractive possibilities of BIT-type arbitrations offered to investors (including occasional temptations to adventure).

The three tendencies I perceive involve the acknowledgment of (i) substantial regulatory margins of appreciation, (ii) the requirement that investors substantiate international delicts by demonstrating reasonable efforts to allow the State to rectify incidents of maladministration, and (iii) high barriers to remedies of specific performance or restitution in kind against States.

The landmark *Methanex*[16] decision, rendered unanimously by a tribunal comprised of V.V. Veeder QC (President), Professor Michael Reisman, and William Rowley QC, makes clear that international arbitrators do not award damages for the detrimental consequences of regulatory changes on the sole grounds that they find governmental policy to be wrongheaded. Foreign investors, like nationals, may have to accept such consequences as a local fact of life. A claimant must go further, and demonstrate bad faith, including arbitrariness, discrimination, or disregard of legitimate expectations. A policy decision, such as the State of California's ban on certain products said to have deleterious effects, will be accepted as compliant with the standards of international

---

15 *Id.* at p. 257.

16 *Methanex v. United States*, UNCITRAL, 3 August 2005.

law if there is a reasonable showing that it was the result of relevant studies undertaken in good faith. Serious government officials are likely to read the award, taken as an indication of standards by which their future acts will be judged, with equanimity.[17] What is required as foundation for regulatory policy is surely the minimum of what principles of decent governance would command; what is tolerated is far more than what the electorate might accept. And why should this not be so?

A second trend makes it impossible to turn investment arbitration into a Court of Common Pleas having the mission of correcting the conduct of every bureaucrat in the world. It is essential that the non-requirement of exhaustion of local remedies does not lead to an uncontrolled expansion of the mission of investment arbitrators. It simply cannot be that each act of every official in every state having signed a BIT is subject to international scrutiny for compliance with international law. This merits elaboration.

It is in the nature of BITs not to require the exhaustion of local remedies. But the concept of exhaustion of remedies needs to be considered with care. It is important to see how differently this concept operates, depending on whether a case arises under a contract or under a BIT.

Consider first a contract between an investor and a state. Before the ICSID Convention was born, if a claim against a state was to be pursued in the domain of public international law it would first have to be unsuccessfully presented to the highest level of national courts. This is not at all how *contractual* arbitration should work. Any contractual breach should be within the exclusive domain of the contractual arbitral tribunal. This is how it is in the realm of private international law, and of course a state's contracts with investors may be subjected to private law arbitration and enforced under the New York Convention. But the ICSID Convention creates arbitration under *public*

---

17 The arbitrators wrote notably as follows, in para. 7 of Part IV, Chapter D:

> "[A]s a matter of general international law, a non-discriminatory regulation for a public purposes, which is enacted in accordance with due process and, which affects, inter alios, a foreign investor or investment is not deemed expropriatory and compensable unless specific commitments had been given by the regulating government to the then putative foreign investor contemplating investment that the government would refrain from such regulation."

(Health Warning for Persons with a History of Excessive Optimism: No, dear Reader, you have not just discovered the Holy Grail—not even a shortcut. This passage too must be considered in light of the parties' pleading, the facts, and the arbitrators' analytical framework, premises, and qualifications. And even then it remains open-textured: "non-discriminatory," "public purpose" and "due process" are not self-defining terms—nor is the qualifier "general" when applied to international law.)

international law. In order to ensure that contractual disputes could immediately go to arbitration, the ICSID Convention necessarily pre-empted the rule of exhaustion of local remedies. What this means is very simple. It means that if investors raise any claim of breach of contract subject to ICSID jurisdiction, they may bring it immediately before ICSID.

But what about investors who have no contract with the State, yet consider that the State has violated a BIT because they have not been treated "fairly and equitably" under international law? May *any* such claim be brought *directly* to ICSID?

The answer is: absolutely not. This should not be surprising. Let us begin by asking: who breaches a contract? In a contractual situation, the identity of the respondent is clear. If their contract is with the Ministry of Public Works, investors are not going to be able to sue the Ministry of Foreign Affairs. If their complaint is that the National Oil Company has not paid royalties, they cannot sue the Ministry of Education. And, most importantly, even if they have a contract that fell within the general scope of authority of a particular Ministry, they cannot go to ICSID claiming that a low-level official has repudiated the agreement without explaining that somehow this position must be deemed to have been that of the Ministry as a whole.

The situation under a BIT is quite asymmetrical, which is clear if one asks the analogous question: who is the respondent to a claim of unfairness or discrimination? The State has signed the BIT; but does that mean that actions by any functionary, anywhere in the public sector, entitle the investor to bring a claim before ICSID?

Several awards evidence sensitivity to this matter. The tribunal presided by Sir Arthur Watts in *Saluka* stated that the BIT relevant in that case:

> "cannot be interpreted so as to penalise each and every breach by the Government of the rules or regulations to which it is subject and for which the investor may normally seek redress before the courts of the host State … something more than simple illegality or lack of authority under the domestic law of a State is necessary to render an act or measure inconsistent with the customary international law."[18]

[18] 17 March 2006, ICSID, paras. 442–443.

Similarly, the arbitrators in *Generation Ukraine* reasoned that:

> … it is not enough for an investor to seize upon an act of maladministration, no matter how low the level of the relevant governmental authority; to abandon his investment without any effort at overturning the administrative fault; and thus to claim an international delict on the theory that there had been an uncompensated virtual expropriation. In such instances, an international tribunal may deem that the failure to seek redress from national authorities disqualifies the international claim, *not because there is a requirement of exhaustion of local remedies but because the very reality of conduct tantamount to expropriation is doubtful in the absence of a reasonable—not necessarily exhaustive—effort by the investor to obtain correction.*[19] (Emphasis added.)

And in *MCI Power Group et al. v. Ecuador*, the ICSID tribunal observed that a party who fails to seek administrative review acquiesces in the revocation of a permit.[20]

The third development is the emerging confirmation of a presumption against the availability of specific performance or restitution in kind as a remedy against States. Such measures are perceived by States as severe constraints. The Libyan nationalization cases in the 1970s made most international lawyers realize that specific performance was difficult to obtain. Of these cases, the *Texaco* (1978) award seemed the outlier, not so much because it was wrong as because it was the product of the very unusual posture adopted in the claimants' pleadings. Nevertheless, the spectre of specific performance was sufficiently worrisome for the States-party to NAFTA that they explicitly limited remedies to monetary recovery. Today it is likely that the decision on provisional measures rendered by the ICSID tribunal in *Occidental v. Ecuador* represents a reliable indication that even in the absence of such a treaty provision specific performance is generally unavailable against states in the area of investor protection.[21] The three unanimous arbitrators, all experienced in the investment field (Fortier, Stern, Williams), did not repudiate the notion

---

19 16 September 2003, ICSID, para. 20.30. (The author was a member of that tribunal.)

20 31 July 2007, ICSID, para. 302; to similar effect, *Parkerings Compagniet v. Lithuania*, 11 September 2007, ICSID, para. 317.

21 Such a presumption may, like others, be reversed by agreement or other special factors, and it is likely that purely conservatory measures, insofar as they are unlikely to impede regulatory coherence beyond the specific case, constitute a different category; see *Tokios Tokelès v. Ukraine*, PO No. 1, 1 July 2003, ICSID; as well as *Enron v. Argentina*, 14 January 2004 (Jurisdiction), ICSID, paras. 76–81.

that specific performance or restitution in kind might be the *preferred* remedy, yet were quick to deem it impossible: "It is well established that where a State has, in the exercise of its sovereign powers, put an end to a contract or a licence, or any other foreign investor's entitlement, specific performance must be deemed legally impossible."[22] In addition to the *British Petroleum* (1974) and *LIAMCO* (1981) ad hoc awards involving Libya, the tribunal cited the more recent *CMS v. Argentina* to the effect that "it would be utterly unrealistic for the Tribunal to order the Respondent to turn back to the regulatory framework existing before the emergency measures were adopted."[23]

In sum, states should conclude that the awards of first-instance tribunals have not caused the sky to fall. That being so, an important reason to endorse a policy of *festina lente* is that states who win investment arbitrations may be as frustrated as investors are when their triumph is wrested away from them by censors they did not select. (I say this, *inter alia*, from my experience as counsel to Cameroon, victim of the first ICSID annulment.) Investors have shown themselves more than ready to seek annulment—*Klöckner*, *Soufraki*, *Lucchetti*, *Fraport AG*, *Bayview Irrigation District*, and even the little *Malaysian Historical Salvors*. In other words, it is far from evident that states today should be anxious for the finality of awards to be eroded.

Indeed, one surmises that only the bitterest of disappointment could have motivated the just-named investors to seek annulment at considerable expense and with the prospects of a long and uncertain road ahead. A successful attack on the award does no more than to place them back on square one. Losing investors may be appalled at their poor fortune, in effect throwing good money after bad in pursuing an unavailing international remedy. Thus, after the U.S. Thunderbird Gaming Corporation had experienced the closure of its facilities in Mexico, had unsuccessfully sought arbitration under NAFTA, and had been ordered to pay US$1.25M in costs to the Government of Mexico, its General Counsel issued a press release the day after the award,[24] complaining that his company:

> "continuously faces similar acts of interference by government officials in developing countries, but believed that NAFTA would level the playing field in Mexico … clearly it did not as this same government that shut down the Thunderbird operations has given permits for hundreds of new locations."

---

22 17 August 2007, ICSID, para. 79.

23 12 May 2005, ICISD, para. 406.

24 UNCITRAL, 26 January 2006. Petition to set aside denied, 14 February 2007, USDC Col.

The CEO of the corporation added the caustic comment that such other permits "were issued in the country while ... the former Secretario de Gobernación was seeking to become the next President of Mexico."

Disappointed litigants everywhere are tempted to rail at the decision-making process. That does not meant they are right. For each of these unhappy investors, there is probably a state which will say that justice was done.

The Illusion of Cure

The debate could end at this point, with the realization that the problem is much exaggerated; that incidental incongruities are likely to resolve themselves in familiar ways as a relatively new system works its way toward maturity; and that prudence overwhelmingly dictates that one should not be quick to jettison a valuable international mechanism and prematurely expose it to transformations which may be stultifying and destructive.

But it is worthwhile examining the potential for detrimental change.

One of ICSID's great objectives was to depoliticize investment disputes.[25] Diplomatic protection was out; tribunals constituted by the two litigants were in. To create new permanent bodies of ultimate decision-makers raises the spectre of re-politicizing this area by reason of the recruitment of its members—with the additional discomfort of knowing that the fact that the parties selected the arbitrators is likely to invest the latter with greater intuitive legitimacy than their putative censors.

The appellate body is in fact unlikely to have greater moral authority than the first-level arbitral tribunal. Every annulment decision is a repudiation of the award made by the arbitrators chosen by the parties (or in accordance with their agreement). Nor is it likely to assist in improving consistency. First of all, the incidence of inconsistency has been vastly exaggerated by critics unable or unwilling to distinguish ratio from dicta. Second, this is a new area where the jurisprudence must and will feel its way toward consensus; there will be some early aberrations. Third, no arbitrator or appellate body can do the legislator's job; some cases fall to be decided under imperfect texts.

---

25 *See* I. Shihata, "Towards a Depoliticization of Foreign Investment Disputes," 1 ICSID Review 1 (1988).

Fourth, some fundamental norms are necessarily open-textured. As noted above, no legal system has thus far achieved the feat of developing a simple definition of the limits of non-compensable regulatory action. Great jurists and academics have struggled mightily with this in the U.S. for many generations; the matter remains maddeningly fact-specific. (The latest brave iteration of U.S. efforts at codification, present, e.g., in the 2004 U.S. Model BIT, begins with a series of apparently objective and painstakingly worded tests but then gives the game away by including a criterion described as "character of the government action"—lifted from *Penn Central*[26] and full of mystery.[27])

The purely structural challenge to the establishment of appellate mechanisms would compound these difficulties. Given the multiplicity of BITs and other instruments underlying investor protection, the plain fact is that one would have to imagine a plethora of distinct appellate mechanisms—each reflecting the desiderata of its drafters, each responsive to different articulations of substantive norms, each with different personnel.[28]

The ICSID Convention does not contemplate an appellate mechanism. To the contrary, being internationally enforceable ICSID awards are inherently unable to accommodate the intrusion of an appellate mechanism. Could one imagine that recourse to such a mechanism would be a matter of consent, in the ICSID context or otherwise? Hardly. Consent to such a thing is unlikely to find its way into contracts, but would more plausibly appear in newly minted BITs. That would lead to different populations of BITs, and we would all have to start comparing (1) awards, (2) ICSID annulments, (3) new expanded annulments, and 4) resubmitted awards. A monster would be set loose.

Conceptually, a practitioner can contemplate any number of innovations. The idea floated in some U.S. circles of an obligation for tribunals to circulate a draft award to the parties for comment before finalization may sound like a radical proposal, but could well, provided it is policed properly and carried out in good faith, have more than one advantage—including the avoidance of error, or the resolution of the dispute on the basis of a constructive and confidence-building accommodation between the parties before the award becomes an implacable res judicata. The idea of preliminary rulings as

---

26 *Penn Central Transportation Co. v. New York City*, 438 US 104 (1978).

27 I say this despite my awareness of the explanations furnished in the Congress Research Service report of 20 January 1995.

28 *See* Mr. Legum's concise and cogent review of structural difficulties (Chapter 15).

described by Professor Schreuer[29] is interesting, although it is not easy to see how the example of national courts referring questions relating to European Community law to the EJC can be transposed to legal issues arising from the thousands of instruments under which investment disputes arise. One might well anticipate that the exhortation in treaties that the States-party shall "consider whether to establish a bilateral appellate body or similar mechanism"[30] might yield many though-provoking variants. Still, even the good innovations would have the defect of being *different*—leading to the distortion of the international rule of law by centripetal forces.

Non-practitioners are tempted to imagine a conceptually satisfying division between issues of law and fact. On that basis, it is easy to toy with the idea of appeals limited to points of law. In reality, the overlap may be considerable. One would have to come to terms with yet another undefinable criterion—i.e., the test of factual vs legal issues. As ICSID experience with ad hoc annulment committees show, even corrective mechanisms intended to be severely restricted (indeed allowing no appeal even on points of law) have a tendency to duplicate the arbitral process itself in terms of duration, cost, complexity and—dare one say it?—decisions exposed to debate and criticism. (The study of the coherence of ICSID annulment decisions among themselves is a subdiscipline of its own.)

What complaint against any award ever rendered pursuant to a BIT could not be cast as an attack on misapplication of law? An inevitably uneven and very possibly politicized group of decision-makers would have difficulty keeping their mitts off awards—rendered by arbitrators who paradoxically have *greater legitimacy* than they do, given their method of appointment. Cases would become endlessly protracted. The fact that tribunal no. 2 would be instructed to decide in accordance with legal propositions propounded by the appellate body would not stop intelligent downstream arbitrators from recasting a decision as factually contingent. And so back to the appeals body. The process might become a costly nightmare, and I would predict its demise or desuetude.

One particularly pernicious strand of thought would graciously allow investors to participate in investment arbitrations, but not at the ultimate appellate level—that would be a matter for the States-party to the BIT (or other relevant

---

29 Chapter 12.

30 *See, e.g.*, the Panama–U.S. Trade Promotion Agreement appearing in the Appendix to this volume.

instrument). This is surely a folly. What investor would have the slightest faith in a system where the ultimate decision would be taken without even hearing the claimant, and quite plausibly be dictated by the objective alliance of two States anxious to minimize their responsibility generally? May one responsibly speak of an "international court" of "tenured judges" who will be free of perceived bias without at least a thought to how they will be recruited? Will it be by means of an election by a body comprising only diplomats after the usual rounds of sterile receptions and purely political horsetrading—sometimes with good intentions, sometimes cynical; but frequently frivolous? Or a "regional" international body from a heavily capital-importing continent staffed entirely by "judges" from that region? "Judges" who have spent their entire working lives as the employees of governmental elites? Do not the proponents of such ideas care about investors' perceptions? It is permissible to answer "no," of course, just as it is permissible to say that international investment flows should be discouraged, presumably because investment is far too important to be left to investors. This is not, however, a line that goes down well with the economic ministries of poor countries, who tend to believe that investments are mobilized by investors.

We would all like to reach a heaven of consistency and accountability, but in our lifetimes are unlikely to build a tower of Babel to get there.

It would be a sad paradox indeed if the quest for greater legitimacy had the result of undermining legitimacy. The existing system, as noted above, entitles the parties to select arbitrators selected by them, or in accordance with the rules to which they have agreed. Parties have used this opportunity to appoint highly distinguished arbitrators. The first investment case not founded on a contract, *SPP v. Egypt*,[31] was chaired by a former President of the ICJ. At least four of his successors from The Hague have also served as ICSID arbitrators. But beyond the inherent qualities of the arbitrators, which may of course be variable and debatable, the fundamental point is that they possess the ultimate legitimacy of the parties' confidence. If an appointing authority steps in to name the presiding arbitrator, the appropriateness of its nomination is a matter of the governance of that institution. Given the primordial role of ICSID and the Permanent Court of Arbitration in the context of investment arbitrations, it merits mention that each of these bodies is subordinate to boards whose memberships are constituted entirely of States.

---

31 ICSID, 14 April 1988 (Jurisdiction) (the author assisted the claimant).

When the ICSID annulment committee in *CMS v. Argentina*[32] criticized aspects of the arbitral tribunal's award dealing with Argentina's necessity defence, it noted that if it were "acting as a court of appeal, it would have to reconsider the Award on that ground." This may rekindle ardours for an appellate mechanism. My objection, however, not only remains the same (with the greatest respect, although I accept that a *garde-fou* is required to police excess of jurisdiction and failures of due process, I fail to see that members of ad hoc committees have greater claim to legitimacy in assessing substantive issues than arbitrators chosen by the parties) but I would add that ad hoc decisions themselves are open to criticism. There is no objective final answer. We have already seen three ICSID ad hoc decisions containing dissenting opinions, including those authored by no lesser figures than Professor Francisco Orrego Vicuña and Sir Frank Berman.[33]

The Promise of Transparency

From a practitioner's point of view, all is certainly not perfect. The problem is not, I believe from my vantage point as advocate for claimants and respondents alike, one of moral hazard. Critics pointing fingers at an imagined self-selecting group of arbitrators, who callously seek their own advantage without regard to legitimacy or public welfare, are simply unacquainted with reality. Arbitrators are selected by the parties, or in accordance with the parties' agreement. States are not helpless victims, incapable of strategy or tactics.[34] Practitioners are no less attached to these questions when representing states than when acting for investors.

The concern is rather one of unevenness in the quality of decision-making in this new field. Some excellent commercial arbitrators seem to have insufficient grounding in public international law. Apart from their unfamiliarity with important recurring issues, they fail to perceive that they are no longer referees in a match which concerns only the participants. Investment arbitrations

---

32 ICISD, 25 September 2007. (The author was not personally involved in the case, but his firm acted for the claimant.)

33 *Siag v. Egypt*, ICSID, 11 April 2007; and *Lucchetti v. Peru*, ICSID, 5 September 2007; respectively. See also *Soufraki v. UAE*, ICSID, 27 May 2007 (Nabulsi).

34 To take the example of Europe's least internationally experienced state, when Albania faced its first ICSID case (a not implausible claim that an investor's agricultural plant had been overrun by local groups, with governmental encouragement or tolerance, or at any rate without any governmental reaction as required in the relevant treaty), the government appointed leading international lawyers to represent it. The eminent arbitral tribunal was presided over by Professor Karl-Heinz Böckstiegel. Albania prevailed; ICSID, 29 April 1999.

generate constant public interest. Awards tend immediately to fall into the public domain and contribute to the broad emerging normative tapestry. It may be a serious mistake to perceive one's duty as selecting which of two parties' arguments are better. Even if there is a clear winner, its arguments are not necessarily correct; often they are not. This requires discernment and hard study, lest the arbitral tribunal lend its authority to propositions which may be intuitively convenient in the particular, but are unsound in the general. Commercial lawyers venturing into finely balanced matters of public international law may also be tempted, perhaps by an excess of self-confidence, to deliver themselves of a broad general exposition with the intent of clearing up a troubling issue, presuming hubristically, as it were, to do the world a favour by accounting for their brief foray into this new area. This often leads to trouble.

Equally, public international lawyers may have an inadequate grasp of the proper way to conduct proceedings, not to mention economics and commercial law. It does not help that parties are generally deferential, and may therefore unfortunately steer arbitrators away from the path of modesty. Another undesirable consequence is that such arbitrators, like surgeons operating on someone who has the flu, do what they know rather than what they should, avoiding areas with which they are not familiar but which are at the core of the task at hand.

Finally, the rapid development of investment arbitration has given rise to a problem of recruitment of arbitrators. The challenge is how to ensure inclusiveness without sacrificing quality and impartiality. Investment arbitration needs decision-makers selected from the fullest range of backgrounds. But that does not make it tolerable for arbitral institutions in any given case to appoint unknown and untested persons merely on the basis of their geographic origin, without regard to their lack of verifiable references. Such reservations are of course themselves problematic; they may serve to frustrate the recognition and emergence of deserving individuals outside the major centers of legal resources.

All of this is significantly related to the issue of transparency. Transparency alone will not ensure quality decision-making. Even without increased transparency, I expect that the second decade of modern investment arbitration will already see the rise of a better second generation of awards. (Everyone can learn: parties, lawyers, institutions—even arbitrators.)

Nor is the objective of transparency solely to improve arbitral decision-making. At stake are also important values of accountability and policy-making freedom to pursue the public interest. But these are vast subjects, much discussed in past and modern literature, and not the direct focus of this volume. Allow me therefore to make a few simple observations about the relationship between transparency and quality of decision-making.

First, what about the perception that confidentiality is per se a valuable *raison d'être* for arbitration? It has already been abundantly pointed out that when the process involves public bodies, secrecy is presumptively suspect. The point I wish to make is broader. Even when the parties are private, the issue is radically different when one compares national settings with the international arena. In the former, the preference for confidentiality may be decisive in the choice between local courts and local arbitrators. The applicable law is neutral, and the question of national discrimination does not arise. So when two parties of the same nationality choose arbitration, they may indeed be seeking confidentiality. When they are of different nationality, on the other hand, they seek neutrality above all. (Seeking to avoid a sidetrack, I propose simply to note that cost and time efficiency, along with the attraction of specialized decision-makers, are features difficult to assess *ex ante* in the international context, and likely to play a minor role as compared to the goal of neutrality.) In other words, investment arbitrations should be transparent not only because they involve states, but also because they are international and therefore above all should be neutral. How can we be satisfied about neutrality unless we can observe this law in action?[35]

Second, the diligence of arbitrators is improved by the awareness that their work is being observed by others. When arbitration is confidential, bad work may be immune from criticism because the winner will in any event praise it, while the loser's plaints are dismissed as sour grapes. To be observed—to have their decisions dissected and criticized—may annoy some arbitrators. It may increase their workload to have to be more punctilious about matters of form, more thoughtful about matters of substance, more painstaking about their drafting in a foreign language, more careful in the accounts they give of the parties' arguments and their own analysis of the law. It will be a challenge to all, perhaps a discouragement to some who may prefer to decline appointment. So be it.

---

[35] There are particular circumstances when parties have legitimate needs for confidentiality, such as matters of intellectual property and national security. For such specific circumstances, specific agreements are called for.

Third, I perceive a danger that the proponents of transparency may harm the good cause by overreaching. Unlimited access by all and sundry to pleadings, evidence and hearing rooms is disruptive, and may indeed have quite unintended and illegitimate consequences. That also goes for the unlimited right to be heard by self-appointed interested parties, because they would of course then require access to the pleadings, evidence, and hearings. To require all presidents of ad hoc tribunals to inform international organizations of the pendency of certain types of cases is a very poor idea, for a multitude of reasons. There are however a number of good solutions. Decisions of tribunals (orders and awards) may simply be de-confidentialized. In order that awards may be properly understood by third parties, pleadings and transcripts (and possibly the evidentiary record) may be de-confidentialized as well—once the case is over. But such solutions are not appropriate for all types of arbitrations, nor for all types of international treaties. We need a scalpel, not a wrecking ball. Secrecy should always have to be justified, but that does not answer all questions of proper legal process. In investment arbitrations, to the extent that the relevant rules allow discretion, this is part of the arbitral craft, as some distinguished tribunals have already shown; to the extent they do not, the issue falls to determination by specific agreement, whether case by case, BIT by BIT, or otherwise.

CHAPTER 17

Implications of an Appellate Body for Investment Disputes from a Developing Country Point of View

Asif H. Qureshi[1] *and Shandana Gulzar Khan*[2]

Most successful judicial systems are accompanied by an appellate process. However, the need for accommodating such a mechanism in disputes processed through arbitration systems has not necessarily been apparent. Thus hitherto, many of the U.S. free trade agreements which dealt with investment issues did not include appellate processes to follow the standard arbitral facility that is included in the agreements. In an international investment system wherein an external conflict resolution system is shopped into (for example, the International Centre for Settlement of Investment Disputes (ICSID)) as and when needed, the introduction of an appellate system in ICSID with potential "precedential" consequences for other bilateral investment systems poses interesting challenges—including a sub-set from a developing country perspective.

The discourse for an appellate process has been mainly informed by the need to ensure consistency and coherence in international arbitral decisions.

---

1 Asif H. Qureshi, Professor of International Economic Law, Law School, University of Manchester, Manchester, UK. I am grateful to F. Ortino for his comments on an earlier version of this chapter. It is based upon, and draws from, a chapter titled "Much ado about a possible appellate system in international investment arbitration?" *in* P. Muchlinski, F. Ortino and Christoph Schreuer ed., *Oxford Handbook of International Investment Law* (Oxford: 2008).

2 Shandana Gulzar Khan, Legal Affairs Officer, Permanent Mission of Pakistan to the WTO, Geneva, Switzerland.

In passing it may be noted here at the outset that the need for transparency in international arbitration, including in an appellate process, is equally an important issue, and one that will need to be addressed sooner rather than later. This brief chapter, however, confines itself to and rehearses some of the arguments for an appellate process in the investment sphere, identifies some of the potential appellate options and focuses on the development perspective to such a proposal. This contribution is not intended to be exhaustive but rather is proffered mainly as a framework paper outlining the developing country perspectives.

The Basis for the Call for an Appellate Process

The call for a possible introduction of an appellate system in international investment arbitration has been particularly attributed to the United States,[3] along with the placing of a proposal for an Appellate Facility under the auspices of ICSID.[4] These developments have led to a number of learned conferences on investment arbitration in which the proposal for an appellate system has been the subject of discussion involving both academics and practitioners in the field.[5] The impetus for an appellate system, however, at the political level seems to have lost its edge since around 2003 or 2004.[6]

The U.S.'s agenda for the introduction of an appellate system in investment arbitration is to be found in the U.S. Trade Promotion Authority under Section 2102 of the U.S. Trade Act 2002. Herein the U.S.'s objectives in negotiations with respect to investment chapters[7] in international trade agreements are expressed as involving the inclusion in these agreements of "meaningful procedures for resolving investment disputes" between an investor and a government, through *inter alia* the provision of "an appellate body or similar mechanism to provide coherence to the interpretations of investment provisions in trade agreements …."In the circumstances, it will be noted that the U.S. justification for an appellate process focuses on the need for

---

3 *See, e.g.,* James Crawford "Is There a Need for an Appellate System?" *in* F. Ortino, A. Sheppard and H. Warner, ed., *Investment Treaty Law,* Current Issues Volume 1 (BIICL: London, 2006).

4 ICSID Secretariat Discussion Paper, 22 October 2004. (Annex 3 in this volume).

5 For example, the 7 May 2004 conference organized by the British Institute of International and Comparative Law on the subject of the feasibility and implications of the establishment of a mechanism for the hearing of appeals from investment. The conference proceedings have been published *in op. cit.* F. Ortino, ed., et al. *Investment Treaty Law*; and Conference on ICSID held at the University of Frankfurt in April 2006.

6 F. Ortino, *supra* note 5..

7 Barton Legum in Ortino et al. *supra* note 5, p. 121.

coherence in interpretation, along with the need to institute proper safeguards in dispute settlement, particularly in case the U.S. is being taken to task in international arbitration.

This approach of the United States is reinforced in Annex D of the New Draft U.S. Model bilateral investment treaty (BIT)[8] which states:

> Within three years after the date of entry into force of the Treaty, the Parties shall consider whether to establish a bilateral appellate body or similar mechanism to review awards rendered under Article 34 in arbitrations commenced after they establish the appellate body or similar mechanism.

It is not surprising therefore that this same agenda is to be found in ICSID. Thus, the ICSID Discussion Paper of October 22, 2004, points out:

> A further, potentially most important, issue that has been raised is whether an appellate mechanism is desirable … in case law generated in ICSID and other investor-to-State arbitrations initiated under investment treaties.[9]

In the same vein there is evidence of a growing consensus amongst investment practitioners and academics that there is a need for an appellate system in the investment sphere.[10] In sum, the initiative and call for an appellate system come mainly for the moment from interests in the developed hemisphere. Developing countries appear not to have addressed the issue and/or developed an articulated position on it.[11]

Indeed, "the coherence in the interpretation of investment provisions" which forms a basis for such a call is somewhat reminiscent of the OECD's failed initiative for a multilateral agreement on investment (MAI) and the failure on the part of developed countries in the WTO to set the agenda on trade and investment issues. These initiatives for an appellate process—coming as they do shortly after these abortive attempts at multilateralizing international

---

8 *See, e.g.*, Doak Bishop *in* Ortino et al. *supra* note 5, p. 15.

9 ICSID Discussion Paper, 22 October 2004, para 6.

10 *See, e.g.*, V.V. Veeder QC "The Necessary Safeguards of an Appellate System" *in* Ortino et al. *supra* note 5, pp. 9–11; and Christian J. Tams "Is There a Need for an ICSID Appellate Structure?" Paper delivered at Conference on ICSID held at Frankfurt University in Frankfurt, Germany, April 2006.

11 A view shared by Karl P. Sauvant (telephone conversation with authors, August 2007).

investment law—beg the question whether they are purely focused on strengthening dispute settlement mechanisms (because initial arbitration decisions could be flawed); or seek to bring about substantive co-ordination in international investment law. However, the possibility that these initiatives may address both concerns cannot be excluded.

In the circumstances, there are several reasons for this call for an improved dispute settlement system in the investment sphere that encompasses an appellate process. First, an appellate system operates as a corrective mechanism in case an arbitration decision is made wrongly.[12] Second, the increased number of ICSID cases has meant that the real and potential risk of inconsistent arbitration decisions is on the increase.[13] Therefore an appellate system is advocated to address the "sustainability" of the existing arbitration system.[14] However, it is necessary to note that the achievement of the objective of consistency is severely limited by the differences in the provisions of different international investment agreements.[15] Furthermore, although there is no formal doctrine of precedent in investment arbitration, it has been noted that the reasons given for (and in) the awards are assuming "greater importance for other disputes."[16] In this respect it is believed that an appellate system would ensure coherence and consistency,[17] predictability, objectivity and sensitivity in judicial decisions.[18] Third, the advent and success of the WTO appellate system has a bearing on the thinking in the investment sphere, in particular given that the international trade and investment regimes operate in each other's shadows. Fourth, certain sectors or origins of investment enjoy dispute settlement systems with built-in appellate processes, e.g., disputes on all services supplied under mode 3 of the GATS agreement (also called "commercial presence investment") are covered by dispute settlement at the WTO. Fifth, while this is heralded by some large developing countries as a flexibility issue (hence the rejection of the proposed Singapore issue for an Agreement on Trade and Investment under the Doha Development Agenda at the WTO), the ability of countries and/or investors to go forum shopping is one of the

---

12 We are grateful to F. Ortino for highlighting this point to us.

13 *See, e.g.,* M. D. Goldhaber, "*Wanted: A World Investment Court*" The American Lawyer/Focus Europe/ Summer 2004 (*See* www.americanlawyer.com/focuseurope/investmentcourt04.html).

14 *See* Doak Bishop in Ortino et al. *supra* note 5, p.17.

15 We are grateful to F. Ortino for this point.

16 *See* V.V. Veeder in Ortino et al. *supra* note 5, p. 9.

17 *See* ICSID Discussion Paper, *supra* note 9, para 21.

18 R. Doak Bishop "The Case for an Appellate Panel and its Scope of Review" Paper delivered on May 7, 2004 at the British Institute of International and Comparative Law, in Ortino et al. *supra* note 5, p. 15.

biggest roadblocks to setting up an appellate body for investment disputes. It is quite difficult to reconcile these views with the growing number of trade agreements that have begun to incorporate references to appellate processes, for example Annex 10-H of the U.S.–Chile FTA and the CAFTA-D.R. Agreement.[19] This growing practice with respect to investment provisions in trade agreements is also to be found in BITs. In this respect, of note is the following statement in the ICSID Discussion Paper:[20]

> There have already been concluded several treaties that envisage, in broad terms, the eventual creation of such a mechanism. Several more such treaties are being negotiated. By mid-2005, as many as 20 countries may have signed treaties with provisions on an appeal mechanism for awards in investor-State arbitrations under the treaties.

In conclusion, while the weight of the opinion within the discourse for an appellate process appears to rest for now with a standing appellate body or system, there are also arguments against the introduction of such a system. To complete the picture, these need to be noted. This side of the case has been eloquently formulated as follows:[21] Significant inconsistencies have not to date been a general feature of the jurisprudence of ICSID. It might also be argued that providing an appeal mechanism could fragment the ICSID arbitral regimes: ICSID arbitrations would in some instances be subject to the mechanism and in other cases remain free of the mechanism. Subjecting ICSID arbitral awards to an appeal mechanism might also detract from the finality of the awards and open opportunities for delays in their enforcement.

As has already been alluded to, one of the frequently advanced reasons for an appellate process is "coherence and consistency." This is the case despite the fact that the whole discourse for an appellate process has been in the setting of *institutional* reform in investment arbitration. Consequently, there are some questions here that precede an evaluation of the case for an appellate process, and which are missing in much of the commentary in this field.

First, it seems to us that deconstructionists would have much to say about proposals for reform in the international investment dispute settlement

---

19 See Annex 10-F of CAFTA-D.R. FTA.

20 ICSID Discussion Paper, *supra* note 9, para 20.

21 *Id.*, para 21.

system, given that it is largely set against a *normative* framework that is bilateral, disorganized and non-multilateral. Is it really possible to meaningfully evaluate the arguments for and the obstacles in setting up an appellate facility in the investment sphere, with the objective of providing normative coherence, in circumstances in which the multilateral consensus on substantive matters is not very evident? Does this institutional debate not partake of concerns and preferences with respect to the normative framework of investment? Indeed, one may even venture to query whether the suggestion for an appellate facility at a multilateral level is not an attempt to force an issue onto the international agenda. Notably, this is an issue that has not received the endorsement of being so negotiated by a significant constituency concerned with international investment law—namely, the developing countries. In recent history, as pointed out earlier, this lack of endorsement has happened twice, first in the context of the negotiations for the previously-mentioned MAI under the auspices of the OECD, and then under the Doha Agenda within the WTO, though the main reason for its failure within the setting of the WTO has been the availability of cross retaliation in case of non-implementation of the rulings and recommendations of the DSB.

As is well recognized, appellate processes are about interpretations of legal norms—and the system that partakes of the ultimate interpreter is also the ultimate legislator. Therefore at the outset it needs to be highlighted that the question posited is not simply a procedural/institutional one—one that is concerned about adjudication and the place and need for appellate processes in that system—but rather very much about the wider and much discussed question as to whether and how the international investment regime should be organised normatively. In short, the advocacy for an appellate system can indirectly partake of the call for a multilateral investment agreement given that the appellate system would operate as a "multilateral quasi-legislative body." Of course, the legislative impact of such an appellate process would depend on its character—for example, its composition, locus and powers.[22]

Second, and in the same vein, it is not possible to engage in constructing dispute settlement mechanisms without reference to the *nature* of the underlying normative structure. The case for an appellate facility must be set against

---

22 We are grateful to F. Ortino for this point.

the objectives and purposes of the provisions of dispute settlement *in the international investment sphere* as it is not possible to de-link institutional building from its substantive sphere and its underpinnings. In this respect it needs to be noted that the objects and purposes of a normative framework in international investment, along with the conflict management system in the field, are not confined to the investors' concerns alone. Thus, "consistency and coherence" in dispute settlement may be significant reasons for institutional reform for both states and investors, but there are other concerns that may seek to trump these considerations: for example, human rights, environmental concerns and of course the development objectives of the host country.

The Choice of Appellate Process?

The discourse for an appellate process is not unconnected with the kind of appellate process that is being sought and its locus. There are in this respect a number of options, viz., appellate processes included in existing dispute settlement mechanisms in BITs; an appellate facility in ICSID; the availability of an appellate process in the framework of the WTO, along with the inclusion of appellate processes in existing trade agreements dealing with investment; and, finally, a Supreme Investment Court (SIC) and/or the International Court of Justice (ICJ) functioning as such.

The thrust of the focus amongst the "investment fraternity" appears to be on ICSID, as a logical extension point in the arbitral process it offers in the investment sphere. It may be more helpful to divide the debate and introduce the idea of an appellate process in all kinds of fora versus an appellate body in ICSID. One major reason for such a division of the concept of an appellate process and its physical manifestation is that, having an appellate body in ICSID, is not necessarily going to bring about the kind of cohesion and consistency that is being aimed for by the proponents. In fact, it may even be resisted by those that prefer UNCITRAL to ICSID.

Nevertheless, this chapter maintains a focus on the creation of an appellate process and a standing body within ICSID. The locus of the arbitration process has a bearing on the question of institutional uniformity (or, conversely, fragmentation of appellate processes) and indeed nuances in approaches stemming from the location of the appellate process—for example with investor, trade/investment liberalization, development, and internationalist orientations, respectively.

An ICSID Appeals Facility?

The ICSID proposal is to set up a single appeal mechanism[23] (the ICSID Appeals Facility) under a set of ICSID Appeals Facility Rules to be adopted by the Administrative Council of ICSID. This would be an alternative to individual appeal processes that may be set up in individual treaties. The Appeals Facility is to be available for "both forms of ICSID arbitration, UNCITRAL Rules arbitration and any other form of arbitration provided for in the investor-to-State dispute-settlement provisions of investment treaties."[24] The introduction of such a Facility would necessitate amendment of ICSID.

The principal features of the proposed facility of note are as follows. First, the availability of the appeals process would "depend on the consent of the parties."[25] Thus, the option to opt for arbitration without recourse to the appeal process would remain.[26] Second, it is proposed that an Appeals Panel would be established "composed of 15 persons elected by the Administrative Council of ICSID on the nomination of the Secretary-General of the Centre."[27] Each appellate member would be from a different country, and "be persons of recognised authority, with demonstrated expertise in law, international investment and investment treaties," as per the WTO Appellate Body conditions.[28] The WTO however has a smaller appellate panel. Each Appeal Tribunal would consist of three members from the Panel of 15.[29] Third, the grounds for appeal would be "clear error of law," or "any of the five grounds for annulment of an award set out in Article 52 of the ICSID Convention" or "serious errors of fact."[30] Fourth, the Appeal Tribunal would be able to uphold, modify, reverse, or annul the award concerned.[31] Finally, access to the Facility would be subject to the approval of the Secretary-General of ICSID.[32]

A number of points may be made about this proposal. First, the appointment of the judges on the panel at the sole behest of a nomination by the

---

23 ICSID Discussion Paper, *supra* note 9, para 21.

24 *Id.*, Annex para 1.

25 *Id.*, para 3.

26 *Id.*

27 *Id.*

28 *Id.*

29 *Id.*, para 6.

30 *Id.*, para 7.

31 *Id.*, para 9.

32 *Id.*, para 10.

Secretary-General without further ado needs more justification. In the WTO, it is the members who nominate individuals for consideration by the WTO for judicial appointments in the Appellate Body. Second, there is no mention of any geographical distribution, or developed/developing, investor home/host state constituencies within this panel. In the WTO, a kind of a representative formula is to be found in practice. Third, the appeal process seems not to be compulsory but based on its consensual user. In the WTO, the appeal mechanism is automatically available to the parties without further ado. Fourth, BITs are international agreements entered into between States. An appellate process allows a non-governmental investor entity to affect the nature of the agreement entered into between two state entities, through the interpretative appellate process—not to mention the fact that such an appellate interpretation could have an impact upon other bilateral agreements. Thus, whatever may be the merits of this argument, it needs to be pointed out nevertheless that such an appellate process may have a further limiting effect on sovereign foreign policy decisions—in particular to engage in "efficient breaches." Fifth, the idea of extension of the existing section on review process in ICSID as a starting point for a gradual evolution to a standing appellate body has not been considered to its fullest extent.

Finally, the proposal appears to be silent with respect to the submission of *amicus* briefs. In contrast, such submissions have been made in the WTO appellate proceedings, and it is worth taking a look at how they have fared there. Even though negotiators from the entire membership of the WTO during the Uruguay Round of negotiations (except the United States) rejected outright the idea and need for *amicus* briefs at the appellate stage (though recognizing the same need for factual input at the Panel stage), and despite the fact that this right is not explicitly granted by the Understanding on the Settlement of Disputes (DSU), the WTO Appellate Body has chosen to accept such briefs. This has in turn drawn much criticism from the entire membership (save the developed countries) as "the appellate body going beyond its mandate and reading into procedural rules, substantive ones."[33] Therefore any such system for the appeals process would have to be very careful in its design as developing countries are unlikely to support additional burdens on already stretched resources and time taken to deal with briefs that may eventually not contribute anything meaningful in the arbitration process.

---

33 Minutes of special general council meeting held in November 2000 as a response to the appellate body's creation of additional procedures in *EC-Asbestos dispute*.

The Development Perspective

There have been, at various points in time, at any rate in this chapter, calls for the development perspective to be taken into account in the establishment of an appellate process in the investment sphere. The development perspective involves ensuring *inter alia* that:

- The review process facilitates the "development objective" in arbitrations. (This looks easier on paper than in reality, a case in point being the stalled DDA negotiations, wherein the development dimensions seem to be floundering.)The review process contributes toward the reduction or alleviation of the burdens that accompany investment liberalization.
- There exist independent, fair and transparent processes in the appellate structure, through, for example, ensuring effective participation of other developing/host countries in the appellate judicial forum.
- The power of multinational corporations (MNCs) is not unduly strengthened through the abusive use of an appellate process. The availability of the process could result in frivolous and vexatious claims paralysing host country action.
- The national legislative "policy space" that developing countries need for their development objectives is not undermined through the introduction of an appellate process. If investor-State appeals are permitted (and in particular where they are successful), this would empower private parties to engage in legislative activity in a sphere in which there may be sound national and public policy arguments for preserving the power of the state.
- The appellate system does not lead to the multilateralization of bilaterally negotiated agreements, and thereby compromise the flexibility afforded by a bilateral system along with the collective decision of developing countries not to engage in a multilateral system that is not development friendly.

Where do Things Stand Today?

Historically, the demandeurs for the appellate process have been primarily the developed countries. But the situation that is now evolving posits NGOs, industry groups and investors as one of the main groups revisiting this issue—the theory of two shots at the same dispute being the simplest reason.

Even developing country domestic investors are looking at the issue as some sort of a security blanket. However, it is worth pointing out that there have been no serious attempts by the above mentioned and/or developing country demandeurs to engage in cost-benefit analysis associated with an appellate process. It has been the experience in the WTO that, while some larger developing country members of the WTO have been able to see a dispute to its last leg, the majority of developing countries does not have the kind of resources needed to go through the same process twice over.

Historically, developing countries have agreed to an unspoken waiver of their right of appealing investment arbitrations under ICSID and have had to content themselves with Section 52 procedures of review, which are rare in annulling decisions. Moreover, as mentioned earlier, political will from the developed countries to amend the ICSID Convention has also trickled off. The chief reason is that developed country corporations fear that "sensible misapplication or refusal to accept" arbitral awards will further be strengthened by an appellate process. In fact, they are actively pursuing their governments to keep the arbitration processes and its results as tight as is possible.

Finally, one of the reasons why the appellate process works smoothly in the WTO is that it is purely intergovernmental. In international investment and/or commercial arbitrations, it has been thus far a marriage of inconvenience between principles of public international law and private commercial laws, with undesirable side effects, for example, forum-shopping, arising from different rules and procedures in different possible forums.

Conclusion

In conclusion, a number of points may be made in the form of questions. First, is the justification for an appellate system on the basis of "consistency and coherence" in judicial outcomes not really an argument for moulding a particular kind of "consistency and coherence" into the disorganized international investment system—given that interpretation in an appellate process is a form of legislation?[34] Is the objection to "inconsistency" not really a call for normative uniformity? Second, should disparate investment norms necessarily be interpreted identically on the basis of equality, fairness, predictably,

34 According to F. Ortino, the very fact of arbitration can involve legislation, albeit in the context of the particular case as opposed to general legislation which comes from an appellate process.

and reliability? Third, if investment involves and is about ultimately ensuring development—should development not be the overriding consideration in the process of interpretation? Should the goal not be constantly to facilitate the "development objective" and better decisions all round, rather than pursuing a fetish for identity of interpretation? Fourth, will a non-ring-fenced appellate system, set against a disorganized bilateral investment normative framework, not add to uncertainty and complexity—given that the beneficiaries of and parties to bilateral agreements will not be clear as to how ultimately their rights and obligations will be "coherently and consistently" interpreted—not to mention the added complexity in interpretation arising from such a system? Finally, will an appellate system not lead to further investor bias in relation to weaker host countries, by augmenting the capacity of multilateral companies (MNCs) to pursue an appeal?

In conclusion, the need to place "consistency and coherence" as sacrosanct—as the basis for an appellate system—needs to be considered with some degree of caution. One should not put it on such a high pedestal as other objectives—particularly the development objective. From a development perspective, until there is agreement on a multilateral investment agreement, a treaty-specific appeal system is better. A principal concern about the efforts to introduce a non-ring-fenced appellate system in the investment sphere is that it seeks to add to the coherence and development of international investment law through a somewhat circuitous non-transparent route. Further, the need to inject the development dimension in any proposed appellate system is important. A development-friendly appellate system requires in particular a focus on its apparatus of interpretation, on participatory rights and technical.

PART V

Report to the Symposium

CHAPTER 18

Examining the Institutional Design of International Investment Law

*Christopher Brummer**

The Columbia Program on International Investment symposium on the law of international investment took place at a critical moment in the development of international rules relating to foreign direct investment (FDI). The past 20 years have seen a dramatic rise not only in FDI flows to developing countries, but also in the number of bilateral and regional agreements granting, among other things, foreign investors the right to sue countries hosting their investment where they fail to honor substantive commitments contained in those agreements. Together, these two trends have led to an exponential rise in investor-State litigation, with at least 219 treaty arbitrations brought between 1987 and 2005, two-thirds of which have been initiated in the past three years, and virtually all of them initiated by firms.

The growing recourse to arbitration by multinational corporations (MNCs) has heightened the concern of a number of scholars, practitioners and government officials who argue that investment treaties and their enforcement institutions are inherently unpredictable and opaque. Substantively, critics argue, obligations agreed to under the myriad agreements in effect are too varied and inconsistently interpreted by ad hoc tribunals to provide clarity and transparency for host countries as to the nature and extent of their commitments; moreover, procedurally, International Centre for Settlement of Investment Disputes (ICSID) tribunal judges are either too ideological or ethically conflicted to act as proper deciders. As a result, some critics of the

---

* Assistant Professor, Vanderbilt University School of Law. Email: chris.brummer@vanderbilt.edu.

current framework argue for an appellate mechanism to review arbitral awards that would provide, through its oversight integrity and consistency, for the interpretation and application of international investment law.

The implications of this debate are enormous. Facing an increasing number of costly claims against them, developing countries are already questioning the rationale of entering into investment treaties that cover nearly US$400 billion of investment worldwide and grant investors private rights of action when a host country engages in what it may believe to be legitimate regulation. If these states additionally identify a lack of transparency and fairness in the interpretation of the rules articulated in investment instruments, fewer states will likely enter into investment commitments in the future, and some countries already parties to investment treaties may denounce their agreements due to the legal risk they present. Though the welfare benefits of such flight might be debated, one consequence is clear: a widespread retreat from commitments and commitment-making would leave foreign investors with diminished comfort for their investments, weaken the system of international economic governance and reduce net world welfare.

To grapple with the important questions arising out of these concerns, the authors of the chapters in this book advance several conversations that lie at the heart of academic and policy debates in international investment law: How does procedure inform the substance of international investment law? What should be the objectives of investor-State arbitration? The rule of law? Liberalization? Fairness, and if so, for whom? To be sure, the complex nature of such queries makes an exhaustive account of the viewpoints put forward during the symposium impractical. Still, a brief sketch of the main arguments made yields important insights that help highlight the debate's normative and practical implications, as well as fruitful areas for future research.

The first group of articles, devoted to recent trends in international investment agreements, explores whether the prevailing legal architecture governing investment achieves the essential institutional requirements of legitimacy and fairness. For the most vehement critics, investment treaties constitute flawed and unjust instruments of international economic law. They argue that, from the standpoint of distributive justice, investment treaties are exceedingly unbalanced. Host countries, usually developing countries, are charged with an at times very wide array of obligations and restrictions as to the treatment of foreign investment, while investors, often important MNCs, assume no responsibilities and get only rights—including the right to sue governments where they are seen to fail to live up to their commitments.

Procedural mechanisms then can exacerbate this unevenness by tilting the resolution of disputes in favor of investors. Treaty provisions permit attorneys to preside over tribunals whose clients may be many of the same companies bringing suit against governments. This situation, critics argue, incentivizes judges to interpret key treaty obligations in a manner that benefits investors—and at times far beyond the reasonable expectations of host country governments. Ultimately, the substantive and procedural deficiencies of investment treaties lead to a rise in investor-State litigation: with no appellate review mechanism provided for under international investment agreements to constrain interpretation and police judicial conflicts of interest, investors are encouraged to pursue expansive interpretations of treaties in court. A legitimacy deficit consequently haunts the entire judicial system.

Not all critics, however, draw normative conclusions from the perennial one-sidedness of the agreements, as investment treaties have as their core objective the promotion of foreign private financings. Instead, their concern involves problems of interpretation that undermine the potential for adequate transparency at the time of treaty formation.

Along the lines of this more limited critique, the fact that many treaty commitments reference only indirectly other commitments spelled out beyond the four corners of a treaty impacts negatively on a state's ability to discern the full nature of the obligations it is incurring. The use of most-favored-nation (MFN) clauses, for example, grants a party all advantages in the treatment of investment that any third nation receives. Since these obligations are only referential and indirect, poorer countries may not at the time of treaty formation have either the technical expertise or resources to review their existing treaties and understand the extent of their outstanding agreements. They may thus enter into agreements not knowing their entire reach, or failing fully to negotiate key terms.

Exacerbating the problem is the fact that tribunals, too, may be faced with what can be viewed as their own capacity problems. Standards-laden commitments like "just" and "fair" treatment may have a meaning when translated outside their original context, and tribunals may not be in a position to decipher these meanings accurately. Judges may consequently extract and impose interpretations that are different from the expectations arising from the legal culture of the host country. Again, because no review mechanism is available to provide clarity as to treaty commitments, predictability is eroded and recourse to arbitration grows.

Proponents of the existing investment framework respond to these critiques in a number of this volume's chapters, arguing that the treaties function *well.* They remind critics that the agreements are designed to encourage foreign investment in developing countries by providing investors with a right of action against states as a defense to prohibited state interference. Given what all scholars acknowledge as an exponential increase in the number of such treaties over the past 20 years, the growth in arbitration—which, at under 250 cases, falls well short of an "explosion" in litigation—reflects not so much a lack of transparency as instead the growing availability of a remedy to unwarranted government conduct where there would otherwise be none. If anything, many argue, the trend in international trade and investment law has been toward increased transparency, particularly in the two most prominent plurilateral frameworks, the WTO and NAFTA. In both forums, arbitration has evolved from a sphere of diplomatic commercial negotiation far removed from public scrutiny to a more inclusive domain that not only allows the publication of various trial documents, but also limited third party intervention in the form of *amicus* briefs.

Investment treaty advocates also resist calls for reforms, particularly the establishment of an appellate tribunal, which they argue would not only add an additional layer of costly litigation, but would also undermine the key principles of consistency and legitimacy that they were envisaged to promote. As to consistency, they contend that, at some 2,500 at times deceptively similar bilateral investment treaties (BITs) negotiated over a 50-year time span, no singular interpretation of the content of commitments could possibly speak to the diverse original intents of all parties to such instruments. An appeals court in the exercise of its binding authority would almost necessarily fail fully to take into consideration the objects and purposes, subsequent practices and rational expectations of all parties to all outstanding investment treaties, effectively frustrating the very goals of predictability that appellate review would at least in part be envisioned to solve.

Skeptics of reform additionally argue that appeals facilities present significant challenges to tribunal authority and legitimacy that would plague the underlying system's efficacy. From the standpoint of lower courts, appellate review would increase documentation and publication of their dealings, a development that (though increasing transparency) would magnify the market and political consequences of what would ordinarily be low profile compromises. As a result, parties would be incentivized to fight longer and harder.

Appellate trials, too, may be protracted. It is unlikely that countries will maintain support for (or perhaps ever agree to) any one institutional design for an appeals court, losers in a litigation will have an incentive to criticize appellate decisions on the basis of judicial staffing or procedural rules employed, and may even delay their compliance or undermine a trial pronouncement. Particularly if an appellate decision has a binding precedential effect, concerns will be all the more amplified since the costs of a "bad" appellate decision would effectively touch all subsequent private financings.

In light of such difficulties, skeptics argue that it is of little surprise, and indeed prudent, that bilateral investment treaties provide at most for only one form of review: annulment. Through such limited oversight, tribunal oversight is checked where, under the terms of the ICSID treaty, it "manifestly exceed[s] its powers"—thereby ensuring the proper jurisdictional exercise of authority. At the same time, the difficulty of achieving and maintaining requisite consensus for deeper institutional review is acknowledged, and thus avenues for additional merits-based decision-making and fact-finding are generally precluded.

The clash of perspectives as to the relative benefits of the governing framework provides a useful theoretical backdrop with which readers can begin to reach their own conclusions as to the challenges facing the law of foreign direct investment. The chapters here demonstrate that investment treaties—the backbone of international investment law—present both promise and peril, substantively as well as procedurally. On the one hand, as primarily bilateral instruments they make consensus between states easier than under larger multiparty configurations, and under optimal conditions they tailor commitments to the legal traditions and expectations of participants. Yet, at the same time, bilateralism provides no anchor to common norms or objectives among treaties, only disparate applications of at times only vaguely defined standards. Consistency in treaty interpretation is consequently difficult to achieve, and ethical questions arise where one party is overwhelmed by either the technical capacity or expertise of the other, or more fundamentally, the complex application of standards in a world of interwoven commitments.

Providing solutions for such challenges is exceptionally difficult, particularly since policy responses, often in the form of greater multilateralism, themselves pose significant structural advantages and disadvantages. As many of the first section's commentators demonstrate, multilateralism—whether embodied in common precedent, claim aggregation or appellate review—likely provides greater transparency of commitments and consistency as to interpretation, lending constancy to what at times appears to be an unstable body of law. Yet, as the second section's authors show, multilateralism also poses unique challenges. With an expanded array of interests, consensus is harder, if not impossible, to reach. Equally important, greater capacity building, even with multilateral reforms, will remain necessary for a variety of actors, as multilateralism might increase the error costs of bad appellate decisions and inadequate counsel or advocacy. More will be at stake in a system that, though perhaps more transparent, challenges countries to an even greater extent in the effective drafting and litigation of agreements that may not speak directly to a party's own legal traditions, interpretations or needs.

As readers thus begin to familiarize themselves with the arguments put forward in this volume, they should keep in mind one commentator's suggestion that scholars look beyond the lofty preambular language of investment treaties to excavate and more precisely assess the underlying objectives of the international investment network. Such conceptual work not only permits legal scholars to gauge the consistency of institutional practice with institutional aims, but it also helps policymakers define the extent to which any trade-offs concomitant to any institutional design feature are acceptable to and congruent with the aims and values of the larger investment framework. The scholars and practitioners who participated in the April 2006 symposium and who have contributed to this volume make an important step in this effort by advancing a range of potentially non-complementary aspirations relating to liberalization, government autonomy, economic development, the rule of law, and personal property rights. In evaluating the existing institutional architecture in light of such values, the authors in this volume make clear that many policy choices are largely mutually exclusive and that all are in some way imperfect.

These challenges identified in the symposium point to important pathways for future research. Perhaps most obviously, they illustrate the need for further empirical assessments of key institutional features, players and problems, not to mention, as one commentator suggests, additional studies of other macro-economic factors that may inform the increasing recourse to arbitration. They also demonstrate the necessity of deeper, more foundational conversations concerning the nature and prioritization of objectives of international investment commitments and the legal architecture better to interpret research data and guide policy responses. To its credit, this volume provides a crucial platform for advancing such a dialog insofar as, by illustrating structural deficits of any one institutional design, commentators have highlighted the importance of the value or standard from which their critique is made.

More such work is, however, needed, as the various perspectives cry out for further normative analysis to address investment treaty structure and institutional concerns, as well as examine, for both comparative and instructional purposes, other relevant regulatory fields like international trade, capital markets and economic development. In the end, an exploration of these authors' insights carries not only tremendous scholarly promise, but also practical significance. Such an inquiry not only makes the insights found in this volume's various chapters all the richer by providing a more comprehensive normative context, but they will also promote, independent of institutional reform, greater transparency and consistency in international investment law.

Selected Bibliography

*Compiled by Brian J. Rapier**

Fredrick M. Abbott, "The Political Economy of NAFTA Chapter Eleven: Equality Before the Law and the Boundaries of North American Integration," 23 HASTINGS INT'L & COMP. L. REV. 303 (2000).

Guillermo A. Alvarez & William W. Park, "The New Face of Investment Arbitration: NAFTA Chapter 11," 28 YALE J. INT'L L. 365 (2003).

Amy K. Anderson, "Individual Rights and Investor Protections in a Trade Regime: NAFTA and CAFTA," 63 WASH. & LEE L. REV. 1057 (2006).

Joel C. Beauvais, "Regulatory Expropriations Under NAFTA: Emerging Principles & Lingering Doubts," 10 N.Y.U. ENVTL. L.J. 245 (2002).

Bipartisan Trade Promotion Authority Act of 2002, 19 U.S.C. §§ 3801 et seq., Senate Rept. 107–139, 107th Cong., 2d Sess., 28 February 2002, at 16.

Doak Bishop, "The Case for an Appellate Panel and its Scope of Review," *in* Federico Ortino et al., eds., *Investment Treaty Law: Current Issues*, Vol. 1:15 (Transnational Dispute Management: 2006).

Nigel Blackaby, "Public Interest and Investment Treaty Arbitration," *in* Albert Jan van den Berg, ed., *International Commercial Arbitration: Important Contemporary Questions, ICCA International Arbitration Conference Series*, No. 11, 362 (2002).

* Brian Rapier is a member of the Class of 2008 at the University of Nebraska College of Law. Email: brapier@bigred.unl.edu.

Nigel Blackaby, "Testing the Procedural Limits of the Treaty System: The Argentinean Experience," *in* Federico Ortino et al., eds., *Investment Treaty Law: Current Issues*, Vol. 1:29 (Transnational Dispute Management: 2006).

Andrea K. Bjorklund, "The Continuing Appeal of Annulment?: Lessons from Amco Asia and CME," *in* Todd Weiler, ed., *Investment Law and Arbitration: Leading Cases from the ICSID, NAFTA, Bilateral Treaties and Customary International Law* (Cameron May: 2005), pp. 471–521, *available at* http://ssrn.com/abstract=911627.

Aron Broches, "The Finality of ICSID Awards," 6 ICSID REVIEW—FOREIGN INVESTMENT LAW JOURNAL 321 (1991).

Charles H. Brower, II, "Structure, Legitimacy, and NAFTA's Investment Chapter," 36 VAND. J. TRANSNAT'L L. 37 (2003).

Charles N. Brower, "A Crisis of Legitimacy," 26 NAT'L L.J. B9 (7 October 2002).

Canada's Model Foreign Investment Promotion and Protection Agreement (2004), *available at* http://www.dfait-maeci.gc.ca/tna-nac/documents/2004-FIPA-model-en.pdf.

Jack J. Coe, Jr., "Domestic Court Control of Investment Awards: Necessary Evil or Achilles Heel Within NAFTA and the Proposed FTAA?," 19 J. INT'L ARB. 185 (2002).

Jack J. Coe, Jr., "Taking Stock of NAFTA Chapter 11 in Its Tenth Year: An Interim Sketch of Selected, Themes, Issues and Methods," 36 VAND. J. TRANSNAT'L L. 1381 (2003).

Bernardo M. Cremades, "Disputes Arising Out of Foreign Direct Investment in Latin America: A New Look at the Calvo Doctrine and Other Jurisdictional Issues," 59 DISP. RESOL. J. 78 (2004), *available at* http://findarticles.com/p/articles/mi_qa3923/is_200405/ai_n9377090.

Bernardo M. Cremades, "Investor Protection and Legal Security in International Arbitration" 60 DISP. RESOL. J. 82 (2005), *available at* http://findarticles.com/p/articles/mi_qa3923/is_200505/ai_n14717721.

Lucien J. Dhooge, "The North American Free Trade Agreement and the Environment: The Lessons of *Metalclad Corporation v. United Mexican States*," 10 MINN. J. GLOBAL TRADE 209 (2001).

William S. Dodge, "Investment Disputes and NAFTA Chapter 11: Remarks," 95 AM. SOC'Y INT'L L. PROC. 207 (2001).

William S. Dodge, "Investor-State Dispute Settlement Between Developed Countries: Reflections on the Australia–United States Free Trade Agreement," 39 VAND. J. TRANSNAT'L L. 1 (2006).

Alejandro A. Escobar, "Procedural Issues Raised by Treaty Interpretation in ICSID Proceedings," *in* Agata Fijalkowski, ed., *International Institutional Reform: Proceedings of the Seventh Hague Joint Conference Held in The Hague, The Netherlands 30 June–2 July 2005* (2007).

Julia Ferguson, "California's MTBE Contaminated Water: An Illustration of the Need For an Environmental Interpretive Note on Article 1110 of NAFTA," 11 COLO. J. INT'L ENVTL. L. & POL'Y 499 (2000).

Susan D. Franck, "The Legitimacy Crisis in Investment Treaty Arbitration: Privatizing Public International Law Through Inconsistent Decisions," 73 FORDHAM L. REV. 1521 (2005).

Susan D. Franck, "The Nature and Enforcement of Investor Rights under Investment Treaties: Do Investment Treaties Have a Bright Future?," U.C. DAVIS J. INT'L L. & POL'Y 47 (2005).

Susan D. Franck, "ICSID Institutional Reform: The Evolution of Dispute Resolution and the Role of Structural Safeguards," *in* Agata Fijalkowski, ed., *International Institutional Reform: Proceedings of the Seventh Hague Joint Conference Held in The Hague, The Netherlands 30 June–2 July 2005* (2007).

Samrat Ganguly, "The Investor-State Dispute Mechanism (ISDM) and a Sovereign's Power to Protect Public Health," 38 COLUM. J. TRANSNAT'L L. 113 (1999).

David A. Gantz, "*The Evolution of FTA Investment Provisions: From NAFTA to the United States–Chile Free Trade Agreement*," 19 AM. U. INT'L L. REV. 679 (2004).

David A. Gantz, "The Free Trade Area of the Americas: An Idea Whose Time has Come–and Gone?," 1 LOY. INT'L L. REV. 179 (2004).

David A. Gantz, "An Appellate Mechanism for Review of Arbitral Decisions in Investor-State Disputes: Prospects and Challenges," 39 VAND. J. TRANSNAT'L L. 39 (2006).

David A. Gantz, "*Settlement of Disputes Under the Central America—United States—Dominican Republic Free Trade Agreement*," 30 BOSTON COLLEGE INT'L & COMP. L. REV. Vol. 30, No. 2 (2007).

James M. Gaitis, "International and Domestic Arbitration Procedure: The Need for a Rule Providing a Limited Opportunity for Arbitral Reconsideration of Reasoned Awards," 15 AM. REV. INT'L ARB. 9 (2004).

Judith Gill, "Inconsistent Decisions: An Issue to be Addressed or a Fact of Life," *in* Federico Ortino et al., eds., *Investment Treaty Law: Current Issues*, Vol. 1:23 (Transnational Dispute Management: 2006).

Michael D. Goldhaber, "Wanted: A World Investment Court," AM. LAWYER (Summer 2004), *available at* http://www.americanlawyer.com/focuseurope/investmentcourt04.html.

Eric Gottwald, "Leveling The Playing Field: Is It Time For A Legal Assistance Center For Developing Nations In Investment Treaty Arbitration?," 22 AM. U. INT'L L. REV. 237 (2007).

Naveen Gurudevan, "An Evaluation of Current Legitimacy-Based Objections to NAFTA's Chapter 11 Investment Dispute Resolution Process," 6 SAN DIEGO INT'L L.J. 399 (2005).

H.E. Judge Howard M. Holtzman, "A Task for the 21st Century: Creating a New International Court for Resolving Disputes on the Enforceability of Arbitral Awards," *in* Martin Hunter et al., eds., *The Internationalisation of International Arbitration: The LCIA Centenary Conference* 109 (Graham and Trotman/Martinus Nijhoff: 1995).

ICSID Secretariat, *Possible Improvement of the Framework for ICSID Arbitration* (22 October 2004), *available at* http://www.worldbank.org/icsid/highlights/improve-arb.pdf.

ICSID Secretariat, *Suggested Changes to the ICSID Rules and Regulations* (2 June 2005), *available at* http://www.worldbank.org/icsid/highlights/052405-sgmanual.pdf.

Convention on the Settlement of Investment Disputes Between States and Nationals of Other States, October 14, 1966, 17 U.S.T. 1270, 575 U.N.T.S. 159.

International Institute for Sustainable Development, *Comments on ICSID Discussion Paper, "Possible Improvement of the Framework for ICSID Arbitration"* (December 2004), *available at* http://www.iisd.org.

Thomas Johnson, "Factual Review," *in* Federico Ortino et al., eds., *Investment Treaty Law: Current Issues*, Vol. 1:59 (Transnational Dispute Management: 2006).

Joanna Kalb, "Creating an ICSID Appellate Body," 10 UCLA J. Int'l L. & Foreign Aff. 179 (2005).

Kevin C. Kennedy, "The FTAA Negotiations: A Melodrama in Five Acts," 1 Loy. Int'l L. Rev. 121 (2004).

William H. Knull, III & Noah D. Rubins, "Betting the Farm on International Arbitration: Is It Time To Offer An Appeal Option?," 11 Am. Rev. Int'l Arb. 531 (2000).

Ian Laird & Rebecca Askew, "Finality Versus Consistency: Does Investor-State Arbitration Need an Appellate System?," 7 J. App. Prac. & Process 285 (2005).

Barton Legum, "Visualizing an Appellate System," *in* Federico Ortino et al., eds., *Investment Treaty Law: Current Issues*, Vol. 1:121 (Transnational Dispute Management: 2006).

René L. Lerner, "International Pressure To Harmonize: The U.S. Civil Justice System In An Era Of Global Trade," 2001 BYU L. Rev. 229 (2001).

Daniel R. Loritz, "Corporate Predators Attack Environmental Regulations: It's Time to Arbitrate Claims Filed Under NAFTA's Chapter 11," 22 Loy. L.A. Int'l & Comp. L. Rev. 533 (2000).

Marrakech Agreement Establishing the World Trade Organization, Understanding on Rules and Procedures Governing the Settlement of Disputes, 15 April 1994, Annex 2, Legal Instruments—Results of the Uruguay Round Vol. 31, 33 I.L.M. 1226 (1994).

Amala Nath, "Comment: The SAFTA Dispute Settlement Mechanism: An Attempt to Resolve or Merely Perpetuate Conflict in the South Asian Region?," 22 Am. U. Int'l L. Rev. 333–359 (2007).

OECD, "Transparency and Third Party Participation in Investor-State Dispute Settlement," *in Making the Most of International Investment Agreements: A Common Agenda* (2005), *available at* http://www.oecd.org/dataoecd/6/25/36979626.pdf.

OECD, *Improving the System of Investor-State Dispute Settlement: An Overview* (2006), *available at* http://www.oecd.org/dataoecd/3/59/36052284.pdf.

Robert K. Paterson, "A New Pandora's Box?: Private Remedies for Foreign Investors Under the North American Free Trade Agreement," 8 Willamette J. Int'l & Disp. Resol. 77 (2000).

Jan Paulsson, "The Practitioner's Perspective on the Need for Reform: 'Hâtez-vous Lentement,'" *in* Agata Fijalkowski, ed., *International Institutional Reform: Proceedings of the Seventh Hague Joint Conference Held in The Hague, The Netherlands 30 June–2 July 2005* (2007).

Philippe Pinsolle, "'Manifest' Excess of Power and Jurisdictional Review of ICSID Awards," *in* Federico Ortino et al., eds., *Investment Treaty Law: Current Issues*, Vol. 1:51 (Transnational Dispute Management: 2006).

Daniel M. Price, "US Trade Promotion Legislation," in Federico Ortino et al., eds., *Investment Treaty Law: Current Issues*, Vol. 1:89 (Transnational Dispute Management: 2006).

Asif Qureshi, "Development Perspectives on the Establishment of an Appellate Process in the Investment Sphere," *in* Federico Ortino et al., eds., *Investment Treaty Law: Current Issues*, Vol. 1:99 (Transnational Dispute Management: 2006).

Noah Rubins, "Judicial Review of Investment Arbitration Awards," *in* Federico Ortino et al., eds., *Investment Treaty Law: Current Issues*, Vol. 1:75 (Transnational Dispute Management: 2006).

Noah Rubins, *Observations of Noah Rubins*, *in* Stockholm Arb. Rep., 2003, at 202 (2003), *available at* http://www.sccinstitute.com/_upload/shared_files/artiklar/tjeckiska_republiken.pdf.

Noah Rubins, "Judicial Review of Investment Arbitration Awards," *in* Todd Weiler, ed., *NAFTA Investment Law & Arbitration: Past Issues, Current Practice, Future Prospects* 354 (Transnational Publishers: 2004).

H.E. Judge Stephen M. Schwebel, "The Creation and Operation of an International Court of Arbitral Award," *in* Martin Hunter et al., eds., *The Internationalisation of International Arbitration: The LCIA Centenary Conference* 109 (Graham and Trotman/Martinus Nijhoff: 1995).

Audley Sheppard & Hugo Warner, "Editorial Note," *in* Federico Ortino et al., eds., *Investment Treaty Law: Current Issues*, Vol. 1:3 (Transnational Dispute Management: 2006).

Bette Shifman, "The Challenges of Administering an Appellate System for Investment Disputes," *in* Federico Ortino et al., eds., *Investment Treaty Law: Current Issues*, Vol. 1:113 (Transnational Dispute Management: 2006).

Abby Cohen Smutny, "Procedural Review," *in* Federico Ortino et al., eds., *Investment Treaty Law: Current Issues*, Vol. 1:65 (Transnational Dispute Management: 2006).

South Centre, "Developments on Discussions for the Improvement of the Framework for ICSID Arbitration and the Participation of Developing Countries," 2(3) TRANSNATIONAL DISPUTE MANAGEMENT (June 2005).

C. Ignacio Suarez Anzorena, "Multiplicity of Claims under BITs and the Argentine Case," *in* Federico Ortino et al., eds., *Investment Treaty Law: Current Issues*, Vol. 1:37 (Transnational Dispute Management: 2006).

C. Ignacio Suarez Anzorena, "Multiplicity of Claims Under BITs: Changing Institutions and Proceedings or Changing the Way we Construe the Treaties," *in* Agata Fijalkowski, ed., *International Institutional Reform: Proceedings of the Seventh Hague Joint Conference Held in The Hague, The Netherlands 30 June–2 July 2005* (2007).

Christian J. Tams, "An Appealing Option? The Debate About ICSID Appellate Structure," *57 Essays in Transnational Economic Law* (2006), *available at* http://www.wirtschaftsrecht.uni-halle.de/Heft57.pdf.

Guido Santiago Tawil, "An International Appellate System: Progress or Pitfall?," *in* Federico Ortino et al., eds., *Investment Treaty Law: Current Issues*, Vol. 1:131 (Transnational Dispute Management: 2006).

U.S. Department of State, Update of U.S. Model Bilateral Investment Treaty, (2004), *available at* http://www.state.gov/documents/organization/29030.doc.

UNCTAD, "Occasional Note: International Investment Disputes on the Rise," UNCTAD/WEB/ITE/IIT/2004/2 (United Nations Publication: 2004), *available at* http://www.unctad.org/sections/dite/iia/docs/webiteiit20042_en.pdf.

UNCTAD, "Research Note: Research Developments In International Investment Agreements," UNCTAD/WEB/ITE/IIT/2005/1 (United Nations Publication: 2005), *available at* http://www.unctad.org/sections/dite_dir/docs/webiteiit20051_en.pdf.

UNCTAD, "Investor-State Disputes Arising From Investment Treaties: A Review," UNCTAD/ITE/IIT/2005/4 (United Nations Publication: 2005), *available at* http://www.unctad.org/en/docs/iteiit20054_en.pdf.

UNCTAD, "Latest Developments in Investor-State Dispute Settlement," IIA Monitor, 2005, No. 4 (United Nations Publication: 2005), *available at* http://www.unctad.org/en/docs//webiteiit20052_en.pdf.

UNCTAD, "Latest Developments in Investor-State Dispute Settlement," IIA Monitor, 2006, No. 4 (United Nations Publication: 2006), *available at* http://www.unctad.org/sections/dite_pcbb/docs/webiteiia200611_en.pdf.

UNCTAD, *International Investment Arrangements: Trends and Emerging Issues*, *in* UNCTAD Series on International Investment Policies for Development UNCTAD/ITE/IIT/2005/11 (United Nations Publication: 2006), *available at* http://www.unctad.org/Templates/Download.asp?docid=6983&lang=1&intItemID=1397.

United States–Dominican Republic–Central American Free Trade Agreement (United States, Costa Rica, Dominican Republic, El Salvador, Guatemala, Honduras, Nicaragua) (5 August 2004), *available at* http://www.ustr.gov/

Trade_Agreements/Bilateral/CAFTA/CAFTA-DR_Final_Texts/Section_Index.html.

V.V. Veeder, "The Necessary Safeguards of an Appellate System," *in* Federico Ortino et al., eds., *Investment Treaty Law: Current Issues*, Vol. 1:9 (Transnational Dispute Management: 2006).

Thomas Wälde, "Alternatives for Obtaining Greater Consistency in Investment Arbitration: An Appellate Institution after the WTO, Authoritative Treaty Arbitration or Mandatory Consolidation?," *in* Federico Ortino et al., eds., *Investment Treaty Law: Current Issues*, Vol. 1:135 (Transnational Dispute Management: 2006).

Thomas W. Walsh, "Substantive Review of ICSID Awards: Is The Desire For Accuracy Sufficient To Compromise Finality?," 24 BERKELEY J. INT'L L. 444 (2006).

Appendix

APPENDIX 1

Selection of BITs and FTAs with Provisions Relating to an Appellate Review Mechanism

Introduction:

The documents in this Appendix reproduce treaty articles dealing with the possibility of an appellate review mechanism. These provisions demonstrate, in particular, the recent policy of the United States on the question of such a mechanism. The U.S. envisages the creation of bilateral appellate bodies which, however, could perhaps be subsumed under a multilateral appellate review mechanism, were one to emerge. The leadership position of the U.S. makes this an interesting and potentially transformative factor in the global regime. The language used in its BITs and FTAs varies slightly treaty-by-treaty, but, as the reader will note, the provisions are virtually identical in form, function and intent.

I. Dominican Republic–Central America–United States Free Trade Agreement (DR-CAFTA)[1]

Chapter 10: Investment
Article 10.20: Conduct of the Arbitration

9. (a) In any arbitration conducted under this Section, at the request of a disputing party, a tribunal shall, before issuing a decision or award on liability, transmit its proposed decision or award to the disputing parties and to the non-disputing Parties. Within 60 days after the tribunal transmits its proposed decision or award, the disputing parties may submit written comments to the tribunal concerning any aspect of its proposed decision or award. The tribunal shall consider any such comments and issue its decision or award not later than 45 days after the expiration of the 60-day comment period.

   (b) Subparagraph (a) shall not apply in any arbitration conducted pursuant to this Section for which an appeal has been made available pursuant to paragraph 10 or Annex 10-F.

10. If a separate multilateral agreement enters into force as between the Parties that establishes an appellate body for purposes of reviewing awards rendered by tribunals constituted pursuant to international trade or investment arrangements to hear investment disputes, the Parties shall strive to reach an agreement that would have such appellate body review awards rendered under Article 10.26 in arbitrations commenced after the multilateral agreement enters into force as between the Parties.

Article 10.26: Awards

6. A disputing party may not seek enforcement of a final award until:
   (a) in the case of a final award made under the ICSID Convention,
      (i) 120 days have elapsed from the date the award was disputing party has requested revision or annulment of the award; or
      (ii) revision or annulment proceedings have been completed; and

---

1 Central American Free Trade Agreement, 5 August 2004, *available at* (http://www.ustr.gov/assets/Trade_Agreements/Bilateral/CAFTA/CAFTA-DR_Final_Texts/asset_upload_file328_4718.pdf).

(b) in the case of a final award under the ICSID Additional Facility Rules or the UNCITRAL Arbitration Rules,
   (i) 90 days have elapsed from the date the award was rendered and no disputing party has commenced a proceeding to revise, set aside, or annul the award; or
   (ii) a court has dismissed or allowed an application to revise, set aside, or annul the award and there is no further appeal.

Annex 10-F
Appellate Body or Similar Mechanism

1. Within three months of the date of entry into force of this Agreement, the Commission shall establish a Negotiating Group to develop an appellate body or similar mechanism to review awards rendered by tribunals under this Chapter. Such appellate body or similar mechanism shall be designed to provide coherence to the interpretation of investment provisions in the Agreement. The Commission shall direct the Negotiating Group to take into account the following issues, among others:

   (a) the nature and composition of an appellate body or similar mechanism;
   (b) the applicable scope and standard of review;
   (c) transparency of proceedings of an appellate body or similar mechanism;
   (d) the effect of decisions by an appellate body or similar mechanism;
   (e) the relationship of review by an appellate body or similar mechanism to the arbitral rules that may be selected under Articles 10.16 and 10.25; and
   (f) the relationship of review by an appellate body or similar mechanism to existing domestic laws and international law on the enforcement of arbitral awards.

2. The Commission shall direct the Negotiating Group to provide to the Commission, within one year of establishment of the Negotiating Group, a draft amendment to the Agreement that establishes an appellate body or similar mechanism. On approval of the draft amendment by the Parties, in accordance with Article 22.2 (Amendments), the Agreement shall be so amended.

II. United States–Chile Free Trade Agreement[2]

Chapter 10: Investment
Article 10.19: Conduct of the Arbitration

9. (a) At the request of a disputing party, a tribunal shall, before issuing a decision or award on liability, transmit its proposed decision or award to the disputing parties and to the non-disputing Party. Within 60 days after the tribunal transmits its proposed decision or award, the disputing parties may submit written comments to the tribunal concerning any aspect of its proposed decision or award. The tribunal shall consider any such comments and issue its decision or award not later than 45 days after the expiration of the 60-day comment period.

   (b) Subparagraph (a) shall not apply in any arbitration conducted pursuant to this Section for which an appeal has been made available pursuant to paragraph 10.

10. If a separate multilateral agreement enters into force as between the Parties that establishes an appellate body for purposes of reviewing awards rendered by tribunals constituted pursuant to international trade or investment arrangements to hear investment disputes, the Parties shall strive to reach an agreement that would have such appellate body review awards rendered under Article 10.25 in arbitrations commenced after the appellate body's establishment.

Article 10.25: Awards

6. A disputing party may not seek enforcement of a final award until:
   (a) in the case of a final award made under the ICSID Convention,
      (i) 120 days have elapsed from the date the award was rendered and no disputing party has requested revision or annulment of the award; or
      (ii) revision or annulment proceedings have been completed; and
   (b) in the case of a final award under the ICSID Additional Facility Rules, UNCITRAL Arbitration Rules, or rules selected pursuant to Article 10.15(5)(d),

---

2 U.S.–Chile Free Trade Agreement, 6 June 2003, *available at* (http://www.ustr.gov/assets/Trade_Agreements/Bilateral/Chile_FTA/Final_Texts/asset_upload_file1_4004.pdf).

(i) 90 days have elapsed from the date the award was rendered and no disputing party has commenced a proceeding to revise, set aside, or annul the award; or

(ii) a court has dismissed or allowed an application to revise, set aside, or annul the award and there is no further appeal.

Annex 10-H
Possibility of a Bilateral Appellate Body/Mechanism

Within three years after the date of entry into force of this Agreement, the Parties shall consider whether to establish a bilateral appellate body or similar mechanism to review awards rendered under Article 10.25 in arbitrations commenced after they establish the appellate body or similar mechanism.

III. United States–Morocco Free Trade Agreement[3]

Chapter 10: Investment
Article 10.19: Conduct of the Arbitration

9. (a) In any arbitration under this section, at the request of a disputing party, a tribunal shall, before issuing a decision or award on liability, transmit its proposed decision or award to the disputing parties and to the non-disputing Party. Within 60 days after the tribunal transmits its proposed decision or award, the disputing parties may submit written comments to the tribunal concerning any aspect of its proposed decision or award. The tribunal shall consider any such comments and issue its decision or award not later than 45 days after the expiration of the 60-day comment period.

   (b) Subparagraph (a) shall not apply in any arbitration conducted pursuant to this Section for which an appeal has been made available pursuant to paragraph 10 or Annex 10-D.

10. If a separate multilateral agreement enters into force between the Parties that establishes an appellate body for purposes of reviewing awards rendered by tribunals constituted pursuant to international trade or investment arrangements to hear investment disputes, the Parties shall strive to reach an agreement that would have such appellate body review awards

[3] U.S.–Morocco Free Trade Agreement, 2 March 2004, *available at* (http://www.ustr.gov/assets/Trade_Agreements/Bilateral/Morocco_FTA/FInal_Text/asset_upload_file651_3838.pdf).

rendered under Article 10.25 in arbitrations commenced after the regional or multilateral agreement enters into force between the Parties.

Article 10.25: Awards

6. A disputing party may not seek enforcement of a final award until:

   (a) in the case of a final award made under the ICSID Convention
      (i) 120 days have elapsed from the date the award was rendered and no disputing party has requested revision or annulment of the award; or
      (ii) revision or annulment proceedings have been completed; and

   (b) in the case of a final award under the ICSID Additional Facility Rules, UNCITRAL Arbitration Rules, or rules selected pursuant to Article 10.15.3(d)
      (i) 90 days have elapsed from the date the award was rendered and no disputing party has commenced a proceeding to revise, set aside, or annul the award; or
      (ii) a court has dismissed or allowed an application to revise, set aside, or annul the award and there is no further appeal.

Annex 10-D
Possibility of a Bilateral Appellate Mechanism

Within three years after the date of entry into force of this Agreement, the Parties shall consider whether to establish a bilateral appellate body or similar mechanism to review awards rendered under Article 10.25 in arbitrations commenced after they establish the appellate body or similar mechanism.

IV. United States–Singapore Free Trade Agreement[4]

Chapter 15: Investment
Article 15.19: Conduct of the Arbitration

9. (a) In any arbitration under this section, at the request of a disputing party, a tribunal shall, before issuing an award on liability, transmit its proposed award to the disputing parties and to the non-disputing Party.

---

4 U.S.–Singapore Free Trade Agreement, 6 May 2003, *available at* (http://www.ustr.gov/assets/Trade_Agreements/Bilateral/Singapore_FTA/Final_Texts/asset_upload_file708_4036.pdf) [Chapter 15] and (http://www.ustr.gov/assets/Trade_Agreements/Bilateral/Singapore_FTA/Final_Texts/asset_upload_file159_4060.pdf) [Side Letter].

Within 60 days after the tribunal transmits its proposed award, the disputing parties may submit written comments to the tribunal concerning any aspect of its proposed award. The tribunal shall consider any such comments and issue its award not later than 45 days after the expiration of the 60-day comment period.

(b) Subparagraph (a) shall not apply in any arbitration conducted pursuant to this Section for which an appeal has been made available pursuant to paragraph 10.

10. If a separate multilateral agreement enters into force as between the Parties that establishes an appellate body for purposes of reviewing awards rendered by tribunals constituted pursuant to international trade or investment arrangements to hear investment disputes, the Parties shall strive to reach an agreement that would have such appellate body review awards rendered under Article 15.25 of this section in arbitrations commenced after the appellate body's establishment.

Article 15.25: Awards

6. A disputing party may not seek enforcement of a final award until:

   (a) in the case of a final award made under the ICSID Convention,
      (i) 120 days have elapsed from the date the award was rendered and no disputing party has requested revision or annulment of the award; or
      (ii) revision or annulment proceedings have been completed; and

   (b) in the case of a final award under the ICSID Additional Facility Rules, UNCITRAL Arbitration Rules, or rules selected pursuant to Article 15.15.5(d),
      (i) 90 days have elapsed from the date the award was rendered and no disputing party has commenced a proceeding to revise, set aside, or annul the award, or
      (ii) a court has dismissed or allowed an application to revise, set aside, or annul the award and there is no further appeal.

Chapter 15, Article 15.16: Status of Letter Exchanges Appellate Mechanism

15.16: The following letters exchanged this day on:

(d) Appellate Mechanism

shall form an integral part of this Agreement.

The Side Letters:

May 6, 2003, Robert Zoellick, United States Trade Representative, to George Yeo, Singapore Minister for Trade and Industry:

> "During the negotiation of the Investment Chapter of the Agreement (Chapter 15), the United States of America and Singapore (collectively, the "Parties") discussed the possibility of establishing a bilateral appellate mechanism to review awards rendered by tribunals under that Chapter. Based on those discussions, I have the honor to confirm the Parties' shared understanding that, within three years after the date of entry into force of this Agreement, the Parties shall consider whether to establish a bilateral appellate body or similar mechanism to review awards rendered under Article 15.25 (Awards) in arbitrations commenced after they establish the appellate body or similar mechanism.
>
> I have the honor to propose that this understanding be treated as an integral part of the Agreement.
>
> I would be grateful if you would confirm that this understanding is shared by your Government."

May 6, 2003, George Yeo, Singapore Minister for Trade and Industry, to Robert Zoellick, United States Trade Representative:

> "I have the honor to confirm receipt of your letter, which reads as follows: [as above].
>
> I have the further honor to confirm that this understanding is shared by my Government and constitutes an integral part of the Agreement."

V. United States–Oman Free Trade Agreement[5]

Chapter 10: Investment
Article 10.19: Conduct of the Arbitration

9. (a) In any arbitration under this section, at the request of a disputing party, a tribunal shall, before issuing a decision or award on liability, transmit its proposed decision or award to the disputing parties and to the non-disputing Party. Within 60 days after the tribunal transmits its proposed decision or award, the disputing parties may submit written comments to the tribunal concerning any aspect of its proposed decision or award. The tribunal shall consider any such comments and issue its decision or award not later than 45 days after the expiration of the 60-day comment period.

   (b) Subparagraph (a) shall not apply in any arbitration conducted pursuant to this Section for which an appeal has been made available pursuant to paragraph 10 or Annex 10-D.

10. If a separate, multilateral agreement enters into force between the Parties that establishes an appellate body for purposes of reviewing awards rendered by tribunals constituted pursuant to international trade or investment arrangements to hear investment disputes, the Parties shall strive to reach an agreement that would have such appellate body review awards rendered under Article 10.25 in arbitrations commenced after the multilateral agreement enters into force between the Parties.

Article 10.25: Awards

6. A disputing party may not seek enforcement of a final award until:
   (a) in the case of a final award made under the ICSID Convention,
      (i) 120 days have elapsed from the date the award was rendered and no disputing party has requested revision or annulment of the award; or
      (ii) revision or annulment proceedings have been completed; and

---

[5] U.S.–Oman Free Trade Agreement, 19 January 2006, *available at* (http://www.ustr.gov/assets/Trade_Agreements/Bilateral/Oman_FTA/Final_Text/asset_upload_file976_8810.pdf).

(b) in the case of a final award under the ICSID Additional Facility Rules, UNCITRAL Arbitration Rules, or the rules selected pursuant to Article 10.15.3(d),
  (i) 90 days have elapsed from the date the award was rendered and no disputing party has commenced a proceeding to revise, set aside, or annul the award; or
  (ii) a court has dismissed or allowed an application to revise, set aside, or annul the award and there is no further appeal.

Annex 10-D
Possibility of a Bilateral Appellate Mechanism

Within three years after the date of entry into force of this Agreement, the Parties shall consider whether to establish a bilateral appellate body or similar mechanism to review awards rendered under Article 10.25 in arbitrations commenced after they establish the appellate body or similar mechanism.

VI. United States–Colombia Trade Promotion Agreement[6]

Chapter 10: Investment
Article 10.20: Conduct of the Arbitration

9. (a) In any arbitration conducted under this Section, at the request of a disputing party, a tribunal shall, before issuing a decision or award on liability, transmit its proposed decision or award to the disputing parties and to the non-disputing Parties. Within 60 days after the tribunal transmits its proposed decision or award, the disputing parties may submit written comments to the tribunal concerning any aspect of its proposed decision or award. The tribunal shall consider any such comments and issue its decision or award not later than 45 days after the expiration of the 60-day comment period.

   (b) Subparagraph (a) shall not apply in any arbitration conducted pursuant to this Section for which an appeal has been made available pursuant to paragraph 10 or Annex 10-D.

10. If a separate multilateral agreement enters into force as between the Parties that establishes an appellate body for purposes of reviewing

---

6 U.S.–Colombia Trade Promotion Agreement, 22 November 2006, *available at* (http://www.ustr.gov/assets/Trade_Agreements/Bilateral/Colombia_FTA/Final_Text/asset_upload_file630_10143.pdf).

awards rendered by tribunals constituted pursuant to international trade or investment arrangements to hear investment disputes, the Parties shall strive to reach an agreement that would have such appellate body review awards rendered under Article 10.26 in arbitrations commenced after the multilateral agreement enters into force as between the Parties.

Article 10.26: Awards

6. A disputing party may not seek enforcement of a final award until:

   (a) in the case of a final award made under the ICSID Convention,
      (i) 120 days have elapsed from the date the award was rendered and no disputing party has requested revision or annulment of the award; or
      (ii) revision or annulment proceedings have been completed; and

   (b) in the case of a final award under the ICSID Additional Facility Rules, the UNCITRAL Arbitration Rules, or the rules selected pursuant to Article 10.16.3(d),
      (i) 90 days have elapsed from the date the award was rendered and no disputing party has commenced a proceeding to revise, set aside, or annul the award; or
      (ii) a court has dismissed or allowed an application to revise, set aside, or annul the award and there is no further appeal.

Annex 10-D
Appellate Body or Similar Mechanism

Within three years after the date of entry into force of this Agreement, the Parties shall consider whether to establish an appellate body or similar mechanism to review awards rendered under Article 10.26 in arbitrations commenced after they establish the appellate body or similar mechanism.

VII. Panama–United States Trade Promotion Agreement[7]

Chapter 10: Investment
Article 10.20: Conduct of the Arbitration

9. (a) In any arbitration conducted under this Section, at the request of a disputing party, a tribunal shall, before issuing a decision or award on liability, transmit its proposed decision or award to the disputing parties and to the non-disputing Party. Within 60 days after the tribunal transmits its proposed decision or award, the disputing parties may submit written comments to the tribunal concerning any aspect of its proposed decision or award. The tribunal shall consider any such comments and issue its decision or award not later than 45 days after the expiration of the 60-day comment period.

   (b) Subparagraph (a) shall not apply in any arbitration conducted pursuant to this Section for which an appeal has been made available pursuant to paragraph 10 or Annex 10-D.

10. If a separate multilateral agreement enters into force as between the Parties that establishes an appellate body for purposes of reviewing awards rendered by tribunals constituted pursuant to international trade or investment arrangements to hear investment disputes, the Parties shall strive to reach an agreement that would have such appellate body review awards rendered under Article 10.26 in arbitrations commenced after the multilateral agreement enters into force as between the Parties.

Article 10.26: Awards

6. A disputing party may not seek enforcement of a final award until:
   (a) in the case of a final award made under the ICSID Convention,
      (i) 120 days have elapsed from the date the award was rendered and no disputing party has requested revision or annulment of the award; or
      (ii) revision or annulment proceedings have been completed; and
   (b) in the case of a final award under the ICSID Additional Facility Rules or the UNCITRAL Arbitration Rules,

---

7 U.S.–Panama Trade Promotion Agreement, signing expected 2007, *available at* (http://www.ustr.gov/assets/Trade_Agreements/Bilateral/Panama_FTA/Draft_Text/asset_upload_file470_10351.pdf).

(i) 90 days have elapsed from the date the award was rendered and no disputing party has commenced a proceeding to revise, set aside, or annul the award; or

(ii) a court has dismissed or allowed an application to revise, set aside, or annul the award and there is no further appeal.

Annex 10-D
Possibility of a Bilateral Appellate Mechanism

Within three years after the date of entry into force of this Agreement, the Parties shall consider whether to establish a bilateral appellate body or similar mechanism to review awards rendered under Article 25 in arbitrations commenced after they establish the appellate body or similar mechanism.

VIII. United States–Peru Trade Promotion Agreement (PTPA)[8]

Chapter 10: Investment
Article 10.20: Conduct of the Arbitration

9. (a) In any arbitration conducted under this Section, at the request of a disputing party, a tribunal shall, before issuing a decision or award on liability, transmit its proposed decision or award to the disputing parties and to the non-disputing Parties. Within 60 days after the tribunal transmits its proposed decision or award, the disputing parties may submit written comments to the tribunal concerning any aspect of its proposed decision or award. The tribunal shall consider any such comments and issue its decision or award not later than 45 days after the expiration of the 60-day comment period.

(b) Subparagraph (a) shall not apply in any arbitration conducted pursuant to this Section for which an appeal has been made available pursuant to paragraph 10 or Annex 10-D.

10. If a separate multilateral agreement enters into force as between the Parties that establishes an appellate body for purposes of reviewing awards rendered by tribunals constituted pursuant to international trade or investment arrangements to hear investment disputes, the Parties shall

8 U.S.–Peru Trade Promotion Agreement, 12 April 2006, *available at* (http://www.ustr.gov/assets/Trade_Agreements/Bilateral/Peru_TPA/Final_Texts/asset_upload_file78_9547.pdf).

strive to reach an agreement that would have such appellate body review awards rendered under Article 10.26 in arbitrations commenced after the multilateral agreement enters into force as between the Parties.

Article 10.26: Awards

6. A disputing party may not seek enforcement of a final award until:
   (a) in the case of a final award made under the ICSID Convention,
      (i) 120 days have elapsed from the date the award was rendered and no disputing party has requested revision or annulment of the award; or
      (ii) revision or annulment proceedings have been completed; and
   (b) in the case of a final award under the ICSID Additional Facility Rules, UNCITRAL Arbitration Rules, or rules selected pursuant to Article 10.16.3(d),
      (i) 90 days have elapsed from the date the award was rendered and no disputing party has commenced a proceeding to revise, set aside, or annul the award; or
      (ii) a court has dismissed or allowed an application to revise, set aside, or annul the award and there is no further appeal.

Annex 10-D
Appellate Body or Similar Mechanism

Within three years after the date of entry into force of this Agreement, the Parties shall consider whether to establish an appellate body or similar mechanism to review awards rendered under Article 10.26 in arbitrations commenced after they establish the appellate body or similar mechanism.

IX. United States–Uruguay Bilateral Investment Treaty[9]

Article 28: Conduct of the Arbitration

9. (a) In any arbitration under this Section, at the request of a disputing party, a tribunal shall, before issuing a decision or award on liability, transmit its proposed decision or award to the disputing parties and to the

---

[9] Treaty Between the United States of America and the Oriental Republic of Uruguay Concerning the Encouragement and Reciprocal Protection of Investment (U.S.–Uruguay Bilateral Investment Treaty), 4 November 2005, *available at* (http://www.ustr.gov/assets/Trade_Agreements/BIT/Uruguay/asset_upload_file748_9005.pdf).

non-disputing Party. Within 60 days after the tribunal transmits its proposed decision or award, the disputing parties may submit written comments to the tribunal concerning any aspect of its proposed decision or award. The tribunal shall consider any such comments and issue its decision or award not later than 45 days after the expiration of the 60-day comment period.

(b) Subparagraph (a) shall not apply in any arbitration conducted pursuant to this Section for which an appeal has been made available pursuant to paragraph 10 or Annex E.

10. If a separate multilateral agreement enters into force between the Parties that establishes an appellate body for purposes of reviewing awards rendered by tribunals constituted pursuant to international trade or investment arrangements to hear investment disputes, the Parties shall strive to reach an agreement that would have such appellate body review awards rendered under Article 34 in arbitrations commenced after the multilateral agreement enters into force between the Parties.

Article 34: Awards

6. A disputing party may not seek enforcement of a final award until:
   (a) in the case of a final award made under the ICSID Convention,
      (i) 120 days have elapsed from the date the award was rendered and no disputing party has requested revision or annulment of the award; or
      (ii) revision or annulment proceedings have been completed; and
   (b) in the case of a final award under the ICSID Additional Facility Rules, UNCITRAL Arbitration Rules, or rules selected pursuant to Article 24(3)(d),
      (i) 90 days have elapsed from the date the award was rendered and no disputing party has commenced a proceeding to revise, set aside, or annul the award; or
      (ii) a court has dismissed or allowed an application to revise, set aside, or annul the award and there is no further appeal.

Annex E
Possibility of a Bilateral Appellate Mechanism

Within three years after the date of entry into force of this Treaty, the Parties shall consider whether to establish a bilateral appellate body or similar mechanism to review awards rendered under Article 34 in arbitrations commenced after they establish the appellate body or similar mechanism.

X. United States Model Bilateral Investment Treaty[10]

Article 28: Conduct of the Arbitration

9. (a) In any arbitration under this Section, at the request of a disputing party, a tribunal shall, before issuing a decision or award on liability, transmit its proposed decision or award to the disputing parties and to the non-disputing Party. Within 60 days after the tribunal transmits its proposed decision or award, the disputing parties may submit written comments to the tribunal concerning any aspect of its proposed decision or award. The tribunal shall consider any such comments and issue its decision or award not later than 45 days after the expiration of the 60-day comment period.

   (b) Subparagraph (a) shall not apply in any arbitration conducted pursuant to this Section for which an appeal has been made available pursuant to paragraph 10 or Annex D.

10. If a separate multilateral agreement enters into force between the Parties that establishes an appellate body for purposes of reviewing awards rendered by tribunals constituted pursuant to international trade or investment arrangements to hear investment disputes, the Parties shall strive to reach an agreement that would have such appellate body review awards rendered under Article 34 in arbitrations commenced after the multilateral agreement enters into force between the Parties.

Article 34: Awards

6. A disputing party may not seek enforcement of a final award until:

   (a) in the case of a final award made under the ICSID Convention,
      (i) 120 days have elapsed from the date the award was rendered and no disputing party has requested revision or annulment of the award; or
      (ii) revision or annulment proceedings have been completed; and

---

10 United States Model Bilateral Investment Treaty, November 2004, *available at* (http://www.state.gov/documents/organization/38710.pdf).

(b) in the case of a final award under the ICSID Additional Facility Rules, UNCITRAL Arbitration Rules, or rules selected pursuant to Article 24(3)(d),
   (i) 90 days have elapsed from the date the award was rendered and no disputing party has commenced a proceeding to revise, set aside, or annul the award; or
   (ii) a court has dismissed or allowed an application to revise, set aside, or annul the award and there is no further appeal.

Annex D
Possibility of a Bilateral Appellate Mechanism

Within three years after the date of entry into force of this Treaty, the Parties shall consider whether to establish a bilateral appellate body or similar mechanism to review awards rendered under Article 34 in arbitrations commenced after they establish the appellate body or similar mechanism.

APPENDIX 2

ICSID Convention, Excerpt

Introduction:

As ICSID is the pre-eminent site for international arbitration, this Appendix reproduces the ICSID Convention's possible approach to an appeals mechanism. Article 53 points to the lack of a current appeals process; the Articles on amendment of the treaty are included to demonstrate the great difficulty of amending the Convention, as unanimity is required.

I. ICSID Convention on the Settlement of Investment Disputes Between States and Nationals of Other States[1]

Chapter IV: Arbitration
Section 6: Recognition and Enforcement of the Award
Article 53

(1) The award shall be binding on the parties and shall not be subject to any appeal or to any other remedy except those provided for in this Convention. Each party shall abide by and comply with the terms of the award except to the extent that enforcement shall have been stayed pursuant to the relevant provisions of this Convention.

(2) For the purposes of this Section, "award" shall include any decision interpreting, revising or annulling such award pursuant to Articles 50, 51 or 52.

---

1 International Centre for Settlement of Investment Disputes, "Convention on the Settlement of Investment Disputes Between States and Nationals of Other States," as amended 10 April 2006, *available at* (http://www.worldbank.org/icsid/basicdoc/CRR_English-final.pdf).

Chapter IX: Amendment
Article 65

Any Contracting State may propose amendment of this Convention. The text of a proposed amendment shall be communicated to the Secretary-General not less than 90 days prior to the meeting of the Administrative Council at which such amendment is to be considered and shall forthwith be transmitted by him to all the members of the Administrative Council.

Article 66

(1) If the Administrative Council shall so decide by a majority of two-thirds of its members, the proposed amendment shall be circulated to all Contracting States for ratification, acceptance or approval. Each amendment shall enter into force 30 days after dispatch by the depositary of this Convention of a notification to Contracting States that all Contracting States have ratified, accepted or approved the amendment.

(2) No amendment shall affect the rights and obligations under this Convention of any Contracting State or of any of its constituent subdivisions or agencies, or of any national of such State arising out of consent to the jurisdiction of the Centre given before the date of entry into force of the amendment.

APPENDIX 3

Possible Improvements of the Framework for ICSID Arbitration*

Introduction:

This Appendix, along with the subsequent Appendixes 4 and 5, contain proposals by the International Centre for Settlement of Investment Disputes to modify its arbitral rules, regulations and procedure with respect to an appellate review mechanism. This process involved two papers discussing proposals for improving the system as well as a period of public comment on the proposals. Here, this first document—prepared by a team led by Antonio R. Parra—addresses head-on the difficulty of amending the Convention, and certain proposals for doing so. Subsequently, ICSID invited public commentary on this document.

---

* Article re-published with approval of the International Centre for Settlement Disputes. Document is publicly available on the website of ICSID, http://icsid.worldbank.org/ICSID/Index.jsp, its original place of publication.

International Centre for Settlement of Investment Disputes

1818 H Street, N.W., Washington, D.C. 20433 U.S.A.
Telephone: (202) 458-1534 Faxes: (202) 522-2615 / 522-2027
Website: http://www.worldbank.org/icsid

POSSIBLE IMPROVEMENTS OF THE FRAMEWORK FOR ICSID ARBITRATION

ICSID Secretariat
Discussion Paper
October 22, 2004

Contact person: Antonio R. Parra
Tel: (202) 458-1534
icsidideas@worldbank.org

POSSIBLE IMPROVEMENTS OF THE FRAMEWORK FOR ICSID ARBITRATION

Contents

		Page
I.	Introduction	323
II.	Preliminary Procedures	326
III.	Publication of Awards and Access of Third Parties	327
IV.	Disclosure Requirements for Arbitrators	330
V.	Mediation and Training	331
VI.	An ICSID Appeals Facility?	331
	Annex	
	Possible Features of an ICSID Appeals Facility	333

I. INTRODUCTION

1. The International Centre for Settlement of Investment Disputes (ICSID or the Centre) is established by the Convention on the Settlement of Investment Disputes between States and Nationals of Other States (the ICSID Convention or Convention).[1] This is a multilateral treaty that was opened for signature in 1965 and came into force the following year. To date, 140 countries have ratified the Convention to become Contracting States.[2] The Convention provides a system, administered by ICSID, for the conciliation and arbitration of investment disputes between Contracting States and nationals of other Contracting States. ICSID itself has a governing body, the Administrative Council, which is composed of one representative of each Contracting State, and a Secretariat, headed by

---

1 The ICSID Convention, ICSID Regulations and Rules and Additional Facility Rules are available in booklet form from the Centre and posted on its website, www.worldbank.org/icsid.

2 *See* List of Contracting States and Other Signatories of the Convention, www.worldbank.org/icsid.

a Secretary-General, responsible for the day-to-day activities of the Centre.

2. The provisions of the Convention are supplemented by various ICSID Regulations and Rules. These include the ICSID Arbitration Rules, which set forth procedures for the conduct of an arbitration proceeding, from the constitution of the arbitral tribunal to the preparation of its award. ICSID also has a set of Additional Facility Rules. They authorize the Secretariat of ICSID to administer, among other types of proceedings between States and foreign nationals that fall outside the scope of the ICSID Convention, arbitration proceedings for the settlement of investment disputes where either the State party to the dispute or the home State of the foreign national is not a Contracting State of the Convention. Such proceedings are conducted in accordance with the Additional Facility Arbitration Rules.

3. The ICSID Convention may be amended only if all Contracting States ratify the amendment.[3] It is thus not surprising that the Convention has never been amended. Obtaining unanimous ratification for an amendment by the 140 Contracting States would at best be a very long process. By contrast, amendment of the ICSID and Additional Facility Arbitration Rules requires only a decision of the Administrative Council of ICSID.[4] Adoption of any new ICSID rules similarly would be done by decision of the Administrative Council.

4. The Administrative Council adopted definitive texts of the ICSID Regulations and Rules in 1967; the Additional Facility Rules were adopted in 1978. Amendments adopted in 1984 updated and streamlined the ICSID Regulations and Rules. In 2002, similar amendments were made to the Additional Facility Rules and a few further changes were made to the ICSID Regulations and Rules. Up until the beginning of 2002, ICSID had registered 85 ICSID Convention cases and 10 Additional Facility cases; of these cases, three were conciliation proceedings and the rest arbitrations. Since then, the caseload of ICSID has grown dramatically, by another 73 arbitration proceedings.[5]

---

3 *See* ICSID Convention, Art. 66.

4 *See id.*, Art. 6.

5 *See* Lists of Pending and Concluded Cases, www.worldbank.org/icsid.

5. Continuing a trend that began in the late 1990s, almost all of the new cases have been initiated pursuant to the investor-to-State dispute-settlement provisions of investment treaties with consents to arbitration under the ICSID Convention or Additional Facility Rules. There are now over 1,500 bilateral investment treaties (BITs) containing such provisions as well as several multilateral treaties, which notably include the NAFTA and the Energy Charter Treaty. In many respects, parties to proceedings seem to have continued to regard the ICSID and Additional Facility Rules as adequately meeting their needs. However, in a number of areas, concerns have been raised and there have been proposals for change.

6. One area involves preliminary procedures, immediately following the registration of a request for arbitration. In an arbitration under the ICSID Convention, interim measures of protection are in principle only available from the arbitral tribunal. It has been suggested that consideration be given to addressing the situation where interim relief is urgently required at the outset of the proceeding, by introducing an expedited procedure for the preparation of submissions on the question so that they may be considered by the arbitral tribunal immediately after its constitution. As the power of ICSID to deny registration of a request for arbitration is closely circumscribed by the Convention, to cases where the request discloses a manifest lack of jurisdiction, it has also been proposed that there be a procedure for a party to seek from the tribunal, once it is constituted, the dismissal on an expedited basis of an unmeritorious claim. It has furthermore been asked whether ICSID could more rapidly publish awards issued under its auspices and whether ICSID arbitral proceedings could be made more accessible to third parties. In addition, some concern has been expressed about the adequacy of the disclosure requirements for ICSID arbitrators. Other suggestions that have been made include making mediation more readily available for investor-to-State disputes and more systematically assisting developing countries to build expertise in investor-to-State arbitration. A further, potentially most important, issue that has been raised is whether an appellate mechanism is desirable to ensure coherence and consistency in case law generated in ICSID and other investor-to-State arbitrations initiated under investment treaties.

7. Many of the above-mentioned issues can be addressed by appropriate provisions in new investment treaties, as a number of them already illustrate, and in amendments of existing investment treaties. This paper examines how such efforts might be complemented by amendments of the ICSID and Additional Facility Arbitration Rules, and by other initiatives

of the Centre. The purpose is to encourage discussion of such possible improvements and to invite any further suggestions for change.

II. PRELIMINARY PROCEDURES

8. Under the ICSID Convention, an arbitral tribunal may, if it considers that the circumstances so require, recommend any provisional measures that should be taken to preserve the respective rights of either party.[6] The ICSID Arbitration Rules make it clear that provisional measures may only be sought from national courts if this is provided for in the consent to arbitration of the parties.[7] Some investment treaties take advantage of this possibility and permit recourse to national courts for provisional measures. Such arrangements are, however, uncommon; parties seeking provisional measures must therefore normally await the constitution of the arbitral tribunal, even if the measures may be urgently required. In addition to the time needed to review and register a request for arbitration, four months or more may be required to constitute an arbitral tribunal. The tribunal, in turn, may only recommend provisional measures after each party has had the opportunity to present its observations.[8] The problem might be addressed by a procedure for the expedited filing of a request for provisional measures and all of the observations of the parties on the request while the tribunal is being constituted so that it may upon its constitution consider and decide on the request within a brief time limit.[9] Such a procedure could be introduced by amendment of ICSID Arbitration Rule 39, on provisional measures.

9. If, on the basis of the information contained in a request for arbitration under the ICSID Convention, the dispute is manifestly outside the jurisdiction of the Centre, the Secretary-General of ICSID will refuse to register the request and the case will proceed no further.[10] The Secretary-General exercises a similar screening power with respect to requests for arbitration under the Additional Facility Rules. The screening power does not extend to the merits of the dispute or to cases where jurisdiction is

---

6 *See* ICSID Convention, Art. 47.

7 *See* ICSID Arbitration Rule 39(5).

8 *See id.*, Rule 39(4).

9 An alternative might be to introduce a pre-arbitral referee procedure along the lines of that of the International Chamber of Commerce Court of Arbitration. *See* www.iccwbo.org.

10 *See* ICSID Convention, Art. 36(3).

merely doubtful but not manifestly lacking. In such cases, the request for arbitration must be registered and the parties invited to proceed to constitute the arbitral tribunal. Registration is, however, without prejudice to the powers and functions of the arbitral tribunal in regard to jurisdiction and the merits of the dispute. The parties are reminded of this in the notice of registration of the request.[11] Once constituted, the tribunal may dismiss the claim on the merits or for lack of jurisdiction. As several cases have demonstrated, if the tribunal considers the claim to have been frivolous, it may also award costs to the respondent.

10. It might in this context be useful to make clear in the ICSID and Additional Facility Arbitration Rules, by provisions establishing a special procedure for the purpose, that the tribunal may at an early stage of the case be asked on an expedited basis to dismiss all or part of the claim. Such provisions could specify that a request for such a dismissal would be without prejudice to the further objections a party might make, if the request were denied. The provisions would be helpful in reassuring parties that consider the screening power of the Secretary-General to be too limited, especially insofar as it does not extend to the merits of the dispute. The provisions could be introduced by amending ICSID Arbitration Rule 41 and Article 45 of the Additional Facility Arbitration Rules, which deal with preliminary objections to jurisdiction.

III. PUBLICATION OF AWARDS AND ACCESS OF THIRD PARTIES

11. Through its conciliation and arbitration registers, ICSID publishes information on procedural developments in all of the cases pending before the Centre.[12] Article 48(5) of the ICSID Convention provides that ICSID shall not publish an award without the consent of the parties. The Centre actively seeks, and usually obtains, the consent of the parties for such publication. It then posts the award on the website of ICSID and reprints it in the *ICSID Review—Foreign Investment Law Journal.* When both parties do not consent to the publication of the award by ICSID, one party commonly releases it for publication by such other sources as *International Legal Materials*, the *Journal du Droit International* or *ICSID Reports.* If the Centre does not have the required consent of both parties

---

11 Pursuant to ICSID Institution Rule 7(e).

12 The registers are maintained pursuant to ICSID Administrative and Financial Regulation 23.

for publication of the full text of the award, and it is not published by another source, ICSID publishes (on its website and in the *ICSID Review—Foreign Investment Law Journal*) excerpts from the legal holdings of the award, pursuant to ICSID Arbitration Rule 48(4). In short, all ICSID arbitral awards, or at least their key legal holdings, are now published.

12. There nevertheless remains the question of the timeliness of publication, an important consideration when many cases involving similar issues are pending. It occasionally is not until several months have passed that ICSID receives the consent of both parties for it to publish an award. ICSID might in such cases promptly publish excerpts of the main holdings, while it awaits the consents for publication of the full text. Arbitration Rule 48(4) authorizes, but does not require, ICSID to publish excerpts from the awards. Their prompt publication would be facilitated by amending ICSID Arbitration Rule 48(4) (and the corresponding provision of the Additional Facility Arbitration Rules, Article 53(3)) to make it mandatory for ICSID to publish the extracts.

13. In two recent investor-to-State arbitrations governed by the Arbitration Rules of the United Nations Commission on International Trade Law (UNCITRAL),[13] a form of arbitration that is also often mentioned in investment treaties, the tribunals confirmed that they had broad authority to accept and consider submissions from third parties. Arbitrations under the ICSID and Additional Facility Arbitration Rules have not yielded similar precedents. There may well be cases where the process could be strengthened by submissions of third parties, not only civil society organizations but also for instance business groups or, in investment treaty arbitrations, the other States parties to the treaties concerned. It might therefore be useful to make clear that the tribunals have the authority to accept and consider submissions from third parties. This could be done by amendments of ICSID Arbitration Rule 34 and Article 41 of the Additional Facility Arbitration Rules, regarding evidence. The amendments could set out conditions for the submissions—for example, as to financial and other disclosures by aspiring friends of the court—or more flexibly leave such conditions for determination by the tribunals in each case.

---

13 For the UNCITRAL Arbitration Rules, see www.uncitral.org.

14. The disputing parties, their counsel and other representatives, and witnesses and experts called upon to testify at hearings held by the tribunal, may attend the hearings. According to the ICSID and Additional Facility Arbitration Rules, the tribunal may allow other persons to attend the hearings only "with the consent of the parties."[14] The notes published with the first edition of the ICSID Regulations and Rules presented this provision in the ICSID Arbitration Rules as reflecting an implication in Article 48(5) of the ICSID Convention "that, as a matter of principle, arbitration proceedings should not be public."[15] However, as indicated earlier, Article 48(5) of the Convention prohibits ICSID from publishing an award without the consent of the parties. The notion that it connotes wider confidentiality or privacy obligations, beyond those of ICSID itself, is not supported by current arbitral practice.

15. Hearings open to the public have been consented to by the parties in two cases administered by ICSID. The Centre has successfully coped with the logistical challenges of hosting such hearings. Some new investment treaties provide for open hearings in all investor-to-State arbitrations under the treaties. It would seem unwise simply to substitute such a blanket provision for the existing provisions of the ICSID and Additional Facility Arbitration Rules. Not all cases under those rules are treaty arbitrations. On the other hand, the present provisions allow a party to veto any wider attendance at hearings that might be considered necessary or desirable not only by the other party but also by the tribunal. The provisions concerned, ICSID Arbitration Rule 32(2) and Article 39(2) of the Additional Facility Arbitration Rules, might be amended so that the consent of both parties would no longer be required for decisions of the tribunal to permit additional categories of persons to attend the hearings or even to open them to the public. Such amendments should require the tribunal, before making the decisions, to consider the views of the disputing parties, as well as those of the third parties concerned, and to consult with the Secretariat of ICSID on the administrative arrangements involved. The amendments should also make clear the authority of the tribunal to prescribe the conditions (for example, to protect proprietary information) of any wider attendance at the hearings.

---

14 ICSID Arbitration Rule 32(2); Additional Facility Arbitration Rules, Art. 39(2).

15 Note C to ICSID Arbitration Rule 31 (now Rule 32) in ICSID Regulations and Rules, Doc. ICSID/4/ Rev. 1(1968).

IV. DISCLOSURE REQUIREMENTS FOR ARBITRATORS

16. Almost invariably, ICSID arbitral tribunals consist of three persons, one appointed by each party and a third (presiding) arbitrator appointed by agreement of the parties or by ICSID if there is no such agreement within a certain time limit. All ICSID arbitrators must be persons of high moral character and recognized competence in the fields of law, commerce, industry or finance, who may be relied upon to exercise independent judgment.[16] The requirement of reliability for independent judgment has been interpreted as encompassing impartiality as well as independence from the parties. At the outset of the proceedings, the arbitrators must sign declarations affirming that they know of no reason why they should not serve as arbitrators in the case, that they will judge fairly between the parties according to the applicable law, and that they will accept no unauthorized instruction or compensation.[17] Arbitrators are required to append to the declarations statements of any past or present professional, business or other relationships with the parties.[18] Once signed, the declarations are transmitted by ICSID to the parties.

17. With the large number of new cases, the disclosure requirements for ICSID arbitrators might usefully be expanded. Under the UNCITRAL Arbitration Rules, an arbitrator is required to disclose to the parties any circumstances likely to give rise to justifiable doubts as to his or her impartiality or independence.[19] The relevant ICSID provisions, ICSID Arbitration Rule 6(2) and Article 13(2) of the Additional Facility Arbitration Rules, could be amended similarly to require the arbitrator to disclose, not only any past or present relationships with the parties, but more generally any circumstances likely to give rise to justifiable doubts as to the arbitrator's reliability for independent judgment. This might in particular be helpful in addressing perceptions of issue conflicts among arbitrators. The ICSID provisions could also be amended to make it clear that the expanded disclosure requirement would apply throughout the entire proceeding and not just at its commencement. Consideration might, in addition, be given to the elaboration by ICSID of a code of

---

16 *See* ICSID Convention, Arts. 14(1) and 40(2); Additional Facility Arbitration Rules, Art. 8.

17 *See* ICSID Arbitration Rule 6(2); Additional Facility Arbitration Rules, Art. 13(2).

18 See *id.*

19 *See* UNCITRAL Arbitration Rules, Art. 9.

conduct for arbitrators like codes elaborated in other intergovernmental settings.[20]

V. MEDIATION AND TRAINING

18. ICSID also provides facilities for the settlement of disputes by conciliation. The Centre now actively promotes conciliation as a relatively low-cost alternative to arbitration that may better preserve business relationships between the parties. On receipt of a request for arbitration, ICSID calls the attention of the parties to the conciliation alternative. Mediation may in some cases be a more effective means of reaching an amicable settlement than the comparatively formal conciliation procedures. In addition to promoting its conciliation facilities, ICSID has therefore begun to examine the possibility of helping to sponsor the establishment of a mediation service for investor-to-State disputes.

19. The ICSID Secretariat has over the years cooperated with such other organizations as the International Development Law Organization and the United Nations Conference on Trade and Development in training programs for officials of developing countries, on the arbitration of investment disputes. The ICSID Secretariat could consider ways of intensifying and further systematizing such training activities.

VI. AN ICSID APPEALS FACILITY?

20. As indicated in the introduction of this paper, interest has been shown in awards in investor-to-State cases under investment treaties being made subject to a mechanism for the appeal of the awards. There have already been concluded several treaties that envisage, in broad terms, the eventual creation of such a mechanism. Several more such treaties are being negotiated. By mid-2005, as many as 20 countries may have signed treaties with provisions on an appeal mechanism for awards rendered in investor-to-State arbitrations under the treaties. Most of these countries are also Contracting States of the ICSID Convention.

21. It was mentioned in the introduction of this paper that the appeal mechanism would be intended to foster coherence and consistency in the case

20 *See, e.g.*, WTO Rules of Conduct for the Dispute Settlement Understanding, www.wto.org.

law emerging under investment treaties. Significant inconsistencies have not to date been a general feature of the jurisprudence of ICSID. It might also be argued that providing an appeal mechanism could fragment the ICSID arbitral regimes: ICSID arbitrations would in some instances be subject to the mechanism and in other cases remain free of the mechanism. Subjecting ICSID arbitral awards to an appeal mechanism might also detract from the finality of the awards and open opportunities for delays in their enforcement.

22. On the other hand, there clearly is scope for inconsistencies to develop in the case law, given the increased number of cases, as well as the fact that under many investment treaties disputes may be submitted to different, ICSID and non-ICSID, forms of arbitration. As to the question of fragmentation, it may be pointed out that there already are different forms of ICSID arbitration (ICSID Convention arbitration and Additional Facility Rules arbitration). With an appeal mechanism, ICSID would be extending a further dispute-settlement option to interested parties. For the cases where there is such interest, the mechanism might enhance the acceptability of investor-to-State arbitration.

23. In any event, as indicated above, a number of countries are committing themselves to an appeal mechanism. It would in this context seem to run counter to the objectives of coherence and consistency for different appeal mechanisms to be set up under each treaty concerned. Efficiency and economy, as well as coherence and consistency, might best be served by ICSID offering a single appeal mechanism as an alternative to multiple mechanisms. It would be on this assumption that the Centre might pursue the creation of such an ICSID Appeals Facility at this stage. The possible features of an ICSID Appeals Facility are set out in the Annex of this paper. If, however, multiple appeal mechanisms are to be established, ICSID might best abstain from pursuing the creation of an Appeals Facility as it might otherwise only add to the number of appeal mechanisms

ANNEX

POSSIBLE FEATURES OF AN ICSID APPEALS FACILITY

1. If ICSID undertakes the creation of a single Appeals Facility, as an alternative to multiple mechanisms under treaties providing for the appeal of awards made in investor-to-State arbitrations, the Facility might be established and operate under a set of ICSID Appeals Facility Rules adopted by the Administrative Council of ICSID. An investment or other treaty (including a treaty amending an earlier one) could then provide that awards, made in cases covered by the treaty, would be subject to review in accordance with the ICSID Appeals Facility Rules. The Facility would best be designed for use in conjunction with both forms of ICSID arbitration, UNCITRAL Rules arbitration and any other form of arbitration provided for in the investor-to-State dispute-settlement provisions of investment treaties.

2. According to Article 53(1) of the ICSID Convention, awards rendered pursuant to the Convention "shall not be subject to any appeal or to any other remedy except those provided for in this Convention." As explained earlier, amendment of the ICSID Convention requires the unanimous ratification of the Contracting States. The assumption, however, is that the submission of an ICSID Convention award to the Appeals Facility would in each case be based on the provisions of a treaty. In accordance with the general treaty law rules reflected in Article 41 of the 1969 Vienna Convention of the Law of Treaties,[1] the treaty with the submission to the Appeals Facility might also modify the ICSID Convention to the extent required, as between the States parties to that treaty, provided that the modification was not prohibited by the ICSID Convention, did not affect the enjoyment of rights and performance of obligations of the other Contracting States under the ICSID Convention and was compatible with the overall object and purpose of the ICSID Convention.[2] The modification would have to be notified to the other Contracting States before the conclusion of the modifying treaty.[3]

3. As just explained, a treaty would appear to be required to make an arbitration under the ICSID Convention subject to the Appeals Facility.

---

1 For the Vienna Convention on the Law of Treaties, see www.un.org/law/ilc/texts/treaties.htm.

2 *See id.*, Art. 41(1)(b).

3 *See id.*, Art. 41(2).

But the Appeals Facility could be incorporated into consents to other forms of arbitration, such as arbitration under the Additional Facility or UNCITRAL Rules, in investment laws and contracts as well as treaties. In any event, availability of the Appeals Facility would in all cases depend on the consent of the parties. Parties wishing instead to provide for arbitration without recourse under the Appeals Facility Rules would simply omit them from the consents to arbitration.

4. In keeping with their consensual nature, the Appeals Facility Rules would be flexible and subject to adjustment in the underlying consent instrument. The following paragraphs describe in further detail a possible set of ICSID Appeals Facility Rules, modeled, in many respects, after provisions of the ICSID Convention, Regulations and Rules.

5. Such a set of ICSID Appeals Facility Rules could provide for the establishment of an Appeals Panel composed of 15 persons elected by the Administrative Council of ICSID on the nomination of the Secretary-General of the Centre. The terms of the Panel members would be staggered. Eight of the first 15 would serve for three years; all others would be elected for six-year terms. Each member would be from a different country. They would all have to be persons of recognized authority, with demonstrated expertise in law, international investment and investment treaties.[4]

6. Under such Appeals Facility Rules, challenges of awards could be referred to an appeal tribunal constituted for each case by appointment by the Secretary-General of ICSID. Unless the disputing parties agreed otherwise, each appeal tribunal would have three members. Appointments of appeal tribunal members would be made from the Panel after consultation with the parties as far as possible.[5]

7. An award could be challenged pursuant to the Appeals Facility Rules for a clear error of law or on any of the five grounds for annulment of an

---

[4] These suggested requirements are based on those applicable to members of the WTO Appellate Body. *See* WTO Dispute Settlement Understanding, Art. 17(3), www.wto.org.

[5] The approach, suggested in this and the preceding paragraph of the text, of appeal tribunals drawn from a limited Appeals Panel, might be compared to the system of subsidiary chambers familiar among international dispute-settlement bodies.

award set out in Article 52 of the ICSID Convention.[6] A further ground for challenging an award might consist in serious errors of fact; this ground would be narrowly defined to preserve appropriate deference to the findings of fact of the arbitral tribunal.

8. An ICSID arbitral tribunal renders just one award, the final award disposing of the case. Earlier decisions of the tribunal will be deemed part of the award and subject at that stage to annulment and other post-award remedies. In some other systems of arbitration, including arbitration under the UNCITRAL Rules, interim decisions of the tribunal may be made in the form of awards and possibly challenged immediately. To avoid discrepancies of coverage between ICSID and non-ICSID cases, the Appeals Facility Rules might either provide that challenges could in no case be made before the rendition of the final award or allow challenges in all cases in respect of interim awards and decisions. It might be best to allow such challenges subject to certain safeguards. These could include a procedure for a party to proceed with the challenge only with permission of a member of the Appeals Panel, chosen in advance by the Panel members to perform this function, and a provision making it clear that the arbitration would continue during the challenge proceeding.

9. Under the possible Appeals Facility Rules, an appeal tribunal might uphold, modify or reverse the award concerned. It could also annul it in whole or in part on any of the grounds borrowed from Article 52 of the ICSID Convention. With the exceptions mentioned in the next sentence, the award as upheld, modified or reversed by the appeal tribunal would be the final award binding on the parties. If an appeal tribunal annulled an award or decided on a modification or reversal resulting in an award that did not dispose of the dispute, either party could submit the case to a new arbitral tribunal to be constituted and operate under the same rules

---

6 These grounds are that the arbitral tribunal was not properly constituted; that it manifestly exceeded its powers; that one of its members was corrupt; that there was a serious departure from a fundamental rule of procedure; and that the award failed to state the reasons on which it was based. Under Article 52 of the ICSID Convention, either party may apply for annulment of an award on one or more of these grounds. An application to annul an award is referred to a three-member ad hoc committee appointed by ICSID from the Panel of Arbitrators of the Centre. The ad hoc committee has the authority to annul the award in whole or in part on any of the five specified grounds. Awards made pursuant to such other rules as the Additional Facility and UNCITRAL Rules are in general subject to the control of the courts at the place of arbitration. The law there may authorize the courts to set aside arbitral awards on the grounds of non-arbitrability of the dispute or conflict with public policy, as well as on grounds similar to those for annulment under Article 52 of the ICSID Convention.

as the first arbitral tribunal. The Appeals Facility Rules might, however, allow appeal tribunals in some such cases to order that the case instead be returned to the original arbitral tribunal.

10. As in the case of annulment proceedings under the ICSID Convention, the party requesting review of the award would, unless the appeal tribunal decided otherwise, be solely responsible for the advances to ICSID to meet the fees and expenses of the appeal tribunal members and other direct costs of the review proceeding, without prejudice to the power that the appeal tribunal would have to decide on the ultimate allocation of costs. The fees and expenses of the appeal tribunal members would be the same as those to which ICSID arbitrators are entitled.[7] The Appeals Facility Rules would also require the party requesting review of the award, unless the appeal tribunal decided otherwise, to provide a bank guarantee, approved by the appeal tribunal, for the amount of the award. This would be similar to the practice that has been developed of requiring applicants for annulment of an award in ICSID Convention cases to furnish such guarantees as a condition of the continued stay of enforcement of the award.

11. As in the case of the Additional Facility, access to the Appeals Facility would be subject to the approval of the Secretary-General of ICSID. Like the Additional Facility Rules, the Appeals Facility Rules would provide for the initiation of proceedings by request to the Secretary-General. The request would have to be made within a specified period after the rendition of the award.[8] After verifying that the request was timely and otherwise within the scope of the Appeals Facility Rules, the Secretary-General would register it and proceed to the constitution of the appeal tribunal.

12. The Secretariat of ICSID would provide to the subsequent proceedings all of the administrative services it gives to ICSID Convention and Additional Facility proceedings. To promote a speedy process, the Appeals Facility Rules might establish in advance time limits, from the date of

---

7 *See* ICSID Administrative and Financial Regulation 14; ICSID Schedule of Fees, para. 3.

8 As in the case of applications for annulment under the ICSID Convention, this might be 120 days after the rendition of the award except for requests based on corruption which could be made within 120 days after discovery of the corruption and in any event within three years. *See* ICSID Convention, Art. 52(2). The Appeals Facility Rules might specify a shorter period for requests for review in respect of errors of law or fact. The shorter period might be 60 days, the period specified for recourse to the WTO Appellate Body. *See* WTO Dispute Settlement Understanding, Art. 16(4).

registration of the request, for the filing of the written pleadings of the parties. The time limits would be subject to any necessary adjustment by the appeal tribunal. The Appeals Facility Rules would also establish a time limit for the appeal tribunal to render its decision. The time limit might be 120 days from the closure of the proceeding.[9] The Appeals Facility Rules could provide that in other respects the proceedings would be conducted, *mutatis mutandis*, in accordance with the ICSID Arbitration Rules.[10]

13. The Appeals Facility Rules could incorporate general undertakings by parties not to seek enforcement of an award pending its review and to comply promptly with the award to the extent it is upheld by the appeal tribunal. The Rules might also make clear that, while recourse to the Facility would supersede other rights to appeal or seek annulment of the award, such post-award remedies as rectification, supplementation and interpretation of the award would, at least in cases governed by the ICSID, Additional Facility and UNCITRAL Rules, remain to be sought from the original arbitral tribunal.[11]

14. The Additional Facility Rules of ICSID were initially adopted by the Administrative Council on a trial basis. Given the novelty of an Appeals Facility, the Administrative Council might be asked similarly to adopt a set of Appeals Facility Rules for an initial period of six years and then possibly modify them in the light of experience.

---

9 This is the basic period the ICSID Arbitration Rules allow arbitral tribunals to make their awards. *See* ICSID Arbitration Rule 46.

10 The expedited procedure for the dismissal of unmeritorious claims would thus be available for proceedings under the Appeals Facility Rules if the ICSID Arbitration Rules are amended as suggested in section II of this paper. The same point may be made with respect to the provisions regarding access of third parties suggested in section III.

11 *See* ICSID Arbitration Rules 49–51; Additional Facility Arbitration Rules, Arts. 56–58; UNCITRAL Arbitration Rules, Arts. 35–37.

APPENDIX 4

Suggested Changes to the ICSID Rules and Regulations*

Introduction:

This document is the complement to that found in the prior Appendix, as it presents ICSID's analysis of the possibility of changing ICSID's arbitral methods and procedures after hearing back from business, civil society, academics, and concerned institutions in response to the October, 2004, document. In this Appendix, Parra's team presents the key results of this public process, as well as continuing to develop some of their own ideas for reform—including the issue of an appellate review mechanism

* Article re-published with approval of the International Centre for Settlement Disputes. Document is publicly available on the website of ICSID, http://icsid.worldbank.org/ICSID/Index.jsp, its original place of publication.

Appendix 4

International Centre for Settlement of Investment Disputes

1818 H Street, N.W., Washington, D.C. 20433, U.S.A.

Telephone: (202) 458-1534 FAX: (202) 522-2615/2027

Website: www.worldbank.org/icsid

Suggested Changes
to the
ICSID Rules
and Regulations

Working Paper of the ICSID Secretariat

May 12, 2005

Contact Person:
Antonio R. Parra
Tel: (202) 458-1534
Fax: (202) 522-2615
EM: aparra@worldbank.org

Suggested Changes to the ICSID Rules and Regulations

CONTENTS

	Page
Suggested Changes to the ICSID Rules and Regulations	342
Annexes	
Preliminary Procedures	
Suggested changes to ICSID Arbitration Rule 39	344
Suggested changes to ICSID Arbitration Rule 41	345
Publication of Awards	
Suggested changes to ICSID Arbitration Rule 48	347
Access of Third Parties	
Suggested changes to ICSID Arbitration Rule 32	348
Suggested changes to ICSID Arbitration Rule 37	349
Disclosure requirements for Arbitrators	
Suggested changes to ICSID Arbitration Rule 6	350
Fees of Arbitrators	
Suggested changes to ICSID Administrative and Financial Regulation 14	351

Suggested Changes to the ICSID Rules and Regulations

1. By letter of October 22, 2004, the Secretary-General of the International Centre for Settlement of Investment Disputes (ICSID or the Centre) sent to the members of the Administrative Council of the Centre an ICSID Secretariat Discussion Paper entitled "Possible Improvements of the Framework for ICSID Arbitration."

2. The Discussion Paper, also dated October 22, 2004, suggested some changes to the ICSID Arbitration Rules and the Additional Facility Arbitration Rules. The suggested changes concerned preliminary procedures; publication of awards; access of third parties to the proceedings; and disclosure requirements of arbitrators. The Discussion Paper also suggested that ICSID might strengthen its conciliation services and expand its training activities. A further possibility considered in the Discussion Paper was the establishment by ICSID of a mechanism for the appeal of awards in investment arbitrations. The Discussion Paper explained that this was a possibility that ICSID might pursue as an alternative to the creation of individual appeal mechanisms under different investment treaties of member countries.

3. In addition to sending the Discussion Paper to members of the Administrative Council for their comments, the Secretariat of the Centre sought comments on the Paper from business and civil society groups and from arbitration experts and institutions around the world. The present Working Paper outlines the results of this extensive consultation and makes several follow up suggestions.

4. The members of the Administrative Council and others who provided comments on the Discussion Paper expressed appreciation for the initiative to review the framework for ICSID arbitration and identify possible improvements. There was general agreement that, if international appellate procedures were to be introduced for investment treaty arbitrations, then this might best be done through a single ICSID mechanism rather than by different mechanisms established under each treaty concerned. Most, however, considered that it would be premature to attempt to establish such an ICSID mechanism at this stage, particularly in view of the difficult technical and policy issues raised in the Discussion Paper. The Secretariat will continue to study such issues to assist member countries when and if it is decided to proceed towards the establishment of an ICSID appeal mechanism.

5. Uniformly positive comments were received on the strengthening of the Centre's conciliation and training activities. These are areas where ICSID might achieve most by joining forces with other organizations working in these fields. A separate paper of the Secretariat on such possible collaborative efforts will be issued in due course.

6. There were generally favorable reactions to the suggestions in the Discussion Paper for changes to the ICSID Arbitration Rules and Additional Facility Arbitration Rules. As mentioned above, these suggested changes concerned preliminary procedures; publication of awards; access of third parties to the proceedings; and disclosure requirements of arbitrators. Although the reactions were generally favorable, the suggestions regarding access of third parties in particular elicited some disagreement. Concerns were expressed that any provisions on access of third parties to proceedings should subject such access to appropriate conditions ensuring, for example, that the third parties do not by their participation unduly burden parties to the proceedings.

7. Attached are drafts of the suggested changes to the ICSID Arbitration Rules which take account of these and other comments received on the Discussion Paper. The drafts are accompanied by explanatory notes giving the background and rationale of each proposed change. Where applicable, the changes would also be incorporated into the Additional Facility Arbitration Rules. This paper also takes the opportunity to make it clear in the ICSID Administrative and Financial Regulations that increases in the applicable arbitrator fee may only be sought through the Centre.

8. Comments on the changes suggested in this Paper may be sent to the ICSID Secretariat by June 30, 2005. A revised set of proposed amendments will then be prepared for submission to the Administrative Council of the ICSID.

Preliminary Procedures – Suggested changes to ICSID Arbitration Rule 39

Rule 39
Provisional Measures

(1) At any time ~~during~~ after the institution of the proceeding a party may request that provisional measures for the preservation of its rights be recommended by the Tribunal. The request shall specify the rights to be preserved, the measures the recommendation of which is requested, and the circumstances that require such measures.

[…]

(5) If a party makes a request pursuant to paragraph (1) before the constitution of the Tribunal, the Secretary-General shall, on the application of either party, fix time limits for the parties to present observations on the request, so that the request and observations may be considered by the Tribunal upon its constitution.

(~~5~~6) Nothing in this Rule shall prevent the parties, …

Note: As noted in the Secretariat's Discussion Paper of October 22, 2004, under the ICSID Arbitration Rules, provisional measures may only be sought from national courts if provided for in the consent to arbitration of the parties. Even where such measures are urgently needed, the parties must await the review and registration of the request for arbitration, and the constitution of the arbitral tribunal, before filing a request. Thereafter, the tribunal would have to allow the parties enough time to file observations before it could recommend provisional measures.

The suggested changes introduce a procedure for the expedited filing of requests for provisional measures, and of all the observations of the parties on such a request, prior to the constitution of a tribunal. Such a procedure would reduce delay and ensure that the tribunal is able to consider the request once it is constituted, especially where the measures are urgently required.

Preliminary Procedures - Suggested changes to ICSID Arbitration Rule 41

Rule 41
Preliminary Objections ~~to Jurisdiction~~

(1) [...]

(2) [...]

(3) Upon the formal raising of an objection relating to the dispute, the Tribunal may decide to suspend the proceeding on the merits ~~shall be suspended~~. The President of the Tribunal, after consultation with its other members, shall fix a time limit within which the parties may file observations on the objection.

(4) [...]

(5) A party may, no later than 30 days after the constitution of the Tribunal, and in any event before the first session of the Tribunal, file an objection that a claim is manifestly without merit. The party shall specify as precisely as possible the basis for the objection. The Tribunal, after giving the parties an opportunity to present their observations shall, at its first session or promptly thereafter, notify the parties of its decision on the objection. The decision of the Tribunal shall be without prejudice to its authority to decide on other objections that the parties may make in the course of the proceeding.

(~~5~~6) If the Tribunal decides that the dispute is not within the jurisdiction of the Centre or not within its own competence, or that all claims are manifestly without merit, it shall render an award to that effect.

Note: The Secretariat's Discussion Paper of October 22, 2004, notes that the Secretary-General's power to screen requests for arbitration does not extend to the merits of the dispute or to cases where jurisdiction is merely doubtful but not manifestly lacking. In such cases, the request for arbitration must be registered and the parties invited to proceed to constitute the arbitral tribunal.

It is suggested to make it clear, by the introduction of a new paragraph (5), that the tribunal may at an early stage of the proceeding be asked on an expedited basis to dismiss all or part of a claim on the merits. The change would be helpful in addressing any concerns about the limited screening power of the Secretary-General.

Preliminary Procedures - Suggested changes to ICSID Arbitration Rule 41 (cont.)

At the same time, this may be an opportunity to introduce some flexibility and make the suspension of the proceeding on the merits of the case, on the raising of a preliminary objection to jurisdiction, discretionary for the tribunal.

Similar changes would be made to the corresponding provisions in the Additional Facility Arbitration Rules, Article 45.

Publication of Awards - Suggested changes to ICSID Arbitration Rule 48

Rule 48
Rendering of the Award

[…]

(4) The Centre shall not publish the award without the consent of the parties. The Centre ~~may~~ shall, however, promptly include in its publications excerpts of the legal ~~rules applied by~~ conclusions of the Tribunal.

Note: As stated in the Discussion Paper of October 22, 2004, Article 48(5) of the ICSID Convention and the first sentence of Arbitration Rule 48(4) preclude the Centre from publishing a Convention award without the consent of the parties. However, the Centre may publish excerpts from the legal holdings of the award.

The suggested changes would facilitate the prompt release of excerpts, by making their early publication mandatory, and clarify the wording of the provision. Prompt publication of the excerpts is particularly important in view of the increase in the number of pending cases at the Centre.

Similar changes would be made to the corresponding provisions in the Additional Facility Arbitration Rules, Article 53(3).

Access of Third Parties - Suggested changes to ICSID Arbitration Rule 32

Rule 32
The Oral Procedure

[…].

(2) After consultation with the Secretary-General and with the parties as far as possible, ~~The~~ the Tribunal ~~shall decide, with the consent of the parties, which~~ may allow other persons, besides the parties, their agents, counsel and advocates, witnesses and experts during their testimony, and officers of the Tribunal ~~may,~~ to attend or observe all or part of the hearings. The Tribunal shall for such cases establish procedures for the protection of proprietary information and the making of appropriate logistical arrangements.

[…]

Note: In certain cases, it could be useful to have hearings open to persons other than those directly involved in the proceeding. The suggested changes would make clear that this might be considered by a tribunal after consultation with the Secretary-General and both parties as far as possible. Such consultation with the parties would ensure that any objection or concern they may have will be taken into account by the tribunal in considering whether to allow any third parties to attend or observe the hearings. The changes would also require the tribunal for such cases to prescribe procedures to protect proprietary information and make the appropriate logistical arrangements.

Similar changes would be made to the corresponding provisions in the Additional Facility Arbitration Rules, Article 39(2).

Access of Third Parties - Suggested changes to ICSID Arbitration Rule 37

Rule 37
Visits and Inquiries; Submissions of Non-disputing Parties

(1) If the Tribunal considers it necessary to visit any place connected with the dispute or to conduct an inquiry there, it shall make an order to this effect. The order shall define the scope of the visit or the subject of the inquiry, the time limit, the procedure to be followed and other particulars. The parties may participate in any visit or inquiry.

(2) After consulting both parties as far as possible, the Tribunal may allow a person or a State that is not a party to the dispute (hereafter called the "non-disputing party") to file a written submission with the Tribunal. In determining whether to allow such a filing, the Tribunal shall consider, among others things, the extent to which:

a) the non-disputing party submission would assist the Tribunal in the determination of a factual or legal issue related to the proceeding by bringing a perspective, particular knowledge or insight that is different from that of the disputing parties;
b) the non-disputing party submission would address a matter within the scope of the dispute;
c) the non-disputing party has a significant interest in the proceeding.

The Tribunal shall ensure that the non-disputing party submission does not disrupt the proceeding, unduly burden or unfairly prejudice either party, and that both parties are given an opportunity of presenting their observations on the non-disputing party submission.

Note: The suggested changes would make clear that ICSID tribunals may accept and consider written submissions from a non-disputing person or a State, after consulting both parties as far as possible. The tribunal would have to be satisfied that any such submissions would assist the tribunal in the determination of a factual or legal issue within the scope of the dispute, that the non-disputing party has a significant interest in the dispute and that this would not disrupt the proceeding or unfairly burden either party.

Similar changes would be made to the Additional Facility Arbitration Rules, by introducing a new paragraph to Article 41.

Disclosure requirements for Arbitrators - Suggested changes to ICSID Arbitration Rule 6

Rule 6
Constitution of the Tribunal

[...]

(2) Before or at the first session of the Tribunal, each arbitrator shall sign a declaration in the following form:

"To the best of my knowledge there is no reason why I should not serve on the Arbitral Tribunal constituted by the International Centre for Settlement of Investment Disputes with respect to a dispute between ____________________ and____________________.

[....]

"<u>Attached is a</u> ~~A~~ statement of <u>(a)</u> my past and present professional, business and other relationships (if any) with the parties ~~is attached hereto~~ <u>and (b) any other circumstance that might cause my reliability for independent judgment to be questioned by a party. I acknowledge that by signing this declaration I assume a continuing obligation promptly to notify the Secretary-General of the Centre of any such relationship or circumstance that subsequently arises during this proceeding</u>."

[...]

Note: As pointed out in the Discussion Paper of October 22, 2004, the suggested changes expand the scope of disclosures of arbitrators to include any circumstances likely to give rise to justifiable doubts as to the arbitrator's reliability for independent judgment. They also extend the period of time over which disclosures are to be made, by requiring that the obligation be continuous. The Secretary-General would upon receiving the declaration transmit it to the other members of the tribunal and to both parties.

Expanding the disclosure requirements for arbitrators has become particularly important with the large number of new cases being registered by the Centre and the increased scope for possible conflicts of interest.

Similar changes would be made to the corresponding provisions in the Additional Facility Arbitration Rules, Article 13(2).

Fees of Arbitrators - Suggested changes to ICSID Administrative and Financial Regulation 14

Regulation 14
Direct Costs of Individual Proceedings

(1) Unless otherwise agreed pursuant to Article 60(2) of the Convention, and in addition to receiving reimbursement for any direct expenses reasonably incurred, each member of a Commission, a Tribunal or an *ad hoc* Committee appointed from the Panel of Arbitrators pursuant to Article 52(3) of the Convention (hereinafter referred to as "Committee") shall receive:

(a) a fee for each day on which he participates in meetings of the body of which he is a member;

(b) a fee for the equivalent of each eight-hour day of other work performed in connection with the proceedings;

[...]

The amounts of the fees referred to in paragraphs (a) and (b) above shall be determined from time to time by the Secretary-General, with the approval of the Chairman, in the expectation that a member of a Commission, a Tribunal or an *ad hoc* Committee will only in exceptional circumstances request higher amounts.~~, and may be changed, not more than once a year, in order to take account of monetary changes in the cost of living~~ Any such request for a higher amount must be made through the Secretary-General and not directly to the parties to the proceeding.

Note: The Secretary-General, under ICSID Administrative and Financial Regulation 14, sets standard daily fees for members of conciliation commissions, arbitral tribunals and annulment committees. In accordance with Article 60(2) of the Convention, however, the parties and the commission, tribunal or committee may agree on a different rate of remuneration than the standard fee. The suggested changes would make it clear that requests for increases in the applicable rate will only be made in exceptional circumstances and must be made through the Centre. At the same time, drafting improvements are suggested to avoid repetition in stating the Secretary-General's power to set the fees.

APPENDIX 5

Comments on ICSID Discussion Paper, "Possible Improvements of the Framework for ICSID Arbitration"*

Introduction:

This commentary, prepared by the International Institute for Sustainable Development (IISD), an NGO based in Winnipeg, Manitoba, is a leading example of the public comment solicited in response to the ICSID reform proposal reproduced in Appendix 3. Howard Mann, one of the contributors to this volume, was a lead author of this IISD commentary.

---

* Reprinted with the permission of the International Institute for Sustainable Development (IISD). IISD is a Canadian-based institute that champions sustainable development around the world through innovation, partnerships, research and communications. Its homepage is http://www.iisd.org.

http://www.iisd.org

Comments on ICSID Discussion Paper, "Possible Improvements of the Framework for ICSID Arbitration"

Howard Mann, Aaron Cosbey, Luke Peterson, Konrad von Moltke

IISD's International Investment and Sustainable Development Team

Mark Halle, Director

December 2004

Published by the International Institute for Sustainable Development

The International Institute for Sustainable Development contributes to sustainable development by advancing policy recommendations on international trade and investment, economic policy, climate change, measurement and assessment, and natural resources management. Through the Internet, we report on international negotiations and share knowledge gained through collaborative projects with global partners, resulting in more rigorous research, capacity building in developing countries and better dialogue between North and South.

IISD's vision is better living for all—sustainably; its mission is to champion innovation, enabling societies to live sustainably. IISD receives core operating support from the Government of Canada, provided through the Canadian International Development Agency (CIDA) and Environment Canada; and from the Province of Manitoba. The institute receives project funding from numerous governments inside and outside Canada, United Nations agencies, foundations and the private sector. IISD is registered as a charitable organization in Canada and has 501(c)(3) status in the United States.

International Institute for Sustainable Development
161 Portage Avenue East, 6th Floor
Winnipeg, Manitoba Canada R3B 0Y4
Tel: +1 (204) 958-7700
Fax: +1 (204) 958-7710
E-mail: info@iisd.ca
Web site: http://www.iisd.org/

International Institute for Sustainable Development
Institut international du développement durable

December 15, 2004

Mr. Antonio Parra
Deputy Secretary General
International Centre for Settlement of Investment Disputes
World Bank
1818 H St NW
Washington, DC 20433
U.S.A.

Dear Antonio,

Attached please find the comments from the International Institute for Sustainable Development, Investment and Sustainable Development Team, on the discussion paper entitled "Possible Improvements of the Framework for ICSID Arbitration."

These comments reflect the collected input from Aaron Cosbey, Luke Peterson, Konrad von Moltke and myself. If you have any questions, please do not hesitate to contact me at your convenience.

Please note that IISD will make these comments available to the public at the same time they are transmitted to you. We believe this is in keeping with the important public process you have initiated.

Warmest regards,

Howard Mann

Howard Mann
Senior International Law Advisor
International Institute for Sustainable Development
424 Hamilton Ave. S. Ottawa,
Ontario Canada K1Y 1E3
tel: (613) 729-0621
e-mail: h.mann@sympatico.ca

WEBSITE: www.iisd.org **E-MAIL: info@iisd.ca**

161 Portage Avenue East, 6th Floor
Winnipeg, Manitoba
Canada R3B 0Y4
TEL: (204) 958-7700
FAX: (204) 958-7710

MIE 2
9, chemin de Balexert
1219 Châtelaine, Geneva, Switzerland
TEL: (41-22) 917-8373
FAX: (41-22) 917-8054

212 East 47th Street, #21F
New York, NY
10017 USA
TEL: (212) 644-0204
FAX: (212) 644-0206

250 Albert St., Suite 1360
Ottawa, Ontario
Canada K1P 6M1
TEL: (613) 238-2296
FAX: (613) 238-8515

Contents

1.	Introduction	358
2.	Limitations on the Issues and Comments	358
3.	The Broader Underpinnings for IISD's Comments	360
	3.1 Principles	360
	3.2 Goals	362
4.	The Issues	364
	4.1 Provisional measures	364
	4.2 Expedited dismissal	364
	4.3 Publication of awards	364
	4.4 Participation of third parties, *amicus curiae*	365
	4.5 Open hearings	366
	4.6 Conflict of interest/disclosure requirements	368
	4.7 Mediation	369
	4.8 Training	369
	4.9 Appellate mechanism	370
	4.9.1 The approach of Administrative Council Rules	371
	4.9.2 Appointment of Appellate Body	372
	4.9.3 Standard and scope of review	373
	4.9.4 Appeal of interim awards	373
	4.9.5 Results of appeal process	374
	4.9.6 Costs and funding	374
	4.9.7 Additional powers of Secretary General	374
	4.9.8 Time period for appeals	375
	4.9.9 Conduct of process	375
	4.9.10 Role of Secretariat	375
	4.9.11 Review of appeals process	375
5.	A Final Note	375

1. Introduction

These comments respond to the International Centre for Settlement of Investment Disputes (ICSID) discussion paper, "Possible Improvements of the Framework for ICSID Arbitration," released for public comment on October 22, 2004.

The International Institute for Sustainable Development (IISD) believes it is important to acknowledge the precedent-setting nature of the process upon which ICSID has embarked. Irrespective of the positions taken by us or by others on the proposals found in the paper, we strongly believe that the simple act of seeking public input into the international investor-state arbitration process marks an important and welcome shift in policy-making in this area.

The application of the principles of public access, stakeholder dialogue and transparency by ICSID is a welcome departure from the historic secrecy surrounding the development of all aspects of the international investment law regime. ICSID and its officials are to be congratulated, without reservation, for taking this step. We look forward to the Centre following this process into the next stage of detailed proposals.

IISD expects there will be a wide variety of views submitted in response to the discussion paper. In keeping with the spirit demonstrated by ICSID, we have made our comments public at the same time they have been submitted to ICSID. We hope others will make their comments public as well.

This response begins with a short note on the limits of the ICSID paper and of these comments. This is followed by a context-setting section where we note the key principles and objectives IISD believes are at stake, and hence should be reflected in the resolution of the issues raised. Subsequently, we turn to each of the issues raised in the discussion paper.

2. Limitations on the Issues and Comments

The issues raised by ICSID are procedural or institutional in nature, as opposed to substantive. This is, of course, consistent with ICSID's mandate; it does not design the substantive obligations, nor does it have a direct say in their interpretation. (We say "direct" here because some of ICSID's procedural roles can have an impact on the interpretations.)

The comments below are thus made with the awareness that, while the dispute settlement process is playing an increasingly important role in setting out the scope of the obligations included in international investment agreements, the latter are not the direct subject of review for this paper. That said, we wish to make it clear that the participation in a discussion on the procedural and institutional elements of dispute settlement do not constitute approval of or support for the current evolution (or *revolution* in some respects) in the interpretation and application of these obligations. Our broader concerns are set out elsewhere, and need not be repeated here.[1] It suffices to say here that improving the defects in the current investor-state process will help address some concerns, but such improvements cannot in themselves fix the wide range of problems arising from the substantive obligations and from the structure of the treaties that create them.

The ICSID paper also seeks to distinguish between the types of rules or issues addressable by changes in the Arbitration Rules and those that require amendment of the ICSID Convention. While we understand the pragmatic reasons behind this, and fully accept the good faith behind this entire project, we reject the limitations this generates on the proposals, which relate only to what can be done in the Rules. Doing what is right for the future should not be constrained by the limitations contained in past agreements. If a change is principled and appropriate, it should be sought regardless of the difficulties.

One reason IISD rejects an approach based on such initial compromises is that we believe it is time for the investor-state process to mature and be based on democratic principles that must be reflected in the emerging role of international law in this area. The observation that "(i)nvestment has overtaken trade in global economic importance, but so far investment has failed to inspire the creation of mature legal institutions"[2] is fundamentally correct. Changes to the dispute settlement process must, we believe, be seen in the context of a developing international law regime rather than simply as a tinkering with the arbitration procedures. Simply put, this cannot be achieved by giving the limitations of yesteryear primacy over the needs of tomorrow.

The ICSID paper raises a number of issues that might, if changes are made, motivate investors to choose fora that are less transparent or less responsive to

---

1 See Aaron Cosbey, Howard Mann, Luke Peterson, Konrad von Moltke, *Investment and Sustainable Development: A Guide to the Use and Potential of International Investment Agreements*, IISD, 2004, available at http://www.iisd.org/publications/publication.asp?pno=627

2 Michael Goldhaber, "Wanted, A World Investment Court," *American Lawyer—Focus Europe—Summer*, 2004. Also at http://www.transnational-dispute-management.com/members/search/welcome.html?search archive=0

basic democratic principles. This is the risk of being a front-runner in this field. At the same time, it is governments alone that sign the international investment agreements. They have the power to amend them and either exclude systems that are not as responsive as ICSID should be to these basic principles, or ensure that they are reformed in an equivalent manner. In short, this is not just an ICSID issue, but one of critical relevance to all governments involved in this area. It is up to them to ensure that positive changes under the ICSID Rules do not lead to the increased use of other systems to avoid these changes. Consistent and complementary changes should be considered for all arbitral rules used for investor-state arbitrations in order to ensure this does not happen.

3. The Broader Underpinnings for IISD's Comments

The views on the specific issues expressed in Section 4 below are guided by certain overriding principles and goals. IISD believes that it is important in the context of redesigning key elements of the dispute settlement system to express those principles that should underlie the system as a whole, and the goals it is meant to achieve. It is not, in our view, sufficient to say one has quietly analyzed and considered such higher level issues; they should be made clear so that others can fully understand where the proposals, and comments on proposals, are rooted.

3.1 Principles

IISD proposes the following critical principles for any sound dispute settlement system in this field. In doing so, we are fully aware that they will tend to diminish the differences between arbitration and judicial proceedings. This is deliberate. The arbitration system in the investor-state context has, quite simply, outlived its original rationale. The primary reason for this is clear: the cases coming before it too often bear no resemblance to traditional commercial or private disputes that arbitration systems are essentially designed to address. Rather, more often than not, they engage key issues of public policy and the balancing of private and public welfare issues.[3] As a result, it is time to reconsider the basic appropriateness of arbitration models. IISD's suggested principles point strongly to a more judicial approach to dispute settlement.

---

3 This public welfare dimension is clearly noted, for example, in the decision of the Methanex tribunal on their jurisdiction to receive *amicus* submissions. Para. 49 of *Methanex Corp. v. United States of America, Decision of the Tribunal on Petitions of Third Persons to Intervene as Amicus Curiae*, January 15, 2001.

IISD proposes five basic principles:

▸ *Legitimacy*

The mere fact that a process is legally constituted or based on the practices of previous decades does not make it legitimate. Legitimacy is, rather, a standard based on good governance and the best practices of democratic institutions of today, not the practices of prior decades. We believe that the legitimate demands of improved democratic institutions and good governance at the international level must be met in the dispute settlement system of international investment law. Its relevance to development, and to sustainable development, demand no less.

▸ *Independence*

A key requirement of a legitimate dispute settlement system in any democratic context is that it must be fully and functionally independent of external pressures and relationships. Conflict of interest is not simply a matter of declarations by arbitrators, but of ensuring that independence is met and appears to be met at every operating level of the system.

▸ *Impartiality*

The impartiality of the process is closely related to its independence. Independence is both a principle in itself and a means to an end here: that end is the most impartial view of the law that can be achieved.

▸ *Accountability*

Accountability requires the institutional capacity to review and respond to the evolution of the law that dispute settlement processes inevitably produce. This is not a process of micromanaging disputes, but of ensuring appropriate responsiveness to the intentions of the parties. The interpretive statement option available to the North American Free Trade Agreement (NAFTA) and other Free Trade Commissions is one example of accountability mechanisms at play. The use of meetings or conferences of the parties to review the evolution of a regime is another. In addition, the proposals must not insulate ICSID from public or governmental scrutiny and accountability, or insulate the investment law regime itself.

▸ *Transparency*

Transparency in any legal regime, including its dispute settlement system, is fundamental to democratic governance today. As a bottom-line principle, this is beyond dispute. As but one example of the need for transparency, we note that the discussion paper states at paragraph 5 that almost all of the new treaty-based investor-state cases in recent years have been initiated under the ICSID Convention or ICSID Additional Facility processes. A recent report by the United Nations Conference on Trade and Development (UNCTAD), however, suggests that as many as one third of the known arbitrations have been outside this system, or over 50 of 160 known cases.[4] What remains unknown is the full number of cases actually initiated to date, as many remain shrouded in secrecy even after decisions are reached. This fact alone makes the ICSID claim in paragraph 5 unsupportable. That one cannot say for sure how many cases have been initiated to date should be understood as a stinging indictment of the failure of the broader investor-state arbitration system (encompassing various non-ICSID rules of arbitration) to meet even the most basic of good governance principles: transparency.

The ICSID discussion paper raises a number of issues from a technical, or operational, perspective. However, it grounds none of the suggested responses in any declared set of principles. IISD believes this is a serious flaw in the paper. The underlying principles, if there are any, should be expressly stated.

3.2 Goals

The goals of a dispute settlement system may vary, depending on the nature of the disputes, the nature of the parties, and the political and economic context of the legal regime being applied. Private contract dispute settlement may have a number of goals that are quite different, therefore, than the settlement of disputes arising from the policy and legal activities of governments.

IISD proposes the following key goals for the investor-state system:

▸ *Consistency*

The ICSID paper refers several times to the goal of consistency between decisions. We agree this is a critical goal. Whatever position one takes on the consistency of today's judgments, consistency in the applicable rules and

---

4 UNCTAD, *International Investment Disputes on the Rise*, Occasional Note, Nov.29, 2004, available online at: http://www.unctad.org/sections/dite/iia/docs/webiteiit20042_en.pdf

obligations is a necessary goal. Of course, every case will call for a specific application of the law to its particular facts, but that does not reduce the need for consistency in the rules and principles being applied.

▸ ***Predictability***

Consistency breeds predictability, itself an important goal for investors, governments and other stakeholders. This goal in itself requires the recognition that decisions in one case should be relevant to decisions in other cases. The mantra of one case not being binding on any other, each one being an individual, one-off, ad-hoc process, has no place in a legal system that passes judgment on a vast range of government measures affecting international investments. It is the antithesis of predictability and consistency. An appeal process, in particular, must play a key part in supporting predictable decisions. This has now taken root in the World Trade Organization (WTO) Appellate process, and should be seen as necessary in the present context as well.

▸ ***Sensitivity to legitimate government interests, balance of interests***

While the cases to date do not deny that governments have legitimate interests, these are often placed, indeed expressly placed in some cases, at a lower level than the legitimate interests of foreign investors. IISD does not argue with the proposition that investors have legitimate interests or expectations. It does have grave concerns as to how well these are balanced with the interests and expectations of governments and other stakeholders in relation to an investment. A reformed dispute settlement system can enhance how this balance is achieved today, though it cannot alter the substantive obligations that are the basis of the disputes, and the one-dimensional focus of these obligations on investor rights. As already noted, changes to the arbitration process will not be a cure-all for what ails the international investment law regime.

▸ ***Expeditious decision-making***

All disputes should be settled as quickly and economically as possible. At the same time, speed should not prevail over all other aspects of the system. It is a legitimate goal, and one that argues against frivolous procedures being developed.

▸ ***Finality***

Finality is a proper goal of any dispute settlement system. Host states, for example, should not be subject to multiple proceedings on the same set of facts from investors, minority investors, investments, under different arbitration agreements, or under domestic and international law. Finality is required to overcome the growing procedural anarchy that a number of recent decisions on jurisdiction and process have induced.

4. The Issues

4.1 Provisional measures

This is not an issue on which IISD has a major concern. Should new provisions be adopted, we would hope they would be equally available to both sides, and would include a provision to factor in the public interest in circumstances where this is warranted. For example, an investor's case based on an air pollution measure could lead to significant public health interests that militate against an application for provisional measures by an investor seeking to prevent its enforcement. This type of public interest should be expressly recognized as a legitimate issue for consideration.

4.2 Expedited dismissal

IISD has no specific comments on this issue.

4.3 Publication of awards

This issue bears an obvious relationship to the principles enunciated above. Indeed it is fundamental to them.

The discussion paper actually raises three related issues: timeliness, accessibility and completeness. This is one example of an area where the proposals are defined by the current limits of the Convention as opposed to the Rules, and inappropriately so in our view. The deficiencies of the current system are highlighted by the reality that there is some informal exchange of arbitral decisions among the practicing international arbitration bar, while others are often deprived of access to the decisions.

IISD believes that only the prompt, complete and accessible publication of all awards, interim and final, meets the basic principles of transparency. Indeed, this is now enshrined in several new U.S. free trade agreements including those with Central America and the Dominican Republic, Chile and Singapore.[5]

---

5 See for example the U.S., Central America and Dominican Republic Free Trade Agreement, Article 10.21; U.S.-Chile FTA, Article 10.20; and U.S.-Singapore FTA, Article 15.20

No other legal dispute settlement system under public international law besides the investor-state process either prevents the publication of its determinations or relies in whole or in part on the publication of selected portions of a decision. Looking forward, it is not acceptable for ICSID (or any other system it may be added) to continue to rely upon anything less than full, prompt and accessible publication of all decisions.

The full publication in Web-accessible versions of all key litigation documents should also be required. Several new agreements have moved in this direction, and NAFTA has evolved to promote such practice, with all three NAFTA parties now maintaining extensive Chapter 11 Web sites. While not all new agreements have adopted this principle, it should be evident by now that applying basic rules of transparency to international arbitrations will be the predominant direction. ICSID, as a leading arbitration body, should be at the front end of meeting this call. Falling back on the distinction between the Rules and the Convention is not a valid reason for not doing so.

4.4 Participation of third parties, amicus curiae

To establish the technical parameters of this issue, we understand it to mean a reference not to third parties to the arbitration *per se*, but the participation of third persons–"parties"–as *amicus curiae.*

IISD in fact initiated the precedent-setting "petition" process for *amicus* standing in the *Methanex v. United States* case under NAFTA's Chapter 11 in August 2000, and was subsequently one of two submitters of an *amicus* brief in the hearing on the merits in that case. We agree with the ICSID paper that the decision in that case and in others now make it clear that such *amicus* briefs are fully consistent with extant rules of procedure under United Nations Commission on International Trade Law (UNCITRAL) or ICSID. Still, making this clear in a specific rule would be of value.

As to conditions for such participation, IISD suggests these should be tests that inform a tribunal as to the reasons why a submission is being offered, and what it seeks to accomplish. *The NAFTA Statement on Amicus Briefs* is a useful starting point in this regard,[6] and is replicated in its essence in the subsequent U.S. Free Trade Agreements with Singapore, Chile, Morocco and now Central America and the Dominican Republic.

---

6 Statement of the Free Trade Commission on non-disputing party participation, October 7, 2003, at http://www.dfait-maeci.gc.ca/nafta-alena/Nondisputing-en.pdf

Beyond this, it is important for Tribunals and parties to understand that *amicus* participation is not in opposition to good practice or to the arbitration process. Rather, it can be a productive and useful part of promoting the transparency and legitimacy of any international process today. Transparency is also, of course, a prerequisite for the *amicus* process: one has to know of an arbitration to be able to consider seeking *amicus* status.

Some fear that allowing *amicus* participation may overwhelm the role or resources of the litigating parties, or distort the process due to overwhelming (but one-sided) third party submissions. In practice, IISD knows this concern to be unfounded. In both the WTO, where *amicus* submissions are now permitted, and in the investor-state process, no instance of an overwhelming number of submissions is known. In fact, potential *amici* will always tend to act responsibly in the face of a responsible and responsive process, and will seek among themselves to avoid undue duplication. In addition, the suggestion that the Tribunal ultimately controls its procedure is apt, and acts as a block against potential distortions to which the process may theoretically lead.

4.5 Open hearings

Like access to documents, decisions and third party submissions, the opening of investor-state arbitrations to the public is another area where the call of democratic process has taken root in the investor-state process today. The trend is as undeniable as it is unstoppable. Open proceedings are now an expectation under the NAFTA, at least for cases involving Canada and the United States.[7] They are similarly included as part of the process under other new U.S. investment and FTA agreements.

Representatives of IISD attended the public hearings on the merits of the *Methanex v. United States* case. The efforts of the Secretariat and litigating parties in that case, the first to be open at a hearing on the merits, should be acknowledged.

The experience in that arbitration, which is highly controversial and one of the best known of all ongoing international arbitrations, is instructive. On the first day, about 30 people were in attendance for half a day. These were predominantly university students on a summer semester. The use of this opportunity to expose students to international proceedings is, in itself, a reason to hold

---

7 http://www.dfait-maeci.gc.ca/nafta-alena/open-hearing-en.asp

open proceedings. After day one, the attendance decreased to three–five observers. Security staff effectively disappeared by the end of the first day. Neither ICSID nor the parties knew precisely what to anticipate for this occasion, which led to an overabundance of caution and high levels of reliance on remote broadcast technologies.

That experience, and a related opening of a hearing on jurisdiction, show that there is no need to fear an open hearing. Observers will generally act with proper decorum, and in the rare instances where problems arise, the panel has resources to deal with them, with the exclusion of observers being the ultimate sanction. There is no need, in reality, for remote sites and broadcasting equipment. Observers can be asked to leave a room for any discussion of confidential business information. And, where specific legal issues the Tribunal decides are appropriately kept *in camera* arise, code words to describe them can be developed just as they were to allow the lawyers in the Methanex hearing to make reference to an issue without disclosing its content or having to start and stop the broadcast.

Some might suggest that small numbers obviate the need for open hearings. IISD believes the numbers are not the key point: the opportunity to be present and witness the hearings, and to hold parties to account for their positions, is what counts. Citizens, media or interested groups may lack the time or resources to attend all hearings—just as they do in many domestic court contexts—but the availability of this option is crucial. Indeed, in the case of the Methanex arbitration, the submission of an (unaccepted) post-hearing brief by all the *amici* acting together following the hearings is one example where attendance at open hearings was indispensable.[8] The U.S. position on a specific issue was revealed in a way that would have been impossible without the open hearings.

The discussion paper suggests there may not be a basis for a blanket approach to all ICSID cases, as some may be contract- rather than treaty-based. To the extent that an investor-state hearing may involve public policy or welfare issues, IISD rejects such a distinction. Challenging contract issues in investor-sate arbitrations as breaches of a state's international obligations inherently raises such public welfare issues, as all cases of the application of these agreements inherently do. The issue should be guided by the principle of transparency and not allow public access to be avoided by an investor basing its claim on a contract as opposed to a treaty. Governments may need to review other

---

8 The post hearing submission is available at http://www.iisd.org/publications/publication.asp?pno=641

treaty provisions, as well as work to ensure contract provisions, do not lead to an evasion of good governance principles for all investor-state cases.

Finally, we see little merit in the idea of allowing "additional categories" of persons to attend as opposed to opening a hearing, as suggested in paragraph 15. There is no need for half measures here, and no principled justification for them in our view. Nor is there a need to "consult" with ICSID Secretariat officials on logistic arrangements prior to taking a decision. ICSID officials carry out the requirements of the procedures and the Tribunals, but should not insert themselves as arbiters of what can or should be done. Certainly, how access is made effective will require Secretariat support, but this should not be a barrier to participation as a matter of principle or practice.

IISD does not dispute the desirability of having a residual capacity of a Tribunal to hold part of a hearing in camera if necessary. But this should be by way of limited exception to be justified against the presumption of an open hearing.

4.6 Conflict of interest/disclosure requirements

Section IV of the discussion paper is entitled "Disclosure Requirements for Arbitrators." IISD submits that this is the wrong issue statement, and in fact confuses means and ends. The end goal is avoiding conflicts of interest. The means used for this purpose today is through disclosure requirements for arbitrators. IISD believes that this means is no longer sufficient to achieve the appropriate ends, and that both the ends and means need to be more thoroughly considered.

The ICSID paper suggests disclosure by any arbitrator be expanded from any relationship to the parties to "any circumstances likely to give rise to justifiable doubts as to the arbitrator's reliability for independent judgment." This would be an improvement, but it is not sufficient.

Arbitrations today raise a wide range of issues of public versus private welfare. To ensure this type of situation does not create a conflict of interest for judges in all democratic countries, no practicing lawyer is permitted to be a member of the judiciary as well. It is one or the other only. The reason is very simple: conflict of interest includes both actual bias and the avoidance of any appearance of bias. Lawyers or their partners cannot sit as a judge one day and as an advocate on a similar issue another day. Judges cannot create decisions that might in some way aid their partners in another case or a firm client in a future potential situation. Yet, this is precisely what happens today in the international arbitration bar. This is not, and can never be, the hallmark of a mature legal system. Indeed, it is the antithesis of one. It must be ended.

The appointment of arbitrators must therefore be revisited *ab initio*. IISD believes that practicing lawyers who either themselves act as counsel in cases or have partners who do by definition have a conflict of interest (actual or perceived) that is inimical to their participation as arbitrators. Nor is the selection process of continued appropriateness: it is well understood today that parties to arbitrations choose arbitrators because of their understood leanings. This is not a circumstance of justice being blind.

Thus, IISD believes that the appropriate route forward is to have rosters of arbitrators who do not have either an actual or perceived conflict of interest, as described above. The legitimacy of the process today depends not just on disclosure documents, but an actual separation between the advocacy and judicial functions, especially when the balance between public and private interests is in dispute. We can no longer apply a lesser standard to international dispute settlement in this regard than we do to domestic dispute settlement. Indeed, the very fact that arbitrators can rule on domestic legal issues, and often do, shows the need to move to a system that reflects the same judicial distance from the practice of law required of domestic judges making rulings on these matters.

IISD recognizes that this would be a very significant departure from current practice. It may be disruptive to some practices. We believe the demands of independence of the judicial function require it take place. The revision of disclosure requirements alone will not accomplish this goal. A clear statement of the scope of possible conflict circumstances requiring disclosure is also needed. A code of conduct that is appropriately expansive may also assist in this regard.

4.7 Mediation

IISD agrees that more mediation would be a good thing. We have no further comments on this, except to note that equality in a mediation processes requires equally well informed parties.

4.8 Training

Training can play an important role in assisting states in the negotiation of agreements as well as in the defense of claims and in responding to potential claims.

However, for training programs to accomplish these ends they must be sufficiently extensive and balanced, and the content must be objective and neutral. Public scrutiny of training material can help ensure this is accomplished.

4.9 Appellate mechanism

The ICSID discussion paper notes that one of the motivating factors for the discussion of an appeal procedure is that several recent international investment agreements have proposed such a mechanism. This raises the risk that ICSID or any other body might proceed quickly in order to be the first to do so, rather than to be principled in doing so. We urge all parties to all agreements to ensure this risk does not materialize.

The ICSID paper also raises the possibility of multiple appeal procedures. ICSID states that it would not allow itself to participate in such a multiplication of processes. IISD believes this is wise. The value of an appeals process would be almost entirely destroyed if it was not designed to meet the principles outlined above, and achieve the goals similarly set out above. IISD hopes that states will work in a cooperative manner rather than a first-past-the post-race in this area.

Whether ICSID should be the forum to house an appellate process depends, in our view, on its willingness to change its institutional structure. This is a difficult subject to address, yet, one cannot avoid the discussion. One can say, however, that the discussion should not reflect negatively on the performance of Secretariat officials, but simply speaks to a need to consider a broader systemic issue.

ICSID is not, today, an independent organization. It is a part of the World Bank Group. It is financially and structurally dependant upon the Bank. The President of the World Bank chairs its Administrative Council. The Legal Vice President of the Bank is also Secretary General of ICSID. At the same time, the Bank routinely expresses specific positions regarding the values of investment agreements, and the interpretation of specific provisions and obligations and goals, and the role of the investor-state process. All of this means that the independence of ICSID as currently constituted is, from a conflict of interest perspective, undeniably compromised.

In addition, it is entirely possible that other parts of the World Bank Group may have a financial stake in a project brought to arbitration or in another project in similar circumstances facing related challenges as the circumstances generating a dispute. Again, this presents the potential for an actual or reasonably apprehended conflict of interest.

Thus, a prerequisite for ICSID operating an appellate facility is its divestiture by the World Bank and re-establishment as a single, independent body with individualized governmental control entirely outside the existing World Bank voting system. While the linkage to the Bank may have been necessary at the beginning of the process, it is not demonstrably necessary now. The linkage to the Vice Presidency of the World Bank is particularly unnecessary.

Of course, the above is equally true for the current role of ICSID in terms of arbitration panels, and most pronouncedly in relation to the annulment panels. An independent organization could house both the leading arbitration panel process and the single appellate process. This would create some additional governance and financing needs, beyond those that could be recovered by arbitration and appeal fees. However, given the vital role of foreign investment in the global economy today, and its critical role in the pursuit of development and sustainable development, this cost is one worth bearing.

A further preliminary note: developing an appellate process must lead to demonstrable improvements in the current situation of unequal review processes, unrealistic review standards, non-transparent appointments to annulment tribunals, and the checkerboard of transparent and non-transparent proceedings and documents. Simply having an appeal process is not a valid objective; the end goal must be a better process than what we have now.

Annex 1 to the ICSID discussion paper raises several specific issues. These are addressed in turn below.

4.9.1 The approach of Administrative Council Rules

Paragraphs 1 to 4 of Annex 1 describe an essentially optional process under a new set of Appeal Facility Rules that would be adopted by the Administrative Council. IISD understands the expediency of this approach, but rejects its efficacy. Indeed, it seems to belie the very goal of consistency and a single appeal process. In addition, it essentially shirks the responsibility of ICSID Convention Parties to address this issue by referring it back to bilateral or regional treaty negotiations and private parties who can potentially accept or reject the appellate process on a treaty-by-treaty or even case-by-case basis. Again, this reflects a situation of the existing decision-making rules acting as a significant constraint of the potential scope of amendments for the future of this vital area of international law. It is no longer an appropriate approach.

The issue of exclusions from the appeals process raised in paragraph 4 requires an additional comment: IISD fails to see how the goals of consistent and predictable results can be achieved without consistent and predictable processes. It appears that the suggestions remain underpinned by the conception of arbitration as a flexible process in the hands of the parties that reflects its commercial origins. As already explained, IISD does not believe this is the appropriate approach to dispute settlement in this area as the regime builds for a mature future.

4.9.2 Appointment of Appellate Body

The number of 15 appointees may be appropriate, though it does seem to be high for a starting position. One immediate reason for this difference in view is the nature of the body: IISD believes that the model used in the WTO Appellate Body, of appointments being essentially full time positions, is the correct model. As already explained, we believe it would be completely inappropriate for members of the body to hold practicing legal positions[9] while participating as members of this body.

The idea of staggered terms is appropriate. The qualifications should, in our view establish that a recognized competence in international law is an appropriate prerequisite, not just in international investment law. One critical attribute of the WTO Appellate Body was that it reached out beyond the closed community of international trade lawyers and practitioners to others with a broader base of expertise. IISD believes this has been critical to much of the WTO success in this area, and that this approach should also be applied in the investment field.

For reasons already explained, IISD does not believe it is appropriate for the Secretary General of ICSID, as currently constituted, to have anything to do with the appointment of the appellate judges. We understand this would essentially replicate its role now on the annulment panels. We reject this role also as

[9] There may be limited exceptions to this, for example academics might continue to teach (subject to other rules on conflict generally applicable in that context already) or members might, time permitting, also have other neutral arbitrator positions. The primary point here is to recognize the very limited additional work an appeals body member might be able to engage in based on our previous submissions of an appropriate view of conflict of interest in this field.

being in clear conflict of interest as well as lacking the required independence for such a process. The appointment process should be managed by all participating states in an independent dispute settlement centre to ensure an appropriate balance geographically, legally and in experience. The prerequisites for ICSID to fulfill this role have already been discussed.

The same holds in relation to paragraph 6, and the appointment of appellate judges for each case. This must be managed in a clearly independent manner. A rotation system, lots or some similar process should be used, subject to the possible exclusion of nationals of the litigating parties and any conflict of interest on the part of a selected judge. The combination of paragraphs 5 and 6 in this proposal reflect, in our view, an inordinate concentration of power in the hands of the Secretary General in any circumstance.

4.9.3 Standard and scope of review

The standard and scope of review is a critical issue for any appeals process. The ICSID proposal appears fairly well developed. Only a few brief comments are made here.

First, IISD believes that the standard for error of law should be just that, no qualifier, such as "clear" or "serious" is needed. An alleged error should be reviewable.

Second, for the review of facts, a higher standard may be warranted. If an error can be shown that might lead to a reversal of the decision, in other words a material or significant error of fact, this should be reviewable.

Third, in the text of footnote 6, the issue of a corrupt arbitrator is raised. IISD believes that this standard is too high. A decision taken by a panel where an arbitrator is in conflict of interest, as defined previously in this comment, should be reviewable as well.

These standards should be understood to broaden the current basis for an annulment panel or a judicial review process. That is the intention of IISD in making these suggestions.

4.9.4 Appeal of interim awards

IISD takes no position on this issue.

4.9.5 Results of appeal process

The results of an appeal process are important. Must an appeal body return a case if it believes the findings are wrong, or may it substitute another result?

IISD believes that an appeal body should have the capacity, and should anticipate making a decision that will dispose of the case with finality. It may uphold, modify or reverse a decision. The only exception that should be foreseen is one where the appellate body reverses a finding of law or fact, and determines it then does not have a sufficient factual record before it to reach a final determination on the matter. Here, a return to the original Tribunal may be warranted.

A major goal of the process is finality. This should be the presumption applied to this issue.

4.9.6 Costs and funding

There should be no presumption that the full costs of a properly constituted, independent appellate process can be recovered from the costs for the appeals themselves. They can go a significant way toward this end, but additional funds will also be needed. With this in mind, ISID has no issue with the proposal for the costs to the parties to parallel the current costs system.

4.9.7 Additional powers of Secretary General

Paragraph 11 suggests that the Secretary General have a form of gatekeeper function for the appeals process similar to that now exercised in relation to the panel process at ICSID. IISD has already stated its view that such a role is inappropriate. Expanding it for the appeals process is even more so for the reasons already stated. In addition, assuming here for the sake of argument that an independent process is established, we believe the right of appeal should come with the agreement to arbitrate. The process should be, in that sense, a single continuing process of the arbitration, not a process with a submission to jurisdiction to a panel and a separate submission to jurisdiction to an appellate body. Thus, the agreement to arbitrate should comprise the agreement to accept the appeal process. Otherwise, the goals of consistency and predictability, in process or substance, will remain elusive. Thus, there would be no similar function to exercise under that conception. The remaining suggested powers for the Secretary General in paragraph 11 have already been discussed and considered as inappropriate in previous sections.

4.9.8 Time period for appeals

Paragraph 11 suggests a time period for filing an appeal of 120 days. We believe 60 days is sufficient, subject to a longer period if the issue is the discovery of a corrupt or conflicted arbitrator. Time should then be measured from the time of discovery of these specific facts.

4.9.9 Conduct of process

Paragraph 12 of the ICSID proposal suggests that the conduct of the appeal should use the same rules as the conduct of the arbitration. IISD believes this would be appropriate if the arbitration is conducted in a fully transparent and accessible manner. We have described these elements *in extenso* above.

4.9.10 Role of Secretariat

Paragraph 12 suggests that the Secretariat of ICSID also be the Secretariat of the appeals process. IISD believes this is inappropriate. Secretariats play an important role as the repository of the history of many processes, and as an ongoing corporate memory. Having the same people service the initial proceedings and the appeals risks, by simple force of personal interaction and both formal and informal discussions of the people involved, tilting the conduct of an appeal away from a direction it may otherwise have taken. There is no suggestion of nefarious activity even remotely implied here, simply the weight of normal human interaction. While one independent institution may house both the panel and the appeal process, there is, we believe, a need to separate the Secretariat services for each. The WTO model for appeals is instructive in this context.

4.9.11 Review of appeals process

IISD fully supports the idea of a review period for the operation of the appeals process. Five or six years should be a sufficient period for this in the first instance. Subsequent reviews every five years should also be conducted.

5. A Final Note

IISD understands that addressing the process issues in dispute settlement will not in itself fix the defects found in the current international investment regime. In the next few weeks, IISD will be tabling a fuller proposal in this respect, one which we believe will address the broader role of international investment law and the international investment regime in today's sustainable development context. This document will be available for public comment through IISD's investment Web site at http://www.iisd.org/investment.

However, IISD does believe that the public process initiated by ICSID is clearly the appropriate method for moving forward on a number of important issues of process, and we applaud the Secretariat of ICSID for its foresight and courage in undertaking it.

APPENDIX 6

Latest Developments in Investor-State Dispute Settlement, 2005*

Introduction:

To help put this volume's discussion and analysis of an appellate review mechanism into context, the Appendixes conclude with three documents surveying the growth of both investment treaties and international disputes. The first of these, reproduced here, comes from the United Nations Conference on Trade and Development (UNCTAD), an important player in the emerging system of international investment law. UNCTAD's International Investment Agreement Monitor (IIA Monitor) from the fourth quarter of 2005 provides data on the wide increase in international investment disputes in recent years.

---

* Reprinted with permission of the United Nations Conference on Trade and Development. More information can be found on the UNCTAD website at www.unctad.org

UNCTAD/WEB/ITE/IIT/2005/2

UNITED NATIONS CONFERENCE ON TRADE AND DEVELOPMENT

Geneva

Latest Developments in Investor-State Dispute Settlement

IIA Monitor No. 4 (2005)

UNITED NATIONS
New York and Geneva, 2005

UNITED NATIONS COFERENCE ON TRADE AND DEVELOPMENT (UNCTAD)

CONFÉRENCE DES NATIONS UNIES POUR LE COMMERCE ET LE DÉVELOPPEMENT (CNUCED)

IIA Monitor
No. 4 (2005)

LATEST DEVELOPMENTS IN INVESTOR-STATE DISPUTE SETTLEMENT*

UNCTAD/WEB/ITE/IIT/2005/2

In 2005, investor-State dispute settlement cases continued to grow ...

Investor-State arbitrations under international investment agreements (IIAs) continue to grow unabated, with at least 42 cases launched in the first 11 months of 2005.[1] This brings the cumulative number of known treaty-based cases to 219 by November 2005 (figure 1).

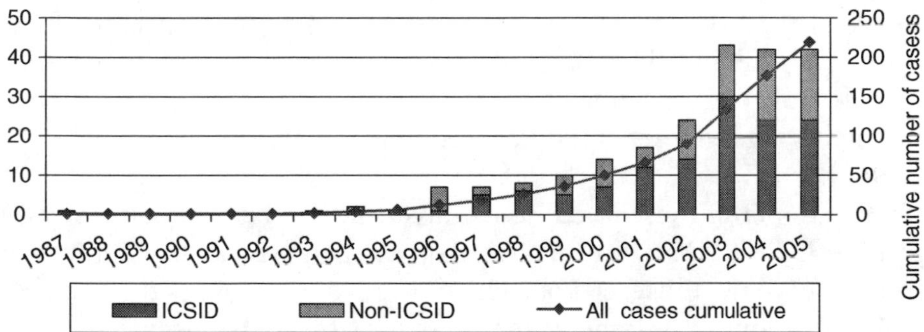

Figure 1 Known investment treaty arbitrations, (cumulative and newly instituted cases, by year) a/
Source: UNCTAD. a/ As of November 2005.

---

* Contact: James Zhan, +41-22-907-5797; e-mail: james.zhan@unctad.org; Joerg Weber, +41-22-907-1124; e-mail: joerg.weber@unctad.org. This note is based on research undertaken by Luke Eric Peterson, Global Arbitration Tracking & Expertise. The final version benefited from comments from Bertram Boie, Anna Joubin-Bret and Joachim Karl

1 International investment disputes can also arise from contracts between investors and governments; a number of such disputes are (or have been) brought under ICSID, other institutional arbitration systems or ad-hoc arbitration but are not included in this data, except where there is also a treaty-based claim at hand.

132 of these have been brought before the World Bank's International Centre for Settlement of Investment Disputes (ICSID) (including ICSID's Additional Facility) and 87 before other arbitration forums (figure 2).[2] Almost two-thirds (69%) of the 219 known claims were filed since the beginning of 2002, with virtually none of them initiated by governments.[3]

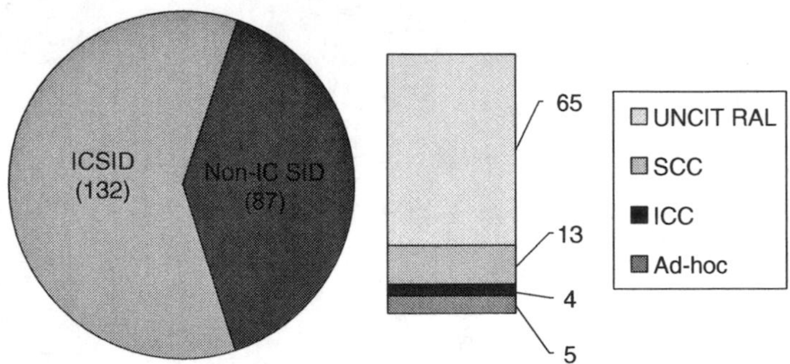

Figure 2 Disputes by forum of arbitration a/
Source: UNCTAD.
a/ As of November 2005.
Note: SCC = Stockholm Chamber of Commerce; ICC = International Chamber of Commerce.

These figures do not include cases where a party signaled its intention to submit a claim to arbitration, but has not yet actually commenced the arbitration; if these cases are ultimately submitted to arbitration, the number of pending claims will grow further. Some disputes are settled either before an arbitration is launched or after the arbitration procedure has started.[4]

The total number of these treaty-based investment arbitrations is impossible to measure; UNCTAD's figures are based on extensive research and interviews, but represent only those claims which were disclosed by the parties or arbitral institutions.[5] Even where the existence of a claim has been made public,

---

2 The new figure of 219 includes new cases launched since UNCTAD's earlier reporting on this issue (see UNCTAD 2004), as well as a number of earlier cases that were only recently uncovered.

3 The sole exception is a 2003 State-to-State dispute between Chile and Peru that was lodged in response to an investor-State claim filed by a Chilean firm, Lucchetti (*Lucchetti S.A. and Lucchetti Peru S.A. v. Republic of Peru*, ICSID Case No. ARB/03/4). The State-State procedure was discontinued, and the investor-State case was only recently decided. In other instances, States have set up claims commissions to deal with investor-to-State cases, such as the Iran-United States Claims Tribunal.

4 UNCTAD's database includes all claims that have been brought to arbitration, including those that were settled after they had been registered.

5 While the ICSID facility maintains a public registry of claims, other arbitral mechanisms do not, meaning that no official records of all claims filed are available. Further, in some cases the investors or governments

such as in the case of a claim listed on the ICSID registry, often the information about such a claim is quite minimal. Similarly, from the information on the ICSID database it is not possible to ascertain whether a claim is based on an investment treaty or on a State contract. Under other arbitration rules, the details of a claim and its resolution are likely to become public only if one of the disputants discloses such information. As such, it is significant that 40% of the discovered claims occur under these rules. The actual number of claims instituted under non-ICSID rules is very likely larger than what is known.

The increase in the number of claims can be attributed to several factors. First, increases in international investment flows lead to more occasions for disputes, and more occasions for disputes combined with more IIAs are likely to lead to more cases.[6] Second, with larger numbers of IIAs in place, more investor-State disputes are likely to involve an alleged violation of a treaty provision and more of them are likely to be within the ambit of a dispute settlement provision.[7] Another reason may be the higher complexity of recent IIAs, and the regulatory difficulties in their proper implementation. Further, as news of large, successful claims spreads, more investors may be encouraged to utilize the investor-State dispute resolution mechanism. Greater transparency in arbitration (e.g. within the North American Free Trade Agreement (NAFTA)) may also be a factor in giving greater visibility to this legal avenue of dispute settlement.

... involving a growing number of countries ...

At least 61 governments—37 of them in the developing world, 14 in developed countries and 10 in Southeast Europe and the Commonwealth of Independent States—have faced investment treaty arbitration (annex). 42 claims have been lodged against Argentina, 39 of which relate at least in part to that country's financial crisis. The number of claims against Argentina peaked in 2003 with 20 claims, and receded to 8 new claims in 2004 and 5 new cases in the first 10.5

---

involved in a dispute wish to keep the dispute confidential, with the result that the disputants themselves may not reveal the existence of a claim

6 The worldwide inward FDI stock has grown from $2.8 trillion at the end of 1995 to $8.9 trillion at the end of 2004 (see www.unctad.org/wir).

7 The universe of IIAs has grown considerably over the past decade. At the end of 2004, it consisted of 2,392 bilateral treaties for the promotion and protection of investment (or bilateral investment treaties/BITs) (compared to 1,097 BITs at the end of 1995), 2,559 treaties for the avoidance of double taxation (or double taxation treaties/DTTs) (1,663 in 1995), and some 215 other bilateral and regional trade and investment agreements as well as various multilateral agreements that contain a commitment to liberalize, protect and/or promote investment (77 in 1995) (see www.unctad.org/iia).

months of 2005. Mexico has the second highest number of known claims (17), most of them falling under NAFTA, and a handful under various BITs. The United States has also faced a sizeable number (11). India (9 claims), the Czech Republic (8), Egypt (8), Poland (7 claims), the Russian Federation (7) and Ecuador (7) also figure prominently, followed by Canada (6) and the Republic of Moldova (5).

In several instances, there have been a multitude of claims lodged in relation to a single investment or against a particular government action. In the Argentine cases, a series of emergency measures and policies have occasioned suits from several dozen companies. In the case of India, the disputed Dabhol Power project lead to a least 2 BIT claims by the project companies, as well as 7 BIT claims by the project lenders. All of these claims against India have since been settled. At other times, a single arbitration may have dozens upon dozens of individual claimants, as is the case in a NAFTA arbitration against Mexico by individual investors in tourist real estate, and in the case of a NAFTA arbitration against the United States brought by more than 100 individual claimants in the beef industry.[8]

2005 saw efforts towards consolidation in major NAFTA cases. On request by the United States, three softwood lumber cases, Canfor Corp. v. United States of America, Terminal Forest Products Ltd. v. United States of America and Tembec Inc. et al. v. United States of America were consolidated. On the other hand, Mexico requested the establishment of a Tribunal to consider the consolidation of three claims, all concerning an excise tax on certain soft drinks. The Consolidation Tribunal in its order of May 2005, however, decided against the consolidation on grounds that the United States based companies involved were in direct and major competition.

... arising in all sectors, and concerning key treaty provisions ...

Recent cases have involved the whole range of investment activities and all kinds of investments, including privatization contracts and State concessions. Measures that have been challenged include emergency laws put in place during a financial crisis, value added taxes, rezoning of land from agricultural use to commercial use, measures on hazardous waste facilities, issues related

---

8 In UNCTAD's database, the beef cases against the United States are counted as one case, rather than 100, following the United States practice on its website. Furthermore, all of these cases pertain to the same facts and the same treaty. By contrast, the 7 Dabhol banks cases are counted as individual cases, because they pertain to the same facts, but different investment treaties.

to the intent to divest shareholdings of public enterprises to a foreign investor, and treatment at the hands of media regulators. Disputes have involved provisions such as those on fair and equitable treatment, non-discrimination, expropriation, and the scope and definition of agreements. These disputes are yielding awards that interpret the legal obligations of the agreements, which in turn has caused some parties to reexamine and reconsider the scope and extent of such obligations.

In 2005, the vast majority of claims have been brought under BITs, several of the cases involving also contractual disputes between the State and the investor. Several recent cases also involve disputes under the Energy Charter Treaty.

... with 2005 seeing important tribunal decisions in terms of interpretation of treaty provisions ...

Tribunals have rendered decisions in the last year that could have significant substantive implications:

- On most-favored-nation treatment, two recent decisions (Salini Costruttori S.p.A. and Italstrade S.p.A. v. The Hashemite Kingdom of Jordan[9] and Plama Consortium Limited v. Republic of Bulgaria[10]) have significantly departed from the broad approach taken by the Maffezini and Siemens cases in 2000 and 2004 on the scope of the MFN provision. These two recent decisions on jurisdiction reaffirm the distinction that must be drawn between substantive and jurisdictional provisions of treaties in order to identify the scope of protection offered by an MFN provision and the importance of the wording of the basic treaty.[11]
- On the umbrella effect of treaties, in recent decisions tribunals have followed a broad approach. However, in an April 2005 decision

9 Decision on Jurisdiction, 9 November 2004 (ICSID Case No. ARB/02/13).

10 Decision on Jurisdiction, 8 February 2005 (ICSID Case No. ARB/03/24).

11 See, for example, the Plama decision, as follows: "... the principle with multiple exceptions as stated by the tribunal in the Maffezini case should instead be a different principle with one, single exception: an MFN provision in a basic treaty does not incorporate by reference dispute settlement provisions in whole or in part set forth in another treaty, unless the MFN provision in the basic treaty leaves no doubt that the Contracting Parties intended to incorporate them" (Plama Consortium Limited v. Bulgaria (ICSID Case No. ARB/03/24), Decision on Jurisdiction, 8 February 2005, paragraph 223).

(Impregilo S.p.A. v. Islamic Republic of Pakistan[12]), the tribunal has limited treaty jurisdiction over contractual claims to claims involving the State itself and not State-owned entities. In the recent Consortium Groupement L.E.S.I. - DIPENTA v. Algeria,[13] the tribunal emphasized the requirement that contractual claims brought before a treaty-based tribunal must also amount to a violation of the treaty standards themselves.[14]

- The ruling on national treatment in the August 2005 decision on Methanex Corporation vs. United States of America[15] takes a narrow approach to the test of the requirement "in like circumstances", comparing the foreign investor to those economic activities comparable in the domestic sphere, rather than taking a broad approach as used for example in the S.D. Myers, Inc. v. Canada decision.[16]
- The first ICSID decision on the question of interpretation of awards as under Article 50 of the ICSID Convention was rendered by an arbitral tribunal. In the case Wena Hotels Limited v. the Arab Republic of Egypt,[17] Wena sought the interpretation of the concept of expropriation as used in the award. The tribunal found that there was indeed a dispute between Wena and Egypt as to the interpretation of the term "expropriation".

Another development worth mentioning is the attention paid by tribunals in two recent NAFTA cases to Amicus Curiae submissions.[18]

... in terms of awards ...

Although the financial implications of the investor-State dispute resolution process can be substantial, the information available thus far does not provide a clear picture of their full nature. Information about the quantum of damages sought by investors tends to be sporadic and unreliable, in part because many claims are still in a preliminary stage and claimants are often not required to

---

12 Decision on Jurisdiction, 22 April 2005 (ICSID Case No. ARB/02/2).

13 Decision on Jurisdiction, 10 January 2005 (ICSID Case No. ARB/03/8).

14 See Emmanuel Gaillard, "Treaty-based jurisdiction: broad dispute resolution clauses" *in International Arbitration Law, New York Law Journal*, 6 October 2005.

15 Final Award, 3 August 2005, UNCITRAL (NAFTA).

16 Final Award, 30 December 2002, UNCITRAL (NAFTA).

17 Decision on Application for Interpretation of Award, 31 October 2005 (ICSID Case No. ARB/98/4).

18 See the Methanex v. United States and UPS v. Canada decisions, Final Award, 3 August 2005, UNCITRAL (NAFTA), and Award on Jurisdiction, 22 November 2002, UNCITRAL (NAFTA).

quantify their claims until a later stage in the proceedings. Nevertheless, it is known that some claims involve large sums, in some cases in the hundreds of millions of dollars. Recent examples include:

- In February 2005, an UNCITRAL tribunal awarded France Telecom $266 million after finding the Republic of Lebanon to be in breach of the France-Lebanon BIT. Lebanon has sought to challenge that verdict in the courts of Switzerland, where the arbitration was sited. The arbitral award has not been published by the parties.[19]
- In May 2005, an ICSID tribunal awarded a United States energy company some $133 million after finding Argentina in breach of its obligations under contracts and the United States-Argentina BIT. In September, Argentina introduced a procedure to annul the tribunal's award under Article 52 of the ICSID Convention.[20]
- In August 2005, an UNCITRAL tribunal dismissed in its entirety a set of claims by the Canadian-based Methanex Corporation, alleging violations of investment protections found in the NAFTA. Methanex had claimed some $970 million in damages.[21]
- Recently, a series of three arbitrations were mounted by the majority shareholders in the Yukos Corporation, alleging a violation by the Russian Federation of the Energy Charter Treaty. These claims are for a reported total of $33 billion, making them the largest known claims in investment arbitration history.[22]

Because the number of awards issued to date is relatively small, it remains unclear how frequently large claims will be successful. Even assuming that a claim is unsuccessful, the cost of defense can be significant.

... and in terms of costs for litigation.

---

19 See Luke Eric Peterson, "France multinational wins treaty arbitration against Lebanon", *Investment Law and Policy News Bulletin*, 10 March 2005, http://www.iisd.org/pdf/2005/investment_investsd_mar10_2005.pdf.

20 See Luke Eric Peterson, "Argentina moves to annul award in dispute with CMS Company over financial crisis", *Investment Treaty News*, 26 October 2005, http://www.iisd.org/pdf/2005/investment_investsd_oct26 _2005.pdf.

21 See http://www.state.gov/s/l/c5818.htm.

22 See Luke Eric Peterson, "Menatep's Yukos claim is largest in investment treaty history, others in offing?", *Investment Law and Policy News Bulletin*, 22 February 2005, http://www.iisd.org/pdf/2005/investment_investsd_feb22_2005.pdf.

Two recent decisions are noteworthy in as far as the allocation of costs and attorney's fees by the tribunals are concerned:

- The Methanex tribunal in its decision of 3 August 2005 on the merits awarded the burden of the full costs to the unsuccessful claimant, including the United States' legal costs.[23]
- The annulment Committee in a recent decision rendered against the Seychelles,[24] has decided that all the costs of the annulment procedures should be borne by the State that had challenged the first award, seemingly in an attempt to discourage frivolous annulment procedures. The Committee made clear that an annulment proceeding does not offer a displeased litigant a fresh opportunity to second-guess an ICSID Tribunal's findings.

In the last year, the number of annulment procedures against ICSID awards has also been on the rise, with some 7 pending procedures introduced before the ICSID secretariat by States but also by investors.

The dramatic growth of investor-State dispute settlement cases has given rise to concerns and triggered several reactions on part of governments.

The surge in investment disputes arising from IIAs in and by itself is not necessarily an unhealthy development—after all, it is an expression of the rule of law, and hence an expression of the fact that IIAs "work" towards creating a favorable investment climate in host countries. However, there have been some concerns with regard to both the substantive aspects of the IIAs that have given rise to arbitrations and some procedural issues of existing investor-State dispute settlement mechanisms (UNCTAD 2004 and 2005).

These concerns have led to calls for a reform of the ICSID system, on the one hand, and to the revision of several model BITs, on the other. The latter include significant innovations regarding investor-State dispute settlement procedures. Greater and substantial transparency in arbitral proceedings, including open hearings, publication of related legal documents, and the possibility for representatives of civil society to submit "*amicus curiae*" notes to arbitral tribunals is foreseen. In addition, other very detailed provisions on investor-State

---

23 See footnote 14.

24 CDC Group plc v. Republic of the Seychelles, Case No. ARB/02/14. Note that this arbitration is not treaty-based.

dispute settlement are included in order to provide for a more legally oriented, predictable and orderly conduct at the different stages of this process. Thus, for example, the Canadian model BIT includes specific standard waiver forms to facilitate the filing of waivers as required by article 26 of the Agreement for purposes of filing a claim. The United States-Uruguay BIT, on the other hand, not only provides for a special procedure available at the early stages of the dispute settlement process aimed at discarding frivolous claims or to seek interim injunctive relief, but also envisages the possibility to set up a mechanism for appellate review, in order to foster a more consistent and rigorous application of international law in arbitral awards.

One key concern for developing countries is to increase their ability to manage the investor-State disputes effectively.

However, some broader development concerns and policy implications for developing countries remain to be addressed. Their vulnerability in this regard is based on their limited technical capacity to handle investment disputes coupled with the increasing number of such disputes, the potentially high costs involved of conducting such procedures, and the potential impact of awards on the budget and a country's reputation as an investment location.

At the same time, the proper functioning of the dispute settlement system is dependent on well-informed partners. Technical assistance seems necessary required to enable countries to make effective and efficient use of the investor-State dispute settlement system as part of an overall endeavor to improve the investment climate, the rule of law and ensuing that IIAs contribute to countries' efforts to attract and benefit from foreign direct investment.

* * *

United Nations Conference on Trade and Development (UNCTAD) (2005). *Research Note: Recent Developments in International Investment Agreements* (UNCTAD/WEB/ITE/IIT/ 2005/1) (30 August).

__________ (2004). *Occasional Note: International Investment Disputes On The Rise* (UNCTAD/WEB/ITE/IIT/2004/2) (29 November).

Annex

Country	**Number of claims**
Argentina	42
Mexico	17
United States	11
India	9
Czech Republic	8
Egypt	8
Ecuador	7
Poland	7
Russian Federation	7
Canada	6
Moldova, Republic of	5
Chile	4
Congo, Democratic Republic of	4
Kazakhstan	4
Romania	4
Ukraine	4
Hungary	3
Pakistan	3
Venezuela	3
Algeria	2
Burundi	2
Estonia	2
Georgia	2
Jordan	2
Latvia	2
Lebanon	2
Morocco	2
Philippines	2
Sri Lanka	2
Turkey	2
United Arab Emirates	2

Country	Number of claims
Albania	1
Bangladesh	1
Barbados	1
Bolivia	1
Bulgaria	1
Croatia	1
El Salvador	1
France/United Kingdom	1
Germany	1
Ghana	1
Guyana	1
Indonesia	1
Kyrgyzstan	1
Lithuania	1
Malaysia	1
Mongolia	1
Myanmar	1
Paraguay	1
Peru	1
Portugal	1
Saudi Arabia	1
Serbia-Montenegro	1
Slovenia	1
Spain	1
Tanzania, United Republic of	1
Trinidad and Tobago	1
Tunisia	1
Viet Nam	1
Yemen	1
Zimbabwe	1
Unknown	9

Source: UNCTAD.

APPENDIX 7

Latest Developments in Investor-State Dispute Settlement, 2006*

Introduction:

This Appendix reproduces, like Appendix 6, an IIA Monitor from UNCTAD. Published by UNCTAD in the fourth quarter of 2006, it provides more analysis than the previous article on the rise in investment disputes. The key arbitral decisions of the past year are examined and considered, categorized by the key legal issue in each.

UNCTAD/WEB/ITE/IIA/2006/11

United Nations Conference on Trade and Development
Geneva

Latest Developments in Investor-State Dispute Settlement

IIA Monitor No. 4 (2006)
International Investment Agreements

UNITED NATIONS
New York and Geneva, 2006

IIA Monitor
No. 4 (2006)

Latest developments in investor-State dispute Settlement*

In the first 11 months of 2006, at least 25 investor-State cases were filed under international investment agreements (IIAs), 18 of which were filed with the International Centre for Settlement of Investment Disputes (ICSID).[1] If confirmed at that level, this would be the lowest number of known treaty-based cases filed since the year 2000, hinting to a considerable slow down in the number of cases launched. However, given the fact that the ICSID arbitration facility is the only facility to maintain a public registry of claims, this could also indicate a shift of arbitration activity into the less public domain of other arbitral venues.

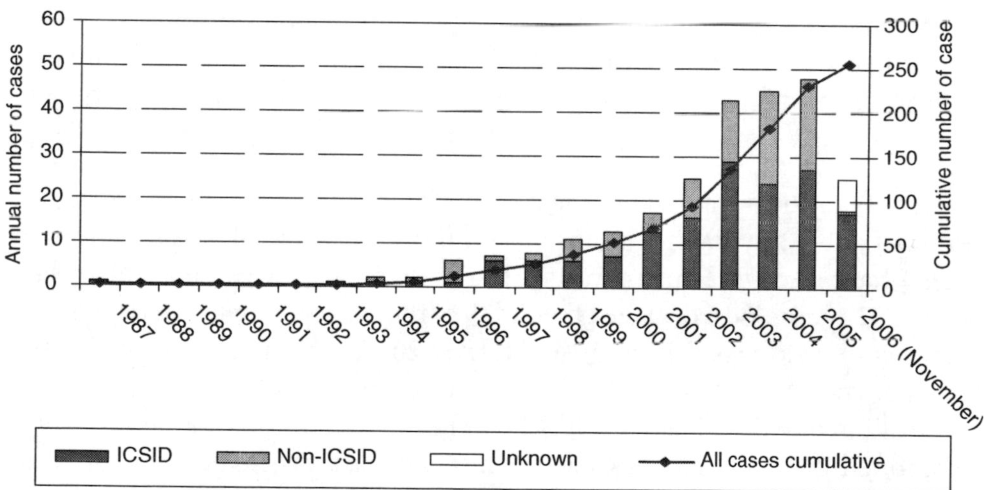

Figure 1. Known investment treaty arbitrations (cumulative and newly instituted cases, 1987–November 2006
Source: UNCTAD.

* Contact: James Zhan, +41-22-907-5797; Joerg Weber, +41-22-907-1124; e-mail: iia@unctad.org. This note is based on a draft prepared by Federico Ortino, Investment Treaty Forum, London. The final version benefited from comments from Hamed El-Kady, Anna Joubin-Bret and Joachim Karl.

1 This number does not include cases where a party signaled its intention to submit a claim to arbitration, but has not yet commenced the arbitration (notice of intent); if these cases are submitted to arbitration, the number of pending cases will increase. See UNCTAD 2005a and 2005b.

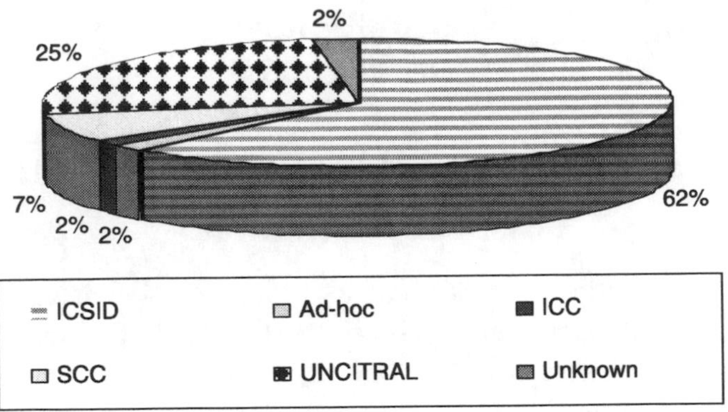

Figure 2. Disputes by forum of arbitration, cumulative as of November 2006 (Percentage)
Source: UNCTAD.
Note: SCC = Stockholm Chamber of Commerce; ICC = International Chamber of Commerce.

The total cumulative number of known treaty-based cases increased to a new peak of 255 (figure 1). These disputes were filed with ICSID (or ICSID Additional Facility) (156), the United Nations Commission on International Trade Law (UNCITRAL) (65), the Stockholm Chamber of Commerce (18), the International Chamber of Commerce (4), and ad-hoc arbitration (4). One case concerned the Cairo Regional Centre for International Commercial Arbitration, and for seven cases the exact venue was still unknown at the time of writing (figure 2).

At least 70 governments—44 of them in the developing world, 14 in developed countries and 12 in Southeast Europe and the Commonwealth of Independent States—have faced investment treaty arbitration (annex). Argentina still tops the list with 42 claims lodged against that it (39 of these disputes relate at least in part to that country's financial crisis) (UNCTAD 2005a). No new arbitration cases were launched against Argentina in the first 11 months of 2006, and only one notice of intent was registered at ICSID in this period. Mexico continues to have the second highest number of known claims (17); also with no new cases in 2006. The United States and the Czech Republic have the third highest number of claims filed against them with 11 each. The Russian Federation (9 claims), the Republic of Moldova (9), India (9), Egypt (8), Ecuador (8), Romania (7), Poland (7), Canada (7) and Ukraine (6) also figure prominently. Nine countries faced arbitration proceedings for the first time in 2006, with one exception all from the developing world (Azerbaijan (2 cases), the Republic of Congo, Grenada, Mali, Nicaragua, Seychelles, the Slovak Republic (2 cases), Thailand and Togo).

A little less than half of the cases (42 %) involved the services sector, including electricity distribution, telecommunications, debt instruments, water services

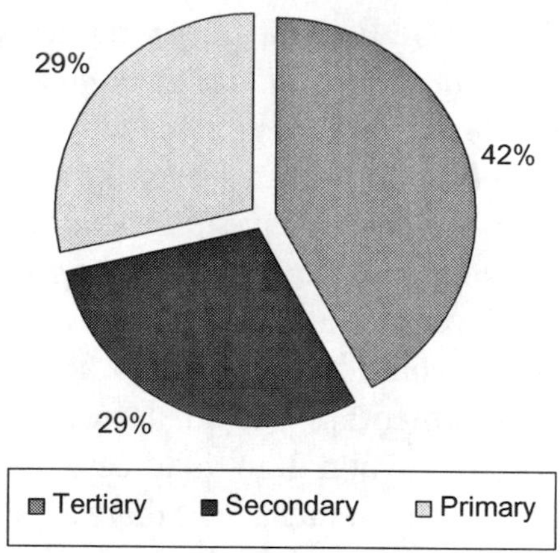

Figure 3 Sectors involved in known investment treaty arbitration (Percentage)
Source: UNCTAD.

and waste management (figure 3). All primary sector cases relate to mining and oil and gas exploration activities.

As far as the substantive implications are concerned, tribunals in 2006 rendered significant decisions:

On most-favoured-nation treatment, two decisions (*Suez, Sociedad General de Aguas de Barcelona SA et al v. The Argentine Republic* and *National Grid plc v. The Argentine Republic)* permitted investors to avail themselves of a more favourable (i.e. shorter) waiting period before launching an international arbitration. This is in line with the approach taken by the *Maffezini* case in 2000. However, two other decisions, *Vladimir Berschader and Michael Berschader v. Russian Federation* and *Telenor Mobile Communications A.S. v. Republic of Hungary* denied the investors' claim to borrow the more favourable consent-to-arbitration clause found in other investment treaties endorsing the more recent approach taken by the *Plama* tribunal in 2005.[2] The two BITs at issue in the latter cases provided in fact for investor-state arbitration for expropriation claims only and the investors had argued that through the most-favoured-nation provision they could expand the tribunal's jurisdiction to include other treaty standards.

On fair and equitable treatment, several recent decisions have upheld and reinforced a broad acceptance of the FET standard in line with the often-cited

---

2 See the *Telenor* decision: "*The tribunal therefore concludes that in the present case the MFN clause cannot be used to extend the tribunal's jurisdiction to categories of claim other than expropriation, for this would subvert the common intention of Hungary and Norway in entering into the BIT in question*" (*Telenor*, paragraph 100).

Tecmed award in 2003. In *LG&E v. the Argentine Republic*, for example, the tribunal affirmed that the *"fair and equitable standard consists of the host State's consistent and transparent behaviour, free of ambiguity that involves the obligation to grant and maintain a stable and predictable legal framework necessary to fulfill the justified expectations of the foreign investor."*[3] This reading is in line with the other awards rendered in 2006 in *Azurix v. The Argentine Republic and Saluka v. The Czech Republic.* [4] Moreover in *Thunderbird v. Mexico*, the breach of the investor's legitimate expectations would have provided the basis for a violation of the minimum standard of treatment as provided for in Article 1105 NAFTA.[5] However, a majority of the tribunal in that case found that the Mexican Government's conduct did not generate a legitimate expectation upon which the foreign investor could reasonably rely. Worth mentioning is also the statement in Saluka that the fair and equitable treatment standard "*cannot easily be assumed to include a general prohibition of State aid*."[6]

On expropriation, decisions rendered in 2006 demonstrate that a claim of expropriation may give rise to two types of issues, one referring to the question of whether a regulation results in expropriation and the other concerning the lawfulness of the expropriation itself. In addressing the first question, one

---

3 See the *LG&E* decision: "[...] *Having created specific expectations among investors, Argentina was bound by its obligations concerning the investment guarantees vis-à-vis public utility licensees, and in particular, the gas distribution licensees. The abrogation of these specific guarantees violates the stability and predictability underlying the standard of fair and equitable treatment*" (*LG&E*, paragraph 133).

4 See the *Azurix* decision: "[...] *there is a common thread in the recent awards under NAFTA and Tecmed which does not require bad faith or malicious intention of the recipient State as a necessary element in the failure to treat investment fairly and equitably.* [...] *It is also understood that the conduct of the State has to be below international standards but those are not at the level of 1927. A third element is the frustration of expectations that the investor may have legitimately taken into account when it made the investment.* [...] *To encourage and protect investment is the purpose of the BIT. It would be incoherent with such purpose and the expectations created by such a document to consider that a party to the BIT has breached the obligation of fair and equitable treatment only when it has acted in bad faith or its conduct can be qualified as outrageous or egregious.*" (*Azurix*, paragraph 372). See also the *Saluka* decision: "*The Czech Republic, without undermining its legitimate right to take measures for the protection of the public interest, has therefore assumed an obligation to treat a foreign investor's investment in a way that does not frustrate the investor's underlying legitimate and reasonable expectations. A foreign investor whose interests are protected under the Treaty is entitled to expect that the Czech Republic will not act in a way that is manifestly inconsistent, non-transparent, unreasonable (i.e. unrelated to some rational policy), or discriminatory (i.e. based on unjustifiable distinctions). In applying this standard, the tribunal will have due regard to all relevant circumstances.*" (*Saluka*, paragraph 309).

5 See the *Thunderbird* decision: "[...] *the concept of 'legitimate expectations' relates, within the context of the NAFTA framework, to a situation where a Contracting Party's conduct creates reasonable and justifiable expectations on the part of an investor (or investment) to act in reliance on said conduct, such that a failure by the NAFTA Party to honour those expectations could cause the investor (or investment) to suffer damages.*" (*Thunderbird*, paragraph 147).

6 *Saluka*, paragraph 445.

recent decision (*LG&E v. The Argentine Republic*) dealing with a case of indirect expropriation focused on balancing two competing interests: the degree of the measure's interference with the right of ownership and the power of the State to adopt its policies. In evaluating the degree of the measure's interference with the investor's right of ownership, the two key elements were the measure's economic impact (i.e. effective change of control or ownership of the investment, interference with the investor's reasonable expectations) and the measure's duration.[7] This approach is in line with previous awards such as those in *SD Myers v. Canada*, *Feldman v. Mexico* and *Tecmed v. Mexico*. To be noted is also the statement of the tribunal in *EnCana v. Ecuador* that places taxation in a special category for purposes of a claim of expropriation, i.e. "*only if a tax law is extraordinary, punitive in amount and arbitrary in its incidence would issues of indirect expropriation be raised*".[8]

In another decision (*ADC Affiliate and ADC & ADMC Management Limited v. The Republic of Hungary*) dealing with a case of direct expropriation, the tribunal focused on whether the expropriation (a) had been taken in the public interest; (b) respected the due process principle; (c) was non-discriminatory; and (d) was accompanied by payment of just compensation. In that case, the tribunal found that the Government's take-over of the investor's activities concerning the operation of two terminals at Budapest airport did not comply with any of the above conditions.[9]

Of the seven decisions rendered in 2006 that examined claims based on expropriation only one decided in favour of the investor (*ADC Affiliate Limited and ADC & ADMC Management Limited v. The Republic of Hungary*), while six rejected such claims (*EnCana v. Ecuador, Saluka v. Czech Republic, LG&E v. Argentina, Azurix v. Argentina, Thunderbird v. Mexico, Telenor Mobile Communications v. Hungary*). Three of the six tribunals that rejected the expropriation claims, nonetheless found that the host countries had violated other treaty provisions, in particular the fair and equitable treatment standard (*Saluka, LG&E* and *Azurix*).

On the "umbrella clause", recent decisions have emphasized once more the divergent views followed by arbitral tribunals since the issue was first decided in *SGS v. Pakistan*. The tribunals in *El Paso v. The Argentine Republic* and *BP-Pan American v. The Argentine Republic* concluded that the so called 'umbrella clause'

---

7 *LG&E*, paragraphs 189–190.

8 *Encana*, paragraph 177.

9 *ADC*, paragraph 476.

in the United States–Argentina BIT could not transform any contract claims into breaches of international law.[10] On the other hand, in *LG&E v. The Argentine Republic*, the tribunal held that Argentina's abrogation of certain contractual undertakings gave rise to international liability under the 'umbrella clause' of that treaty. The tribunal in *Azurix v. The Argentine Republic* rejected the investor's claim based on the umbrella clause emphasizing that the claimants were not party to the original contract with the State.[11]

On the "state of necessity", in the *LG&E* award the tribunal accepted Argentina's defense that its actions following the financial crisis in the late 1990s were taken due to a state of necessity that imperiled the essential interests of the country at the time. Although the tribunal found that Argentina's actions breached some of the investment protection provided for in the relevant BIT, it absolved Argentina from liability for losses caused during the period of necessity (which the tribunal estimated to have lasted for eighteen months). This decision notably contradicts the 2005 award in *CMS v. The Argentine Republic* which, although based on almost identical facts, had not accepted the 'state of necessity' defense ruling that the essential interests of the state do not include economic issues and in any event the crisis was not severe enough to warrant the measures taken (the annulment proceedings against the CMS award are still pending).

In terms of damages, a few awards in 2006 are noteworthy, among which:

- In July 2006, an ICSID tribunal awarded *Azurix* $165 million after finding the Argentine Republic to be in breach of the United States–Argentina BIT. The investor had originally claimed $665 million.
- In October 2006, an ICSID tribunal awarded Cyprus-based *ADC Limited* $76.2 million after finding Hungary in breach of its obligation under the Cyprus–Hungary BIT. The investor had originally claimed $244.3 million.

---

10 See the decision in *El Paso*: "*These far-reaching consequences of a broad interpretation of the so-called umbrella clauses, quite destructive of the distinction between national legal orders and the international legal order, have been well understood and clearly explained by the first tribunal which dealt with the issue of the so-called 'umbrella clause' in the SGS v. Pakistan case and which insisted on the theoretical problems faced. It would be strange indeed if the acceptance of a BIT entailed an international liability of the State going far beyond the obligation to respect the standards of protection of foreign investments embodied in the Treaty and rendered it liable for any violation of any commitment in national or international law 'with regard to investments'.*" (*El Paso*, paragraph 82).

11 *Azurix*, paragraph 384.

Although in *LG&E* and *Saluka* the tribunals decided in favour of the investor, the respective tribunals have yet to determine the amount of damages to be awarded at a subsequent stage.[12]

An interesting development with regard to determination of damages may be found in the *ADC* award. The ADC tribunal determined that Article 4 of the Cyprus–Hungary BIT on expropriation stipulated only the standard of compensation payable in case of a *lawful* expropriation and that applying this standard to a case of *unlawful* expropriation (as in the case at hand) would have been inappropriate.[13] Accordingly, the tribunal applied the customary international law standard set out in the decision of the PCIJ in the *Chorzów Factory* case and on that basis decided to assess the value of the expropriated property at the date of the award rather than at the date of expropriation (1 January 2002).[14]

Looking at the 21 disputes that have reached a conclusion in 2006 (either rejecting the investor's claims or awarding damages to the affected investor),[15] out of a total of $1.63 billion in claimed damages, tribunals have awarded a total of $241.2 million (approximately 15 %).[16]

As far as ***the allocation of costs and attorney's fees*** by tribunals are concerned, a few recent decisions are also noteworthy. At least four decisions seem to reinforce the recent trend that allocates (at least part of) the legal fees and arbitration costs to the losing party, whether the State or the investor.

- The *ADC* tribunal in its decision of 2 October 2006 awarded the burden of the full costs totaling $7.6 million to the defending country

---

12 In November 2006, the parties have reached a settlement according to which the tribunal cannot award damages higher than 7 billion Czech crowns (equivalent to $332 million).

13 *ADC*, paragraphs 480–482.

14 The tribunal noted that this case was "unique" since the value of the investment after the date of expropriation increased very considerably, while usually the value of the investment declined after the interference of the State. The tribunal reasoned that "*to put the Claimants in the same position as if the expropriation had not been committed*" (as required by the *Chorzów Factory* standard), in the present, *sui generis*, type of case the date of valuation should be the date of the Award and not the date of expropriation. In support of this approach, the tribunal referred to the statement of the PCIJ in the *Chorzów Factory* case, according to which damages are "*not necessarily limited to the value of the undertaking at the moment of dispossession.*" (*ADC*, paragraphs 496–497).

15 *EnCana* (claims rejected on the merits), *Thunderbird* (claims rejected on the merits), *Telenor* (claims rejected on the merits), *Salini v. Jordan* (claims rejected on the merits), *Inceysa* (tribunal lacked jurisdiction), on the one hand, and *ADC* and *Azurix*, on the other hand.

16 *Azurix* and *ADC*.

that had been found to have breached its treaty obligations, including the investor's legal costs.

- The *Telenor* tribunal in its decision of 13 September 2006 awarded the burden of the full costs totalling $1.25 million to the unsuccessful claimant, including Hungary's legal costs.
- In *Thunderbird*, a majority of the tribunal required the losing claimant to cover three quarters of the arbitration costs and the legal fees incurred by Mexico in its successful defense.
- In *Azurix*, the tribunal required each party to bear its own legal costs but awarded the burden of all the arbitration costs to be borne by the losing State.

However, in *EnCana v. Ecuador* and *Salini v. Jordan*, the tribunal required each party to bear its own costs (in both cases, the tribunal had rejected the investor's claims).

A new development worth mentioning is the final award rendered on 2 August 2006 in the *Inceysa Vallisoletana S.L. v. Republic of El Salvador* case. The tribunal accepted that El Salvador's consent to ICSID jurisdiction embodied in the Spain–El Salvador BIT did not extend to investments that were made fraudulently, and therefore not in accordance with the law. The tribunal relied both on the express language of the Spain–El Salvador BIT and on references in the *travaux preparatoires* to investments complying with local law as a precondition to benefiting from that treaty's protection. Although prior ICSID decisions (*Tokios Tokeles v. Ukraine* and *Salini Construttori S.p.A. v. Kingdom of Morocco*) had briefly addressed the function of 'accordance with law' clauses in investment treaties, the decision in this case is believed to be the first to apply such clauses for purposes of determining the tribunal's jurisdiction.[17] It is interesting to note that out of the fourteen decisions on jurisdiction rendered in 2006[18] the award in *Inceysa* is only one of two instances in which the

---

17 In a similar vein, in *WDF v. Kenya*, a contract dispute (i.e. not based on an investment treaty), the tribunal acknowledged that international law will not allow either party to enforce a contract obtained through corruption as a matter of public policy. This decision resulted in the country avoiding liability under the contract even though the Head of State was complicit in accepting the bribe.

18 *Suez et al v. Argentina, Continental Casualty v. Argentina, Suez, Vivendi et al v. Argentina, Pan American Energy et al v. Argentina, National Grid v. Argentina, El Paso Energy International v. Argentina, Metalpar et al v. Argentina, Grand River Enterprises Six Nations v. United States, Jan de Nul et al v. Egypt, Canfor Corp v.United States, L.E.S.I. S.p.A. et al v. Algeria, Inceysa v. El Salvador, Telenor v. Hungary,* and *Duke EnergyInternacional Peru Investments No 1 v. Peru.*

tribunal upheld in full the respondent State's objections to jurisdiction dismissing the investor's claims in their entirety.[19]

On Third-Party participation, the trend towards admitting (at least in principle) the submission of *amicus curiae* briefs continued. The tribunal in *Suez & InterAguas v. The Argentine Republic* noted that a tribunal has the power to accept such briefs if certain conditions are present. With regard to oral submissions by third parties (including NGOs), however, the *Suez* tribunal recognized that this is not in a tribunal's discretionary power unless disputants give express permission.

This trend is reflected in the recent changes to ICSID Arbitration Rules, which will apply to ICSID arbitrations in which the date of consent to arbitration is on or after 10 April 2006. Amendments to Rule 37 add, for the first time, procedures and standards by which tribunals shall consider requests from third parties to file *amicus curiae* briefs to address issues that may not adequately be addressed by the parties (e.g. environmental or other public policy issues). Notably, a tribunal can decide to accept the submission of an amicus brief by a third party even if the parties object. The tribunal is, however, required to consult both parties before ruling on the amicus request. In determining whether to accept a third-party submission, the tribunal must consider: (a) whether the non-party has a "significant interest" in the proceeding; (b) whether the submission addresses "*a matter within the scope of the dispute*"; and (c) how the submission would help resolve a legal or factual issue before the tribunal by "*bringing a perspective, particular knowledge or insight*" different from those provided by the parties.

Amendments to Arbitration Rule 32 authorize tribunals to allow third parties to attend or observe oral hearings, but only if none of the parties to the proceedings object. An earlier version of the amendment to Rule 32, which proposed allowing tribunals to open hearings to the public over the parties' objections, was rejected. In addition, the new rule requires tribunals presiding over open proceedings to "*establish procedures for the protection of proprietary or privileged information*".

Noteworthy in this respect is Order n°3 in *Biwater Gauff (Tanzania) Ltd. v. United Republic of Tanzania* rendered on 29 September 2006. This Order represents the first ruling in an ICSID proceeding on public availability of

---

19 The award in *Telenor* also rejected the investor's claim for lack of jurisdiction.

records of hearings, documents produced by the parties, party submissions and correspondence, orders and awards subsequent to the Amendments to ICSID Arbitration Rules. The Tribunal emphasized that in the absence of any agreement between the parties regarding confidentiality, there is no general rule imposing either a general duty of confidentiality or transparency in ICSID arbitration.[20]

In terms of ***review of arbitral awards***, in 2006 two annulment proceedings under ICSID were concluded with at least one application for annulment being successful. In *Patrick Mitchell v. Democratic Republic of the Congo*, the *ad hoc* Committee annulled the 2004 arbitral award in its entirety on the grounds of "manifest excess of powers" and "failure to state reasons" owing to the decision of the original arbitral tribunal to accept its jurisdiction on the basis of the existence of an investment within the meaning of the ICSID Convention.[21] At the time of writing, there are at least five other annulment proceedings still pending before ICSID (*MTD v. Chile*, *Repsol v. Ecuador*; *Soufraki v. UAE*; *Lucchetti v. Peru*; *CMS v. Argentina*).

Furthermore, the last fifteen months have also witnessed a relative increase in the number of domestic court decisions reviewing arbitral awards on the basis of a limited set of grounds under domestic law (usually the law where the arbitration took place or *lex arbitri*). Most of these challenges have been brought by the losing State[22] and none has so far been successful.

* * *

The surge in investment disputes arising from IIAs in and by itself is not necessarily an unhealthy development—after all, it is an expression of the rule of law, and hence an expression of the fact that IIAs "work" towards creating a favorable investment climate in host countries. Obviously, increases in international investment flows lead to more occasions for disputes, and more

---

20 See Biwater, paragraph 121.

21 The other decision was rendered in January 2006 in the annulment proceeding in *Consortium R.F.C.C. v. Kingdom of Morocco*. However, the decision on annulment is not publicly available.

22 The cases brought by States include: *Czech Republic v. Saluka Investments* (Swiss Supreme Court, 17 September 2006); *Republic of Ecuador v. Occidental Export and Petroleum* (London High Court, 2 March 2006; pending before Court of Appeal); *Lebanon v. France Telecom* (Swiss Supreme Court, 10 November 2005); *The Russian Federation v. Sedelmayer* (Svea Court of Appeal, 15 June 2005); *Poland v. Eureko* (Brussels District Court, 24 November 2006). On the other hand, the investor challenged the jurisdiction decision in *Nagel v. Czech Republic* before Swedish courts (Svea Court of Appeal, 30 May 2005).

occasions for disputes combined with more IIAs are likely to lead to more cases. Furthermore, the greater complexity of recent IIAs leads to more regulatory difficulties in their proper implementation.

However, there have been some concerns and implications for developing countries. Their vulnerability is based on their limited technical capacity to handle investment disputes, the potentially high costs involved of conducting such procedures, and the potential impact of awards on the budget and a country's reputation as an investment location. Technical assistance seems required to enable countries to manage effectively and efficiently investor-State disputes as part of an overall endeavor to improve the investment climate and ensure that IIAs contribute to their efforts to attract and benefit from foreign investment for development.

REFERENCES

United Nations Conference on Trade and Development (UNCTAD) (2005a). "Latest developments in investor-State dispute settlement", *IIA Monitor No. 4* (Geneva: United Nations), available at (http://www.unctad.org/en/docs/webiteiit20052_en.pdf).

__________(2005b). *Investor-State Disputes Arising from Investment Treaties: A Review*. UNCTAD Series on International Investment Policies for Development (New York and Geneva: United Nations), United Nations publication, Sales No. E.06.II.D.1.

Annex 1: Known investment treaty claims, by defendants (November 2006)

Defendant	Number of claims
Argentina	42
Mexico	17
Czech Republic	11
United States	11
Moldova, Republic of	9
Russian Federation	9
India	9
Ecuador	8
Egypt	8
Canada	7
Poland	7
Romania	7
Ukraine	6
Chile	4
Congo, Democratic Republic of	4
Kazakhstan	4
Venezuela	4
Estonia	3
Hungary	3
Kyrgyz Republic	3
Pakistan	3
Turkey	3
Algeria	2
Azerbaijan	2
Bangladesh	2
Bolivia	2
Burundi	2
Georgia	2
Jordan	2
Latvia	2
Lebanon	2
Malaysia	2
Morocco	2
Peru	2
Philippines	2
Slovak Republic	2
Slovenia	2
Sri Lanka	2
United Arab Emirates	2
Albania	1
Barbados	1
Bulgaria	1

Defendant	Number of claims
Congo, Republic of	1
Croatia	1
El Salvador	1
France/United Kingdom	1
Germany	1
Ghana	1
Grenada	1
Guyana	1
Indonesia	1
Lithuania	1
Mali	1
Mongolia	1
Myanmar	1
Nicaragua	1
Paraguay	1
Portugal	1
Saudi Arabia	1
Serbia–Montenegro	1
Seychelles	1
Spain	1
Tanzania, United Republic of	1
Thailand	1
Togo	1
Trinidad and Tobago	1
Tunisia	1
Viet Nam	1
Yemen	1
Zimbabwe	1
Unknown	9
Total	**255**

Source: UNCTAD.

Annex 2: List of cases reviewed

ADC Affiliate Limited and ADC & ADMC Management Limited v. Republic of Hungary, ICSID Case No. ARB/03/16, Award, 2 October 2006.

Azurix Corp. v. Argentine Republic, ICSID Case No. ARB/01/12, Award, 14 July 2006.

Berschader & Berschader v. The Russian Federation (Arbitration Institute of the Stockholm Chamber of Commerce).

Biwater Gauff (Tanzania) Ltd. v. United Republic of Tanzania, ICSID Case No. ARB/05/22, Procedural Order No. 1, 31 March 2006; Procedural Order No. 3, 29 September 2006.

Canfor Corp. v. United States of America, UNICITRAL, Decision on Preliminary Question, 6 June 2006.

CMS Gas Transmission Company v. Argentine Republic, ICSID Case No. ARB/01/8, Decision on Jurisdiction, 17 July 2003; Award, 12 May 2005.

Consortium R.F.C.C. v. Kingdom of Morocco, ICSID Case No. ARB/00/6, Decision on Annulment, 18 January 2006 (not public).

Continental Casualty Company v. Argentina, ICSID Case No. ARB/03/9, Decision on Jurisdiction, 22 February 2006.

Duke Energy International Peru Investments No. 1, Ltd. v. Peru, ICSID Case No. ARB/03/28; Decision on Jurisdiction, 1 February 2006.

El Paso Energy International Company v. The Argentine Republic, ICSID Case No. ARB/03/15, Decision on Jurisdiction, 27 April 2006.

Emilio Agustin Maffezini v. The Kingdom of Spain, ICSID Case No. ARB/97/7, Decision on Jurisdiction, 25 January 2000; Award, 13 November 2000; Rectification of Award, 31 January 2001.

EnCana Corporation v. Republic of Ecuador, LCIA Case No. UN3481, UNCITRAL, Award, 3 February 2006.

Grand River Enterprises Six Nations, Ltd., v. United States, UNCITRAL, Decision on Objections to Jurisdiction, 20 July 2006.

Inceysa Vallisoletana S.L. v. Republic of El Salvador, ICSID Case No. ARB/03/26, Award, 2 August 2006.

International Thunderbird Gaming Corp. v. The United Mexican States, UNCITRAL, Award, 26 January 2006.

Jan de Nul N.V. and Dredging International N.V. v. Arab Republic of Egypt, ICSID Case No. ARB/04/13, Decision on Jurisdiction, 16 June 2006.

LESI, S.p.A. and Astaldi, S.p.A. v. People's Democratic Republic of Algeria, ICSID Case No. ARB/05/3, Decision on Jurisdiction, 12 July 2006.

LG&E Energy Corp., LG&E Capital Corp. and LG&E International Inc. v. Argentine Republic, ICSID Case No. ARB/02/1, Decision of the Arbitral Tribunal on Objections to Jurisdiction, 30 April 2004, Decision on Liability, 3 October 2006.

Marvin Roy Feldman v. The United Mexican States, ICSID Case No. ARB(AF)/99/1, Award on Merits, 16 December 2002.

Metalpar S.A. and Buen Aire S.A. v. Argentine Republic, ICSID Case No. ARB/03/5, Decision on Jurisdiction, 27 April 2006.

National Grid plc v The Argentine Republic, UNCITRAL, Decision on Jurisdiction, 20 June 2006.

Pan American Energy LLC and BP Argentina Exploration Company v. Argentine Republic, ICSID Case No. ARB/03/13 and *BP America Production Co. and Others v. Argentine Republic,* ICSID Case No. ARB/04/8. Decision on Preliminary Objections, 27 July 2006.

Patrick Mitchell v. Democratic Republic of the Congo, ICSID Case No. ARB/99/7, Decision on Annulment, 1 November 2006.

Plama Consortium Limited v. Republic of Bulgaria, ICSID Case No. ARB/03/24, Decision on Jurisdiction, 8 February 2005.

S.D. Myers, Inc. v. Canada, UNCITRAL, First Partial Award, 13 November 2000.

Salini Construtorri S.p.A. and Italstrade S.p.A. v. Morocco, ICSID Case No. ARB/00/4, Decision on Jurisdiction, 23 July 2001.

Salini Costruttori S.p.A. and Italstrade S.p.A. v. Jordan, ICSID Case No. ARB/02/13, Decision on Jurisdiction, 9 November 2004.

Saluka Investments BV v. The Czech Republic, Swiss Federal Tribunal Decision, 7 September 2006.

SGS Société Générale de Surveillance S.A. v. Islamic Republic of Pakistan, ICSID Case No. ARB/01/13, Decision on Jurisdiction, 6 August 2003.

Suez, Sociedad General de Aguas de Barcelona S.A. and Interagua Servicios Integrales de Agua S.A. v. Argentine Republic, ICSID Case No. ARB/03/17, Decision on Jurisdiction, 16 May 2006.

Tecnicas Medioambientales Tecmed S.A. v. United Mexican States, ICSID Case No. ARB(AF)/00/2, Award, 29 May 2003.

Telenor Mobile Communications AS v. Republic of Hungary, ICSID Case No. ARB/04/15 Award, 13 September 2006.

Tokios Tokelės v. Ukraine ICSID Case No. ARB/02/18, Decision on Jurisdiction, 29 April 2004; Dissenting Opinion, 29 April 2004, Procedural Order No. 3, 18 January 2005

APPENDIX 8

Novel Features In OECD Countries' Recent Investment Agreements: An Overview*

Introduction:

This research report from the OECD, written by Marie-France Houde at the Organisation for Economic Co-operation and Development, addresses new features in international investment agreements, comparing several of the most prominent bilateral and model treaties. It is forward-looking, considering what might and might not be most prominent in future treaties. The charts at the back of the article are particularly useful for comparing treaties.

* Reprinted with approval of OECD, from the public domain. *See* the OECD website at www.oecd.org for more information and publications.

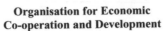

International Centre for
Settlement of Investment Disputes

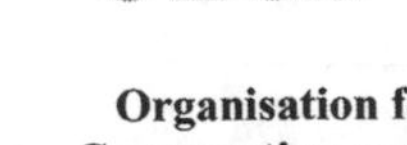

Organisation for Economic
Co-operation and Development

UNITED NATIONS
CONFERENCE
ON TRADE AND
DEVELOPMENT

SYMPOSIUM CO-ORGANISED BY ICSID, OECD AND UNCTAD

MAKING THE MOST OF INTERNATIONAL INVESTMENT AGREEMENTS: A COMMON AGENDA

12 December 2005, Paris Room 1, OECD Headquarters, Paris

NOVEL FEATURES IN OECD COUNTRIES' RECENT INVESTMENT AGREEMENTS: AN OVERVIEW

This document by the OECD Secretariat has been reviewed and approved for derestriction by the OECD Investment Committee as background information for the Symposium.

Contact: OECD Investment Division: marie-france.houde@oecd.org; ayse.bertrand@oecd.org (FDI statistics).

Novel Features in OECD Countries' Recent Investment Agreements: An Overview[1]

I. Introduction

1. As major actors in the globalisation process, OECD countries have, as of July 2005, entered into 1,240 bilateral investment treaties (BIT) and 36 trade agreements with investment content (TAs) [hereafter referred to as international investment agreements (IIAs)] with some 140 non-Member countries. OECD IIAs account for over half of the agreements in existence. But how much foreign direct investment is actually protected by these agreements? And what are their most novel features?

2. This Note presents an overview of developments that have occurred during the last decade, and more particularly since 2000. Section II provides an assessment of how much investment is currently being covered by OECD IIAs as well as how much more investment is expected to be covered by agreements under negotiation or awaiting ratification (see also Annex 1). Section III highlights the most interesting trends in the main investment provisions found in a representative sample of IIAs. Annex 2 provides synoptic tables of their main features.

II. How much FDI is covered by OECD investment agreements?

3. *The amount of FDI covered by OECD IIAs is significant.* It is estimated that at the present time, OECD IIAs cover 18% and 14% of total OECD countries' outward and inward foreign direct investments (FDI) stocks, respectively. These seemingly modest percentages need to be seen, however, against the fact that a large proportion of OECD FDI inflows from and outflows to the world take place between OECD countries in the absence of investment agreements between them. At the same time, around 60% of the total FDI stock invested by OECD countries into the non OECD countries are covered by the OECD countries' IIAs with these countries (according to 2002–2003 estimates). There are also important differences between countries and agreements, particularly when forthcoming new TAs are accounted for.

---

1 The present note covers bilateral investment treaties and bilateral and regional trade agreements with investment content concluded by OECD countries. It does not cover the investment provisions of the Treaty on European Union.

4. *A new dynamic in favour of trade agreements with investment content is emerging.* While BITs dominate the OECD IIA landscape in quantitative terms, TAs are rising in importance both in terms of numbers and volume of investment (Figure 1 and Annex 1). Only 10 new BITs have been contracted by OECD countries this year as compared to 107 BITs in the peak year of 1996. There are, however, 36 OECD TAs in place and 40 new TAs under consideration.

5. *European countries account for the largest number of BITs.* While European countries are responsible for the largest number of BITs, in many cases they cover less than 10% of their outward investment. But there are exceptions. Poland, Turkey, Hungary, Greece and the Slovak Republic on the other hand, direct a larger share of their investments outside the EU area and show a higher treaty coverage of their investment abroad—88%, 66%, 64%, 49% and 48%, respectively. In Asia, Korea, whose BIT tradition goes back to 1967, also has a relatively high level of BIT protection—53.5%. Japan, on the other hand, which very recently embarked on this process, records a comparatively lower percentage—8%.

6. *Non-European countries are increasingly turning to TAs.* Mexico, the United States, Australia and Canada account for 90% in the increase of the number of OECD TAs. These agreements also constitute the main source of outward investment protection—namely 60% of outward

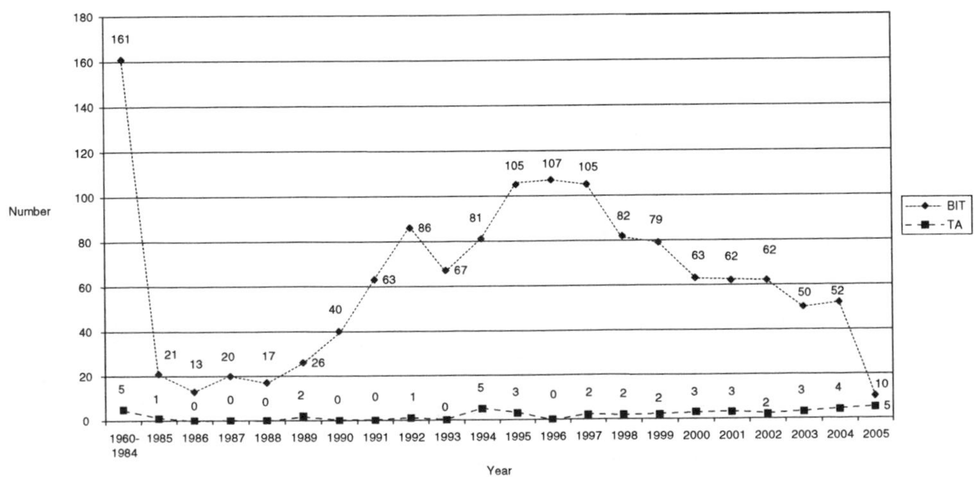

Figure 1 BITs and TAs newly contracted by OECD countries (as of July 2005)

investment in Australia, 44% in Canada and 20% in the United States (as compared with less than 5% in the case of BITs)—and more is in the making. New TAs could potentially increase the treaty coverage of the United States up to 24%, of Australia to around 61% and of Canada to 51%. New Zealand and Japan provide typical examples of the shift in favour of trade agreements from BITs. The proportion of outward investment to be captured by future New Zealand FTAs is to rise from 1.5 % to 61%. and new Japanese TAs from 3.8% to 12%.

7. *OECD countries are providing protection to a growing share of inward investment.* OECD agreements are not a one-way street. Apart from the new EU member states, BITs cover a very limited share of inward investment into Europe. At the same time, in respect of the direct investment received Mexico (86%), Norway (79%), Iceland (71%), Korea (65%), Canada (64%) and Hungary (60%) are committed to upholding treaty standards. The highest level is recorded by Poland's BITs however (94%). Future TAs are also expected to be the source of incremental treaty coverage, notably in New Zealand (by 46%), Australia (by 9%), Korea (by 5%) and Japan (by 4%).

III. What are the main novel features of recent OECD IIAs

8. *The pursuit of high standards.* The pursuit of high standards in investment policy has historically been a major driving force behind OECD investment agreements. Never before, however, has this quest been so far reaching than that of the OECD agreements negotiated in recent years. This can be assessed by the gradual broadening, deepening and clarification of the scope of application of the substantive and procedural provisions of the agreements, the increased attention paid to regulatory transparency, investment promotion and investment facilitation, and the inclusion of new liberalisation commitments. While this movement has largely been led by TAs, such as United States Free Trade Agreements (FTAs), Japan's "New Age" Economic Partnership Agreements (EPAs), Australia's FTAs and Chile–Korea FTA, it has also spread to path-breaking new BITs (Japan–Korea and Germany–China in the OECD survey's sample).

9. *High standards are spreading worldwide.* Developing countries are the main partners of OECD agreements. While diversity can be observed between agreements reflecting different country situations, developing

countries' growing acceptance of OECD standards is contributing to the propagation of these high standards worldwide and is reflected in agreements concluded among non-OECD countries. This trend is also contributing to the improvement of countries' domestic investment policies as well as their investment policy capacity.

10. *More public interest safeguards have been introduced.* An increasing number of agreements refer to the role of governments to pursue other policy goals. Specific provisions have been incorporated, in particular, that address governments' regulation to pursue certain objectives such as health, safety, the environment and internationally recognized labour standards. This is the case, for example, with respect to recent TAs negotiated by Canada and the United States and BITs recently negotiated by Belgium–Luxembourg. Often these agreements also recognize that it is inappropriate to encourage investment by weakening or reducing the protections afforded in domestic environmental or labour laws (US and Canadian TAs and preambles of Japan–Korea and Japan–Vietnam BITs).

11. There is also an increased recourse to various sorts of general exceptions pertaining to taxation, essential security, the protection of human, animal or plant life or health, the conservation of exhaustible natural resources, prudential measures for the financial sector and culture (European BITs, Canadian Model BIT, and US Model BIT as regards essential security…). Although not a generalized practice, greater use is also being made of safeguards affecting transfer obligations to deal with serious short-term balance of payments difficulties (French BIT Model, Mexico FTAs, Japan–Korea BIT and Japan–Singapore EPA).

12. *From the traditional focus of investment protection towards the inclusion of more extensive liberalisation disciplines.* The rise in recent IIAs standards can largely be attributed to the guarantees provided by recent TAs (and replicated in some BITs—Japan–Korea and Japan–Vietnam and US–Uruguay BIT) in the pre-establishment phase, as well to new liberalisation commitments such as in the agreements signed by the United States with the Dominican Republic and Central America (DR-CAFTA), the Singapore–Australia Free Trade Agreement (SAFTA) and the Australia–United States Free Trade Agreement (AUSFTA). In general, the guarantees apply to national treatment and MFN treatment and to other core provisions (key personnel and performance requirements) but there are exceptions (SAFTA, for example, does not contain an MFN treatment

obligation and the obligations on pre-establishment are less demanding than on post-establishment).

13. Increased liberalisation is also promoted by the wider use of the negative list approach and the increased application of the standstill principle and ratchet effect to country exceptions—which facilitates broader coverage, progressiveness and transparency to liberalisation. Practically all IIAs contain provisions on key personnel while the prohibition of certain performance requirements appears to be less frequent (mainly limited to the US, Canada or Japan IIAs). Interestingly enough, a relatively large number of BITs covering the post-establishment phase contain regional or economic integration clauses (notably all European BITs) while none of the TAs reviewed contain such clauses.

14. *New attempts have been made to provide greater precision to the asset-based definition of "investment".* The broad asset-based definition of investment has now become the norm in recent IIAs. Because of its far reaching implications, however, there has been a move away from a totally open-ended definition so as not to cover operations which are not deemed to be "real" investments. Different approaches have emerged. The new US Model has adopted a circular definition which defines "investment" as those assets that have the characteristics of an investment (US–Chile FTA, AUSFTA...). At the other end, the 2004 Canada Model defines "investment" in terms of a finite list of categories of assets. Other BITs (such as the 2000 Mexico–Greece BIT) define investment as assets used for economic purposes.

15. *Key investment protection provisions have also been redefined.* The new Canadian and US Model BITs and recent TAs now define the protection accorded under the "fair and equitable standard" (and "full protection and security") as not going beyond the minimum standard of treatment to aliens in accordance to customary international law. This clarification has been incorporated into some other FTAs (US–Singapore FTA, Mexico–Japan TA, DR-CAFTA) but not in others. Some other IIAs also link the standard with international law. But the fair and equitable standard is not included in all agreements. It has been included in AUSFTA and Thailand–Australia Free Trade Agreement (TAFTA) but not in SAFTA.

16. *New language has been added to guide the application of the expropriation articles.* Virtually all new OECD IIAs contain clauses describing the

conditions under which a lawful expropriation may be made and a standard for compensation of the expropriated property. There is a debate, however, on what degree of interference with property rights is required for a government action or a series of government actions to constitute an "indirect", "creeping" or "de facto" expropriation. Recent Annexes in FTAs negotiated by the US, Singapore, Chile and Australia or those found in the new Canadian and US Model BITs identify criteria on how to distinguish between compensable and non-compensable regulatory actions on a case-by-case basis. The inclusion of interpretative notes and clarifications is concomitant to the growing body of experience with investor/state arbitration (see below).

17. *A more widely shared recognition of the values of transparency.* Until recently, transparency was limited to the exchange of information between States. More recent IIAs, notably those listing liberalisation commitments, also include obligations on the publication of laws and decisions respecting investment. They may, in addition, contain provisions to enhance the transparency of the regulatory process and provide a reasonable opportunity to interested investors to be consulted on proposed regulatory changes and to obtain from contacts points information on matters covered by the agreement (2004 Canada and US Model BITs). These latter obligations are typically not subject to investor-state dispute settlement however.

18. *Investment promotion and facilitation is becoming an important dimension of investment agreements.* An increasing larger number of agreements, notably European agreements and Japanese EPAs, provide for identification of investment opportunities and exchange of information, the establishment of mechanisms for the encouragement and promotion of investment and work towards harmonized and simplified administrative procedures.

19. *Investor-state dispute settlement (ISDS) is becoming more widely accepted.* Most recent OECD IIAs concluded with developing countries provide for "prior consent" without "prior exhaustion of local remedies" or establishing a "fork on the road" foreclosing recourse to international arbitration. Furthermore, fewer exceptions are also applied to the ISDS coverage. This can represent a major shift of policy (as in the case of China in the Germany–China BIT). The Australia–US Free Trade Agreement, on the other hand, which is the second TA after the Canada–US FTA (1988)

with substantive provisions on investment to have ever been concluded between two developed countries, contains no ISDS provisions.

20. The cumulative number of known treaty-based cases brought before ICSID or other arbitration facilities under IIAs in the last ten years was estimated at approximately 174 at the end of June 2005 as compared to two at the end of 1994. Well over half of the known claims were filed within the past there years. Almost all of them were initiated by investors. Some claims have involved large sums and the arbitration proceedings costs are usually very high.

21. *Innovations have also been brought to the arbitration process.* Three new trends are also emerging in the new generation of BITs and some other investment chapters of TAs (US–Singapore, US–Chile FTAs, US and Canada Model BITs). First, there is concern for greater predictability and control over the arbitration process by means of more detailed guidance on arbitral proceedings and binding interpretations on tribunals. Recent US agreements foresee, in addition, the possibility of creating an appeal mechanism. Second, judicial economy is encouraged by special provisions dealing with frivolous claims, multiple or parallel proceedings or consolidation of claims. Third, increased attention is being given to allowing civil society scrutiny through increased transparency of arbitral proceedings and awards, and the institutionalisation of the possibility of non-disputing parties to make their views known through "amicus curiae".

Annex 1

Table 1. Coverage of OECD Outward and Inward Investment by IIAs 1)

Country	*Number of agreements*						*Outward FDI positions covered by BITs and TAs 2) (as % of total outward FDI positions)*						*Inward FDI positions covered by BITs and TAs 2) (as % of total inward FDI positions)*					
	existing agreements			*future agreements 3)*			*existing agreements*			*future agreements 3)*			*existing agreements*			*future agreements 3)*		
	BITs	*TAs*	*Total*	*BITs*	*TAs*	*Total*	*BITs*	*TAs*	*Total*	*BITs*	*TAs*	*Total*	*BITs*	*TAs*	*Total*	*BITs*	*TAs*	*Total*
Australia	19	4	23	6	4	10	2.6	60.1	62.7	-	1.1	1.1	1.3	32.3	33.6	-	8.8	8.8
Austria	55	-	55	2	-	2	37.2	-	37.2	-	-	-	3.8	-	3.8	-	-	-
BELU	57	-	57	63	-	63	4.2	-	4.2	0.3	-	0.3	2.0	-	2.0	0.1	-	0.1
Canada	22	4	26	5	9	14	4.1	43.5	47.6	0.2	7.5	7.7	-	63.9	63.9	0.2	3.1	3.3
Czech Republic	72	-	72	12	-	12	5.6	-	5.6	-	-	-	8.9	-	8.9	-	-	-
Denmark	43	-	43	7	-	7	10.6	-	10.6	1.1	-	1.1	1.1	-	1.1	-	-	-
Finland	50	-	50	5	-	5	5.6	-	5.6	0.3	-	0.3	1.1	-	1.1	-	-	-
France	84	-	84	12	-	12	6.1	-	6.1	1.1	-	1.1	0.9	-	0.9	0.03	-	0.03
Germany	115	-	115	21	-	21	12.4	-	12.4	0.9	-	0.9	1.0	-	1.0	0.1	-	0.1
Greece	33	-	33	14	-	14	49.3	-	49.3	0.1	-	0.1	10.4	-	10.4	0.03	-	0.03
Hungary	52	-	52	6	-	6	64.2	-	64.2	0.04	-	0.04	60.2	-	60.2	0.01	-	0.01
Iceland	2	2	4	0	1	1	0.6	79.4	80.0	-	-	-	0.8	70.7	71.5	-	-	-
Ireland	1	-	1	0	-	0	-	-	-	-	-	-	-	-	-	-	-	-
Italy	70	-	70	21	-	21	5.5	-	5.5	1.3	-	1.3	0.9	-	0.9	0.1	-	0.1
Japan	11	2	13	0	14	14	7.8	3.8	11.6	-	12.3	12.3	2.4	1.2	3.6	-	3.8	3.8
Korea	55	1	56	9	7	16	53.5	0.1	53.6	0.9	2.4	3.3	64.4	-	64.4	0.02	4.9	4.9
Mexico	17	12	29	1	1	2	n.a.	n.a.	n.a.	n.a.	n.a.	n.a.	18.6	67.7	86.3	0.03	3.5	3.6
Netherlands	79	-	79	12	-	12	8.9	-	8.9	1.7	-	1.7	0.6	-	0.6	0.1	-	0.1

New Zealand	2	1	3	1	7	8	0.3	1.5	1.8	-	60.6	60.6	1.2	2.1	3.3	-	45.6	45.6
Norway	16	2	18	0	-	0	2.0	70.4	72.4	-	-	-	-	78.5	78.5	-	-	-
Poland	56	-	56	5	-	5	87.7	-	87.7	1.5	-	1.5	94.4	-	94.4	2.5	-	2.5
Portugal	35	-	35	8	-	8	3.9	-	3.9	27.1	-	27.1	7.3	-	7.3	1.7	-	1.7
Slovak	37	-	37	3	-	3	48.4	-	48.4	-	-	-	91.5	-	91.5	-	-	-
Spain	47	-	47	23	-	23	24.8	-	24.8	1.4	-	1.4	1.5	-	1.5	0.1	-	0.1
Sweden	54	-	54	2	-	2	6.2	-	6.2	-	-	-	0.04	-	0.04	-	-	-
Switzerland	102	2	104	5	1	6	8.3	43.6	51.9	0.9	1.9	2.8	-	56.5	56.5	-	0.6	0.6
Turkey	54	7	61	17	12	29	66.2	3.7	69.9	0.2	-	0.2	82.3	3.6	85.9	0.01	-	0.01
United Kingdom	93	-	93	7	-	7	6.9	-	6.9	0.7	-	0.7	1.6	-	1.6	0.01	-	0.01
United States	39	6	45	8	8	16	1.3	20.6	21.9	0.1	3.1	3.2	-	10.2	10.2	-	0.4	0.4
Gross Total (4)	1372	43	1415	275	64	339												
Net Total (5)	1240	36	1276	273	40	313												

1) The number of BITs and TAs are based on available information as July 2005.
2) Stock positions are based on OECD data available for the most recent year available, 2002 or 2003. Data for BELU, Mexico (inward), Spain, Norway (Outward) and Korea (Inward) accumulated FDI flows
3) "Signed" but not "ratified" or under "negotiation" or "scheduled or envisaged".
4) Gross total: BITs between OECD countries are counted twice and TAs are counted according to the number of parties involved.
5) Net total: BITs and TAs between OECD countries are counted only once to avoid double counting.

Source: OECD Investment Division, International Direct Investment database

Annex 2
Summary Tables of Substantive and Dispute Investor-to State Provisions in IIAs (Sample)*

* *Among the criteria used for the selection of the sample were the following: the date of the agreements (concluded after 2000), the relative importance of the partner countries (as host or home country of investment), including their regional or cross continental dimension; differences between the levels of development of the contracting parties; the 2005 German Model BIT has been examined because Germany was the first country to enter into such agreements and has today the largest number of BITs; a special attempt has been made to include major players in non-Member countries, such as Singapore, India and China.*

Table 1. Substantive provisions in recent BITs

	Definitions/Scope/Coverage					*Admission*			*Post Admission*			*Investment Protection*			
	Asset based		*Investment*											*Expropriation*	
	Open list	*Closed list*	*Direct*	*Indirect*	*Umbrella clause*	*NT*	*MFN*	*Perfor-mance require-ments*	*NT*	*MFN*	*Perfor-mance require-ments*	*Standard of treat-ment*	*Transfers*	*Direct*	*Indirect*
German Model	+				+				+	+		+	+	+	+
French Model	+		+	+					+	+		+	+	+	+
Belgium-Luxembourg Model	+		+	+	+				+	+		+	+	+	+
Canadian Model		+	+	+		+	+	+	+	+	+	+	+	+	+
US Model	+		+	+		+	+	+	+	+	+	+	+	+	+
Germany-China BIT	+		+	+	+				+	+		+	+	+	+
Germany-India BIT	+				+				+	+		+	+	+	+
Japan-Korea BIT	+		+	+		+	+	+	+	+	+	+	+	+	+
Mexico-Korea BIT	+								+	+		+	+	+	+

	Key personnel	*Transparency*	*Exceptions*					*Financial Services*	*Taxation*	*Environment*	*Labour*	*Investment facilitation*	*CR*
			EIA[1]	*General Exceptions*	*Security Interests*	*Prudential measures*	*Country exceptions*						
German Model	+		+						+				
French Model	+		+			2			+				
Belgium-Luxembourg Model	+		+		+				+	+	+		
Canadian Model	+	+		+	+	+	+	+	+	+			
US Model	+	+			+	+	+	+	+	+	+		
Germany-China BIT	+		+						+				
Germany-India BIT	+		+	+	+				+				
Japan-Korea BIT	+	+	+	+	+	+[3]	+		+	+			
Mexico-Korea BIT			+			4			+				

Notes:
1) Economic Integration Agreements (i.e. membership or association with a custom or economic union, a common market or a free trade area).
2) Article on BOP (Balance of Payment) safeguards.
3) The same Article also includes a BOP Clause.
4) BOP Clause provided in the Protocol.
Source: OECD Investment Division.

Table 2. Substantive provisions in investment chapters of recent TAs

	Definitions/Scope/Coverage				*Umbrella clause*	*Admission*			*Post Admission*			*Investment Protection*			
	Asset based		*Investment*											*Expropriation*	
	Open list	*Closed list*	*Direct*	*Indirect*		*NT*	*MFN*	*Performance requirements*	*NT*	*MFN*	*Performance requirements*	*Standard of treatment*	*Transfers*	*Direct*	*Indirect*
SAFTA	+		+	+		+			+	+			+	+	+
AUSFTA	+		+	+		+	+	+	+	+	+	+	+	+	+
TAFTA	+		+			+			+	+		+	+	+	+
US-Singapore FTA	+		+	+		+	+	+	+	+	+	+	+	+	+
JSEPA	+		+	+		+		+	+		+	+	+	+	+
Japan-Mexico EPA		+	+	+		+	+	+	+	+	+	+	+	+	+
US-DR-CAFTA	+		+	+		+	+	+	+	+	+	+	+	+	+
Chile-US FTA	+		+	+		+	+	+	+	+	+	+	+	+	+
Chile-Korea FTA	+		+	+		+		+	+	+	+	+	+	+	+

	Key personnel	*Transparency*	*Exceptions*					*Financial Services*	*Taxation*	*Environment*	*Labour*	*Investment facilitation*	*CR*
			EIA	*General Exceptions*	*Security Interests*	*Prudential measures*	*Country exceptions*						
SAFTA		+		+	+	+	+						
AUSFTA	+				±	±	+	±	±	+	±		
TAFTA						1							
US-Singapore FTA	+				±	±	+	=	±	+	±		
JSEPA				+		+2	+		3				
Japan-Mexico EPA	+					+4	–			+			
US-DR-CAFTA	+				±	±	+	±	±	+	±		
Chile-US FTA	+				±	±	+	±	±	+	±		
Chile-Korea FTA	+					+	+			+			

Note:
1) A BOP clause is contained in Chapter 16 as an exception to Chapter 8 (Trade in services) and Chapter 9 (Investment).
2) Separate BOP clause also included.
3) Article 87 on Taxation Measures as Expropriation.
4) BOP clause included.
± These provisions are located in other chapters, but apply or relate to investment.
Source: OECD Investment Division

Table 3A. Dispute Settlement in recent BITs

	State/ State	*Investor/ State*						
			Claims by an investor of a Party on its own behalf and on behalf of an Enterprise	*Prior Consent*	*Waivers of initiating/ continuing a proceeding before local courts/ Non-Exhaustion of local remedies*	*Participation by the non-disputing Party*	*Transparency (access to filing, minutes, transcriptions and decisions)*	*Open hearings*
German Model	+	+						
French Model	+	+						
Belgium–Luxembourg Model	+	+		+	+ (Non-Exhaustion of host state remedies)			
Canadian Model	+	+	+	+	+	+	+	+
US Model	+	+	+	+	+	+	+	+
Germany–China BIT	+	+						
Germany–India BIT	+	+						
Japan–Korea BIT	+	+		+				
Mexico–Korea BIT	+	+	+	+	+			

Specific Investosr/State provisions								
Protection of sensitive information	***Amicus curiae submissions***	***Monetary awards and No punitive damages***	***Comment period before effectiveness of awards/delay of enforcement***	***Enforcement***	***Interim measures***	***Express***	***Consolidation***	***Applicable law***
				+				
				+				
+	+	+	+ (delay of enforcement)	+	+	+	+	+
+	+	+	+ (delay of enforcement)	+	+	+	+	+
				+				
				+				
				+				
		+	+ (delay of enforcement)	+			+	+

Table 3B. Dispute Settlement in recent TAs

	State/ State	*Investor/ State*	*Claims by an investor of a Party on its own behalf and on behalf of an Enterprise*	*Prior Consent*	*Waivers of initiating/ continuing a proceed-ing before local courts/ Non-Exhaustion of local remedies*	*Participation by the non-disputing Party*	*Transparency (access to filing, minutes, transcriptions and decisions)*	*Open hearings*
SAFTA	+	+		+	+			
AUSFTA	+							
TAFTA	+	+						
US–Singapore FTA	+	+	+	+	+	+	+	+
JSEPA	+	+		+				
Japan–Mexico EPA	+	+	+	+	+	+	+	
US–DR–CAFTA	+	+	+	+	+	+	+	+
Chile–US FTA	+	+	+	+	+	+	+	+
Chile–Korea FTA	+	+	+	+	+			

Source: OECD Investment Division

	Specific Investosr/State provisions								
	Protection of sensitive information	***Amicus curiae submissions***	***Monetary awards and no punitive damages***	***Comment period before effectiveness of awards/delay of enforcement***	***Enforcement***	***Interim measures***	***Express***	***Consolidation***	***Applicable law***
						+			
									+
	+	+	+	+ (delay of enforcement)	+	+	+	+	+
			+ (only reference to monetary awards)		+				
	+		+		+	+	+	+	+
	+	+	+	+ (delay of enforcement)	+	+	+	+	+
	+	+	+	+ (delay of enforcement)	+	+	+	+	+
			+	+ (delay of enforcement)	+	+	+	+	+

Index

Note to Index: An *f* following a page number indicates a figure on that page; an *n* after a page number indicates a note on that page; a *t* following a page number indicates a table on that page.

A

AAPL v. Sri Lanka, 39–40, 52, 57n65

Abs-Shawcross draft, 91

accountability, 214

ADC Affiliate Limited and ADC & ADMC Management Limited v. Republic of Hungary, 397

Additional Annulment Facility, 226

ADF Group v. U.S., 65–66, 65n86, 67

ad hoc arbitration, 109, 168, 214

advisory appropriate dispute resolution, 183–185

AES Summit Generation v. Hungary, 167

Aguas del Trigas, 57–58

Aguas del Tunari v. Bolivia, 53n52, 54n57, 74n110, 190

Alabama Claims case, 152

Albania, 262n34

Algeria, 86–87

- *Dipenta v. Algeria*, 94, 95, 96, 97, 101

amicus curiae briefs, 218–219, 275, 284

Angola–U.K. BIT, 234, 235

annulment, 41, 77–78, 224, 247, 258

- costs of procedures, 351, 386
- ICSID, 31–32, 134–135, 257, 259, 260, 262, 274, 285, 402
- ICSID Appeals Facility rules, 334, 335-336, 337
- in ICSID treaty articles, 302-303, 304-305, 306, 307, 309-310, 311

anomie, 43n16

APEC, 25

appellate body, developing country view of

- basis for call for appellate process, 268-273
- choice of appellate process, 273
- current perspective on, 276-277
- and ICSID Appeals Facility, 274-275
- implications of, 267-278
- *see also* appellate review mechanisms

appellate review mechanisms, 231-239, 284-285, 301-314

- Canada-U.S. FTA, 197
- disadvantages of, 238
- DR-CAFTA, 302-303
- lack of options for, 234-239
- lack of options for, structural reasons, 234-236
- need not yet established for, 236-238
- options to establish, 231-234
- Panama-U.S. FTA, 312-313
- U.S. Model BIT, 316-317
- U.S.-Chile FTA, 271, 304-305

appellate review mechanisms (continued)
- U.S.–Colombia FTA, 310–311
- U.S.–Morocco FTA, 305–306
- U.S.–Oman FTA, 309–310
- U.S.–Peru FTA, 313–314
- U.S.–Singapore FTA, 71–72, 76–77, 202, 306–308
- U.S.–Uruguay BIT, 314–316

appropriate dispute resolution (ADR), 158–191
- advisory, challenges related to, 184–185
- advisory, opportunities for, 183–184
- advisory ADR, 183–185
- arbitrator neutrality, 187
- challenges for future, 191–192
- conciliation, 174–177
- conciliation *vs.* mediation, 171–174, 171n108
- confidentiality issues, 188–188
- direct negotiation benefits, 167–168
- discretion issues, 189–190
- facilitated, challenges for, 177–179
- facilitated ADR, 171–179
- fact-finding, benefits of, 180–182
- fact-finding, challenges of using, 182–183
- fact-finding ADR, 179–183
- "good offices," 161
- imposed, benefits of, 185–186
- imposed, costs of, 186
- imposed ADR, 185–186
- indirect negotiation, utility of, 166–167
- lost time and money, 186–187
- negotiated, challenges for, 168–171
- negotiated ADR, 165–170
- negotiated rulemaking, 160
- ombudspersons, 161–164
- party control over outcome, 187–188
- preventative, challenges with, 164–165
- preventative ADR, 160–165

"arbitration addition," 150

arbitration, investment treaty. *See* expansionary trends, in investment treaty arbitration; foreign investment arbitration, expansionary trends in; preliminary rulings, in investment arbitration; treaty-based investment dispute settlement, reasons for increase in

Argentina, 41n8, 55, 55n59, 73, 76n113, 396, 396n4, 400
- claims against, 113, 381–382, 394, 395
- financial crisis, 75, 122
- increase in number of investment treaties, 46
- legitimacy issues, 42
- umbrella clauses, 397–398
- U.S.–Argentina BIT, 398

Asian financial crisis, 75, 122

Australia–U.S. FTA, 41, 41n7, 77, 154n47

awards
- and annulment (*see* annulment)
- appeals procedures for, 26
- changes in interpretation of, 384
- increase in sums, 384–385

Azerbaijan, 394

Azinian v. Mexico, 59n71

Azurix Corp. v. Argentine Republic, 396, 396n4, 397, 398, 400

B

Bahrain, 249

Barcelona Traction, Light and Power Company, Limited, 105–106, 133

Basel Convention on the Transport of Hazardoub Wastes, 50, 63

Beecher, Henry Ward, 143

Berschader & Berschader v. The Russian Federation, 395

bilateral investment treaties (BITs), 7, 9*f*, 10–11, 18–21, 149

- Annex A, international customary law, 89
- arbitral tribunals, consistency of outcomes, 93–97
- Article 4, 89–90
- Article 5, 89
- awards, continuing conflict in, 97–100
- Canadian model, 41, 43, 101
- consistency of tribunal outcomes, 93–97
- dispute settlement in recent, 426*t*–427*t*
- dispute settlement mechanism diversification, 20–21
- fair and equitable treatment clause, 20, 88–89, 138
- general consensus lack, 86–88
- general model, 91–92
- German model, 153–154
- as imbalanced instruments, 82–84
- inconsistency, 100–103
- inconsistency, as caused by arbitral tribunals, 100–103
- inconsistency, in interpretation, 90–93
- inconsistency, in treaties/proceedings/awards, 127–136
- and litigation increase, 20
- as missing object and purpose, 84–86
- most-favored-nation clauses, 20
- as not harmonization instrument, 88–90
- proliferation, 19, 47, 86, 107, 112, 127, 137–138
- pros/cons of, 81–90
- Sornarajah on, 81–82
- South-South, 19, 86, 139, 252
- and sovereignty, 19–20, 83
- substantive provisions in recent, 422*t*–423*t*
- Swiss model, 91
- umbrella clause, 59–61, 91, 92, 98–100, 248, 383–384, 397–398
- unratified, 44n20, 47
- U.S. model, 43, 44n14
- U.S. model, 2004, 83, 88, 89, 97
- U.S. *vs.* European model, 92
- U.S. *vs.* French model, 88–89, 92–93
- variations in seemingly identical provisions, 103
- Bipartisan Trade Promotion Authority Act of 2002 (TPA Act), 202, 232

Biwater Gauff (Tanzania) Ltd. v. United Republic of Tanzania

Bolivia, 54n57, 190

BP, 42n12

Brazil, 44n20

Brett, Jeanne M., 145–147, 146n10, 148, 159n67

British Petroleum, 257

Bulgaria, 55n60, 383

C

CAFTA (Central American Free Trade Agreement), 232–233, 271

Calvo Doctrine, 45n22, 46, 64n83, 73, 87

Camuzzi v. Argentina, 55n59

Canada, 40n4, 42n30, 50, 62–63, 63, 67n91, 382, 394, 415

- Canada–U.S. FTA, 197

Canadian Bill of Rights, and property, 49

Cancun Ministerial, 21

Canfor Corporation v. United States of America, 206n23

Central America, Dominican Republic–Central America–United States FTA (DR-CAFTA), 302–303

Central Europe
- investment treaty increase, 46
- *see also* individual country

challenges, in investment disputes, 143–192
- dispute resolution options, 147–157
- dispute systems design, 144
- efficiency of arbitration, 156–157
- evolution of investment dispute resolution, 148–152
- institutional legitimacy for arbitration, 154–156
- interest-based dispute resolution, 146
- power-based method, 146
- reconsidering conflict, 144–145
- rights-based method, 146
- status quo for resolving disputes, 152–154
- systemic approach to dispute resolution, 145–146

Champion Trading Company v. Egypt, 56n63

Chile, 202, 380n3
- U.S.–Chile FTA, 271, 304–305

China, 47, 75

China National Off shore Oil Corporation (CNOOC), 72n108

CME v. Czech Republic, 73, 127, 128, 129, 133, 228, 237

CMS Gas Transmission Company v. Argentine Republic, 62, 67–68, 67n95, 75–76, 257, 262

Code for the Liberalisation of Capital Movements (OECD), 22

Coe, Jack, 191

Cohen, Amy, 159

Colombia, 202
- U.S.–Colombia FTA, 310–311

colonialism, 33–34

compliance pull, 243

Comprehensive Economic Agreement between India and Singapore, 40, 43

conciliation, 119–120, 174–177

confidentiality issues, 188–188

consent to negotiate, host country, 169

Consolidation Tribunal, 382

Consortium R.F.C.C. v. Kingdom of Morocco, 402n21

Costantino, Cathy, 146n10, 147n11, 148, 159

Costa Rica, 202

costs
- of annulment procedures, 351, 386
- cost allocation and attorney fees, 399–401
- increase in litigation, 385–386

Court of Common Pleas, 254

Court of Justice of the European Communities, 210

creeping expropriation, 68

C.S.O.B. v. Slovak Republic, 101

Cyprus–Hungary BIT, 398, 399

Czech Republic
- BITs, 44n20
- claims against, 113, 114, 382, 394
- *CME v. Czech Republic*, 73, 127, 128, 129, 133, 228, 237
- *Lauder v. The Czech Republic*, 41n8, 56, 73, 127, 128–129, 133, 228, 237, 247
- legitimacy issues, 42
- *Saluka Investments BV v. The Czech Republic*, 255, 396, 397, 399

D

Dabhol Power Project, 117

Danino, Roberto, 217

Declaration and Decisions on International Investment and Multinational Enterprises (OECD), 22

denial of justice, 64–66, 244

Dillingham Moore v. Murphyores, 41n7

Dipenta v. Algeria, 94, 95, 96, 97, 101

diplomacy, 166
- gunboat, 149

direct negotiation, 167–168

Dispute Settlement Understanding (DSU; WTO), 30, 31, 196, 275

dispute resolution. *See* appropriate dispute resolution

dispute systems design, 144

distributional bargaining, 166n89

distributive justice, 282

Dogger Bank, 181–182

Doha Declaration, 103

Doha Development Agenda, 270, 272

Doha Round, 88, 197

Dominican Republic, 202
- Dominican Republic–Central America–United States FTA (DR-CAFTA), 302–303

Dunkel, Arthur, 197n3

Dunkel Text, 197

Dutch Antilles, 57

E

Eastern Europe, 46, 74
- *see also* individual country

ECLAC, 25

economic patriotism, 22

Ecuador, 113, 256–257, 382, 394

effective control, 14

Egypt, 50, 52n47, 56n63, 60, 71n107, 94, 95–96, 97, 252, 261, 382, 394

El Paso Energy International Company v. The Argentine Republic, 397–398, 398n10

El Salvador, 202

E.L.S.I. (*United States of America v. Italy*), 102

Emilio Agustin Maffezini v. The Kingdom of Spain, 55–56, 90, 235

EnCana Corporation v. Republic of Ecuador, 397, 400

Energy Charter Treaty (ECT), 21, 108, 149, 325, 383

English common law, and third parties, 52

Enron, 56n61, 117–118

environmental issues, 20, 23, 50, 110, 199, 273, 416

environmental takings, 70–72

Ethyl Corporation v. the Government of Canada, 69, 199

Europe
- property rights in, 49
- *see also* individual country

European Communities—Antidumping Duties on Malleable Cast Iron Tube or Pipe Fittings from Brazil, 133n18

European Communities—Measures Affecting Asbestos and Asbestos-Containing Products, 197

European Community, 260
- preliminary rulings, 209–210

European Convention on Human Rights, and property rights, 49n36

European Court of Justice, 129, 211

European Court on Human Rights, 72

expansionary trends, in investment treaty arbitration, 39–79
- balance restoration, 73–78
- confining to purely commercial issues, 78
- crisis of legitimacy and, 41–45
- foreign investment arbitration (*see* foreign investment arbitration, expansionary trends in)
- other measures, 77–78
- regulatory space preservation, 74–77
- theoretical basis of problem, 45–51
- *see also* foreign investment arbitration, expansionary trends in expropriation, 417–418
- creeping, 68
- direct takings, 68
- indirect takings, 68
- regulatory takings and, 70–71, 72
- tantamount to property, 70
- tantamount to taking, 68, 69–70

F

facilitated appropriate dispute resolution, 171–179

fact-finding appropriate dispute resolution, 179–183

fair and equitable treatment, 20, 138, 204nn12–13
- 2006 developments, 395–396
- and NAFTA, 40
- *vs. traitement juste et équitable*, 88–89, 97

Fedax v. Venezuela, 53, 53n52, 56n61, 94, 101

festina lente policy, 257

finality principle, 225, 363–364

Fiss, Owen, 170

foreign direct investment (FDI)
- amount covered by IIAs, 413–415
- defining, 3n1
- difference from WTO agreement, 30–31
- positive/negative effects of, 11
- and responsible corporate conduct, 18
- rise in flows of, 3–6, 281
- rules framework for, 17–18
- textual differences among investment agreements, 30–31

foreign investment arbitration, expansionary trends in, 51–73
- arbitration without privity, 51–54
- courses of action, 61–68
- expropriation, 68–73
- failure to provide national treatment, 62–63
- fair and equitable treatment, 66–68
- international minimum standard of treatment, 63–66
- jurisdiction umbrella clause, 59–61
- treatment standards, 61–62
- use of corporate nationality, 56–58
- use of most-favored-nation clause, 55–56
- waiver clauses, 58–59

Franck, Thomas, 32, 156, 242n3

Friedman, Gary, 173

frivolous lawsuits, 116

funds transfer, 11, 169

G

Gabon v. Société Serte, 111

Gaillard, Emmanuel, 95

Gas Natural v. Argentina, 55n59

General Agreement on Tariffs and Trade (GATT)
- and Mexico, 131–132
- number of disputes under, 12, 193
- and transparency, 194–197, 214

Generation Ukraine, 255

Genin v. Estonia, 67

Glamis Gold Ltd. v. United States of America, 204n12

Goetz v. Burundi, 167

Goldberg, Stephen B., 145–147, 146n10, 148, 159n67

Grand River Enterprises Six Nations, Ltd., v. United States

Great Barrier Reef, 71n107

Greece, 414, 415

Grenada, claims against, 394

Grid System, 173

Grueslin v. Malaysia, 47n31, 75

Guatemala, 202

gunboat diplomacy, 149

H

Hague Conference on Private International Law, 130

Himmelstein, Jack, 173

Honduras, 202

human rights, 48, 49, 53n49, 273

Hungary, 167, 395, 395n2, 397, 414, 415
- Cyprus–Hungary BIT, 398, 399

Hunter, Martin, 171n108

I

Iceland, 415

ICSID
- Additional Facility, 13, 31, 184, 274–275
- Additional Facility Conciliation Rules, 175–176, 226
- Additional Facility Fact Finding, 180–181, 182n161–183n161
- annulment in treaty articles, 302–302, 304–305, 306, 307, 309–310, 311
- Appeals Facility, 331–332
- Appeals Facility, possible features of, 332–337
- Appeals Facility rules, 334, 335–336, 337
- Appellate Facility, 268
- caseload, 324
- conciliation services, 174–178, 331
- Constitution of Tribunal, 350
- direct negotiations, 167–168
- harmonization issues, 209, 212
- introduction, 323-326
- investment Web site, 376
- lack of mediation services, 174
- open hearings, 218n7
- oral procedure, 348
- preliminary objections, 345–346
- provisional measures, 344
- Regulation 14, 351
- rendering of award, 347
- submissions of non-disputing parties, 349
- suggested appellate system, 44n14
- visits and inquiries by Tribunal, 349

ICSID (continued)
- *see also* ICSID, arbitration framework, possible improvements; ICSID, possible framework improvements; ICSID, suggested changes to rules and regulations

ICSID, arbitration framework, possible improvements, 321–337
- Appeals Facility, 331–332
- disclosure requirements for arbitrators, 330–331
- mediation, 331
- preliminary procedures, 325, 326–327
- publication of awards, 327–328
- third party access, 329
- training, 331

ICSID, possible framework improvements, 353–376
- additional powers of Secretary General, 374
- Administrative Council Rules approach, 371–372
- *amicus curiae*, 365
- appeal of interim awards, 373
- appeal process results, 374
- appeals process review, 375
- appellate mechanism, 370–375
- appointment of appellate body, 372–373
- broader underpinnings for IISD comments, 360–364
- conduct of process, 375
- conflict of interest/disclosure, 368–369
- costs and funding, 374
- expedited dismissal, 364
- final note, 375–376
- goals, 362–364
- introduction, 358
- issues, 364–375
- limitations on issues and comments, 358–360
- mediation, 369
- open hearings, 366–368
- principles, 360–362
- provisional measures, 364
- publication of awards, 364–365
- role of secretariat, 375
- standard and scope of review, 373
- third parties, 365
- time period for appeals, 375
- training, 369–370

ICSID, suggested changes to rules and regulations, 339–351
- disclosure requirements for arbitrators, 350
- fees of arbitrators, 351
- preliminary procedures, 344–346
- publication of awards, 347
- third party access, 348–349

ICSID Convention on the Settlement of Investment Disputes Between States and Nationals of Other States, 319–320

imposed appropriate dispute resolution, 185–186

Impreglio, 61n75

Inceysa Vallisoletana S.L. v. Republic of El Salvador, 400

India, 40, 43, 86–87, 382, 394

Indonesia, legitimacy issues, 42–43

"in like circumstances" requirement, 14, 384

institutional design of international investment law, 281–287

integrative bargaining, 166n90

Interagua Servicios Integrales de Agua S.A. v. Argentine Republic, 395

interest-based dispute resolution, 146

International Centre for Settlement of Investment Disputes. *See* ICSID

International Chamber of Commerce (ICC), 119, 120, 226

International Court of Justice (ICJ), 102, 149, 156, 235, 273

international investment agreements (IIAs)
- dispute settlement in recent, 428*t*–429*t*
- growing diversity and inconsistency, 137–139
- and OECD outward and inward investments, 420*t*–421*t*
- preferential, 10*f*–11
- rise of, 7–11, 381n7
- substantive provisions of recent, 424*t*–425*t*

see also bilateral investment treaties; challenges, in investment disputes

International Investment Agreements Monitors, 139

international investment disputes
- damages awarded, 14–15
- disputes, by arbitration forum, 13*f*
- known investment treaty arbitrations (1987–2006), 12*f*–13, 393*f*
- known investment treaty claims, by defendants (2006), 405–406
- leading defendants in, 13*t*–14
- rise in, 11–15
- sectors involved in known arbitrations, 14*f*, 393–394*f*, 395*f*

international investment law
- awards appeals procedure, 26
- bilateral treaty network, 18–21
- dispute settlement mechanisms, 26
- draft Multilateral Agreement on Investment, 22–24
- future of, 29–35
- improving transparency and coherence, 25–27
- legal concept clarification, 25–26
- multifaceted nature of, 17–27
- multilateral approach, 26–27
- piecemeal approaches at pluri-/multilateral levels, 21–22
- Policy Framework for Investment, 24–25
- regulatory changes, 1991-2006, 6–7, 8*t*
- rise of, 6–7

international minimum standard of treatment, 14, 45n22, 63–66

International Monetary Fund (IMF), and Malaysia, 75

International Thunderbird Gaming Corporation v. United Mexican States, 114, 257–258

International Trade Organization (ITO), 194

International Tribunal on the Law of the Sea, 235–236

Investment Compact for South East Europe, 25

Investment dispute challenge. *See* challenges, in investment disputes

investment promotion agencies (IPAs), 6

investment treaties
- increase in number of, 46–47
- *see also* bilateral investment treaties; international investment agreements; preliminary rulings, in investment arbitration; OECD

investor-State dispute settlement, 2005 developments, 377–389
- award size increase, 384–385
- breadth of cases, 382–383
- calls for reform/revision, 386–387
- disputes by arbitration forum, 380*f*

investor-State dispute settlement, 2005 developments (continued)
- growing number of countries involved, 381–382, 388–389
- introduction, 377–379
- litigation cost increase, 385–386
- proliferation of cases, 379–381, 388–389
- significant substantive decisions, 383–384
- technical capacity of developing countries, 387
- treaty provision interpretation, 383–384
- *see also* investor-State dispute settlement, 2006 developments

investor-State dispute settlement, 2006 developments, 391–409
- award review, 402
- cost allocation and attorney fees, 399–401
- disputes by arbitration forum, 393–394f
- on expropriation, 396–397
- on fair and equitable treatment, 395–396
- introduction, 391
- list of cases reviewed, 407–409
- most-favored-nation treatment, 395
- state of necessity, 398
- terms of damages, 398–399
- third-party participation, 401–402
- umbrella clause, 397–398
- *see also* investor-State dispute settlement, 2005 developments

investor-State dispute settlement: OECD government perspective on improving, 223–228

Iran, 156n54

Iran–U.S. Claims Tribunal, 68, 156, 185, 380n3

Italy, 102

J

Japan, 11, 47, 62, 77, 182

Jordan, 55n60, 94, 101, 400

Joy Mining Machinery v. Egypt, 60, 94, 95–96, 97

Juillard, Patrick, 137, 138

jura novit curia, 247

K

Karaha Bodas v. Perusahaan, 42n14

Karah Bodas v. Pertamina, 42–43

Korea. *See* Republic of Korea

L

labor issues, 23, 416

Latin America
- conservation of regulatory space in, 74
- increase in number of investment treaties, 46

Lauder v. The Czech Republic, 41n8, 56, 73, 127, 128–129, 133, 228, 237, 247

law, international investment. *see* international investment law

legitimacy issues, 41–45, 154–156

Lemire v. Ukraine, 167

LG&E Energy Corp., LG&E Capital Corp. and LG&E International Inc. v. Argentine Republic

LIAMCO, 42n12, 257

Lianco, 42n12

lis pendens principle, 129, 135–136

Llewellyn, Karl, 107

Loewen Group v. United States, 66n87, 121, 251

Lucchetti v. Peru, 250, 257

M

Maffezini v. Kingdom of Spain, 55–56, 90, 235

Maharashtra State Electricity Board (MSEB), 117

Malaysia, 47n31, 75, 77

Malaysian Historical Salvors, SDN, BHD v. Malaysia, 71n107

Mali, 394

Marvin Roy Feldman v. The United Mexican States, 397

Mauritius–India treaty, 56n61

MCI Power Group et al. v. Ecuador, 255

MENA-OECD Investment Program, 25

Merchant, Christina Sickles, 146n10, 147n11, 148, 159

Merton, Robert, 43n16

Metalclad, 67n91, 69

Metalpar S.A. and Buen Aire S.A. v. Argentine Republic

Methanex Corporation v. The United States of America, 40, 73, 199, 218n8, 251, 253, 365, 366, 384, 386

Mexico, 382, 394, 415

- *Azininian v. Mexico*, 59n71
- *Tecnicas Medioambientales Tecmed S.A. v. United Mexican States*, 71, 90, 396, 397

Mexico—Tax Measures on Soft Drinks and Other

- Beverages, 131–132

Middle East Shipping and Handling Co v. Egypt, 68

"migrating" by companies, 57–58

Millennium Development Goals (UN), 17, 25

mini-trials, 183–184

Mitsubishi v. Soler Chrysler Ltd., 63n79

Mixed Claims Commissions, 237

Mondev International v. U.S., 65, 66, 205n15, 251

Monterrey Consensus, 17

Morocco, 202, 400, 402n21

- U.S.–Morocco FTA, 305–306

most-favored-nation (MFN) provision, 248, 283

- and appeals, 234–235
- interpretation of, 383

most-favoured-nation treatment, 395

Multilateral Agreement on Investment (MAI; OECD), 18, 22–24, 103, 214, 269

multilateral quasi-legislative body, 272

multinational corporations (MNCs), 4–6, 11, 33

- and appellate process, 276
- inconsistency in treatment, 90–91
- inherent rights of, 48–49
- and migration, 57–58

N

NAFTA (North American Free Trade Agreement), 20, 21, 107–108, 149, 325

- access to documents, 365
- accountability, 361
- amicable resolutions, 153
- *amicus curiae* briefs, 219
- beef industry, 382
- Chapter 11, investor-State dispute settlement mechanism, 29, 88, 193, 198–200, 202, 204n13

NAFTA (North American Free Trade Agreement) (continued)
- Chapter 20, State-State dispute settlement mechanism, 197–198
- clarification of legal concepts, 26
- costs of arbitrations, 114
- expropriation under, 61, 68–69
- "fair and equitable" treatment, 40, 67–68
- lumber industry, 382
- minimum standard of treatment, 396
- multiple proceedings, 131, 134, 206
- national treatment under, 62–63
- open hearings, 218n6, 366–367
- property rights, 70
- third parties, 365
- transparency issues, 197–200, 203–205, 217, 218, 381

The NAFTA Statement on Amicus Briefs, 365

National Grid plc v The Argentine Republic, 395

Neer Claim, 64, 64n81

negotiated appropriate dispute resolution, 165–170

NEPAD, 25

New International Economic Order, 251

New York Convention for the Enforcement of Foreign Arbitral Awards, 130, 151

Nicaragua, 202, 394

Noble Ventures v. Romania, 59n71

non-government organizations (NGOs), 24, 25, 83, 196–197, 199, 276, 401

normlessness, 43, 43n16

Norway, 395n2, 415

O

obligation de moyens, 85

obligation de résultat, 85

Occidental v. Ecuador, 256–257

OECD, 18, 22, 91
- acceptance of ISDS, 418–419
- amount of FDI covered by IIAs, 413–415
- arbitration innovations, 419
- clarification of legal concepts, 26
- consolidation of claims, 228
- current appeal mechanism, advantages of, 224–225
- current appeal mechanism, disadvantages of, 225–226
- definition of investment, 417
- definition of key investment protection provisions, 417
- expropriation issues, 417–418
- increase in number of claims, 419
- investment promotion and facilitation, 418
- liberalisation commitments, 416–417
- main novel features of recent IIAs, 415–419
- Multilateral Agreement on Investment, draft, 22–24
- novel features in recent investment agreements, 411–419
- Policy Framework for Investment, 24–25
- public interest safeguards, 20, 416
- standards in investment policy, 415–416
- transparency issues, 227, 418
- *see also* bilateral investment treaties

Oman, 202

ombudspersons, 161–164

Organisation for Economic Co-operation and Development. *See* OECD

OSPAR Convention, 235

P

Pakistan, 42, 59–60, 91, 98, 101, 246–247

Palma Consortium Limited v. Republic of Bulgaria, 55n60, 383

Panama–U.S. FTA, 312–313

Pan American Energy LLC and BP Argentina Exploration Company v. Argentine Republic, 397–398

Parra, Antonio R., 321

Patrick Mitchell v. Democratic Republic of the Congo, 402

Permanent Court of Arbitration, 261

Peru, 202, 234–235, 250, 257, 380n3
- U.S.–Peru FTA, 313–314

Philippines, 44n20, 52n48, 60–61, 91, 98–99, 101, 246–237

platform State, 57, 58n67

Poland, 382, 394, 414

Policy Framework for Investment (PFI), 24–25

policy space, 276

Pope & Talbot, Inc. v. Canada, 67, 69–70, 204n12, 204n13

positional bargaining, 166n89

power-based method, 146

preferential trade and investment agreements (PTIAs), 10*f*–11

preliminary rulings, in investment arbitration, 207–212
- appeals procedure, 209–210
- most-favored-nation, 208
- and permanent courts, 209
- umbrella clause, 207–208

preventative appropriate dispute resolution, 160–165

principled bargaining, 166n90

problem-solving, 166n90

procedural fairness, 20–21, 26

property rights, 49–50, 49n36
- intellectual property, 21

public interest safeguards, 20, 416

Pyramids Case, 121–122

Q

Qatar, 249

R

Rainbow Warrior, 178

Redfern, Alan, 171n108

regulatory takings, 14, 20, 40–41, 70–72

Reisman, Michael, 253

Republic of Congo, 394, 402

Republic of Korca, 47, 62, 415

Republic of Moldova, 382, 394

res judicata principle, 129, 259

resolution, dispute. *See* appropriate dispute resolution

rights-based method, 146

Riskin, Len, 173

Romania, 59n71, 394

Roman law, and third parties, 52–53

round tripping, 53–54, 56–57, 56n63

Rowley, William, 253

Russia
- claims against, 382, 394, 395
- *Dogger Bank* case, 181–182
- financial crisis, 122

S

Salacuse, Jeswald, 85

Salini Construtorri S.p.A. and Italstrade S. p.A. v. Morocco, 400

Salini Costruttori S.p.A. and Italstrade S.p.A. v. Jordan, 55n60, 94, 101, 400

Saluka Investments BV v. The Czech Republic, 255, 396, 397, 399

Santa Elena v. Costa Rica, 70–71

Santa Helena v. Costa Rica, 50

Schreuer, Christian, 153–154

SD Meyers, Inc. v. Canada, 42n30, 50, 62–63

SEDITEX Engineering Beratungsgesellschaft für die
- *Textilindustrie m.b.H. v. Madagascar*, 176, 177

Seychelles, 394

SGS Société Générale de Surveillance S.A. v. Islamic Republic of Pakistan, 59–60, 91, 98, 101, 246–247

SGS v. Philippines, 60–61, 91, 98–99, 101, 246–237

Shariff, Khalil, 146n10

shuttle diplomacy, 172

Siemens v. Argentina, 55n59

Singapore, 40, 43
- Singapore–U.S. FTA, 71–72, 76–77, 202, 306–308

Slovak Republic, 113, 394, 414

small claims, special procedures for, 26

Sociedad General de Aguas de Barcelona S.A., 395

socket provision, 232

Sornarajah, M., on bilateral investment treaties, 81–82

South Africa, 44n20, 217

Southeast Asia, conservation of regulatory space in, 74–75, 76

South-South investment, 19

Spain, 55–56, 90, 235, 395

Spain–Argentina treaty, 55

SPP v. Egypt, 50, 52n47, 71n107, 252, 261

“stakeholder problem,” 170

state of necessity, 14

stipulatio alteri, 52–53, 54

substantive justice, 18, 26

Suez & InterAguas v. The Argentine Republic, 401

Sullivan, Nicholas P., 85

Supreme Investment Court (SIC), 273

Swedish Arbitration Act (1999), 129

T

takings jurisprudence, 41, 61n77–62n77

Tanzania Electric Supply Company Limited v. Independent Power Tanzania Limited, 111

TEC Article 234, 210–211

Tecnicas Medioambientales Tecmed S.A. v. United Mexican States, 71, 90, 396, 397

Telenor Mobile Communications AS v. Republic of Hungary, 395, 397

Tembec et al. v. United States of America, 206n23

Ténicas Medioambientales Tecmed S.A. v. Mexico, 71, 90

Terminal Forest Products Ltd. v. United States of America, 206n23

Tesoro Petroleum Corp. v. Trinidad and Tobago, 120, 176, 177

Texaco, 42n12, 256

TG World Petroleum Ltd. v. Niger, 176, 177

Thailand, claims against, 394

third parties, 53, 118–120, 169, 173, 227, 284, 401–402

Togo, claims against, 394

Togo Electricité v. Republic of Togo, 176

Tokio-Tokelés v. Ukraine, 54n56, 56–57, 250

Tokyo Round DSU, 195

trade-related intellectual property rights (TRIPs), 21

trade-related performance requirements (TRIMS), 21

transparency

- international dispute settlement, 193–200
- mandate for in U.S. investment agreements, 205–206
- *see also* transparency, GATT and WTO; transparency, international dispute settlement; transparency, NAFTA

transparency, avoiding unintended consequences, 241–265

- disclosures and premises, 242–244
- illusion of cure, 258–262
- incoherences of incoherence complaint, 244–252
- natural corrections, 252–258
- promise of transparency, 262–265

transparency, GATT and WTO, 194–197

- access to documents, 195–196
- evolution of, 194–195
- increased transparency, 195–197
- non-disputing party participation (*amicus curiae*), 196–197

transparency, in international investment law, 213–221

- appellate system, 219–220
- conflicts of interest, 215–217, 220
- document publication, 217–218
- double booking, 215–216
- investor-State arbitration rule of law, 221
- major law firm lawyer as arbitrator, 216
- public access to hearings, 218–219

transparency, NAFTA, 203–205, 217, 218, 381

- investor-State dispute settlement mechanism, 198–200
- State-State dispute settlement mechanism, 197–198

"Treaties of Friendship, Commerce and Navigation, 149

treaty-based investment dispute settlement, reasons for increase in, 105–125

- acceptance and internal adjustment, 115–116
- availability of arbitration, 111–114
- background, 105–107
- facilitating factors, 123–124
- investor-State dispute settlement, 108–111
- lack of other satisfactory remedy, 114–121

treaty-based investment dispute settlement, reasons for increase in (continued)
- local courts, 120–121
- movement toward treatification, 107–108
- negotiation, 116–118
- occurrence of economic crises, 122
- politics of investor-State disputes, 121–122
- transformation of global investment climate, 122–123
- voluntary third-party intervention, 118–120

Treaty Establishing the European Community (TEC), 210–211

Trinidad and Tobago, 120, 176

Turkey, 414

U

U.K.–Philippines treaty, 52n48

Ukraine, 54n56, 56–57, 250, 394

U.K.–Angola BIT, 234, 235

U.K.–Sri Lanka treaty, 52

umbrella clauses, 59–61, 91, 92, 98–100, 248, 383–384, 397–398

UNCITRAL Model Law on International Commercial Arbitration, 156

UNCTAD (United Nations Conference on Trade and Development)
- capacity building role, 84
- clarification of legal concepts, 26
- mediation, 174
- use of "good offices," 161

understanding model of mediation, 173

Understand on Rules and Procedures Governing the Settlement of Disputes (the *DSU*), 196, 197

United Nations Commission on International Trade Law (UNCITRAL), 13*f*, 31

United Nations' Millennium Development Goals, 17, 25

United States—Import Prohibition of Certain Shrimp and Shrimp Products, 196n1

United States (U.S.)
- Model Bilateral Investment Treaty, 316–317
- number of claims against, 382, 394
- property rights in, 49
- *see also* U.S. investment agreements, transparency and coherence in

UPS v. Canada, 40n4, 63, 67n91

Uruguay Round, 21, 197, 236, 275

Uruguay–U.S. BIT, 314–315

Ury, William L., 145–147, 146n10, 148, 159n67

U.S.–Argentina BIT, 398

U.S.–Argentina treaty, 76n113
- U.S.–Canada FTA, 197

U.S.–Chile FTA, 271, 304–305

U.S.–Colombia FTA, 310–311

U.S.–Egypt treaty, 56n63

U.S. investment agreements, transparency and coherence in, 201–206
- appellate mechanism potential, 202–203
- CAFTA-DR, 202, 203
- interim reviews, 203–204
- NAFTA minimum standard of treatment article, 204–205
- other provisions to achieve, 203–206
- transparency mandate, 205–206
- U.S. Model BIT, 316–317

U.S.–Morocco FTA, 305–306

U.S.-Pakistan negotiations, 217

U.S.–Peru FTA, 313–314

U.S.–Singapore FTA, 71-72, 76-77, 202, 306–308

U.S. Trade Act (2002), 268–269

U.S. Trade Promotion Authority, 268–269

U.S.–Uruguay BIT, 314–316

V

Veeder, V. V., 253

Vernon, Raymond, 106

Vienna Convention on the Law of Treaties, 84, 205, 333

W

Washington Consensus, 46

Washington Convention, 93–97, 101–102

Watts, Arthur, 255

Wena Hotels Limited v. the Arab Republic of Egypt, 384

World Association of Investment Promotion Agencies (WAIPA), 6, 7*f*

World Bank Group, 370–371

World Heritage Convention, 50

World Investment Report, 2006 (UNCTAD), 109–110

World Trade Center (WTO), and transparency, 194–197

World Trade Organization (WTO), 21
- Appellate Body, 31, 32–33, 220, 236, 274–275, 372
- conflicts with other international jurisdiction, 131
- failure to complete Doha Round, 88
- multilateral investment negotiations, 18
- multiple proceedings, 131–134
- number of disputes from inception to 2007, 12–13

WTO Agreement on Subsidies and Countervailing Measures (SCM), 131
- WTO Appellate Body, 31, 32–33, 220, 236, 274–275, 372

Y

Yaung Chi Ooo v. Myanmar, 47n31, 54n56, 56n63, 75